Teaching
Gender and
Multicultural
Awareness

Teaching Gender and Multicultural Awareness

Resources for the Psychology Classroom

Edited by
Phyllis Bronstein and
Kathryn Quina

American Psychological Association • Washington, DC

Published by
American Psychological Association
750 First Street, NE
Washington, DC 20002
www.apa.org

To order
APA Order Department
P.O. Box 92984
Washington, DC 20090-2984
Tel: (800) 374-2721; Direct: (202) 336-5510
Fax: (202) 336-5502; TDD/TTY: (202) 336-6123
On-line: www.apa.org/books/
E-mail: order@apa.org

In the U.K., Europe, Africa, and the Middle East, copies may be ordered from
American Psychological Association
3 Henrietta Street
Covent Garden, London
WC2E 8LU England

Typeset in Goudy by Page Grafx, St. Simons Island, GA

Printer: Port City Press, Baltimore, MD
Cover Designer: Naylor Design, Washington, DC
Technical/Production Editor: Casey Ann Reever

The opinions and statements published are the responsibility of the authors, and such opinions and statements do not necessarily represent the policies of the American Psychological Association.

Library of Congress Cataloging-in-Publication Data
Teaching gender and multicultural awareness : resources for the psychology classroom / edited by Phyllis Bronstein and Kathryn Quina.
    p. cm.
  Includes bibliographical references and index.
  ISBN 1-55798-991-5 (pbk. : alk. paper)
    1. Psychology—Study and teaching. 2. Pluralism (Social sciences)—Study and teaching. 3. Minorities—Psychology—Study and teaching.
4. Women—Psychology—Study and teaching. I. Bronstein, Phyllis.
II. Quina, Kathryn.

BF77.T4 2003
150'.71'1—dc21

2002154560

British Library Cataloguing-in-Publication Data
A CIP record is available from the British Library.

Printed in the United States of America
First Edition

To the pioneering scholars who have worked to construct
a psychology of all people, transforming and enriching the field
and helping to create an indisputable place for new voices.

To the next generation, in particular, those dearest to us—
Laila, Geoff, Elise, and Jolie.

CONTENTS

CONTRIBUTORS

Adrienne Asch, PhD, Henry R. Luce Professor in Biology, Ethics and the Politics of Human Reproduction, Wellesley College, Wellesley, MA

Augustíne Barón, Jr., PsyD, Associate Director, Counseling, Learning and Career Services, The University of Texas at Austin and Walden University

Evelyn Torton Beck, PhD, Professor Emerita, Women's Studies Department and Meyerhoff Center for Jewish Studies, University of Maryland, College Park

Su L. Boatright, PhD, Assistant Professor, Department of Psychology, University of Rhode Island, Kingston

Lynne A. Bond, PhD, Professor, Department of Psychology, University of Vermont, Burlington

Lisa Bowleg, PhD, Assistant Professor, Department of Psychology, University of Rhode Island, Kingston

Phyllis Bronstein, PhD, Professor, Department of Psychology, University of Vermont, Burlington

Connie S. Chan, PhD, Department of Human Services and Institute for Asian American Studies, University of Massachusetts, Boston

Royda Crose, PhD, Lifecycle Consultants, Columbia, MO

Elizabeth Davis-Russell, EdD, PhD, Provost and Vice President for Academic Affairs, State University of New York College at Cortland

Cynthia de las Fuentes, PhD, Associate Professor, Department of Psychology, Our Lady of the Lake University, San Antonio, TX

Florence L. Denmark, PhD, Robert Scott Pace Distinguished Research Professor, Department of Psychology, Pace University, New York

Halford H. Fairchild, PhD, Professor, Department of Psychology and Intercollegiate Department of Black Studies, Pitzer College, Claremont, CA

Laurel Furumoto, PhD, Professor Emerita, Department of Psychology, Wellesley College, Wellesley, MA

Julie L. Goldberg, PhD, Staff Psychologist, Coordinator Community Wellness Services, Pace University, New York

Beverly J. Goodwin, PhD, Director, Center for Applied Psychology, Indiana University of Pennsylvania, Indiana

Kathleen S. Gorman, PhD, Director, Feinstein Center for a Hunger Free America; Associate Professor of Psychology, University of Rhode Island, Kingston

Vonda Dionne Jones-Hudson, PhD, Psychologist, NorthKey Community Care, Chicago, IL

Elizabeth A. Klonoff, PhD, Professor and Co-Director, Joint Doctoral Program in Clinical Psychology, San Diego State University, San Diego, CA

L. Lee Knefelkamp, PhD, Professor of Higher Education, Department of Organization and Leadership, Columbia University, New York

Janet M. Kulberg, PhD, Department of Psychology, University of Rhode Island, Kingston

Hope Landrine, PhD, Adjunct Research Professor, Joint Doctoral Program in Clinical Psychology, San Diego State University, San Diego, CA

Robert W. Levenson, PhD, Professor and Director of the Institute for Personality and Social Research, Department of Psychology, University of California, Berkeley

Sara S. Little, PhD, School Psychologist, Rhode Island Training School, Cranston, RI

Walter J. Lonner, PhD, Director, Center for Cross-Cultural Research, Department of Psychology, Western Washington University, Bellingham

Albert J. Lott, PhD, Professor Emeritus, Psychology and Women's Studies, University of Rhode Island, Kingston

Henry McCarthy, PhD, Associate Professor, Rehabilitation Counseling Department, Louisiana State University Health Sciences Center, New Orleans

Maureen C. McHugh, PhD, Professor, Department of Psychology, Indiana University of Pennsylvania, Indiana

Nnamdi Pole, PhD, Assistant Professor, Department of Psychology, University of Michigan, Ann Arbor

Kathryn Quina, PhD, Professor, Department of Psychology and Women's Studies Program, University of Rhode Island, Kingston

Harriette W. Richard, PhD, Assistant Professor, Department of Psychology, North Georgia College and State University, Dahlonega

Sondra E. Solomon, PhD, Assistant Professor, Department of Psychology, University of Vermont, Burlington

Stanley Sue, PhD, Professor of Psychology, Psychiatry, and Asian American Studies, University of California, Davis

Ethel Tobach, PhD, Curator Emerita, Department of Mammalogy, American Museum of Natural History; Adjunct Professor, Psychology and Biology, The City University of New York

Lisa Osachy Touster, PsyD, Facilitator, Stanford School of Business, Governor's Corner Office, Stanford, CA

Jennifer J. Treuting, PhD, Department of Psychology, University of Illinois at Chicago

Joseph E. Trimble, PhD, Professor, Center for Cross-Cultural Research, Department of Psychology Western Washington University, Bellingham

Melba J. T. Vásquez, PhD, ABPP, Private Practice, Austin, TX

Jacqueline S. Weinstock, PhD, Associate Professor, Integrated Professional Studies, University of Vermont, Burlington

Lisa Whitten, PhD, Associate Professor, Department of Psychology, State University of New York College at Old Westbury

Gale Young, PhD, Professor, Department of Communications, California State University, Hayward

Mary Zahm, PhD, Chair, Department of Psychology and Sociology, Bristol Community College, Fall River, MA

FOREWORD

CREATING A PSYCHOLOGY
OF ALL PEOPLE

FLORENCE L. DENMARK

The past few years have borne witness to the increasing diversification of U.S. society. Today, more opportunities abound for contact with other cultures and ways of life than have ever existed before. As our world population continues to grow, and our already-small world grows smaller, there will be ever-increasing contact with people whose customs and experiences differ greatly from our own. Population estimates projected for the new millennium indicate that within the next few decades, the demographics of the United States will shift so that the majority of Americans will find themselves as part of a minority group. As a result, the opportunities to associate, work, and learn with others from a multitude of backgrounds and traditions will increase, and there will be a proportionally greater need to foster understanding of and respect for our similarities and differences.

Psychology is touted as a discipline devoted in large part to the study of human thought and behavior. However, in the past, psychological theory was solely based on the thoughts and behaviors of White males. The women's movement and the civil rights movement certainly played a role in broadening the horizons of our collective conscience, and over the years the realm of psychology has expanded to include women and men from different ethnic and racial backgrounds. Although the field of psychology has grown to focus attention on diverse individuals, studies of these populations have always been regarded as "special topics" within psychology. By establishing the study of women or ethnic minorities as elective courses, we are in essence saying that these individuals will not be studied in mainstream psychology courses. As the title of the editors' earlier volume, *Teaching a*

Psychology of People, attests, psychology is the study of *people*, and all human beings who populate this earth fall into this category.

I believe that the importance of multicultural awareness should be paramount in psychology. Our cultural and ethnic backgrounds affect us all in different ways, and it behooves all psychologists, especially those who work with students (or clients) of different nationalities, ethnicities, or lifestyles, to consider the impact of one's unique life experiences within the larger cultural context. Instructors and clinicians alike must remember that not all theories or treatment modalities will be equally effective when applied blindly across all races and ethnicities.

In keeping with the growing need for students entering the field of psychology to develop multicultural skills and an appreciation for diversity, courses must be made relevant to include the experiences of all people. It is no longer sufficient for students to take a single class on gender, multiculturalism, or cross-cultural studies and believe they have gained a true understanding of their fellow humans. Such issues should also be incorporated into each psychology course. Concordant with this, the authors of the chapters in *Teaching Gender and Multicultural Awareness* have provided a pre-eminent book that will be helpful to all individuals in psychology who are attempting to integrate recent sociocultural issues into a variety of courses and programs of study. Chapters not only discuss those groups traditionally considered in multicultural courses, such as African Americans, Latinos/Latinas, American Indians, and Asian Americans, but also include such diverse groups as disabled, elderly, and lesbian, gay, and bisexual people, who are often overlooked in such discussions. The chapters in this volume provide not only information about social and cultural groups but also creative resources and projects by which such issues may be integrated into the most basic introduction to psychology or graduate students' clinical experiences. The book encourages instructors to review and select texts and materials with a critical eye, judging their relevance not only to one particular course but also to a class composed of members of a diverse society. In addition, classroom techniques are suggested to encourage the students to gain an in-depth understanding of the different people and the changing world around them. *Teaching Gender and Multicultural Awareness* is a wonderful resource for preparing students as well as faculty to be members of a growing and diverse international community.

As someone who benefited from the original *Teaching a Psychology of People*, I am eager to make use of this new volume, which includes the most current ideas and materials on multiculturalism and gender across the psychology curriculum. I encourage all instructors to make use of this valuable resource.

FOREWORD

THE RICHNESS OF HUMAN REALITIES

STANLEY SUE

Psychology courses are among the most popular at colleges and universities in the United States. Given that the vast majority of college students enroll in one or more of these courses, it is essential that students develop a full understanding of people and human behavior. This understanding has been difficult to achieve, for two major reasons. First, psychology has traditionally presented a culturally limited perspective of human beings. Issues such as culture, ethnic minority groups, gender, sexual orientation, and disability were often viewed as peripheral or outside of the mainstream of psychology. Past textbooks in psychology provided little more than a glimpse of diversity research and issues. Second, when prompted to integrate topics such as ethnicity, culture, and gender into their courses, many instructors felt that the material should be covered in special courses, such as those addressing race relations or the psychology of women. They argued that these topics could not be easily included in basic psychology courses such as neuroscience, experimental psychology, or psychological methods and statistics. Thus, it has been difficult to provide students with a full understanding of human beings and all of their diversity.

Teaching Gender and Multicultural Awareness offers a compelling case for changes in the way psychology has traditionally viewed human beings and presents creative examples of how diversity issues can be integrated into the curriculum. Contributors to the book cover issues such as culture, ethnic minority groups, gender, sexual orientation, and disability. In addition to content concerning culture, we learn about methodological and theoretical biases that have permeated psychology. The book informs us of the nature of the field—how views are guided by traditional assumptions that are now being questioned. Most psychological research has been conducted on North Americans (and male college sophomores in particular), who represent less than 5% of the world's population. In the process, cultural issues have been seriously ignored.

The chapter authors provide several insights into how instructors can expose their students to human diversity. First, there are forthright discussions of ethnocentrism, racism, sexism, and homophobia that are usually not covered in textbooks. Second, the book chapters are interwoven by groups (ethnic minority groups, women, gays, lesbians, etc.), courses (e.g., developmental, social, personality, experimental, health, and clinical–counseling), topics (masculinity and disability), and type of students (undergraduate and graduate). Instructors who use this book can approach the teaching of diversity in a variety of different ways. This interweaving also reinforces the basic theme that the study of human beings cannot be valid without an appreciation of the range of human diversity.

Third, the book contributors provide concrete examples of how diversity issues can be integrated into each and every psychology course. In the past, some instructors resisted the incorporation of diversity issues into their courses because they lacked knowledge of such issues or felt that certain courses, such as statistics and methodology or neuroscience, were "basic" in nature, cutting across all human beings. The book contributors, who are authorities in their own areas of expertise, present the substantive knowledge of diversity issues that has developed, so that instructors can use this book as a reference text. Moreover, creative tactics are presented for the integration of diversity topics into every course. For instance, the diversity of human beings can be introduced even into statistics/methodology courses by using it to illustrate basic concepts. For example, in discussing reliability and validity of assessment tools, instructors can point to ethnic differences and the meaning of ethnic differences in measurement and evaluation. Also, biological processes that were once considered universal in nature are being reexamined, and researchers have found, for example, ethnic differences in the pharmacokinetic and pharmacodynamic effects of psychotropic medication. Why do these differences exist? What kinds of hereditary or environmental–cultural factors can account for the findings? These are important questions to address because they reveal to students the nature of human beings. Finally, the contributors also encourage instructors to select textbooks that enhance the theme of diversity, in that textbooks vary widely in their coverage of diversity, their illustrations and photographs that depict the range of human beings to students, and their understanding of the diverse nature of human beings.

It is important to note that the inclusion of these diverse issues should not be construed as a matter of political correctness. (In fact, I dislike the term *political correctness*. People who want to dismiss rather than examine issues often use the term. Furthermore, what is correct changes over time.

In fact, it is now politically correct to say that things are politically correct.) Rather, psychology as well as other social sciences has a history of ethnocentrism that has failed to reflect the diverse nature of human beings. The contributors to this book point to these ethnocentric biases and the ways in which certain groups and issues have been invisible. By giving these groups and issues visibility they settle on a philosophy that is inclusive and more reflective of human reality. Thus, the underlying rationale for the book has to do with reality rather than political correctness. It is a reality that we should appreciate and enjoy.

PREFACE

In 1986, when we began work on our original volume, *Teaching a Psychology of People: Resources for Gender and Sociocultural Awareness*, we and our chapter authors were working with little more than ideas and a few resources. We had come together over a concern that too many students were entering our upper-level classes with no prior exposure to some of the most innovative scholarship of the time—specifically, research and writings about underrepresented groups. At that point, aside from a growing number of introductory-level Psychology of Women courses, there was little attention to women in the curriculum, and there was almost no attention to social or cultural minorities in any psychology course or text. In the rare instances in which they were included, women and minorities were viewed as abnormalities or variations from the norm, to be considered in an isolated chapter at the end of a text or in a single class with "outside readings."

During this period, new research was beginning to challenge the traditional psychological knowledge base. Scholars were arguing that concepts such as constructivism belonged in the language and consciousness of psychology, and some brave individuals were introducing innovative classroom approaches that could expand students' awareness of the world around them. Even so, it was an amazingly difficult task we set out for the chapter authors: Provide useful resources and exercises to illuminate the lives of people not included in the traditional psychology curriculum. But provide they did, and the field was enriched as a result. Many of the early transformations our authors had wrought through their scholarship and teaching had been brought about at great personal cost; some of them had been denied tenure or promotions and had suffered criticism and isolation for their efforts—so much so that we devoted the final chapter to alerting readers to the challenges, costs and, ultimately, the rewards of working to create a true psychology of people.

We were delighted that some of the original authors joined us for this new book. The array of multicultural resources that we encountered as we began work on this book owes much to their efforts before and since the publication of the first volume. We are also indebted to our new contributors, including some who made us aware of the inadequacies in the first volume. This time, the challenge for contributors was not the same as the one they took on in 1986. This time, they had to whittle down a wealth of materials, myriad creative exercises, and another decade of experience into relatively few pages. They are to be applauded for doing this so well, and with such equanimity, when we were forced to trim and compress so much of their great work. Because there is so much more that could be said, we urge readers to view this volume as a resource that can be annotated, expanded, altered, and taken into account as the field evolves into an ever-more-exciting discipline. In any project such as this, arbitrary decisions are made about people and materials to include or exclude. We were fortunate to know many outstanding teachers who ably rose to the challenges of this text. There are many others with equally exciting ideas.

We are honored that two outstanding scholars and leaders in the field have provided forewords to this volume. Florence Denmark is a pioneer in the psychology of women, who has led the way in making it a recognized and respected field of study. Denmark is an author of one of the earliest texts, a founder of both the American Psychological Association (APA) Division 35 (Society for the Psychology of Women) and the Association for Women in Psychology, a former editor of the *Psychology of Women Quarterly*, and former president of APA, and she has received many awards for her leadership and distinguished work in the field. Stanley Sue is a leading authority on ethnic minority issues whose research has been influential in shaping mental health policy for providing effective treatment for ethnic minority clients. He has served as president of APA Division 9 (Society for the Psychological Study of Social Issues) and has received two major awards from APA, for distinguished contributions to psychology in the public interest and for research on public policy.

We were gratified that the first volume won the Distinguished Publication Award from the Association for Women in Psychology, and even though some of its references are out of date it continues to be used by teachers and learners across the world. We are pleased that APA Divisions 9 and 35 were able to fund more innovative work with the royalties from the book, all of which were donated to them. We hope that the proceeds from *Teaching Gender and Multicultural Awareness: Resources for the Psychology Classroom* will help fund another generation of scholarship and activism as well. When we look back, what we produced in 1988 seems in some ways naïve and simplistic; we can only begin to imagine what another 10 years may bring.

We hope that the ideas contained in this volume will make it easier to think of our field as a fascinating one, our teaching as a learning process, and our students as diverse and eager to learn about themselves and others. Most important, we hope readers will find themselves engaged in a process of curriculum transformation that is enlightening, enriching, and just plain fun.

Teaching Gender and Multicultural Awareness

INTRODUCTION

GENDER AND MULTICULTURALISM IN PSYCHOLOGY: TRANSFORMATIONS AND NEW DIRECTIONS

KATHRYN QUINA AND PHYLLIS BRONSTEIN

Extraordinary changes have taken place in psychology over the last 20 years. The people being studied are more diverse, as are the scholars studying them. Researchers, practitioners, and theorists have created a rich body of knowledge extending across gender, social, and cultural lines, along with an unprecedented range of approaches for acquiring and interpreting information. In addition, a new generation of students and faculty has increased the personal diversity within the field: The percentage of minorities receiving undergraduate psychology degrees has increased 58% since 1992, and more than 60% of undergraduate psychology degrees go to women (Kyle & Williams, 2000). Among entering doctoral psychology students, 70% are women, and 18% are African American, Latino, Asian American, or American Indian. Among faculty in doctoral programs, 36% are women, and 11% are minority group members (Pate, 2001).

In contemporary education, the question of whether to include material on diversity is no longer an intellectual debate. As Hall (1997) pointed out, given the number of people of color and other diverse groups in the United States, failure to address issues of diversity constitutes "cultural malpractice" (p. 642). Transforming the curriculum is not just a matter of adding specific courses or sections within courses on one or two minority populations, or devoting one class to "minority issues" (Kowalski, 2000; Yoder & Kahn, 1993). Indeed, such a "ghetto-ized" approach may isolate and devalue scholarship on nonmajority groups rather than offering students the kind of curriculum that "present[s] psychological information accurately" (American Psychological Association [APA], 2002a). True curricular transformation involves the recognition of gender and multiculturalism as important aspects of everyday human functioning and interaction and the infusion of this recognition into all areas of psychology. At the same time, there is a place in the curriculum for special foci; recent scholarship has provided exciting new materials for courses that focus specifically on individual groups, multicultural and cross-cultural psychology, and the psychology of gender.

DEFINING GENDER AND MULTICULTURALISM

In 1988, when our first volume, *Teaching a Psychology of People: Resources for Gender and Sociocultural Awareness*, was published, the terms *gender* and *multiculturalism* had very limited application. Most literature treated *gender* as a code word for women and *culture* as a code word for minority groups—as if these constructs were not relevant to men and majority-culture people. If women were included in a research study or theoretical work, it was considered gender relevant; when more than two ethnicities were represented, the study or work was by definition multicultural.

Nowadays, the definitions of those terms have expanded. *Gender* refers not merely to women or to women's issues but to the characteristics and behaviors a culture associates with being female or male and the characteristics and behaviors people may take on as they identify with one gender or the other. The study of men and masculinity has become well established. As well, the boundaries defining gender have become more fluid; for example, an individual may regard her- or himself as transgendered, with a gender identity that is traditionally associated with the other sex (Burke, 1996; Stryker, 1998). In addition, sexual identity is no longer assumed to be related to gender identity—for example, being gay might be associated with either conformity or nonconformity to a traditional gender role. Even the notion of there being only two biological sexes has been challenged (Fausto-Sterling, 1993).

Similarly, the term *multicultural* has expanded to include characteristics in addition to race and ethnicity. Sexual identity, socioeconomic level, physical and mental (dis)abilities, size, age, and religion, to name a few, are now being incorporated into contemporary multicultural definitions. In addition, far more "minority groups" have been recognized than the traditional handful of categories included in questionnaire demographic checklists. Scholars have learned that grouping together "Hispanics" or "Asians" fails to recognize the many cultures and language groups subsumed under each category and that people of mixed heritage often are left out altogether.

Societies tend to generate and label social categories, a process that emphasizes differences between groups and fosters social inequality—what West and Fenstermaker (1995) termed *doing difference*. On the basis of evidence that a very wide range of behaviors and lifestyles can be found within each gender and racial or ethnic group, scholars are beginning to consider gender, race, and ethnicity as social constructions rather than biological characteristics (Gergen, 1985; Unger, 1995). If these groups (and the differences between them) are socially constructed, characteristics attributed to gender, race, or ethnicity cannot be viewed as fixed or universal. Furthermore, the sociohistorical as well as the immediate situational context become critical to examinations of gender, race, ethnicity, or other characteristics (Landrine, 1995).

Feminist and multicultural scholars have also challenged the field of psychology to consider "culture" in a more complex way, addressing the intersections of identities (e.g., African heritage, female, and lesbian, Greene, 1994; women living in poverty, Lott & Bullock, 2001) as well as the experiences of those whose identities—such as biracial, multi-ethnic, bisexual, transsexual, transgendered, and intersexed—defy single categorization (Burke, 1996; Root, 1992). Brown (1994) discussed the need to be aware that people interact with each other as amalgams of characteristics, with stereotypes and expectations along many dimensions. Finally, multiculturalism has come full circle to allow White people to recognize that they, too, have an ethnicity, shaped by skin color, heritage, and cultural patterns, which in turn influences their perceptions, behaviors, and opportunities (Fine, Weis, Powell, & Wong, 1997; Unger, 1995).

BEYOND GROUP DIFFERENCES: NEW DIRECTIONS FOR RESEARCH

On the basis of a growing body of empirical and theoretical literature generated by feminist and multicultural scholars, most researchers have come to recognize the inadequacy of relying on biological sex or race as the explanation for differences observed between groups of men and women or among racial categories (Caplan & Caplan, 1999; Yee, Fairchild, Weizmann, & Wyatt, 1993). There is an increasing acknowledgment that factors such as ethnicity, economic means, country of origin, fluency in the majority language, education, regional factors, and skin color may interact with or even supplant race and gender as key variables that can affect differences in behavior and attainment. Although gender differences in particular are still a topic of fascination, researchers are now devoting attention to the questions of effect size, situational effects (i.e., are differences magnified by the particular context of the study or the particular task?), and the problem of overinterpretation of differences (e.g., see the debate in the *American Psychologist*, March 1995 [vol. 50, no. 3] and February 1996 [vol. 51, no. 2]).

The effects of inequities due to minority group membership have also been explored in new and creative ways. Analyses and discussions of stereotyping (e.g., stereotype threat; Steele, 1997), oppression (Brown, 1994), discrimination and stigma (Oyserman & Swim, 2001), and privilege (McIntosh, 1998) help convey what it means to be a member of a "different" group in U.S. culture. A body of literature on resilience in the face of these negative influences (e.g., Masten & Coatsworth, 1998) is also developing. In addition, there are indicators of a growing activist movement within psychology, toward increasing majority-culture members' awareness of discrimination, oppression, and White privilege, coupled with efforts to effect change in this area (e.g., Adelman & Enguidanos, 1995; Tatum, 2000).

DISSEMINATION OF NEW KNOWLEDGE

The increasing awareness about gender and multicultural issues within psychology has been accompanied by a burgeoning of materials for scholars, practitioners, and teachers. Journals such as the *American Psychologist* and the *Journal of Social Issues* regularly include thought-provoking and informative contributions on these topics. There are also new journals, such as *Cultural Diversity and Ethnic Minority Psychology*, *Psychology of Men and Masculinity*, *Journal of Lesbian Studies*, *Journal of Bisexuality*, *Culture and Psychology*, and *Feminism and Psychology*, as well as the free online *Electronic Magazine of Multicultural Education* (http://www.eastern.edu/publications/emme). These resources join a fine collection of older journals dealing with women and gender (e.g., *Psychology of Women Quarterly*, *Women and Therapy*, *Sex Roles*), minority groups (*Journal of Black Psychology*; *Hispanic Journal of Behavioral Sciences*; and *Disabilities Studies Quarterly*, which recently became available for free on-line at http://www.cds.hawaii.edu/DSQ/), and curricular reform (e.g., *Transformations: A Resource for Curriculum Transformation and Scholarship*). In addition, there are numerous collections of readings, as well as films and videos, that cover a wide range of gender-related and multicultural topics (see resources collected by The Society for the Teaching of Psychology at http://teachpsych.lemoyne.edu/). Many such resources are also cited throughout this volume.

The practice of psychology has changed as well, giving impetus for graduate programs to teach about gender and multiculturalism. APA (2002b) policy includes a detailed set of guidelines for multicultural teaching, research, and practice (http://www.apa.org/pi/), and gender-aware therapeutic approaches that were once considered radical are now regarded as part of quality care for any client (Brown, 1994). Dozens of organizations and individuals have developed Web sites that offer ideas for innovative teaching approaches and culturally sensitive course materials (e.g., the Curriculum Collection on Prejudice and Intergroup Relations, available from the Web site of the Society for the Psychological Study of Social Issues, http://www.spssi.org/teach_cc.html), and many departments offer (and some require) a multicultural course. Textbook authors have begun to include gender and multicultural content, sometimes throughout the book, not merely in a token chapter. Feminist pedagogical approaches have provided transformative ways to conceptualize the classroom process (Forrest & Rosenberg, 1997; Kimmel et al., 1997) as well as ways to deal with ethical challenges in the classroom (Worrell & Oakley, 2000).

Professional organizations, notably APA and its divisions, have also taken leadership roles in public and professional arenas. A plethora of useful reports, position papers, and other resources are available from the Public Interest Directorate, which can be accessed at http://www.apa.org/pi. Several divisions have instituted a biennial National Multicultural Conference and Summit (Sue, Bingham, Porché-Burke, & Vasquez, 1999). Multiculturalism is a strong and vital movement within psychology, not a mere knock at the door.

OVERALL DESIGN OF THIS BOOK

Our goal for the original volume, *Teaching a Psychology of People: Resources for Gender and Sociocultural Awareness* (Bronstein & Quina, 1988), was to gather hard-to-find information in relatively undeveloped areas, to provide instructors with resources to increase their students' awareness of diversity. Our goal this time around, for *Teaching Gender and Multicultural Awareness: Resources for the Psychology Classroom*, is similar—but instead of collecting scarce information our task has been to create a road map to help instructors find their way among the many new theories, approaches, and resources in each area of psychology. We have tried to provide practical materials as well as scholarly ones and a variety of approaches designed to help instructors integrate this new gender and multicultural scholarship into their courses. The suggestions, exercises, and resources the book offers are designed both to engage students in the classroom and to increase their awareness of and knowledge about themselves and other people, in the broadest sense. The chapter authors are teachers and scholars in various higher education settings, with a wide variety of backgrounds and interests. We have brought them together in this volume to share resources that they have found useful and innovative ideas that have worked in their classrooms.

There are a few things that are unchanged from the first book; a number of the original authors rejoined us, and the overall structure is approximately the same. Beyond that, however, this is a new book. Chapters by first-book authors have been completely updated, expanded, and rewritten, to include the latest research, scholarship, and teaching resources in their fields. Authors new to the current book have brought fresh perspectives to the topics at hand, reflecting expanded definitions of multiculturalism and gender; in addition, we have included chapters on American Indians, Jews, men, aging, and cross-cultural psychology, which were absent from the original volume.

The book is divided into three parts. The authors in part I take an integrative approach and present strategies for infusing gender and multiculturalism into basic undergraduate courses. For example, Su L. Boatright and Sara S. Little (chapter 1) present a comprehensive coverage of typical introductory psychology topics, with examples of research in each area that can expand traditional conceptions and increase multicultural awareness. Sondra E. Solomon (chapter 2) offers a list of specific steps instructors can take to infuse multiculturalism into abnormal psychology courses, with readings and resources accompanying each step, and guidance for creating a safe and open classroom environment. Lynne A. Bond and Kathleen S. Gorman (chapter 3) provide many engaging classroom strategies for making developmental psychology students aware of both the commonality of developmental processes and the uniqueness of each individual. Hope Landrine and Elizabeth A. Klonoff (chapter 9) provide thought-provoking examples from their own and others' research to illustrate the links between sociocultural context and health outcomes. Beverly J. Goodwin, Maureen C. McHugh, and Lisa Osachy Touster (chapter 10) provide an in-depth examination of issues for African American women, working-class and poor women, and obese women as illustrations of a multicultural approach to teaching the psychology of women.

Part II includes chapters on courses designed to focus specifically on multiculturalism or to heighten the awareness of cultural, ethnic, and gender issues related to a particular population. For example, Nnamdi Pole, Jennifer J. Treuting, and Robert W. Levenson (chapter 11) present a blueprint for teaching an ethnic psychology course on U.S. populations that can engage an entire department, including undergraduates, graduate students, and faculty. Chapters 13–17 focus on specific ethnic–cultural groups, while chapters 18–21 address disability issues; the psychology of aging; lesbian, gay, bisexual, transgender, and intersex issues; and the psychology of men. The information can be infused into more general courses, or it can be used to teach courses on these particular topics.

Part III goes beyond individual course content and presents models that have been developed and implemented for integrating gender and multicultural issues into the curriculum on a program- or department-wide basis. Vonda Dionne Jones-Hudson (chapter 22) and Elizabeth Davis-Russell (chapter 24) describe the steps and challenges in moving from monoculturalism to multiculturalism, for an entire psychology department and a graduate clinical program, respectively. In chapter 23, Mary Zahm and Kathryn Quina describe ways to enhance the teaching of students from diverse backgrounds in continuing education programs, including the use of distance learning and other technological innovations.

In the final chapter, 25, Gale Young presents guidelines and techniques for dealing with classroom dialogue. Topics related to gender and multicultural issues can become highly charged and emotional as participants struggle to express and understand diverse opinions. If faculty are unaware of this possibility and unskilled in helping the class deal with difficult dialogues, the content may be lost, and barriers may arise between students with different worldviews. Young discusses ways instructors can facilitate the exchange of ideas, views, and perceptions in a positive, ethical, and educational manner that fosters a climate of civility and respect. We hope that this information, along with additional perspectives offered by other authors (e.g., Lisa Bowleg [chapter 4] and Sondra E. Solomon [chapter 2]), will foster faculty skills for defusing difficult situations and encouraging students' openness to one another's views.

We also hope that these approaches, as well as the general informational content of the book, will help instructors overcome any hesitancy they may feel about including diversity issues in their teaching. Many faculty question their own qualifications in this area and may also be afraid that they will make mistakes, that their attempts at inclusion will be seen as perpetuating stereotypes or in some other way misrepresenting a particular group. Faculty may sense students' reluctance to think and talk about race and class and may be worried about arousing defensiveness if students are led to consider their own roles in a racist society. In addition, they may be fearful of discovering or revealing their own biases and may feel vulnerable to criticism or attack should they make a "slip." We believe that when listening and learning are involved mistakes can be a valuable part of the educational process, for faculty as well as for students. Instructors who are willing to enter this new territory, and in the process discover some of their own areas of bias and ignorance, can provide powerful models for their students. We hope that the material in this volume will foster instructors' interest and enthusiasm for infusing multiculturalism into their teaching and that the suggestions (and caveats) provided herein will given them useful tools for moving forward with confidence.

REFERENCES

Adelman, J., & Enguidanos, G. M. (Eds.). (1995). *Racism in the lives of women: Testimony, theory, and guides to antiracist practice.* New York: Haworth.

American Psychological Association. (2002a). *Ethical principles of psychologists and code of conduct* (Principle 7.04[a]). Retrieved January 2, 2003, from http://www.apa.org/ethics/code.html

American Psychological Association. (2002b). *Guidelines on multicultural education, training, research, practice, and organizational change for psychologists*. Retrieved January 3, 2003, from http://www.apa.org/pi

Bronstein, P., & Quina, K. (Eds.). (1988). *Teaching a psychology of people: Resources for gender and sociocultural awareness*. Washington, DC: American Psychological Association.

Brown, L. (1994). *Subversive dialogues: Toward a theory of feminist therapy*. New York: Basic Books.

Burke, P. (1996). *Gender shock: Exploding the myths of male and female*. New York: Anchor Books/Doubleday.

Caplan, P. J., & Caplan, J. (1999). *Thinking critically about research on sex and gender* (2nd ed.). Needham Heights, MA: Addison Wesley Longman.

Fausto-Sterling, A. (1993, March–April). The five sexes. *The Sciences*, 20–24.

Fine, M., Weis, L., Powell, L. C., & Wong, L. M. (Eds.). (1997). *Off white: Readings on race, power, and society*. New York: Routledge.

Forrest, L., & Rosenberg, F. (1997). A review of the feminist pedagogy literature: The neglected child of feminist psychology. *Applied and Preventive Psychology, 6,* 179–192.

Gergen, K. (1985). The social constructionist movement in modern psychology. *American Psychologist, 40,* 266–275.

Greene, B. (1994). Lesbian women of color: Triple jeopardy. In L. Comas-Diaz & B. Greene (Eds.), *Women of color: Integrating ethnic and gender identities in psychotherapy* (pp. 389–427). New York: Guilford Press.

Hall, C. C. I. (1997). Cultural malpractice: The growing obsolescence of psychology with the changing U.S. population. *American Psychologist, 52,* 642–651.

Kimmel, E., Worrell, J., Daniluk, J., Gawalek, M. A., Lerner, K., Stahley, G., & Kahoe, S. (1997). Preaching what we practice: Principles and strategies of feminist pedagogy. In J. Worrell & N. G. Johnson (Eds.), *Shaping the future of feminist psychology: Education, research, and practice* (pp. 121–153). Washington, DC: American Psychological Association.

Kowalski, R. M. (2000). Including gender, race, and ethnicity in psychology content courses. *Teaching of Psychology, 27*(1), 18–24.

Kyle, T. M., & Williams, S. (2000, April). *1998–99 APA Survey of Undergraduate Departments of Psychology*, Retrieved June 28, 2001, from http://research.apa.org/9899undergrad.html

Landrine, H. (1995). Introduction: Cultural diversity, contextualism, and feminist psychology. In H. Landrine (Ed.), *Bringing cultural diversity to feminist psychology: Theory, research, and practice* (pp. 1–20). Washington, DC: American Psychological Association.

Lott, B., & Bullock, H. (Eds.). (2001). Listening to the voices of poor women [Special issue]. *Journal of Social Issues, 57*(2).

Masten, A. S., & Coatsworth, J. D. (1998). The development of competence in favorable and unfavorable environmments: Lessons from research on successful children. *American Psychologist, 53,* 205–220.

McIntosh, P. (1998). White privilege: Unpacking the invisible knapsack. In M. McGoldrick (Ed.), *Revisioning family therapy: Race, culture, and gender in clinical practice* (pp. 147–152). New York: Guilford Press.

Oyserman, D., & Swim, J. K. (Eds.). (2001). Stigma: An insider's perspective [Special issue]. *Journal of Social Issues, 57*(1).

Pate, W. E. (2001, April). *Data from graduate study in psychology: 1999–2000*. Retrieved June 28, 2001, from http://research.apa.org/grad00contents.html

Root, M. (Ed.). (1992). *Racially mixed people in America*. Newbury Park, CA: Sage.

Steele, C. M. (1997). A threat in the air: How stereotypes shape intellectual identity and performance. *American Psychologist, 52,* 513–629.

Stryker, S. (Ed.). (1998). The transgender issue [Special issue]. *Journal of Lesbian and Gay Studies, 4*(2).

Sue, D. W., Bingham, R. P., Porché-Burke, L., & Vasquez, M. (1999). The diversification of psychology: A multicultural revolution. *American Psychologist, 54,* 1061–1069.

Tatum, B. D. (2000). *"Why are all the Black kids sitting together in the cafeteria?" And other conversations about race*. New York: Basic Books.

Unger, R. K. (1995). Conclusion: Cultural diversity and the future of feminist psychology. In H. Landrine (Ed.), *Bringing cultural diversity to feminist psychology* (pp. 413–431). Washington, DC: American Psychological Association.

West, C., & Fenstermaker, S. (1995). Doing difference. *Gender & Society, 9,* 8–37.

Worrell, J., & Oakley, D. R. (2000). Teaching as transformation: Resolving ethical dilemmas in feminist pedagogy. In M. M. Brabeck (Ed.), *Practicing feminist ethics in psychology* (pp. 167–188). Washington, DC: American Psychological Association.

Yee, A. H., Fairchild, H. H., Weizmann, F., & Wyatt, G. E. (1993). Addressing psychology's problems with race. *American Psychologist, 48,* 1132–1140.

Yoder, J. D., & Kahn, A. S. (1993). Working toward an inclusive psychology of women. *American Psychologist, 48,* 846–850.

I

INTEGRATING DIVERSITY INTO GENERAL PSYCHOLOGY COURSES

1

THE INTRODUCTORY PSYCHOLOGY COURSE FROM A BROADER HUMAN PERSPECTIVE

SU L. BOATRIGHT AND SARA S. LITTLE

The introductory psychology course is usually students' first formal exposure to the field of psychology. For many, it is the only exposure they will have, apart from the media or involvement in the mental health system. Issues, facts, questions, and possible biases that students encounter in the introductory course can have lasting effects on their views of psychology and their perceptions of human nature. Such a course has the potential to enhance their understanding of their own motivations, shape their beliefs about mental illness, inform their behaviors as parents and as citizens, and affect their social perceptions of and attributions about others.

As students face the prospect of structuring their lives and developing their careers in the 21st century with the real possibility that they will become members of a global village, it seems particularly important that the introductory psychology course clarify the effects of social context and culture on human behavior. To do this, instructors must make students aware of similarities and differences across cultures and prepare them for encounters in which their own customs, beliefs, and social expectations will be challenged. At the same time, students' local communities are becoming increasingly multicultural. Thus, it is important that introductory courses cover a broad range of human experiences—including issues related to ethnicity, gender, sexual orientation, religion, disabilities, and aging—so that undergraduates can come to appreciate group differences and increase their awareness and sensitivity when interacting with people who are physically or culturally different from themselves.

Like others (e.g., Nieto, 2000), we favor a twofold approach to achieving a multicultural curriculum. In some areas, diversity needs to be addressed directly, as in a lecture or unit on prejudice. However, because limiting discussions of multicultural issues to one or two class periods can marginalize and isolate these topics, we also advocate an infusion of gender and multicultural information across the whole course. In this chapter we address some of the biases and omissions that we have observed in current introductory psychology textbooks, provide suggestions for supplementing these materials, and offer ideas for engaging students, with some consideration of classroom dynamics. Instructors may also wish to consult other chapters in this volume for additional information about specific content areas.

Many schools use large lecture formats for the introductory course, with smaller recitation sections led by teaching assistants. The topics and exercises in this chapter can easily be introduced during recitation sessions; however, the course instructor needs to make sure that teaching assistants, who may have had no previous experience in facilitating groups, receive training in handling difficult dialogues (see chapter 25, this volume). In addition, it is important to have frequent contact with teaching assistants, to help them handle any problems that may arise.

BIOLOGICAL FOUNDATIONS

Beginning college students tend to exhibit *dualistic* thinking (Erickson & Strommer, 1991), viewing behavior as the result of either biological factors or environmental influences. Therefore, a major goal of every introductory psychology course should be to help students avoid these simplistic and inadequate explanations of behavior. This is particularly important because biological reductionism—attributing complex behavioral tendencies to genetic or biochemical causes—has historically been associated with societal inequities, and has been used to foster prejudice and discrimination (Beckwith, 1993) and to promote irresponsible social agendas, such as eugenics (e.g., Gould, 1991).

Discussions of social and cultural influences on behavior can challenge stereotypical thinking and give students tools to question explanations for diversity that are primarily biological. For instance, researchers have implicated neuroendocrine and genetic factors in the development of women's sexual orientations (Veniegas & Conley, 2000). However, biological differences between groups need not imply a causal link. It is often difficult to identify the direction of causality; even if a biological factor is present initially, environmental influences may also have biochemical or biological effects (Greenberg & Bailey, 1993). Instructors can guide students in interpreting biological findings in a broader context, pointing out that homosexuality and heterosexuality are neither dichotomous (Bem, 1995) nor mutually exclusive categories of behavior (Garnets & Kimmel, 1991). Instead, sexual behaviors can be described as involving multiple dimensions based on ideation and activities, as well as sociocultural factors, with sexual preference or sexual identity sometimes evolving or changing across the life span (Garnets & Kimmel, 1991; Kitzinger & Wilkinson, 1995). It is also useful to point out to students that research regarding romantic relationships tends to be heterosexist (Rose, 2000) and that labels may have specific implications—for example, that *sexual orientation* implies an underlying assumption that one's choice of sexual partners is a fixed biological characteristic, in contrast to the terms *sexual preference* and *sexual identity*.

Instructors can also emphasize that sexual norms may vary dramatically across cultures. For example, according to Levine and Silk (1997), polyandry is the most common marital arrangement among the Nyinba of northwestern Nepal. In this social system, brothers jointly wed a single woman who is expected to be sexually active with her various husbands. For Nyinban girls, marriages with three brothers are viewed as highly desirable; in fact, both young girls and their parents view these to be the most stable marital arrangements. Using examples such as this one, instructors can help students recognize that although one may feel compelled to endorse or censure certain cultural practices, objective assessments should take into account the benefits or harm (or both) to individuals within the context of culture. It is rarely the case that a cultural practice is simply "good" or "bad."

Instructors can also encourage students to avoid dualistic thinking in the context of human sexuality by discussing categorizations of biological sex that go beyond "male" versus "female." In the United States, surgical procedures and hormonal treatments usually force people who have some of the physical characteristics of both sexes into male or female physical appearance, often resulting in genital scarring and reduced sexual sensitivity, and most parents reinforce gender-stereotypical social roles, beginning in infancy (Fausto-Sterling, 2000). Students can consider whether discussions of gender should focus less on genitalia and instead include a wider range of sexual identities and characteristics that would allow for gender multiplicity and greater cross-cultural perspective (Kessler, 1998).

DEVELOPMENTAL PSYCHOLOGY

Important themes in the study of human development include attachment, child-rearing practices, gender role socialization, and the development of ethnic or racial identities, yet these topics often receive very narrow coverage in introductory psychology textbooks.

Attachment

Virtually all textbooks discuss the attachment between caregiver and child, as assessed through the Strange Situation Test (Ainsworth, Blehar, Waters, & Wall, 1978), but few contain full discussions of attachment—or ways of assessing attachment—in cross-cultural contexts. Thus, it is helpful for instructors to introduce students to other cultural patterns, such as the cosleeping arrangements for children that are prevalent around the world (Okami, 1995), the rarity of separation anxiety in Beng infants (Gottlieb, 2000), and the potential effects of multiple (Ivey, 2000) or nonparental caregivers (Lev-Wiesel, 2000). Instructors can invite students to consider the role of culture in development, especially as it relates to current controversies about attachment and the secure-base phenomenon (e.g., Posada & Jacobs, 2001).

Child-Rearing Practices

In the absence of cross-cultural comparisons, introductory psychology students are likely to view the child-rearing practices of their own social groups as more "normal" than, or even superior to, others. Instructors might encourage them to step outside of their cultural backgrounds in order to view U.S. practices from the perspective of other cultures. For instance, undergraduate students are typically surprised to learn that it is rare, outside of U.S. society, for infants to sleep in their own beds or children to sleep alone in their own rooms (Okami, 1995)—practices that are presumed to promote independence and self-reliance. It seems even more surprising to students that people from other countries (e.g., the Mayans in Guatemala) tend to view this American practice as a cruel and heartless treatment of young children, who need the security of an adult presence at bedtime (Morelli, Rogoff, Oppenheim, & Goldsmith, 1992). Stearns, Rowland, and Giarnella (1996) provided a historical overview of the topic. McKenna (1996) discussed the relationship between bed sharing and Sudden Infant Death Syndrome, a controversy informed by cross-cultural data.

Gender Role Socialization

Most introductory psychology textbooks today discuss gender role socialization in young children. However, the research that is presented tends to reflect White, middle-class American experiences, with only a few texts addressing ethnic–racial or cross-cultural perspectives on gender. It is useful to point out to students that across cultures, acceptance of traditional gender stereotypes appears to be related to the culture's dominant religion, the degree of urbanization, and levels of socioeconomic development (Best, 2001). Furthermore, within the United States, similarities in gender role socialization seem to be greater than differences for some ethnic or racial groups (DeLeon, 1993), and gender role ideology can differ significantly as a function of geographical location within a single ethnicity or culture (Chang, 1999). Instructors might encourage their students to examine the specific elements of each culture that create and perpetuate gender role differences, such as family dynamics, educational practices, historical and socioeconomic factors, religious beliefs, and government policies.

Ethnic Identity Development

Despite the fact that more than one in four Americans have a cultural heritage associated with nonmajority status (U.S. Bureau of the Census, 2001), many introductory psychology textbooks give little coverage to issues related to the development of ethnic self-awareness. Members of U.S. minority populations seem to develop stronger ethnic identities than do European Americans (Pellebon, 2000). Although one needs to be careful about making generalizations across subgroups, the literature indicates that minority individuals in the United States who have an awareness of racism and who have developed a strong sense of ethnic identity also seem to have higher global self-esteem (Carlson, Uppal, & Prosser, 2000) and show higher achievement (Oyserman, Gant, & Ager, 1995). This has led many psychologists today to suggest that a strong sense of ethnic identity and cultural mistrust (Phelps, Taylor, & Gerard, 2001) can serve as a psychological buffer, mitigating the detrimental effects of racism and negative stereotyping (Franklin, 1999; Quintana & Vera, 1999). U.S. majority-culture students in particular can benefit from consideration of their own ethnic identities (Roediger, 1999), because they tend to view themselves as cultureless—an attitude that can reflect unconscious assumptions of racial superiority (Perry, 2001). Such consideration can facilitate an examination of negative stereotypes, an appreciation of cultural differences, and a greater awareness of the privileges their identities have automatically accrued for them (Lawrence & Tatum, 1997).

While discussing ethnic identity it is important to include information about the psychological dynamics for individuals with multiple ethnic identities (Pittinsky, Shih, & Ambady, 1999) as well as the general nature of biracial or multiracial experiences in the United States (e.g., Fukuyama, 1999; Herring, 1995). The number of multiracial individuals continues to increase in the United States, and there is a growing tendency for these individuals to claim both aspects of their heritages (U.S. Bureau of the Census, 2001). Multiracial students can become very frustrated about omission of their situations in discussions of ethnicity, perhaps because it reflects the way they are treated in the larger society.

INTELLIGENCE AND ACADEMIC PERFORMANCE

Definitions of intelligence and the interpretation of intelligence measures are among the most controversial topics in the field of psychology (Daniel, 1997; Gould, 1996), in part because of their serious political and societal ramifications (Ryan, 1997). Whereas most introductory psychology textbooks address concerns about within- and between-group variability, the role of heredity in intelligence, and potential biases in testing, they rarely discuss criteria for assessing bias in testing (e.g., Brown, Reynolds, & Whitaker, 1999) or cross-cultural perspectives (Bleichrodt, Hoksbergen, & Khire, 1999; Helms, 1992).

It is useful to point out to students that IQ test items may be biased in that they may embody assumptions about life experience that do not apply to individuals from particular subgroups. For example, in the Kaufman Assessment Battery for Children (Kaufman & Kaufman, 1983), an intelligence test that is actually designed to be culturally sensitive, content is derived from television, which is a forbidden activity for American Hassidic Jews. There is also an assumption that everyone knows who Santa Claus is—ignoring the fact that "Santa" is a Christian construction (Little, 1992). In addition, scores on intelligence tests may be affected by visual or other sensory impairments. Wyver and Markham (1999) identified items on the Wechsler Intelligence Scale for Children (Wechsler, 1991) that seem to rely heavily on sighted experiences—for example, a question about finding a lost wallet.

Although for the purpose of protecting secure tests the actual content of standardized test items should not be disclosed (American Psychological Association, 1999), instructors can construct their own examples using comparable items.

An additional problem with intelligence testing is *stereotype threat*, whereby students' performances on tests of academic ability may be hampered by internalized stereotypic views of their capabilities. For example, Steele and Aronson (1995) demonstrated that scores for African American students were significantly reduced by seemingly minor changes in wording (i.e., an intelligence test presented as a measure of their "verbal abilities and limitations," as opposed to a test of the "psychological factors involved in solving verbal problems," p. 799), particularly if race was made salient. Subsequent research has demonstrated that stereotype threat can affect other groups as well, including women (Quinn & Spencer, 2001), White males (Aronson et al., 1999), and persons of lower socioeconomic status (Croizet

& Claire, 1998). Because stereotype threat can conceivably affect the learning environment in the psychology classroom, both teachers and students can benefit from an understanding of this phenomenon. Moreover, intervention strategies that are designed to overcome the effects of stereotype threat have achieved some preliminary success with college students, increasing grade-point averages and retention rates for both African American and European American students (Wolfe & Spencer, 1996).

Finally, few textbooks provide full discussions of the many sociocultural and economic factors that can be confounded with minority status, ultimately affecting children's intelligence scores and their academic performance, such as poverty, stereotypes of marginalized children as less capable, inadequate prenatal care, and special education services (Forness et al., 1998; McLoyd, 1998; also see chapter 7, this volume). It is important for students to learn that researchers have identified a number of environmental factors that can increase a child's likelihood of succeeding socially and academically in school, but only comprehensive, intensive, culturally relevant interventions have yielded long-term results (Ramey & Ramey, 1998). A brief yet cogent review of this issue is available in Wickelgren's (1999) article, which can serve as the basis for class discussion regarding the relationship between research and public policy.

PERSONALITY THEORY

Most introductory psychology textbooks point out that the methods used to assess personality may not be applicable to people from other cultures because of differences in language, motivation, and cultural norms. However, presentations of personality theories are generally restricted to traditional perspectives (psychodynamic, dispositional, humanistic, learning, cognitive, biological), which can be criticized for being culturally isolated (Ehrenreich, 1997) and representing a western European, male-centered perspective. For instance, in many other cultures selfhood seems to be more interdependent—that is, more flexible and public, and dependent on social context, with self-satisfaction based on one's ability to maintain harmonious relations with others (Markus & Kitayama, 1991). According to these authors, "the squeaky wheel gets the grease" in America, while for the Japanese, "the nail that stands out gets pounded down" (p. 224). Furthermore, many introductory texts mention *collectivist* and *individualistic* societies, in the context of personality, yet they often treat collectivism and individualism as dichotomous variables, which may be too simplistic (Chiou, 2001).

Introductory psychology textbooks generally include some personality research and theories that are relevant to women and marginalized groups within the United States, but a number of gaps remain. Whereas texts often include feminist criticisms of mainstream personality theories that were based on males but applied to women, they do not examine different feminist personality theories (Enns, 1993) or include research and theory related to the development of a feminist identity (Carpenter & Johnson, 2001; Fischer, Tokar, Mergl, Good, Hill, & Blum, 2000). Instructors might also introduce students to the Afrocentric paradigm (Mazama, 2001) as an example of an approach to human personality conceptualized outside of the field's predominately Eurocentric focus. Afrocentrism is based on the view that the African experience is central to understanding African American lives and involves a systematic effort to avoid assumptions that can be traced to Western or European conceptual frameworks. Students could then be asked to identify other cultural groups (e.g., Latina/Latino) for whom an exclusively Eurocentric approach may be inappropriate.

SOCIAL PSYCHOLOGY

Instructors can focus on selected topics within social psychology that will foster students' understanding of ethnocentrism and prejudice and help them to function more effectively in a diverse society.

Interpersonal Communication

There is a growing literature regarding interpersonal communication as a function of age, gender, ethnicity, status, and cultural context. For example, the use of nonverbal cues, such as gaze direction or nodding the head, can differ between genders (Bailenson, Blascovich, Beall, & Loomis, 2001; Campbell, Wallace, & Benson, 1996; Hall & Friedman, 1999), ethnicities (Asante & Davis, 1985), and cultures (Burgoon, 1985). For some people, direct gaze into another person's face is a sign of disrespect (Burgoon, 1985); for others, it can heighten the perception that a person is confident, competent, and truthful (Asante & Davis, 1985; Droney & Brooks, 1993; Knackstedt & Kleinke, 1991). The meaning of hand gestures can vary dramatically across cultures, and an awareness of this can reduce the likelihood of accidentally giving offense during social interactions with others. As Kirch (1979) pointed out, spoken errors can provide cues that the speaker has limited mastery of a language, mitigating any negative impressions. In contrast, errors in non-verbal communications provide few such cues and it may be difficult to identify the specific factors that give rise to social discomfort or insulted feelings. Furthermore, even subtle differences in gestures can have dramatically different meanings across cultures. For instance, the "OK" sign in America (thumb touching forefinger) is an insult for Brazilians, for whom it means the same thing as the American upthrust middle finger. Likewise, using the fingers to form a V sign (palm facing oneself) is extremely offensive to many people in England, yet the same gesture with the palm facing outward means "Victory," just as it does in America (Marco, 1998).

Interpersonal distances are also important forms of communication that can differ between groups. In a recent field study examining naturally occurring dyadic interactions around the world, Remland, Jones, and Brinkman (1995) demonstrated that the Irish and Scots tend to stand more closely during their conversations than the English, French, Italians, or Greeks. Students can easily imagine, or role play, an interaction between individuals who differ in their preferred proximities. As one person keeps approaching, the other person keeps backing away, and insulted feelings and negative perceptions of each other can increase, regardless of the verbal messages.

Verbal styles of expression also may vary among genders, age groups, ethnicities, and cultures. For instance, in one preschool study girls were found to use more collaborative speech than did boys (Thompson & Moore, 2000). Research with U.S. adults suggests that women often speak more tentatively than men and that these speech differences can have a significant impact on the success of persuasive arguments made to male or female audiences—for example, men are more readily persuaded by women who speak in a tentative fashion (Carli, 1999). Instructors can underscore these differences by asking students to observe how the behavior of their friends' and their own behavior may vary depending on the gender, ethnicity, or age of the other person, as well as the situation—for example, women may use a more assertive voice when they are seeking care for their children.

Prejudice

Because it is rare for textbooks to adequately identify the many attributes that are linked with discrimination—such as gender, ethnicity, age, sexual identity, socioeconomic status, geographical location of birth, and disability—instructors may wish to supplement textbook presentations of this topic (e.g., see Lott & Maluso, 1995). There are a number of illustrative videos on prejudice and discrimination. For example, *A Class Divided* (Peters, 1985) presents Jane Elliott's techniques for teaching young children about these issues. A useful assignment is to ask students to write reaction papers indicating whether they think that Elliott's methods should be a routine part of the educational curriculum in the United States today; then, in a subsequent class period, they can then discuss their views in relation to some of their own experiences with prejudice or discrimination. Another relevant video is *True Colors* (Sawyer, 1991), a provocative report of a field experiment contrasting the treatment encountered by two men (one Black and one White) in a number of everyday situations. It provides powerful evidence of the pervasiveness of racism and discrimination in this culture and, as such, can generate intense discussion. In addition, instructors can help nonminority students begin to understand the subtleties of racism through a discussion of White privilege (McIntosh, 1988) as well as its effects on the mental health of targeted individuals (Klonoff, Landrine, & Ullman, 1999).

Overall, instructors should expect strong student reactions, including anger, when discussing racism in U.S. society. Some nonminority students may feel that they are being accused of wrongdoing or that their families and social networks are being attacked. Many believe that racial prejudice and discrimination are no longer important factors in U.S. society and may even argue that there is now reverse discrimination against persons of majority status. Minority students may experience anger or hopelessness in response to ignorance, insensitivity, or lack of awareness of racism from nonminority peers. The challenge for instructors is to create a safe learning environment in which the topic can be fully explored, with every individual feeling respected and valued. We have found it useful to assign brief readings that address questions such as "Why are all the Black students sitting together in the cafeteria?" (O'Neil, 1997–1998; Tatum, 1997) and "What do you do when you're called a racist?" (Tatum, 1999), which stimulate lively discussion. It is also useful for students to learn about White role models who have resisted the role of oppressor and protested against racism (Tatum, 1994).

ABNORMAL AND CLINICAL PSYCHOLOGY

Another major theme that instructors may want to address involves the changing definitions of psychiatric diagnoses as they have been presented in the various editions of the *Diagnostic and Statistical Manual of Mental Disorders* (DSM; American Psychiatric Association, 1994). A powerful illustration of this phenomenon is the history of the DSM's perspective on homosexuality. This is effectively conveyed in the video *Changing Our Minds: The Story of Evelyn Hooker* (Harrison & Schmiechen, 1992), which describes earlier medical treatments such as electroconvulsive shock therapy, castration, hysterectomies, massive hormone injections, and lobotomies for this supposed psychiatric disorder.

Critiques of the DSM suggest that sexism, racism, ageism, classism, and homophobia may be inherent in a number of diagnostic criteria (Caplan, 1995). For instance, in the context of learning disabilities, Caplan argued that sexism gives rise to the common perception that boys, more than girls, are prone to learning disabilities. She pointed out that even today it is considered more important for boys to succeed academically and that girls are socialized to express their frustrations with failure less overtly than are boys; therefore, it makes sense that learning disabilities will be diagnosed more often in boys than in girls. Instructors may also want to inform students about current controversies regarding the impact of gender stereotyping and bias in psychiatric diagnoses of personality, anxiety disorders, and judgments of client dangerousness (e.g., Becker & Lamb, 1994; Bornstein, 1996; Elbogen, Williams, Kim, Tomkins, & Scalora, 2001).

In addition, it is important to make students aware of why the *DSM* may be inappropriate for diagnosing individuals from other cultures. For example, syndromes that are typically North American (e.g., anorexia nervosa and chronic fatigue syndrome) are in the main text, whereas syndromes that seem linked to specific cultural minority groups—for example, the Latino *ataque de nervios* (attack of nerves)—are included in an appendix, thereby marginalizing the role of culture in psychiatry (López & Guarnaccia, 2000). As with the assessment of intelligence, students need to be aware that evaluators of psychological and behavioral problems should be culturally competent and cautious in their interpretations. For discussions of therapeutic issues related to the treatment of ethnic minorities and immigrants, see chapters 13–16 in this volume.

CONCLUSIONS

The overall focus of this chapter has been to provide materials that can supplement the introductory psychology course; however, we hope that teachers will use these materials with sensitivity and caution. Students differ in their sophistication and comfort levels in discussions of gender, race, sexual preferences, ethnicity, and culture. Those who are part of a minority group may respond positively to a more inclusive curriculum, but they may also experience discomfort if they feel that they are repeatedly the focus of attention in class discussions. A balance must be achieved in which students feel safe enough to contribute comments about their own cultural contexts yet there is no expectation that they speak as a representative of any particular group and there is no obligation for any one student to take on the role of "teacher." Knowing that our ability to maintain this balance will vary from semester to semester, or even from day to day, we try to resist the occasional discouragement that accompanies a social activist approach to teaching.

We also try to model sensitivity and respect for cultural differences, even as we propose that certain cultural practices should be eliminated or changed. In doing this we realize that we can affect the lives of individual students, influencing how they perceive themselves and their own cultural backgrounds. Recently, following a class discussion of cultural relativism, a student privately expressed anger that *infibulation* (female circumcision) was mentioned in relation to his family's culture. Despite his heritage, the student apparently knew nothing about this cultural practice, and he felt that the class discussion perpetuated negative stereotypes about his culture. He therefore decided to consult his grandfather who, to his dismay, confirmed that this procedure did, in fact, take place in the grandfather's country of origin. The grandfather defended the practice by saying that it was sometimes necessary for young girls to undergo this surgery for hygienic reasons, because of the dry and sandy climate. The student reacted with shame, as many people do when confronted with evidence that one's ancestors or family members have engaged in cultural practices that one finds unacceptable. The student realized that although he loved his grandfather, he could not accept this particular cultural practice.

Perhaps this student's experience shows how the cultural relativism paradox can be resolved. Students can come to realize that they disapprove of an action, belief, or practice, without condemning the people themselves. In the classroom, we model this approach, challenging students to critically examine their beliefs about their own cultural practices, and encouraging them to be more sensitive, while making it clear that we value them as people. In this way we hope to create an experiential example of what it means to embrace and respect multiculturalism.

REFERENCES

Ainsworth, M. S., Blehar, M. C., Waters, E., & Wall, S. (1978). *Patterns of attachment: A psychological study of the Strange Situation.* Hillsdale, NJ: Erlbaum.

American Psychiatric Association. (1994). *Diagnostic and statistical manual of mental disorders* (4th ed.). Washington, DC: Author.

American Psychological Association. (1999). Test security: Protecting the integrity of tests. *American Psychologist, 54,* 1078.

Aronson, J., Lustina, M. J., Good, C., Keough, K., Steele, C. M., & Brown, J. (1999). When White men can't do math: Necessary and sufficient factors in stereotype threat. *Journal of Experimental Social Psychology, 35,* 29–46.

Asante, M., & Davis, A. (1985). Black and White communication: Analyzing workplace encounters. *Journal of Black Studies, 16,* 77–93.

Bailenson, J. N., Blascovich, J., Beall, A. C., & Loomis, J. M. (2001). Equilibrium theory revisited: Mutual gaze and personal space in virtual environments. *Presence, 10,* 583–598.

Becker, D., & Lamb, S. (1994). Sex bias in the diagnosis of borderline personality disorder and post-traumatic stress disorder. *Professional Psychology: Research and Practice, 25,* 55–61.

Beckwith, J. (1993). Thinking of biology: A historical view of social responsibility in genetics. *BioScience, 43,* 327–333.

Bem, S. L. (1995). Dismantling gender polarization and compulsory heterosexuality: Should we turn the volume down or up? *Journal of Sex Research, 32,* 329–334.

Best, D. L. (2001). Gender concepts: Convergence in cross-cultural research and methodologies. *Cross-Cultural Research, 35,* 23–43.

Bleichrodt, N., Hoksbergen, R. A. C., & Khire, U. (1999). Cross-cultural testing of intelligence. *Cross-Cultural Research, 33,* 3–25.

Bornstein, R. F. (1996). Sex differences in dependent personality disorder prevalence rates. *Clinical Psychology: Science and Practice, 3,* 1–12.

Brown, R. T., Reynolds, C. R., & Whitaker, J. S. (1999). Bias in mental testing since "Bias in Mental Testing." *School Psychology Quarterly, 14,* 208–238.

Burgoon, J. K. (1985). Nonverbal signals. In M. L. Knapp & G. R. Miller, *Handbook of interpersonal communication* (pp. 344–390). Beverly Hills, CA: Sage.

Campbell, R., Wallace, S., & Benson, P. J. (1996). Real men don't look down: Direction of gaze affects decisions on faces. *Visual Cognition, 3,* 393–412.

Caplan, P. J. (1995). *They say you're crazy: How the world's most powerful psychiatrists decide who is normal.* Reading, MA: Addison Wesley.

Carli, L. L. (1999). Gender, interpersonal power, and social influence. *Journal of Social Issues, 55,* 81–99.

Carlson, C., Uppal, S., & Prosser, E. C. (2000). Ethnic differences in processes contributing to the self-esteem of early adolescent girls. *Journal of Early Adolescence, 20,* 44–67.

Carpenter, S., & Johnson, L. E. (2001). Women derive collective self-esteem from their feminist identity. *Psychology of Women Quarterly, 25,* 254–257.

Chang, L. (1999). Gender role egalitarian attitudes in Beijing, Hong Kong, Florida, and Michigan. *Journal of Cross-Cultural Psychology, 30,* 722–741.

Chiou, J. (2001). Horizontal and vertical individualism and collectivism among college students in the United States, Taiwan, and Argentina. *Journal of Social Psychology, 141,* 667–678.

Croizet, J., & Claire, T. (1998). Extending the concept of stereotype threat to social class: The intellectual underperformance of students from low socioeconomic backgrounds. *Personality and Social Psychology Bulletin, 24,* 588–594.

Daniel, M. H. (1997). Intelligence testing: Status and trends. *American Psychologist, 52,* 1038–1045.

DeLeon, B. (1993). Sex-role identity among college students: A cross-cultural analysis. *Hispanic Journal of Behavioral Sciences, 15,* 476–489.

Droney, J. M., & Brooks, C. I. (1993). Attributions of self-esteem as a function of duration of eye contact. *Journal of Social Psychology, 133,* 715–722.

Ehrenreich, J. H. (1997). Personality theory: A case of intellectual and social isolation? *Journal of Psychology, 131,* 33–44.

Elbogen, E. B., Williams, A. L., Kim, D., Tomkins, A. J., & Scalora, A. J. (2001). Gender and perceptions of dangerousness in civil psychiatric patients. *Legal and Criminological Psychology, 6,* 215–228.

Enns, C. Z. (1993). Twenty years of feminist counseling and therapy: From naming biases to implementing multifaceted practice. *The Counseling Psychologist, 21,* 3–87.

Erickson, B. L., & Strommer, D. W. (1991). *Teaching college freshmen.* San Francisco: Jossey-Bass.

Fausto-Sterling, A. (2000, July–August). The five sexes, revisited. *The Sciences, 40*(4), 18–23.

Fischer, A. R., Tokar, D. M., Mergl, M. M., Good, G. E., Hill, M. S., & Blum, S. A. (2000). Assessing women's feminist identity development: Studies of convergent, discriminant, and structural validity. *Psychology of Women Quarterly, 24,* 15–29.

Forness, S. R., Cluett, S. E., Ramey, C. T., Ramey, S. L., Zima, B. T., Chuanchieh, H., et al. (1998). Special education identification of Head Start children with emotional and behavioral disorders in second grade. *Journal of Emotional and Behavioral Disorders, 6,* 194–204.

Franklin, A. J. (1999). Invisibility syndrome and racial identity development in psychotherapy and counseling African American men. *The Counseling Psychologist, 27,* 761–793.

Fukuyama, M. A. (1999). Personal narrative: Growing up biracial. *Journal of Counseling & Development, 77*(1), 12–14.

Garnets, L., & Kimmel, D. (1991). Lesbian and gay male dimensions in the psychological study of homosexuality. In L. Garnets & D. Kimmel (Eds.), *Psychological perspectives on human diversity in America* (pp. 144–189). Washington, DC: American Psychological Association.

Gottlieb, A. (2000). Where have all the babies gone? Toward an anthropology of infants (and their caretakers). *Anthropological Quarterly, 73,* 121–132.

Gould, S. J. (1991). The smoking gun of eugenics. *Natural History, 100*(12), 8–14.

Gould, S. J. (1996). *The mismeasure of man* (rev. ed.). New York: W. W. Norton.

Greenberg, A. S., & Bailey, J. M. (1993). Do biological explanations of homosexuality have moral, legal, or policy implications? *Journal of Sex Research, 30,* 245–251.

Hall, J., & Friedman, G. (1999). Status, gender, and nonverbal behavior: A study of structured interactions between employees of a company. *Personality and Social Psychology Bulletin, 25,* 1082–1091.

Harrison, J. (Producer), & Schmiechen, R. (Director). (1992). *Changing our minds: The story of Dr. Evelyn Hooker* [Videotape]. (Available from Changing Our Minds, Inc., 170 West End Avenue, Suite 25R, New York, NY 10023)

Helms, J. E. (1992). Why is there no study of cultural equivalence in standardized cognitive ability testing? *American Psychologist, 47,* 1083–1101.

Herring, R. D. (1995). Developing biracial ethnic identity: A review of the increasing dilemma. *Journal of Multicultural Counseling & Development, 23,* 29–38.

Ivey, P. K. (2000). Cooperative reproduction in Ituri forest hunter-gatherers: Who cares for Efe infants? *Current Anthropology, 41,* 856–866.

Kaufman, A. S., & Kaufman, N. L. (1983). *Kaufman Assessment Battery for Children.* Circle Pines, MN: American Guidance Service.

Kessler, S. J. (1998). *Lessons from the intersexed.* New Brunswick, NJ: Rutgers University Press.

Kirch, M. S. (1979). Non-verbal communication across cultures. *Modern Language Journal, 63,* 416–423.

Kitzinger, C., & Wilkinson, S. (1995). Transitions from heterosexuality to lesbianism: The discursive production of lesbian identities. *Developmental Psychology, 31*, 95–104.

Klonoff, E. A., Landrine, H., & Ullman, J. B. (1999). Racial discrimination and psychiatric symptoms among Blacks. *Cultural Diversity and Ethnic Minority Psychology, 5*, 329–339.

Knackstedt, G., & Kleinke, C. L. (1991). Eye contact, gender, and personality judgments. *Journal of Social Psychology, 131*, 303–304.

Lawrence, S. M., & Tatum, B. D. (1997). Teachers in transition: The impact of antiracist professional development on classroom practice [Electronic version]. *Teachers College Record, 99*, 162–178.

Levine, N. E., & Silk, J. B. (1997). Why polyandry fails: Sources of instability in polyandrous marriages. *Current Anthropology, 38*, 375–398.

Lev-Wiesel, R. (2000). The effects of children's sleeping arrangements (communal vs. familial) on fatherhood among men in an Israeli kibbutz. *Journal of Social Psychology, 140*, 580–588.

Little, S. S. (1992, November). *Cultural issues in interpreting cognitive tests: Examples from an American Hassidic community.* Paper presented at the 32nd annual meeting of the New England Psychological Association, Fairfield, CT.

López, S. R., & Guarnaccia, P. J. (2000). Cultural psychopathology: Uncovering the social world of mental illness. *Annual Review of Psychology, 51*, 571–598.

Lott, B., & Maluso, D. (Eds.). (1995). *The social psychology of interpersonal discrimination.* New York: Guilford Press.

Marco, D. (1998, September). Doing business overseas: It's a whole new ballgame. *USA Today Magazine, 127*(2640), 20–22.

Markus, H. R., & Kitayama, S. (1991). Culture and the self: Implications for cognition, emotion, and motivation. *Psychological Review, 98*, 224–253.

Mazama, A. (2001). The Afrocentric paradigm: Contours and definitions. *Journal of Black Studies, 31*, 387–405.

McIntosh, P. (1988). *White privilege and male privilege: A personal account of coming to see correspondences through work in women's studies.* Working Paper 189, Wellesley College Center for Research on Women, Wellesley, MA.

McKenna, J. J. (1996). Sudden Infant Death Syndrome in cross-cultural perspective: Is infant–parent cosleeping protective? *Annual Review of Anthropology, 25*, 201–216.

McLoyd, V. C. (1998). Socioeconomic disadvantages and child development. *American Psychologist, 53*, 185–204.

Morelli, G. A., Rogoff, B., Oppenheim, D., & Goldsmith, D. (1992). Cultural variation in infants' sleeping arrangements: Questions of independence. *Developmental Psychology, 28*, 604–613.

Nieto, S. (2000). *Affirming diversity: The sociopolitical context of multicultural education* (3rd ed.). New York: Longman.

Okami, P. (1995). Childhood exposure to parental nudity, parent–child co-sleeping, and "primal scenes": A review of clinical opinion and empirical evidence. *Journal of Sex Research, 32,* 51–64.

O'Neil, J. (1997–1998, December–January). Why are all the Black kids sitting together? *Educational Leadership, 55*(4), 12–17.

Oyserman, D., Gant, L., & Ager, J. (1995). A socially contextualized model of African American identity: Possible selves and school persistence. *Journal of Personality and Social Psychology, 69,* 1216–1232.

Pellebon, D. A. (2000). Influences of ethnicity, interracial climate, and racial majority in school on adolescent ethnic identity. *Social Work in Education, 22,* 9–19.

Perry, P. (2001). White means never having to say you're ethnic. *Journal of Contemporary Ethnography, 30,* 56–91.

Peters, W. (Producer, Director). (1985). *A class divided* [Videotape]. Yale University Films for Frontline, produced for the Documentary Consortium by WGBH, Boston. (Available from PBS Home Video Catalogue Mail Order Center, P. O. Box 751089, Charlotte, NC 28275-1089).

Phelps, R. E., Taylor, J. D., & Gerard, P. A. (2001). Cultural mistrust, ethnic identity, racial identity, and self-esteem among ethnically diverse Black university students. *Journal of Counseling and Development, 79,* 209–216.

Pittinsky, T. L., Shih, M., & Ambady, N. (1999). Identity adaptiveness: Affect across multiple identities. *Journal of Social Issues, 55,* 503–518.

Posada, G., & Jacobs, A. (2001). Child–mother attachment relationships and culture. *American Psychologist, 56,* 821–822.

Quinn, D. M., & Spencer, S. J. (2001). The interference of stereotype threat with women's generation of mathematical problem-solving strategies. *Journal of Social Issues, 57,* 55–71.

Quintana, S. M., & Vera, E. M. (1999). Mexican American children's ethnic identity, understanding of ethnic prejudice, and parental ethnic socialization. *Hispanic Journal of Behavioral Sciences, 21,* 387–404.

Ramey, C. T., & Ramey, S. L. (1998). Early intervention and early experience. *American Psychologist, 53,* 109–120.

Remland, M. S., Jones, T. S., & Brinkman, H. (1995). Interpersonal distance, body orientation, and touch: Effects of culture, gender, and age. *Journal of Social Psychology, 135,* 281–297.

Roediger, D. R. (1999). Is there a healthy White personality? *The Counseling Psychologist, 27,* 239–244.

Rose, S. (2000). Heterosexism and the study of women's romantic and friend relationships. *Journal of Social Issues, 56,* 315–328.

Ryan, P. J. (1997). Unnatural selection: Intelligence testing, eugenics, and American political cultures. *Journal of Social History, 30,* 669–685.

Sawyer, D. (1991, September 26). True colors. In M. Lucasiewicz (Producer), *Primetime live* [Television series episode]. New York: American Broadcasting Company.

Stearns, P. N., Rowland, P., & Giarnella, L. (1996). Children's sleep: Sketching historical change. *Journal of Social History, 30,* 345–366.

Steele, C. M., & Aronson, J. (1995). Stereotype threat and the intellectual test performance of African Americans. *Journal of Personality and Social Psychology, 69,* 797–811.

Tatum, B. D. (1994). Teaching White students about racism: The search for White allies and the restoration of hope. *Teachers College Record, 95,* 462–476.

Tatum, B. D. (1997, October). "Why are all the Black kids sitting together in the cafeteria?" [Electronic version]. *Brown University Child & Adolescent Behavior Letter, 13*(10), 1–3.

Tatum, B. D. (1999, September). When you're called a racist. *Education Digest, 65*(1), 29–32.

Thompson, R. B., & Moore, K. (2000). Collaborative speech in dyadic problem-solving: Evidence for preschool gender differences in early pragmatic development. *Journal of Language and Social Psychology, 19,* 248–255.

U.S. Bureau of the Census. (2001). *United States Census, 2000.* Retrieved June 14, 2002, from http://www.census.gov

Veniegas, R. C., & Conley, T. D. (2000). Biological research on women's sexual orientations: Evaluating the scientific evidence. *Journal of Social Issues, 56,* 267–282.

Wechsler, D. (1991). *Manual for the Wechsler Intelligence Scale for Children* (3rd ed.). San Antonio, TX: Psychological Corporation.

Wickelgren, I. (March, 1999). Nurture helps mold able minds. *Science, 283,* 1832–1834.

Wolfe, C. T., & Spencer, S. J. (1996). Stereotypes and prejudice: Their overt and subtle influence in the classroom. *American Behavioral Scientist, 40,* 176–185. Wyver, S. R., & Markham, R. (1999). Visual items in tests of intelligence for children. *Journal of Visual Impairment & Blindness, 93,* 663–665.

2

TEACHING ABNORMAL PSYCHOLOGY: DIVERSIFYING STRUCTURE AND CONTENT

SONDRA E. SOLOMON

Contemporary views of abnormal behavior and theories regarding mental illness cannot be viewed as universal or culture-free. Human thought and action certainly have biological bases in genetics, neurochemistry, and anatomy; however, cultural schemas, developmental experiences, and personal privilege contribute vastly to the shape of human behavior, including those behaviors considered abnormal. In recent years, a few undergraduate textbooks in Abnormal Psychology have begun to incorporate sociocultural issues (e.g., ethnicity, gender, sexual orientation, socioeconomic status, and education) into their discussions regarding the prevalence, etiology, and treatment of major mental illnesses and the personality disorders. Although this is an encouraging trend, it is still the case that "the need to study, understand, and ultimately teach the role of culture in Abnormal Psychology represents a major challenge to mainstream psychology" (Betancourt & Lopez, 1997, p. 9).

In this chapter I introduce some considerations for teaching a more inclusive course in Abnormal Psychology. The intent is to provide a blueprint for instructors to better integrate issues of gender, race, culture, ethnicity, and sexual orientation into the Abnormal Psychology curriculum. My goals in the chapter are threefold: (a) to provide instructors with options and resources for curriculum transformation, (b) to facilitate the development of cultural awareness in students, and (c) to demystify the notion of cultural competency.

LIMITATIONS WITHIN
TRADITIONAL ABNORMAL PSYCHOLOGY

Much of the empirical data that support our understanding of abnormal behavior and the way in which deviant behavior is assessed and treated is based on a Western analytic scientific paradigm. The importance attributed to heredity and race, which can be found in the earliest writings of Western philosophy, has influenced the deterministic bias found in some contemporary perspectives (Guthrie, 1998). Psychological research and practice were developed and have taken place mainly in the industrialized world, in Europe and North America, and countries colonized by those societies, with the general exclusion of the vast populations of Africa, Asia, South America, and the South Pacific (Berry, Irvine, & Hunt, 1988). When studies have been conducted in other countries, they have often merely been replications of the studies conducted in the United States and Europe, with little attention paid to the culture-bound aspects of the research (Segall, Dasen, Berry, & Poortinga, 1990). Thus psychology, as a science, has often excluded cultural, racial, and ethnic groups in developing theories and systems that attempt to explain and categorize human behavior.

Similar concerns exist with respect to diagnosing and to designing interventions that attempt to modify behavior. Castillo (1997) expressed a widely shared concern that the *Diagnostic and Statistical Manual of Mental Disorders* (4th ed. [DSM–IV]; American Psychiatric Association, 1994) considers mostly western European and North American concepts of normative modern behavior and personality development. As a result, the mental health field has generally been unable to provide culturally supportive explanations of abnormal behavior or to offer culturally responsive treatment to ethnic minority clients. European American practitioners tend either to be unfamiliar with the cultures and lifestyles of their ethnic minority clients or to lack the ability to translate relevant information into specific therapeutic interventions (Porter, 1995).

In addition, contributions of ethnic minority psychologists and scholars have largely been disregarded in undergraduate Abnormal Psychology textbooks, thus depriving students of an opportunity to learn about human behavior problems from a variety of cultural perspectives.

TOWARD A MORE INCLUSIVE
ABNORMAL PSYCHOLOGY COURSE

Sue and Sue (1999) aptly noted that there is an intricate balance between the need to understand cultural differences and the need to know how the clinical application of "traditional" psychology is used to categorize individuals. The following sections comprise suggestions that may help instructors achieve greater balance in introductory Abnormal Psychology courses.

Make a Vigorous Attempt to Weave Cultural Data Into Every Lecture and Each Aspect of the Course Material

It is important to resist the temptation to relegate the discussion of culture and abnormal behavior to a special-topics lecture or series of lectures. Although there are few textbooks that contain sufficient information, instructors can rely on journal articles. For example, when illustrating the mood disorders, it is useful to present current research on the differences in optimism, pessimism, and coping in various racial or cultural groups. A review of the literature I recently conducted on depression among various ethnic groups within the last 4 years yielded 16 articles on American Indians, 12 on Asian Americans, and 69 on African Americans. Incorporating these research findings into a lecture on the mood disorders can broaden students' understanding of the complexities of cultural variations in emotion.

It may also be useful to routinely review culturally focused journals for current clinical research. Excellent resources are the *American Journal of Community Psychology, Journal of Black Psychology, Journal of Cross-Cultural Psychology, Cultural Diversity and Mental Health, Ethnicity and Health, Hispanic Journal of Behavioral Sciences, Journal of Multicultural Counseling and Development,* and *Women and Therapy.* Relevant articles may also be found in general-interest journals which, on occasion, include multicultural research; for example, Gray-Little and Hafdahl's (2000) work on self-esteem among different racial groups and Clark, Anderson, Clark, and Williams's (1999) review of the psychosocial sequelae of interethnic and intra-ethnic racism on African Americans.

Let the Students Know That the Class is Intended to Broaden Their Vision and Challenge Assumptions

During the first few classes I describe some ways in which the worldview of psychology is limited. Letting students know that most psychological research was produced in the United States underscores the reality that traditional psychological theories were designed to categorize and treat a specific population—and that the theories may not be appropriate for individuals whose cultural origins are not from western Europe or North America.

As a further illustration, I use a dream exercise described by Segall et al. (1990) that shows the limited applicability of psychodynamic theory in explaining the anxiety of 12-year-old boy from Papua, New Guinea. The intent of the exercise is not to instruct students in dream interpretation per se but to illustrate the fact that widely accepted psychological theories and interventions are not universal and may be insufficient or inaccurate when applied to people from non-Western cultures. Examples from other non-Western countries and from marginalized groups within the United States can be found in Pederson's (1999) book.

Emphasize the Work of Researchers of Color

Brown and Root (1990), Comas-Díaz and Greene (1994), hooks (1981), Steele (1997), Sue and Sue (1999), and Trimble and Bagwell (1995) have offered scholarship and research findings on women, minority, and cross-cultural populations. Guthrie (1998) described the historical contributions of African American psychologists and provides data regarding questions of racial and other biases in psychological theories, research, and testing. Students can seek out scholars of color as a class assignment, or the instructor can provide a list.

Consider At-Risk Groups

Although mental illness and problems in living occur throughout the world's population, some groups are at higher risk than others. A consideration of the effects on mental health of societal roles, discrimination, poverty, and inadequate living conditions enables students to understand the broader social context of psychological problems, rather than presuming individual psychopathology or inherent gender or ethnic weaknesses. A well-documented discussion of these issues can be found in Brown's (1994) book.

Analyze the Controversies Over "Intelligence"

When introducing the provocative data concerning intelligence, IQ, and the nature–nurture debate, I have found it useful for students to first read articles that summarize the flawed research on differences in intellectual performance among European populations. Students become quite adept at discovering methodological errors, critiquing findings, and dismissing recommendations that shaped social policy and fueled prejudicial attitudes toward certain groups. Benson's (1995) critique is particularly useful in this regard. After the students have developed an appreciation of the history of the debate regarding racial superiority and intelligence, I introduce current data that extend this unfortunately biased area of research.

Discuss Limitations of Treatment

Many Abnormal Psychology textbooks do a fine job in their discussions of state-of-the-art treatment for various psychiatric disorders from a number of different perspectives (e.g., medically based interventions and psychotherapeutic interventions). However, in most cases, the books fail to address the difficulties that people of color and people with limited economic means or limited access to medical insurance have in benefiting from state-of-the-art treatments. Kaplan's (1980) book is a particularly useful resource for enhancing one's understanding of the dilemma from a cost-analysis perspective. Most treatment options that are discussed in undergraduate Abnormal Psychology textbooks, such as medication and inpatient and outpatient psychotherapy, are available only to people with insurance coverage or personal financial resources. Government-funded sources (Medicaid and Medicare) and managed-care or health maintenance organizations severely limit the kinds of mental health services that will be covered and the duration (number of sessions, number of days in the psychiatric hospital or rehabilitation facility) of that treatment. Large segments of the population remain underserved or not served at all, notably women, the poor, the elderly, and children.

Consider the DSM in Current Cultural and Political Contexts

DSM–IV (American Psychiatric Association, 1994), although a widely accepted and convenient nosological tool, is based on the Western analytical scientific perspective, which is largely a medical model focusing on presumed biological bases of behavior. Undergraduate Abnormal Psychology textbooks use *DSM–IV* when discussing the Axis I and Axis II disorders, and most never question its accuracy or examine potential biases.

It is useful to discuss the evolution of the *DSM* and how current conceptions of normalcy and deviance are based on economic and political as well as medical factors. When discussing a particular mental disorder (e.g., schizophrenia, trichotillomania, eating disorders, major depression), I ask students to consider and discuss popular stereotypes and common myths and misconceptions they may harbor regarding abnormal behavior, focusing in particular on how these myths are reinforced in popular culture. I then explore with them the myths, particularly as they relate to gender and culture, to determine whether the belief is supported in the literature. Excellent resources that can be used to frame this discussion are *Contemporary Directions in Psychopathology: Toward the* DSM–IV (Millon & Klerman, 1986) and *They Say You're Crazy: How the World's Most Powerful Psychiatrists Decide Who's Normal* (Caplan, 1995), as well as research by Klonoff, Landrine, and Campbell (2000). These works provide useful insights regarding the label of mental illness and the ways in which such labels are applied to the survivors of social injustice.

Castillo's (1997) book also is a first-rate resource, with an excellent discourse on the ways in which "cultural systems shape the experience of self through the construction of cultural schemas" (p. 252) and the ways in which behaviors—psychotic, somatic, dysphoric, or otherwise—occur within a specific cultural context. The interpretation of culturally specific behavior and the subsequent labeling of those these behaviors as dysfunctional have important and often negative consequences for communities of color. Castillo's discussion of culture and psychosis, personality disorders, and somatization disorders is particularly useful for enhancing cultural competence regarding schizophrenia among communities of color.

The current edition of the DSM acknowledges the challenges involved when a clinician from one ethnic or cultural group attempts to assess an individual from a different cultural group (American Psychiatric Association, 1994, p. xxxiv); however, it provides little in the way of guidance as to how these challenges should be addressed. Furthermore, the framers of the DSM presume that culture is the most important distinction between client and clinician, with scant attention paid to other factors (e.g., gender, sexual orientation, and socioeconomic status) that may affect the etiology and course of a mental or personality disorder. For example, the effects of sexual, racial, or homophobic harassment, restricted participation in activities due to lack of handicap accessibility, and the daily struggles of poverty are not considered, although individuals whose ability to function in the world has been affected by such factors may be pathologized (Caplan, 1995; Clark et al., 1999).

Establish a Safe Climate for the Consideration of New Ideas

Regardless of class size or makeup, it is important to establish and maintain a sense of safety, so that students can learn and accept new ideas and have sufficient intellectual "wiggle room" to question traditional models and paradigms. Some students may experience a sense of cultural incompetence or be mystified by cultural material, and as a result, be reluctant to ask important questions. To overcome this hurdle, an instructor can suggest that students submit questions in writing before class and then use these questions to begin the class discussion or lecture.

Other students may simply feel overwhelmed. It can be very helpful to them if the instructor acknowledges this feeling and places it into an easily understood frame of reference. The instructor might compare the anxiety that may accompany the process of acquiring a sense of cultural competency to the anxiety students may have experienced when they first learned the rules of geometry or French grammar. It is also helpful to point out that the anxiety attenuates as more skill is acquired.

Many students may express the "I didn't know that" phenomenon. Students often will say, for example, "I didn't know that being a member of a minority group increases an individual's risk for mental illness"; a common misconception that students harbor is that a marginalized status and mental illness have no connection. I attempt to engage students in a discussion of the interaction between social forces and mental illness, using examples from Halpern (1993) and Castillo (1997). In effect, individuals from stigmatized groups (e.g., ethnic minorities, economically disadvantaged people, sexual minorities, religious minorities, etc.) are particularly prone to the social causes of mental distress. "Cultural schemas stigmatizing certain groups can be internalized to the point where individuals subjectively experience that they really are the wrong race, gender, religion, sexual orientation" (Castillo, 1997, p. 202). The work of Steele (1997) and Clark et al. (1999) also informs such discussions.

I vigorously resist the temptation to rely on students of color, gay and lesbian students, or functionally impaired students to share their experiences with other members of the class; it is often experienced as insulting and burdensome by those students and may interfere with their own learning opportunities and heighten their own sense of personal exposure and vulnerability.

Provide Students With an Opportunity to Notice Changes in Their Conceptions of Culture and Abnormal Behavior

I take the opportunity right at the beginning of the course to learn more about who the students are and why they are taking the course. This also provides an initial opportunity for students' voices to be heard. During the first class I ask students to complete a brief questionnaire that asks the student to answer the following questions:

- How would you define deviance or abnormal behavior?
- Give some examples of abnormal behavior.
- How do people become mentally ill?
- Who becomes mentally ill?
- Are some groups of people more likely to become mentally ill than other groups of people? Can you name those groups?
- Are some cultures more mentally healthy than others?
- Are people born mentally ill, or do other factors cause them to become mentally ill?
- What is the best way to treat mental illness?
- What do you want to learn from this course?

I collect this exercise and review the responses to obtain a notion of how sophisticated the students' ideas are about the prevalence, etiology, and treatment of mental illness. I also report back to the class about how the other students in the class answered these questions. I hold onto these exercises and, during the last class of the semester, I return them to the students. I ask them to complete the questionnaire again and to compare their answers so they can recognize how their conceptions of culture and abnormal behavior have changed.

When Possible, Incorporate Interactive Exercises

In smaller classes, I use a brief exercise that is intended to promote a sense of commonality. I ask all of the students to state their names, majors, reason for taking the course, places where they spent their developmental years, and their parents' and grandparents' cultural group or ethnicity. Finally, I ask them to disclose one important thing for the class to know about them. I spend some time modeling a response before I ask the first student to begin their "report." My model report can diffuse any anxiety that might arise and provides a framework for crafting their response. This exercise usually fosters an appreciation of the diversity that exists within the classroom (beyond the obvious one of skin color), a norm for class discussion, and a feeling of safety.

Use the Media to Illustrate the Role of Culture in Abnormal Behavior

I have used novels, music, films, and videos to foster a better understanding of abnormal behavior across cultural groups. It is useful to present discussion questions to students before they view a video or film, to prime them for the important cultural elements they are about to see and to set aside sufficient class time for discussion afterward. A large class size need not be an impediment to lively discussion, as it is always possible to break students into small interactive groups. One of my favorite instructional videos is *Medicine at the Crossroads: Disordered States* (Montagnon, Moore, & Freeth, 1994), which explores conceptions of schizophrenia from three different cultural perspectives: Italy, India, and the United States Examples of questions I have used for class discussion follow:

- What was the role of the patient's family in the urban U.S. treatment model? In the Italian model?
- How did the role of the family in these two models differ from role of the family in the Indian treatment model?
- What role did the community play in the Italian treatment model?
- What barriers do you think mental health providers would face in establishing that kind of community role in New York City? In your hometown community? How would you go about addressing these barriers?

Popular films are a potent and integral part of U.S. society that convey important information about contemporary culture. They can be very effective in bringing to life students' perceptions of mental illness, both accurate and inaccurate. I point out that although many films offer inaccurate or humorous portrayals of abnormal behavior and treatment, such as *What About Bob?* (Schulman, Oz, Williams, & Zuban, 1991), others are more accurate, such as *Born on the Fourth of July* (Juban & Stone, 1989/1998). It is challenging to find films that discuss aspects of mental illness and present minority group characters in affirming leading or supportive roles; the contemporary film industry still portrays characters of color in the clichéd roles of crack addict and drug dealer. Thus, whereas films may be useful tools for providing examples of mental illness, it is extremely important to choose them carefully and to provide a structured discussion after a film's conclusion. Wedding and Boyd (1999) compiled an impressive list of films that incorporate mental illness as the central theme; students who are frequent moviegoers can also suggest the latest films.

I have found written assignments to be particularly useful in getting students to understand how the print, film, and music industries shape people's conceptions of normal and abnormal behavior and how the media are central to the construction of social identity. I assign a brief (8–10 pages) media watch paper, the purpose of which is to enhance the students' understanding of a specific topic in psychopathology by analyzing how a particular aspect of abnormal behavior (e.g., obsessive–compulsive disorder, substance abuse, borderline personality disorder) is portrayed in some form of media, such as magazine or newspaper articles, television programs, poems, plays, films, music, or performance art. I provide the following list of questions to help sharpen students' awareness of sociocultural factors in analyzing the portrayal of abnormal behavior. I ask them to address several of these questions and invite them to develop a few of their own.

1. *Nature of the disorder.* What is the behavioral disorder being discussed or portrayed (e.g., schizophrenia, depression, anxiety, etc.)?
2. *How are individuals portrayed?* How are the characters depicted in your selection? How do they look? What do they do? Are they married, single, divorced, heterosexual, lesbian, gay, transgendered, old, young, functionally impaired or disabled, and so on? Is there a difference between the way in which women and men are characterized with a particular mental disorder? Is there any evidence of stereotyping the individual with a particular mental disorder? Are there groups of people that are excluded entirely or have minimal roles (African Americans, Asians, Latinas, Pacific East Islanders, American Indians, the elderly, children, etc.)?

3. *Etiology of the disorder.* In your selection, what role is attributed to each of the following in the course of the disorder: premorbid functioning, environment, development or family experience, biological or genetic bases, environmental stress, drugs and alcohol?
4. *Treatment issues.* What statement is made about treatment? Is treatment affordable? Is treatment accessible? Is treatment relevant for this character's race, gender, ethnicity, or sexual orientation? What role does economic privilege play in the character's recovery? How effective is the therapeutic alliance? What statement does your selection make about prevention or early intervention?
5. *Message and impact.* What do you think, and how do you feel, about the images in your selection? What would you change, and how would you change the image? How do you think this particular form of the media shapes attitudes about this particular disorder? Does the image portrayed relate to current health policies or therapy practices?

SOME CLOSING COMMENTS

Fifteen years ago, textbooks in Abnormal Psychology paid no attention to people of color, gays and lesbians, and other marginalized groups. Although there has been some movement to be more inclusive, it remains the individual instructor's responsibility to be creative and pioneering in pulling together resources that introduce students to important cultural material. In doing so, it is useful to view syllabi, readings, and teaching methodologies as dynamic, in that each new idea or perspective can fuel innovation and foster new knowledge. Diversifying the traditional structure and content of the introductory Abnormal Psychology course is a small step toward providing students with the cultural competency they will need.

REFERENCES

American Psychiatric Association. (1994). *Diagnostic and statistical manual of mental disorders* (4th ed.). Washington, DC: Author.

Benson, C. (1995). Ireland's "low" IQ: A critique. In R. Jacoby & N. Glauberman (Eds.), *The bell curve debate: History, documents, opinions* (pp. 222–233). New York: Random House.

Berry, J. W., Irvine, S. H., & Hunt, E. B. (1988). *Indigenous cognitions: Functioning in cultural context.* Dordrecht, The Netherlands: Martinus Nijhoff.

Betancourt, H., & Lopez, S. R. (1997). The study of culture, ethnicity, and race in

American psychology. In L. A. Peplau & S. E. Taylor (Eds.), *Socio-cultural perspectives in social psychology* (pp. 3–19). Englewood Cliffs, NJ: Prentice Hall.

Brown, L. S. (1994). *Subversive dialogues: Theory in feminist therapy*. New York: Basic Books.

Brown, L. S., & Root, M. P. P. (Eds.). (1990). *Diversity and complexity in feminist therapy*. New York: Haworth.

Caplan, P. (1995). *They say you're crazy: How the world's most powerful psychiatrists decide who's normal*. Reading, MA: Addison-Wesley.

Castillo, R. J. (1997). *Culture and mental illness: A client centered approach*. Pacific Grove, CA: Brooks/Cole.

Clark, R., Anderson, N. B., Clark, V. R., & Williams, D. R. (1999). Racism as a stressor in African Americans. *American Psychologist, 54*, 805–816.

Comas-Díaz, L., & Greene, B. (1994). *Mental health and women of color*. New York: Guilford Press.

Gray-Little, B., & Hafdahl, A. R. (2000). Factors influencing racial comparisons of self-esteem: A quantitative review. *Psychological Bulletin, 126*, 26–54.

Guthrie, R. V. (1998). *Even the rat was white: A historical view of psychology* (2nd ed.). Boston: Allyn & Bacon.

Halpern, D. (1993). Minorities and mental health. *Social Science and Medicine, 36*, 597–607.

hooks, b. (1981). *Ain't I a woman: Black women and feminism*. Boston: South End Press.

Juban, L. V. (Producer), & Stone, O. (Director). (1998). *Born on the Fourth of July* [Videotape]. Universal City, CA: Universal Home Video. (Original motion picture release 1989)

Kaplan, H. B. (1980). *Deviant behavior in defense of self*. New York: Academic Press.

Klonoff, E. A., Landrine, H., & Campbell, R. R. (2000). Sexist discrimination may account for well-known gender differences in psychiatric symptoms. *Psychology of Women Quarterly, 24*, 92–98.

Millon, T., & Klerman, G. E. (Eds.). (1986). *Contemporary directions in psychopathology: Toward the DSM–IV*. New York: Guilford Press.

Montagnon, P. (Producer), Moore, S., & Freeth, M. (Directors). (1994). *Medicine at the crossroads: Disordered states* [Videotape]. Alexandria, VA: PBS Video.

Pederson, P. (Ed.). (1999). *Multiculturalism as a fourth force*. Philadelphia: Brunner/Mazel.

Porter, N. (1995). Supervision of psychotherapists: Integrating anti-racist, feminist, and multicultural perspectives. In H. Landrine (Ed.), *Bringing cultural diversity to feminist psychology* (pp. 163–175). Washington, DC: American Psychological Association.

Schulman, T. (Writer), Oz, F. (Director), Williams, B., & Zuban, L. (Producers). (1991). *What about Bob?* [Videotape]. Orlando, FL: Walt Disney Home Video.

Segall, M. H., Dasen, P. R., Berry, J. W., & Poortinga, Y. H. (1990). *Human behavior in global perspective: An introduction to cross-cultural psychology*. Boston: Allyn & Bacon.

Steele, C. M. (1997). A threat in the air: How stereotypes shape intellectual identity and performance. *American Psychologist, 52,* 613–629.

Sue, D. W., & Sue, D. (1999). *Counseling the culturally different: Theory and practice.* New York: Wiley.

Trimble, J., & Bagwell, W. (Eds.). (1995). *North American Indians and Alaska Natives: Abstracts of psychological and behavioral literature, 1967–1995* (No. 15, Bibliographies in Psychology). Washington, DC: American Psychological Association.

Wedding, D., & Boyd, M. A. (1999). *Movies and mental illness: Using films to understand psychopathology.* Boston: McGraw-Hill College.

3

TEACHING DEVELOPMENTAL PSYCHOLOGY: CELEBRATING THE DIALECTICS OF DEVELOPMENT

LYNNE A. BOND AND KATHLEEN S. GORMAN

Every person, regardless of culture, ethnicity, gender, or life experience, shares certain commonalities in developmental processes with the rest of humankind. At the same time, each person, however similar to others in genetic and experiential history, introduces a degree of diversity into the course of development. One of the greatest challenges of developmental psychology is to explore the general rules and principles of behavior that unite people, while simultaneously acknowledging and celebrating the diversity and uniqueness of each individual. This core dialectic is our fundamental premise in the Developmental Psychology courses we teach.

Efforts to make Developmental Psychology courses more inclusive have typically taken the form of added "highlights" and "special topics," both in textbooks and in class lectures and discussions. Too often these topics have been presented as supplements to existing theories and models of normative development that are based on studies of economically privileged populations with unusual access to educational and political resources—in particular, White, middle-class males who reside in the United States (see the introduction to Tavris, 1992, for an excellent discussion of these issues).

Overall, developmental psychologists continue to think and speak in terms of deviations from a norm and the impact of those deviations on development. For example, they consider gay and lesbian parents, single parents, stepparents, and even fathers in terms of the degree to which they replicate—or fail to replicate—the child-rearing practices and outcomes of heterosexual, first-marriage, biological parents. When they consider the effects of mothers' employment on children's development, they treat nonemployment as the norm—even though over half of married-couple families are those with children and with both parents working at least part time (*Fertility of American women*, U.S. Census Bureau, 1998). They examine the effects of poverty but rarely, if ever, the effects of affluence; of teen childbearing but rarely of childbearing in one's 30's or 40's. They ask what causes people to develop a homosexual or bisexual self-identity, but rarely do they ask the same about heterosexual self-identity (for exceptions see Kitzinger, Wilkinson, & Perkins, 1992; Rochlin, 1995; Rust, 2000). This biased view—that there is one standard path of development from which certain groups deviate—has carried over to everyday language; labels such as *underprivileged*, *deprived*, *broken home*, and *illegitimate child* reflect a focus on deficits rather than an emphasis on the potential assets associated with diverse behaviors and environments.

In a similar vein, developmental psychologists have tended to treat certain terms as virtually synonymous with others, ignoring the dialectic of sameness and uniqueness that people share. For example, discussions of the effects of poverty on development frequently equate ethnic minority group membership with being poor. Yet, in their review of developmental research conducted between 1982 and 1991, MacPhee, Kreutzer, and Fritz (1994) found that only a small number of studies actually analyzed data separately for ethnicity and social class, whereas a large percentage of studies did not report family background characteristics at all. It is, of course, important to acknowledge the disproportionate representation of certain ethnic and racial groups in the lower socioeconomic levels and the significance of such environments to development. However, the oversimplified equating of minority status with poverty both perpetuates stereotypes and obscures the factors that actually contribute to the relations among ethnicity–race, socioeconomic level, and developmental outcomes. It is also useful to remind students that whereas poverty disproportionately affects various ethnic–racial groups in the United States (e.g., African Americans and Latinos), the largest number of poor children in this nation are White (Children's Defense Fund, 2002).

In teaching about development, it is very useful for instructors to focus on the dialectic of sameness and difference. On the one hand, they can underscore the universality of much of human experience, emphasizing that common developmental processes and factors are enmeshed in everyone's life—for example, the creation of learning strategies, rules, and problem-solving techniques, as well as the influences of culture, family, and peers. At the same time, instructors can affirm the uniqueness of each individual that contributes to the diversity of humankind. Categories such as the lesbian parent, the American Indian, or the adolescent male do not refer to homogeneous groups of individuals; development is far too complex to think in such generalities. Moreover, it is the variation among individuals that strengthens humans as a collective group and permits one of the universals that they share: the ability to adapt and grow in ever-changing contexts.

COURSE CONTENT

There are a number of ways that we incorporate this dialectical perspective into our course content as we consider the transactions among the social, cognitive, biological, and affective factors that shape human development. One is to emphasize that the effect of a particular factor may depend to a large extent on specific contextual variables (e.g., Elder, Modell, & Parke, 1993; Lerner, Castellino, Terry, Villarruel, & McKinney, 1995; Sameroff, 1993). For example, the strong link between parent income and developmental outcomes in U.S. society is a function of the degree to which U.S. culture makes access to many resources (e.g., health care and higher education) dependent on income (Bronfenbrenner, 1986; Garbarino & Kostelny, 1995). Evidence from other countries, where the link between income and access to services has been modified, illustrates just how powerful these associations can be. For example, the low infant mortality rates across race and geographic region in Cuba (in contrast to the United States) can be explained in part by more widespread access to health care for pregnant women. Similarly, in a study of an endemically malnourished population living in poverty, the expected relationship between socioeconomic status and adolescent achievement was found for the adolescents in the control group, but reduced to zero for the group that had received nutritional supplementation early in life (Pollitt, Gorman, Engle, Martorell, & Rivera, 1993).

Similarly, Bem (1993) described the ways in which U.S. society views the world through "lenses of gender" that, in turn, dramatically increase the degree to which girls and boys have developmental experiences and outcomes that are distinct from one another. When individuals in this culture look at another person, they do not merely see a human being; they instead almost instantly see a girl/woman or a boy/man. Gender appears to have great meaning, so that people use it regularly to shape their own behaviors as well as to interpret others' behaviors toward them, which contributes to developmentally distinct experiences for males and females.

Another way that we incorporate a dialectical perspective is in considering the "shared meaning" of experience (e.g., Bruner, 1990). Across varied contexts and cultures, apparently discrepant acts may convey similar meaning; for example, in much of North America, children use eye-to-eye contact with elders and authorities to convey respect, whereas in many Asian cultures children avert their gaze to communicate such respect. In a related vein, seemingly identical behaviors may take on distinct meaning, with repercussions for developmental outcomes. For example, authoritative parenting has been found to predict academic success among European American adolescents, but not among Asian Americans and African Americans (Steinberg, Mounts, Lamborn, & Dornbusch, 1991).

We also consider the fluidity and multiplicity of developmental trajectories. It is clear that different life circumstances may lead to similar outcomes, just as apparently similar developmental experiences may lead to divergent outcomes. The varied paths to becoming a parent or arriving at a particular profession can provide an excellent context for examining these notions. We have found that including first-person narratives or interviews in the course readings can provide rich data that allow students to consider the common yet unique means by which individuals and groups may arrive at similar outcomes (e.g., Chesler, Rothblum, & Cole, 1995). Recent work analyzing sexual self-identity provides a good example of the ongoing fluidity and change in that particular aspect of development (e.g., Kitzinger & Wilkinson, 1995; Zinik, 2000).

In teaching a multicultural Developmental Psychology course, we also include a strong cross-cultural component. Cross-cultural analyses can be applied to all developmental phenomena, including those in one's own culture (Lamb, Sternberg, Hwang, & Broberg, 1992), thus making more visible for students "the 'invisible' culture of which the reader or researcher is a member" (Harkness & Super, 1996, p. 10). Such analyses can highlight common developmental processes that prevail across highly distinct cultures. For example, although mothers' practices with infants range from strapping them to their backs to leaving them with day care providers, the process of adapting infant care practices to the daily work habits of mothers and other family and community members occurs everywhere. Simultaneously, cross-cultural analyses can illustrate a surprising degree of variation in practices that students may have long assumed are universal. For example, cross-cultural comparisons can challenge assumptions regarding the exclusive primacy of the mother–child relationship by demonstrating the benefits of multiple-caregiver patterns in other cultures (e.g., Harkness & Super, 1996; Tronick, Morelli, & Ivey, 1992).

Along with the cross-cultural content, we emphasize intracultural variability (Palacios & Moreno, 1996). Students learn that commonly held assumptions about the homogeneity of specific environments are often erroneous. For example, in a study of "high risk" communities characterized by poverty, high rates of crime, and unemployment, distribution of these factors actually varied considerably from one neighborhood to the next

(Caughy, O'Campo, & Brodsky, 1999). We have also found that a consideration of demographics within and beyond the United States can generate memorable class discussions. For example, a discussion of teen pregnancy can be enhanced with a comparison of European and U.S. statistics on sexual practices, use of contraception, abortion, and pregnancy and adoption rates. In addition to public census data (see http://www.census.gov and http://ferret.bls.census.gov), a variety of excellent and continually updated sources of comparative, demographic information are available on Web sites. For example, the Children's Defense Fund (2002) provides a wide range of national and state data as well as "key facts" about children in the United States. The Web sites of UNICEF (http://www.unicef.org) and the United Nations Development Programme (1995) have an international focus. Each of these sites provides access to policy reports, publications, media resources, and information regarding programs for children and families.

Finally, it is important for students to know that certain research methods affirm diversity while others do not. Research methods can be oppressive or empowering both in their direct effects on the research participants and in their indirect effects through the findings that emerge. Thus, in class, we consider who decides which areas of knowledge and experience are important enough be studied (researchers? granting agencies? the public?) and the processes by which these decisions are made (Goldberger, 1996; Reinharz, 1992; Trickett, Watts, & Birman, 1994). Reinharz (1994) maintained that "When people do not name their own experience, others name it for them and obliterate it" (p. 182). With this perspective in mind, we examine advantages and disadvantages of research methods that vary in the degree to which respondents are invited to describe their own experience in their own terms, rather than feeling confined to the researcher's language (e.g., semi-structured interviews vs. multiple-choice options, respectively). The goal is not to portray one methodology as always superior to another but rather to raise awareness of the manner in which different methodologies themselves contribute to participants' experience. Primary source materials from a variety of cultures and subcultures offer students an opportunity to hear voices often left out of traditional developmental research. We have found anthologies of personal narratives to be particularly engaging and informative (e.g., Findlen, 1995; Pérez Sarduy & Stubbs, 2000).

CLASSROOM TECHNIQUES

Classroom techniques that encourage students to actively discover, analyze, and revise knowledge provide a powerful context for learning about the dialectics of development. We have found the following activities to be both engaging and productive. Many of them we developed in the context of a large introductory Developmental Psychology course and subsequently adapted for smaller, upper level classes (e.g., Social Development, Cognitive Development); a few we created and subsequently adapted in the reverse direction. Each can be tailored to address a variety of formats as well as diverse topics within and beyond Developmental Psychology.

Dialectics of Sameness and Difference

There are a number of exercises that can help students examine their sameness and diversity within the subculture of the classroom. In one, we simply ask them, early in the semester, to write a brief description of some of the ways in which they feel they are different from nearly everyone in the class and then the ways in which they feel they are similar to the other students. In a course on Social Development, the question might be cast in terms of social influences and experiences; in a course on Parenting, the students might reflect on ways in which their parents are probably different from or similar to everyone else's. The responses can be handed in anonymously, to be summarized by the instructor. We have found that students are often amazed at the number of their presumed differences that are, in reality, common to others—such as the questioning of sexual self-identity, experiences of sexual abuse, suicide attempts, or feeling stigmatized by poverty. At the same time, students are astonished by the number of presumed commonalties that are much more individual than they had assumed, such as the belief that classmates are all in regular contact with their families or that they all have well-defined career plans.

We have also found it useful to administer an anonymous survey during the first class, asking about students' experiences that are related to topics that will be covered in the course. We then introduce relevant survey results throughout the semester to stimulate discussion and illustrate students' homogeneity or heterogeneity (or both) of experience. This technique can be used to acquire information for later discussions of such topics as divorce, single parenting, day care issues, language learning, and socialization. It can also help students recognize that classmates have both shared and highly differentiated perspectives and developmental histories.

Another exercise is to ask students to reflect on personal examples of the major developmental concepts that we cover. When classmates share these examples with one another, the diversity of experience becomes clear. For example, common assumptions about the similarities in college students are challenged when students share their experiences of growing up with single, divorced, or homosexual parents, particularly when students with similar backgrounds contribute different points of view. Comparisons based on other types of student characteristics and experiences (e.g., economic background, peer or sibling relationships, religious or ethnic affiliation) can similarly illustrate the multiplicity of developmental trajectories, showing the ways in which very different experiences have led to relatively common outcomes.

Recognizing Privilege

To help students understand the ways that status in society may affect development, we provide an exercise that is a self-examination of privilege. We ask students to identify on a confidential worksheet three groups with which they feel affiliated and which they believe cause them to be denied certain privileges simply because of the affiliation. If the exercise is used at the beginning of the course, its scope might be broad; when the course addresses more specific topics—such as social, cognitive, or gender role development—the questions can focus directly on privilege in these domains. Typical examples that students offer include gender, academic major, year in school, physical characteristics, religion, race–ethnicity, income, language, and nationality. We ask them to list three disadvantages of each of those group affiliations (e.g., lack of respect, stereotyped assumptions about their skills or interests) and then three advantages (e.g., camaraderie with similar others, empathy with other targets of discrimination). We then ask them to do the converse—to list three group affiliations that grant them special privileges and to elaborate on the benefits and disadvantages of each.

Students share their responses on a voluntary basis during class discussion. They invariably are struck by the fact that the same affiliations that some classmates associate with privileges are linked by others to a denial of privileges and oppression (e.g., being female, an engineering major, blonde, Catholic, or Puerto Rican). In addition, they are often surprised to find they can identify benefits of the affiliations that deny them privileges, and disadvantages of the affiliations that grant them privileges—and many of them find themselves listing one or more of the same affiliations as both bringing and denying privileges. In concluding this activity, we invite the class to examine the distinctions among the different affiliations: for example, the extent to which each is visible or not, voluntary or not, stable or changing, and consistent across time and situation in the responses it elicits. This highlights the fact that certain developmental processes and experiences (e.g., sense of identity and feelings of affiliation and alienation) are powerful forces in everyone's life. It also very clearly demonstrates that affiliations, and the privileges or disadvantages that may accompany them, vary widely in the degree to which they are optional and available to any one individual (e.g., skin color vs. club membership).

Examining Misperceptions and Biases

To encourage students to examine misperceptions and biases they may have regarding specific topics and groups, we have sometimes administered 10- to 20-item "quizzes" (multiple choice or fill in the blank) that ask them what they think or know about those subjects. Seavey's (1996) *The Current State of Welfare* provides a good example, but instructors can also create their own. We have found excellent material in census reports; in public media surveys, such as those presented in Sunday newspaper magazine supplements or in some television news programs; and in popular magazine articles. We have used these quizzes at the beginning of a course as well as intermittently throughout the semester and sometimes repeat a quiz at a later point, to allow students to reflect on their revised perspectives. The quizzes provide a provocative focus for small-group or whole-class discussion, which not only causes students to examine their own assumptions and biases but also often reveals a wide diversity of perspectives among what may have appeared to be a homogeneous group of classmates.

Becoming a Cultural Specialist

To help students understand other cultural perspectives, instructors can ask them at the beginning of the semester to become a specialist on a particular nation, culture, or population. After students have selected their specialty, they are required to become familiar with that group's distinctive experiences, needs, and characteristics. Throughout the semester, students are then asked to represent their group's culture through participation in small groups, discussions, or written work. For example, during a class discussion the instructor might ask the Ghanian specialist, "How do the women of Ghana see this issue of early child care?" Or the instructor might ask specialists to work in subgroups organized by continent (e.g., South American countries), to determine the degree to which their nations vary in approaches to the topic of discussion. Alternatively, students might be asked to debate an issue (e.g., single-gender education programs, or distribution of nutritional supplements to infants), speaking as a representative of their assigned nation or culture.

Applying Theories and Models: What If?

This exercise, a class favorite, encourages students to consider the implications and limitations of developmental theories and models. We ask students to assume that a given theory or model is true, and then, in small-group discussions (or individually, in writing), to describe the implications of that position for a particular set of developmental conditions. For example, we ask students

> What if Freud's theory of gender role development is accurate? What would you then expect to find in the development of: (a) a girl raised in a single-mother-headed household all her life with no contact with her father? (b) a boy raised with his heterosexual mother and father until age 9, when his mother leaves and his father and his father's male partner then raise him?

We then ask them to examine these scenarios from the perspective of other gender role theories (e.g., gender schema or social learning theory). The exercise sparks intense discussion, as students consider the varied human realities that must be explained by developmental models. It is especially effective when it incorporates scenarios that a number of the students have themselves experienced, such as divorce, single parenting from birth, and stepparenting; this allows them to see firsthand the contradictions between overgeneralized rules and the realities of their individual lives. A variation on this task is a 5-min writing assignment we sometimes give at the end of class, posing just one "what if" question. We then begin the following class with examples of student answers that reflect different perspectives, which generates lively discussion.

Journals

We have found journal writing to be a useful way to stimulate interest and capture student insights. Depending on the goals and interests of the instructor and students, journals may take different forms, such as typed sheets to be handed in each week, e-mail (to the instructor or to a class-based Web site), or contributions to an anonymous "suggestion–question" box. Entries can provide opportunities for students to react to lectures and readings, raise questions and speculations, respond to questions they (or the instructor) have posed, and examine and perhaps revise their own assumptions.

Journals are extraordinarily useful for helping students to reflect on powerful influences in their own and others' lives. Much to their surprise, students find themselves writing about persons, pressures, and experiences that they had not previously recognized as important. We sometimes ask students to volunteer to read specific entries to the class, to respond in their own journals to some of those that have been read, or to compare and integrate the varied perspectives they have heard (but not to judge their appropriateness or validity). The opportunity to hear classmates' entries highlights the shared and diverse perspectives that exist, even within a small, apparently homogeneous class. Journal writing also leads to more active, thoughtful class participation in that it requires students to reflect on the readings; to identify important themes, questions, and disagreements with the text or instructor; and to consider connections between their lives and the course. Thus they come to class well-primed for discussion.

Interviews

Interviewing people from the community is a very effective way to help students think deeply about influences and subtleties in their own and others' lives. We usually involve the class in constructing the interview questions, so that everyone thinks about the kinds of knowledge and information that will be valuable to obtain. Within a large class, students can work in small groups; the instructor can then integrate the groups' suggestions to create a final draft. Alternatively, the instructor can provide a sample interview and ask students to modify it according to their own specific interests and needs.

Once the interview questions are finalized, we sometimes ask students to speculate how people will respond to their questions, thereby identifying any preconceptions and providing a framework for subsequent analyses of actual responses. After the interview, students write an analysis of the interviewees' responses, considering how they compare to the information from the readings, class lectures, and discussions, and to students' own personal perspectives. As a final step, students get to share their data in small groups or whole-class discussions (with the interviewees' anonymity carefully protected). It is enlightening for them to discover important factors (e.g., socioeconomic status, age, gender, ethnicity, or marital status) that seem to be associated with different types of responses. They are also surprised at the common reactions of apparently diverse interviewees—but also struck by the uniqueness of each interviewee's responses, even among those who appear to lead relatively similar lives. By the end of the activity, it has become clear to students that it is very difficult to predict any individual's responses from group-based research and theory.

To provide diverse interview participants from the community (e.g., teachers, single mothers, social workers, elders), the instructor can make arrangements with schools, community agencies, continuum-of-care communities, and the like. Another possibility is to arrange an exchange with an instructor from a nearby (or far away) institution that has very different demographics, so that the students from both institutions can interview one another (by phone or e-mail if necessary) and gain additional awareness of developmental commonalties and diversity.

Pilot Research

We have found that pilot research projects help students learn about data collection and interpretation while also fostering critical skills for evaluating research questions and approaches. Such projects help students not only to become more aware of the benefits of research that is well designed and executed, and the limitations of that which is not, but also to recognize the ways that the variability and intricacy of data are often masked by summary statements of findings.

The instructor can design the activity to highlight some of the limitations that characterize existing research. For example, she or he can divide the class into groups and assign each group a select sample of subjects (defined narrowly by such characteristics as gender, age, socioeconomic status, and academic level) from whom to collect and interpret data. The class data can subsequently be combined, reanalyzed, and reinterpreted as a whole, which will often provide a substantially different perspective. This exercise helps students discover the ways that selected samples bias both the data and the models that they generate. Students can speculate on additional topics covered in the course (e.g., day care, divorce, single parenting) that may suffer from similar but as yet undocumented limitations. Once generated, these topics can then be explored further through classroom discussions or subsequent analyses of the data.

Because institutional review of research involving human participants is required, it is important for the instructor to plan ahead for this kind of pilot study. On the other hand, simulated studies (in which, e.g., the instructor creates fictitious data) and "recycled" data can provide useful alternatives.

CONCLUSION

As we encourage teaching a developmental psychology of all people, we frequently hear of many obstacles to doing so: Instructors speak of time constraints, the inability to cover "everything," and lack of information on varied populations. However, these do not need to be barriers; we are not calling for a longer course or a larger amount of information to be covered, and relevant information is readily available. Rather, we are proposing a restructuring of the fundamental premises that underlie so many developmental courses. We are advocating the acknowledgment and celebration of the dialectics of development—the coexistence of sameness and diversity—that we believe should serve as the framework for the content and activities of all courses in Developmental Psychology.

REFERENCES

Bem, S. L. (1993). *The lenses of gender: Transforming the debate on sexual inequality.* New Haven, CT: Yale University Press.

Bronfenbrenner, U. (1986). Ecology of family as a context for human development. *Developmental Psychology, 22,* 723–742.

Bruner, J. S. (1990). *Acts of meaning.* Cambridge, MA: Harvard University Press.

Caughy, M. O., O'Campo, P. J., & Brodsky, A. E. (1999). Neighborhoods, families, and children: Implications for policy and practice. *Journal of Community Psychology, 27,* 615–633.

Chesler, P., Rothblum, E. D., & Cole, E. (Eds.). (1995). *Feminist foremothers in women's studies, psychology and mental health.* New York: Harrington Park Press.

Children's Defense Fund. (2002). *Child poverty: Characteristics of poor children in America–2000.* Retrieved December 18, 2002, from http://www.childrensdefense .org/fs_cptb_child00.php

Elder, G. H., Jr., Modell, J., & Parke, R. D. (Eds.). (1993). *Children in time and place: Developmental and historical insights.* Cambridge, England: Cambridge University Press.

Findlen, B. (Ed.). (1995). *Listen up: Voices from the next feminist generation.* Seattle, WA: Seal Press.

Garbarino, J., & Kostelny, K. (1995). Parenting and public policy. In M. H. Bornstein (Ed.), *Handbook of parenting: Vol. 3. Status and social conditions of parenting* (pp. 419–436). Mahwah, NJ: Erlbaum.

Goldberger, N. R. (1996). Cultural imperatives and diversity in ways of knowing. In N. R. Goldberger, J. M. Tarule, B. M. Clinchy, & M. F. Belenky (Eds.), *Knowledge, difference, and power: Essays inspired by* Women's Ways of Knowing (pp. 335–364). New York: Basic Books.

Harkness, S., & Super, C. M. (1996). Introduction. In S. Harkness & C. M. Super (Eds.), *Parents' cultural belief systems* (pp. 1–23). New York: Guilford Press.

Kitzinger, C., & Wilkinson, S. (1995). Transitions from heterosexuality to lesbianism: The discursive production of lesbian identities. *Developmental Psychology, 31,* 95–104.

Kitzinger, C., Wilkinson, S., & Perkins, R. (Eds.). (1992). Theorizing heterosexuality [Special issue]. *Feminism & Psychology, 2*(3), 293–324.

Lamb, M. E., Sternberg, K. J., Hwang, A. G., & Broberg, A. G. (Eds.). (1992). *Child care in context: Cross-cultural perspectives.* Hillsdale, NJ: Erlbaum.

Lerner, R. M., Castellino, D. R., Terry, P. A., Villarruel, F. A., & McKinney, M. H. (1995). Developmental contextual perspective on parenting. In M. H. Bornstein (Ed.), *Handbook of parenting: Vol. 2. Biology and ecology of parenting* (pp. 285–309). Mahwah, NJ: Erlbaum.

MacPhee, D., Kreutzer, J. C., & Fritz, J. J. (1994). Infusing a diversity perspective into human development courses. *Child Development, 65,* 699–715.

Palacios, J., & Moreno, M. C. (1996). Parents' and adolescents' ideas on children: Origins and transmission of intracultural diversity. In S. Harkness & C. M. Super (Eds.), *Parents' cultural belief systems: Their origins, expressions, and consequences* (pp. 215–253). New York: Guilford Press.

Pérez Sarduy, P., & Stubbs, J. (Eds.). (2000). *Afro-Cuban voices: On race and identity in contemporary Cuba.* Gainesville: University Press of Florida.

Pollitt, E., Gorman, K., Engle, P., Martorell, R., & Rivera, J. (1993). Early supplementary feeding and cognition: Effects over two decades. *Monographs of the Society for Research in Child Development, 58*(7), Serial No. 235.

Reinharz, S. (1992). *Feminist methods in social research.* New York: Oxford University Press.

Reinharz, S. (1994). Toward an ethnography of "voice" and "silence." In E. J. Trickett, R. J. Watts, & D. Birman (Eds.), *Human diversity: Perspectives on people in context* (pp. 178–200). San Francisco: Jossey-Bass.

Rochlin, M. (1995). The heterosexual questionnaire. In M. S. Kimmel & M. A. Messner (Eds.), *Men's lives* (3rd ed., p. 405). Boston: Allyn & Bacon.

Rust, P. C. R. (2000). Alternatives to binary sexuality: Modeling bisexuality. In P. C. R. Rust (Ed.), *Bisexuality in the United States* (pp. 33–54). New York: Columbia University Press.

Sameroff, A. J. (1993). Models of development and developmental risk. In C. H. Zeanah Jr. (Ed.), *Handbook of infant mental health* (pp. 3–13). New York: Guilford Press.

Seavey, D. (1996). *The current state of welfare—1996. Back to basics: Women's poverty and welfare reform.* Working Paper CRW13, Center for Research on Women, Wellesley College, Wellesley, MA.

Steinberg, L., Mounts, N. S., Lamborn, S. D., & Dornbusch, S. M. (1991). Authoritative parenting and adolescent adjustment across varied ecological niches. *Journal of Research on Adolescence, 1,* 19–36.

Tavris, C. (1992). *The mismeasure of woman.* New York: Simon & Schuster.

Trickett, E. J., Watts, R. J., & Birman, D. (Eds.). (1994). *Human diversity: Perspectives on people in context.* San Francisco: Jossey-Bass.

Tronick, E. Z., Morelli, G. A., & Ivey P. K. (1992). The Efe forager infant and toddler's pattern of social relationships: Multiple and simultaneous. *Developmental Psychology, 28,* 568–577.

United Nations Development Programme. (1995). *Human development report 1995.* New York: Oxford University Press.

U.S. Census Bureau. (1998). *Fertility of American women: June 1998.* Retrieved January 14, 2003, from http://www.census.gov/population/www/socdemo/fertility.html

Zinik, G. (2000). Identity conflict or adaptive flexibility? Bisexuality reconsidered. In P. C. R. Rust (Ed.), *Bisexuality in the United States* (pp. 55–60). New York: Columbia University Press.

4

VARYING ANGLES AND WIDER LENSES: A MULTICULTURAL TRANSFORMATION OF THE UNDERGRADUATE SOCIAL PSYCHOLOGY COURSE

LISA BOWLEG

"Imagine that you wanted simultaneously to photograph this room and the people in it," I say to students on the first day of my undergraduate Social Psychology course. Using my hands to simulate a camera, I peer through the viewfinder and say, "Now, if I stand here at the front of the class, I can get a few of the students in the front row, but not those in the middle or back, or even those seated at the end of the front rows." As I move around the room—even climbing onto chairs for utmost effect—I engage students in the exercise of imagining who might be captured or missed by my vantage point in the room. Inevitably, a student notes that a wide-angled lens would allow me to capture more of the room and the people in it. "Bravo!" I usually exclaim, "that's precisely the point." Using photography as a metaphor

59

for multicultural perspectives, I demonstrate in this introductory exercise how social psychology gains a more comprehensive view of people when one relies on a variety of lenses and angles. The exercise sets the stage for a social psychology course in which multicultural perspectives are integral to the course rather than peripheral to it.

Kitano's (1997) model of multicultural course change has proven invaluable to the transformation of my undergraduate social psychology course from one that merely "adds and stirs" multicultural issues or populations (i.e., a course that is "inclusive") to one that uses multiculturalism as a foundation from which to challenge social psychology's traditional assumptions about individuals and social behavior. Moreover, I use multiculturalism as a means to reconceptualize social psychology in light of the new knowledge that is gained when one uses wider lenses and varying angles to view the cultural context of humans and their social behaviors. Using Kitano's model as a conceptual framework, I present in this chapter strategies and examples for making the undergraduate social psychology course multicultural, not only in terms of content but also in terms of learning approaches, assessment procedures, and classroom dynamics.

MULTICULTURALISM: WHAT'S IN A WORD?

Multiculturalism is gaining increasing attention as an integral component of contemporary psychology curricula (Mays, 2000; D. W. Sue, Bingham, Porche-Burke, & Vasquez, 1999), albeit without a clear definition of the term (Helms, 1994). Within social psychology, textbook authors variously use words such as *diversity, inclusiveness, cross-cultural,* and *sociocultural* in their introductory chapters to describe this new and noteworthy shift in the discipline. Yet, with the exception of Moghaddam (1998), few textbook authors provide in-depth coverage or integrate these topics throughout the texts. Furthermore, I have found that most authors view multiculturalism primarily in terms of race–ethnicity or nationality, while paying scant attention to other multicultural identities that shape social behavior, such as class, sexual identity, or disability.

The problems involved in defining multiculturalism notwithstanding, throughout this chapter, I use the word *multicultural*, because I believe that it best encompasses similarities and differences among groups within cultures (e.g., racial and ethnic minorities; gay, lesbian, and bisexual people; people with disabilities). Yet, as Helms (1994) noted, the breadth of these boundaries is at once one of the greatest strengths and weaknesses of the multicultural perspective. On the one hand, the multicultural perspective advocates for the inclusion of a multitude of sociocultural identities and differences. On the other hand, however, such broad inclusiveness often obfuscates critical psychological, historical, and political differences among these sociocultural identities, particularly race. Indeed, multiculturalism is not simply about recognizing cultural similarities and differences. In teaching social psychology, it involves critically examining how people with economic, political, and social power and privilege (historically White, Western, middle-class males) have shaped the perspectives, assumptions, and theories on which our understanding of human social behavior is based. Although cross-cultural perspectives (i.e., similarities and differences across cultures) are also an important component of my course, in this chapter I focus on multicultural perspectives.

Infusing the traditional social psychology curriculum with multicultural perspectives is challenging and exciting. However, for instructors who have not examined their views about different multicultural issues or assessed their level of comfort with teaching these issues, the transformed curriculum provides ample opportunity for pitfalls, large and small. For example, one mistake of which instructors of multicultural perspectives must be mindful, and of which they should repeatedly warn students, is the presumption that cultures are monoliths. Because it is easy to exaggerate or oversimplify cultural characteristics, it is critically important to stress within-group differences. Thus, I often respond to students' overgeneralizations with probes of within-cultural or individual differences. For example, if a student provides an example of something that "Asians do," I might ask, "Which Asians? Cambodians, Japanese, or Asian-Americans?" and continue with further probes, such as "Would that be true of Chinese people who live in urban areas as well as those who live in rural areas? How might age mediate that assumption?" Comas-Diaz's (2001) article on the vast heterogeneity of social identity among people commonly called *Latinos* or *Hispanics* illustrates this well.

FROM EXCLUSIVE TO INCLUSIVE TO TRANSFORMED: LEVELS OF MULTICULTURAL COURSE CHANGE

Kitano (1997) proposed three levels of multicultural course change: (a) exclusive, (b) inclusive, and (c) transformed. An *exclusive* course "presents and maintains traditional, mainstream experiences and perspectives of the discipline" (p. 23). If multicultural perspectives are included at all, they are done so to confirm stereotypes. Exclusive classes typically rely on lecture formats with little or no room for discussion, and student performance is evaluated by means of written examinations. By contrast, the *inclusive* classroom focuses on active learning and uses a variety of teaching methods and assessment to ensure that students learn course content. An inclusive course adds alternative perspectives but often does so without elaboration or any exploration of the reasons why alternative perspectives have traditionally been excluded from the discipline.

The *transformed* course represents a radical departure from the inclusive and exclusive courses. The transformed course "challenges traditional views and assumptions; encourages new ways of thinking; and reconceptualizes [social psychology] in light of new knowledge, scholarship, and ways of knowing" (Kitano, 1997, p. 23).

FROM SYLLABUS TO CLASSROOM: ELEMENTS OF THE TRANSFORMED SOCIAL PSYCHOLOGY COURSE

Kitano's (1997) model of a transformed social psychology course includes four elements: (a) course content, (b) instructional strategies, (c) assessment tools, and (d) classroom dynamics. Using my undergraduate social psychology course as an example, I next highlight various strategies and resources that I have used to transform each aspect of the course.

Element 1: Content, or "What's This Course About Anyway?"

Whenever possible, I try to arrange to have all of my courses meet in our campus's new Multicultural Center. This building, dedicated to fostering a respect for and celebration of multiculturalism, serves as an ideal setting in which to disseminate my goals to students. Meeting there also serves another purpose: It welcomes students who might not otherwise be drawn to the Multicultural Center to visit, become comfortable, and claim their space in the multicultural fabric of the campus. In my welcoming remarks on the first day of class, I discuss the significance of holding class in the Multicultural Center and inform students how the site is related to the course goals I have articulated in the syllabus. These goals are (a) to encourage students to critically analyze the impact of multicultural and cross-cultural identities on social behavior; (b) to introduce students to the contributions of people of color, White women, gay, lesbian, bisexual, and transgendered people, and others not historically recognized in traditional social psychology; and (c) to promote social change through increased awareness about multicultural issues.

My syllabus begins with a description of the course, using a traditional textbook definition of *social psychology*. Because traditional definitions inevitably focus on individuals with little or no mention of the role of culture, this presents a perfect opportunity to mention how multicultural and cross-cultural perspectives provide a richer understanding of the cultural contexts that shape human behavior in social situations. I also include the entire titles of all articles and the names and descriptions of the films I will show, so that students can assess their multicultural content. Thus, for example, a cursory glance at the syllabus will reveal that under the social influence section of the course we will read about different cultures' notions of personal control

(Weisz, Rothbaum, & Blackburn, 1997), or we will view the film *A World of Differences: Understanding Cross-Cultural Communication* (Archer & Silver, 1997). Formatting the schedule in this manner often generates excitement about the content of the course, and someone generally comments on the "cool things" they will be reading and seeing that semester.

I use a textbook that is consistent with the multicultural focus. I initially used *Social Psychology: Exploring Universals Across Cultures* (Moghaddam, 1998), which is unique not only in terms of its content but also in terms of the author's philosophy that social psychology should become more international and incorporate cultural diversity to provide more accurate explanations of human behavior. However, the main focus of the text is on cultural, racial, and ethnic differences rather on than the breadth of multicultural perspectives. I now use *Social Psychology* (Brehm, Kassin, & Fein, 2002), which does incorporate the breadth and depth of topics, as well as an integration of multicultural and cross-cultural perspectives. Even so, although this integration is a welcome development, the coverage of those topics remains, for the most part, scant and inconsistent.

Thus, instructors wishing to transform their courses will need to find other books and articles by and about populations historically underrepresented in social psychology. I adopt a supplemental text, *Sociocultural Perspectives in Social Psychology: Current Readings* (Peplau & Taylor, 1997), and compile a course reading packet that includes articles on a variety of multicultural topics relevant to social psychology. For example, Herek's (2002) review of research on negative attitudes toward gays, lesbians, and bisexual people is an ideal complement to the chapters that students read on perceiving groups and on attitudes. Lott's (2002) recent article challenges students to think about the influence of socioeconomic class and classism on attitudes and behaviors toward people who are poor. To find readings on underrepresented groups, I conduct literature searches of journals such as *Cultural Diversity and Ethnic Minority Psychology*, *Journal of Homosexuality*, *Journal of Cross-Cultural Psychology*, *Journal of Social Issues*, *Psychology of Men and Masculinity*, and *Psychology of Women Quarterly*. I do not limit my search to the field of psychology; disciplines such as anthropology, women's studies, Latino/Chicano studies, and queer studies offer a variety of readings that are ideally suited for social psychology courses. In addition, readers and edited volumes can be excellent resources, such as *The Disability Reader: Social Science Perspectives* (Shakespeare, 1998), *In Our Own Words: Writings from Women's Lives* (Crawford & Unger, 2000), *Hispanic Psychology: Critical Issues in Theory and Research* (Padilla, 1995), and *Social Perspectives in Lesbian and Gay Studies: A Reader* (Nardi & Schneider, 1998).

Alternatives to traditional forms of knowledge are also essential to a transformed course. Materials such as oral histories, diaries, personal narratives, quilts, clothing, works of art, and poetry relevant to groups who have historically been excluded from psychology can enliven a class (Josephine

Moreno, personal communication, April 7, 1999). For example, a personal narrative such as that of French (2000), in which she describes her childhood and adult experiences of having a visual disability, is ideal for teaching about stereotypes, prejudice, and perceptions of groups. Similarly, Ortiz-Cofer's (2000) description of the impact of her skin color and Puerto Rican ethnicity on her feelings about her physical appearance can inform a lesson about attraction in relation to racial and ethnic differences in beauty standards. The inclusion of these materials may also be used to prompt a class discussion about traditional and multicultural epistemologies.

Element 2: Instructional Strategies and Activities— Encouraging Critical Thinking

A multicultural social psychology course includes a pedagogy in which the instructor "is thoroughly grounded in critical education theory and committed to empowering students and correcting social inequities" (Kitano, 1997, p. 27). Various dialectical methods that promote critical discourse and thinking are thus central to the course. To accommodate a variety of learning styles, I use an array of instructional methods. Although I do some lecturing, I never use an all-lecture format, because I believe that it is crucial for students to assist in the creation of knowledge. In particular, I promote class discussions and provide opportunities for individual expression (as in personal-reflection papers) and small-group work.

Because I am committed to altering traditional power dynamics in the classroom, I offer students the opportunity to design or choose different instructional strategies. For example, groups of students can choose a topic that interests them, research it, and then present their findings to the class. I encourage them to be as innovative as possible in designing their presentation and to consider multicultural perspectives. A health psychology group designed a Web site on their topic and used skits to demonstrate how key topics in social psychology such as persuasion and conformity relate to teen smoking. A business and psychology group used a morning television show format as a means of introducing role plays of their topic. One of the student announcers introduced the skit by saying something like, "And now, we turn to this segment on cultural norms governing business practices between Japanese and American businesspeople." Then other members from the group role played a business negotiation, illustrating key social psychological topics such as etics, emics, and norms.

I also include learning activities that combine theoretical, multicultural, and practical applications of social psychology. For example, I showed an excerpt from a morning news program on the racial profiling of Arab Americans in the wake of the September 11, 2001, attacks in the United States. I then divided the class into small discussion groups and provided them with a set of questions testing their knowledge of Arab American cultures, adapted from the Web site of the American-Arab Anti-Discrimination Committee (2001), which led them to recognize how little they knew about this diverse group of people. Armed with this new awareness, they then applied the material from the text on stereotyping, prejudice, and discrimination to the current treatment of Arab Americans.

Another activity involves a consideration of the history of social psychology. This provides an opportunity for them to think critically about the culture-bound nature of the discipline—that it reflects the theories, views, and experiences of its founders and the populations on whom those theories were tested. After considering the founders of the discipline, I ask who is missing, and why. Students are swift to answer that the contributions of women, racial and ethnic minority men, members of Eastern cultures, and poor people are absent. At this point, I divide students into groups of five and ask them to theorize, consulting their texts, how our understanding of different topics in social psychology might be different if these populations were represented as researchers or research participants. As an individual extra credit assignment, I challenge students to turn in the names of as many social psychologists from underrepresented groups that they can find, with a brief description of their contributions. I then compile these findings into a single list and disseminate it to the entire class.

To further encourage critical thinking, I introduce students to the notion that the questions and topics that people choose to study—and indeed, what they consider to be knowledge—are socially constructed. My goal is to prompt students to consider how knowledge has traditionally been used to reinforce and legitimate the status quo of people with power (historically, White, heterosexual, middle-class, Christian men) and to define and control people without it (i.e., people who do not fit those demographics). I begin the discussion with the social construction of homosexuality as an illness. Students inevitably chuckle when I tell them how, in 1974, the American Psychiatric Association cured thousands of Americans of homosexuality overnight when that association removed homosexuality from the *Diagnostic and Statistical Manual of Mental Disorders–II* (Bayer, 1987).

There are many ways to illustrate the social construction of knowledge in psychology. One of my favorites is to ask students to define the following conditions: drapetomania, neurasthenia, and masturbatory insanity. Students can typically guess the meaning of masturbatory insanity (Showalter, 1987). However, few students can define drapetomania, an 18th-century condition marked by the tendency of slaves to run away from plantations (Kitzinger, 1987); or neurasthenia, a 19th-century condition characterized by blushing, vertigo, headaches, insomnia, depression, and uterine irritability, believed to be caused by women's increased mental activity (Showalter, 1987).

I also encourage students to think critically about the research process. In addition to reading the textbook's chapter on research methods, I assign a wonderful article about using qualitative methods to conduct social psychological research (Maracek, Fine, & Kidder, 1997) and engage students in a discussion about the advantages and disadvantages of qualitative, quantitative, and mixed methods. I also devote a separate class to the issue of bias and stigma in psychological research, assigning Herek's (1998) excellent article on how a group of researchers' blatant heterosexist biases produced methodologically flawed, but nonetheless socially influential research, and Guthrie's (1998) review of the influence of racism on standardized testing in psychology. In class, students watch, and then discuss, a video recording of a keynote address delivered by Stanley Sue (1999) on science, ethnicity, and bias, which was delivered at a national multicultural conference of the American Psychological Association.

Element 3: Assessing Student Performance

To assess students' ability to analyze, evaluate, and apply what they have learned, I include two examinations and two 5- to 10-page minipapers. For the first minipaper, which is entitled "Who Am I?" and which coincides with the social self section of the course, students first read the relevant chapter in the text, plus an article on the complexity of multicultural aspects of identity (Tatum, 1997). They then describe themselves in a paragraph or two, discussing the concept of self as it relates to themselves, in terms of topics from the readings that they find relevant. Finally, they discuss their self-concepts within the context of at least one multicultural or cross-cultural identity. For the second minipaper students may choose one of three options:

1. *Exploring attitudes about social issues and problems*. Students find a recent newspaper or magazine article focused on a course-relevant topic. In the paper they summarize the article, discuss the main findings of the article within the context of the attitude theory and research that they have read, and then consider the influence of multicultural and cross-cultural perspectives on the attitudes about which they wrote.
2. *Evaluation of social psychology concepts and theories*. Students must select a concept or theory from their text, such as attribution theory, conformity and obedience, or liking and loving. For the paper, they summarize and evaluate that concept or theory within the context of the individualistic and collectivist cultures they have read about (e.g., Dion & Dion, 1998; Si, Rethorst, & Willimczik, 1999) and provide detailed examples of the assumptions that people in these cultures make about traits and behaviors.
3. *Multicultural interview*. Students choose a topic or theory that appeals to them (e.g., group dynamics or self-perception),

design a set of interview questions (which I review prior to the interview), and then conduct an interview with a person who is different from them on some multicultural dimension relevant to the theory (such as race, ethnicity, gender, sexual orientation, socioeconomic class, disability, nationality). The assignment requires students to analyze how well the theory fits the interviewee's perspectives or experiences. This exposes students to different cultural perspectives, prompts them to critically evaluate and analyze social psychological theory in regard to cultural context, and provides them with an opportunity to use qualitative research methods.

Element 4: Classroom Dynamics

The interaction both between instructor and students and among students can be one of the most exciting aspects of a multicultural Social Psychology course. However, for instructors new to teaching multicultural issues, it can be intimidating; as students begin to explore important social issues and their own preconceptions, intense emotions may be aroused, and exchanges may become heated. It is best for instructors to adopt proactive strategies for dealing with classroom dynamics in anticipation of such interactions; these will be invaluable when difficult dialogues arise. Foremost among my concerns in the classroom is the creation of a safe space that affirms each student's identity and views and promotes respectful dialogue. To foster such a space, on the first day of class, I distribute a list of 12 ground rules for class discussion. I explain to students that the purpose of these ground rules is to facilitate a classroom atmosphere in which each student feels comfortable and welcome to participate in all discussions. They include things such as being respectful, particularly in times of disagreement; acknowledging that classmates may be ignorant about certain multicultural topics, but trusting that they are well intentioned; avoiding language that stereotypes or demeans; and not singling out a member of a group to speak for an entire group's experience. I have the students review the ground rules in class and then solicit feedback about any with which they disagree or about any rules that we should add. It is important to do this as a group, because it facilitates a shared understanding of the norms for class interactions.

Class participation is a fundamental component of my Social Psychology course. In the syllabus, I tell students that class participation is not just desired, it is essential. They can contribute to classroom interactions in a variety of ways, including talking in class, participating in small-group or whole-class discussions, announcing currents events relevant to course material, handing in discussion questions based on the readings, and participating in and reporting to the class on relevant out-of-class activities such as lectures and conferences.

Students may also participate by posting questions or comments on an electronic mailing list for the course, which I establish each semester through the university's computer and technology department. They can post a question or comment about course material to the list, and their classmates can view it and respond. An electronic list is an ideal forum for extending class discussions beyond the class period; moreover, it provides students who may be reticent or shy about speaking in class a more comfortable way to participate.

Classroom dynamics also require instructor vigilance about aspects such as who speaks in class, how often, and for how long (e.g., do women speak less than men? Are students of color more reticent than White students?); how classmates respond to certain speakers; and whether certain groups of students are more likely to "segregate" in class. It is important that instructors be proactive about these dynamics and inform students about how and why these dynamics occur before they happen. Indeed, I advocate addressing these issues as early as the first or second day of class. In some cases (e.g., a student monopolizing class discussions), it is best to meet with the student on an individual basis. In others (as when students express disapproval of a guest speaker or topic), the issue should be addressed as a class. Instructors may use a variety of strategies to prompt such a discussion, such as asking the students directly for their feedback, listening carefully to it, and then encouraging them to find links between their concerns and relevant course materials (e.g., attitudes, prejudice, the fundamental attribution error). Alternatively, an instructor could ask students to hand in anonymous feedback about the speaker or topic and then use some time during the following class period to address their concerns. However, such strategies are not foolproof. In the end, openly and directly confronting classroom dynamics is more advantageous to students' personal and academic growth than ignoring them. Of course, instructors must also pay keen attention to their own conscious or unconscious biases and how they may surface in interactions with students. Some questions for introspection are "How comfortable am I teaching students who are racially/ethnically different from myself, or who are from different socioeconomic backgrounds?", "How comfortable am I with students who have disabilities?", "How do I feel about students whose primary language is not English?" (Prenger, 1999).

REFLECTING ON THE COURSE: A BETTER DEVELOPED PICTURE OF SOCIAL BEHAVIOR

One of the most fulfilling aspects of my role as an instructor is teaching undergraduates both to critique social psychology and to recognize how it is enriched by examining social behaviors within the context of multicultural identities. At the end of the semester, the students also affirm this aspect of the course was especially gratifying for them. As a concluding activity, I conduct an exercise entitled "A Few Thoughts About What I Learned This Semester," which asks students to complete six statements such as: "When I began taking this class, I thought _____ about _____, but I now think _____;" and "Now that the course is over, I believe that I know more about _____, but I feel that I know even less about _____." As we go around the class sharing these reflections, a recurrent theme emerges: that students have a new appreciation for the benefits, challenges, and complexities of viewing social behavior through a multicultural lens. In the end, students leave the course with a wide-angled, multihued picture of social behavior, instead of the black-and-white snapshot that they might have gotten from a more traditional approach to teaching social psychology.

REFERENCES

American-Arab Anti-Discrimination Committee. (2001). *100 questions and answers about Arab Americans: A journalists' guide.* Retrieved October 12, 2002, from http://www.adc.org

Archer, D. (Producer), & Silver, J. (Director). (1997). *A world of differences: Understanding cross-cultural communication* [Film]. Available from University of California Extension, Center for Media and Independent Learning, 200 Center Street, Fourth Floor, Berkeley, CA 94704-1223.

Bayer, R. (1987). *Homosexuality and American psychiatry: The politics of diagnosis.* Princeton, NJ: Princeton University Press.

Brehm, S. S., Kassin, S. M., & Fein, S. (2002). *Social psychology* (5th ed.). Boston: Houghton Mifflin.

Comas-Diaz, L. (2001). Hispanics, Latinos, or Americanos: The evolution of identity. *Cultural Diversity and Ethnic Minority Psychology, 7,* 115–120.

Crawford, M., & Unger, R. (Eds.). (2000). *In our own words: Writings from women's lives.* New York: McGraw Hill.

Dion, K. K., & Dion, K. L. (1998). Individualistic and collectivistic perspectives on gender and the cultural context of love and intimacy. In D. L. Anselmi & A. L. Law (Eds.), *Questions of gender: Perspectives and paradoxes* (pp. 520–531). Boston: McGraw Hill.

French, S. (2000). "Can you see the rainbow?" The roots of denial. In K. E. Rosenblum & T. M. Travis (Eds.), *The meaning of difference: American constructions of race, sex and gender, social class, and sexual orientation* (pp. 194–201). Boston: McGraw Hill.

Guthrie, R. V. (1998). *Even the rat was white: A historical view of psychology* (2nd ed.). Boston: Allyn & Bacon.

Helms, J. E. (1994). The conceptualization of racial identity and other "racial" constructs. In E. J. Trickett, R. J. Watts, & D. Birman (Eds.), *Human diversity: Perspectives on people in context* (pp. 285–311). San Francisco: Jossey-Bass.

Herek, G. M. (1998). Bad science in the service of stigma: A critique of the Cameron Group's survey studies. In G. M. Herek (Ed.), *Psychological perspectives on lesbian and gay issues: Stigma and sexual orientation. Understanding prejudice against lesbians, gay men, and bisexuals* (pp. 223–255). Thousand Oaks, CA: Sage.

Herek, G. M. (2002). The psychology of sexual prejudice. *Current Directions in Psychological Science, 9,* 19–22.

Kitano, M. K. (1997). What a course will look like after multicultural change. In A. I. Morey & M. K. Kitano (Eds.), *Multicultural course transformation in higher education: A broader truth* (pp. 18–34). Boston: Allyn & Bacon.

Kitzinger, C. (1987). *The social construction of lesbianism.* London: Sage.

Lott, B. (2002). Cognitive and behavioral distancing from the poor. *American Psychologist, 57,* 100–110.

Maracek, J., Fine, M., & Kidder, L. (1997). Working between worlds: Qualitative methods and social psychology. *Journal of Social Issues, 53,* 631–644.

Mays, V. M. (2000). A social justice agenda. *American Psychologist, 55,* 326–327.

Moghaddam, F. M. (1998). *Social psychology: Exploring universals across cultures.* New York: Freeman.

Nardi, P. M., & Schneider, B. E. (Eds.). (1998). *Social perspectives in lesbian and gay studies: A reader.* New York: Routledge.

Ortiz-Cofer, J. (2000). The story of my body. In T. E. Ore (Ed.), *The social construction of difference and inequality: Race, class, gender and sexuality* (pp. 495–503). Mountain View, CA: Mayfield.

Padilla, A. M. (Ed.). (1995). *Hispanic psychology: Critical issues in theory and research.* Thousand Oaks, CA: Sage.

Peplau, L. A., & Taylor, S. E. (Eds.). (1997). *Sociocultural perspectives in social psychology: Current readings.* Upper Saddle River, NJ: Prentice Hall.

Prenger, S. (1999, January–February). Steps toward teaching for diversity: Some challenges and solutions. *Teaching at University of Nebraska Lincoln, 20*(4), 1–2.

Shakespeare, T. (Ed.). (1998). *The disability reader: Social science perspectives.* London: Cassell Academic.

Showalter, E. (1987). *The female malady: Women, madness, and English culture, 1830–1980.* New York: Pantheon.

Si, G., Rethorst, S., & Willimczik, K. (1999). Causal attribution perception in sports achievement: A cross-cultural study on attributional concepts in Germany and China. In B. J. Caskey (Ed.), *Stand! Social psychology: Contending ideas and opinions* (pp. 40–50). St. Paul, MN: Coursewise.

Sue, D. W., Bingham, R. P., Porche-Burke, L., & Vasquez, M. (1999). The diversification of psychology: A multicultural revolution. *American Psychologist, 54,* 1061–1069.

Sue, S. (1999). *Science, ethnicity and bias: Where have we gone wrong?* [Videotape]. Available from Microtraining Associates, 25 Burdette Avenue, Framingham, MA 01702.

Tatum, B. D. (1997). *Why are all the Black kids sitting together in the cafeteria? And other conversations about race*. New York: Basic Books.

Weisz, J. R., Rothbaum, F. M., & Blackburn, T. C. (1997). Standing out and standing in: The psychology of control in America and Japan. In L. A. Peplau & S. E. Taylor (Eds.), *Sociocultural perspectives in social psychology: Current readings* (pp. 75–99). Upper Saddle River, NJ: Prentice Hall.

5

PERSONALITY, GENDER, AND CULTURE

PHYLLIS BRONSTEIN

Like fiction and drama, the study of personality seeks to reveal aspects of human nature—the strengths and frailties we may all share, as well as the individual quirks, struggles, and dreams that distinguish us from one another. A key difference, however, is that in literature, the motivations, perceptions, and behaviors of memorable characters are shaped by factors such as gender, race, and socioeconomic level, against a backdrop of the particular culture and time in which the stories are set—whereas in the study of personality, that richness of context is almost entirely absent. Perhaps because of ethnocentrism and androcentrism, or an attempt to make personality psychology as scientific as possible, theorists and researchers have tended to narrow their focus to measuring individual differences within select homogeneous groups (e.g., U.S. majority-culture college students). This approach has been based on the largely unsupported assumption that the findings from such studies will reveal universalities of human nature.

The traditional Personality course reflects this narrow focus. Despite the increasing infusion of gender and multiculturalism into many other areas of the curriculum, the course remains essentially culture bound, in that it focuses on theories and research developed mainly by and about White males of European heritage. Although in recent years, some textbooks have included a chapter on sociocultural factors such as gender and ethnicity, and have featured a few women (Karen Horney, and sometimes Melanie Klein), overall, the content of most Personality textbooks has remained a traditional march through the graveyard of hallowed male theorists, such as Freud, Jung, Adler, Erikson, Sullivan, Murray, Allport, Maslow, Cattell, and Kelly, with an occasional visit to contemporary researchers such as Mischel and Bandura. Most of these textbooks take no notice of either feminist or multicultural perspectives on personality.

Over the years, in an attempt to broaden students' understanding of the factors that make people feel, think, and behave as they do, I have incorporated more material related to gender and sociocultural factors into my teaching of Personality. Recently, I renamed the course "Personality, Gender, and Culture," to distinguish it from the traditional model and to alert students from the beginning about what the focus would be. In this chapter, I discuss this approach, including readings, assignments, exercises, and additional resources that may be useful for teaching Personality from a sociocultural perspective.

OVERALL STRUCTURE

In recognition of the fact that students have different ways of processing new information, and different tolerances for openness and self-exploration, I provide a menu of assignments (some required but most optional), which offers students a variety of ways to accrue points toward their final grade. This approach also gives them control over the final grade, in that the more optional assignments they choose to do, the more points they earn. In addition, it allows me to incorporate campus and community events into the course. For example, if there is a lecture at a local synagogue on psychological issues for children of Holocaust survivors, or an on-campus colloquium on assimilation issues for Southeast Asian immigrants, students can earn a few points of credit by attending the presentation and handing in a 2-page write-up, relating it to some of the personality issues covered in the course. I also watch for relevant television segments (from PBS programs or news shows such as *Nightline* or *60 Minutes*) that might illustrate a topic and stimulate discussion and that are often available from the networks at fairly low cost. Information on obtaining such segments can be found on the Internet (e.g., the ABC New Store Web site: http://www.abcnewsstore.com) or by phoning the network.

COURSE CONTENT

In teaching the course, I cover some of the traditional areas, incorporating gender and multiculturalism into each of them. In addition, I include gender and sociocultural factors related to personality development as topics in their own right. I do not use a textbook but instead assign books and reading selections that are original source material. Although many instructors may prefer to use a textbook, they may also find it effective to use supplementary materials such as these to enhance students' understanding of underrepresented perspectives on personality.

Psychoanalytic Theory

I assign some of Freud's writings, followed by selections that consider his theories within social and cultural contexts. For example, students read *The Girl Who Couldn't Breathe* (Freud, 1895/1937) and *The Aetiology of Hysteria* (Freud, 1896/1989), in which they encounter Freud's early theory that hysterical symptoms in adolescence were caused by childhood sexual abuse. They then read an excerpt from Masson's (1984) book that supports this theory and posits why Freud later renounced it—which provides a fascinating example of how sociocultural factors shaped the psychoanalytic understanding of female personality (see also Westerlund, 1986). Related to this, I assign a reading on the present-day debate about the validity of recovered memories of sexual abuse (e.g., Butler, 1996; Freyd & Quina, 2000), to demonstrate the contemporary relevance of the controversy that surrounded Freud when he first proposed his theory. In addition, I have sometimes invited psychotherapists with expertise in this area to come and share their views and experiences with the class.

To learn about psychoanalytic perspectives on gender identity formation, students first read Freud's (1925/1989) *Some Psychical Consequences of the Anatomical Distinction Between the Sexes*, and then several challenges to his Oedipal theory (e.g., Fast, 1993; Mead, 1974; Stiver, 1991). Given that Freud believed that he was describing universal human development, it is informative for students to learn about applications in other cultures, such as a study conducted by Whiting, Kluckhohn, and Anthony (1958) that supported Freud's Oedipal ideas, and a later reconsideration of those findings that provided an alternative explanation (Munroe, Munroe, & Whiting, 1980). In addition, instructors may wish to include contemporary psychoanalytic perspectives on female development and gender identity formation (Bernay & Cantor, 1986; Chodorow, 1974; Jordan, 1997; Jordan, Kaplan, Miller, Stiver, & Surrey, 1991; Miller, 1976), as well as feminist (Heenan, 2002; Weskott, 1989) and multicultural (Segura & Pierce, 1993) critiques of some of these perspectives.

The Nature–Nurture Controversy

I begin a consideration of the nature–nurture controversy with an overview of early biological frameworks such as humors of the body, types of physiques, physiognomy, phrenology, and palmistry, which are mentioned in many Personality textbooks. This enables students to see that there have been numerous attempts to attribute individual differences in personality and behavior to innate biological factors, and that those theories have not withstood the test of time. It also opens the way to questioning contemporary biological explanations of personality differences. Bleier (1984) and Fausto-Sterling (1992) have provided excellent critiques of hormonal and genetic explanations for gender differences in characteristics such as aggression, dominance, and emotional stability. They have also effectively refuted sociobiologists' evolutionary rationales for traditional gender role behaviors and "reproductive strategies" such as male promiscuity and rape (see also Katz et al., 2000). Hrdy's (1998) analysis of bias in primate research provided an incisive challenge to the use of animal "evidence" in explaining gender differences in human behavior. Zuckerman (1998) presented a compelling cross-cultural challenge to purported connections between race and personality.

It is important to ask students to consider not only the degree to which biopsychological theories and research reflect biases about gender or race/ethnicity (Lewontin, Rose, & Kamin, 1984; Rose, 1998; chapter 7, this volume; Zuckerman, 1998), but also the implications and uses of findings that may emerge. Instructors might acquaint students with the recent controversy surrounding Raymond B. Cattell, which arose when the American Psychological Associaion at the last minute cancelled plans to award him the Gold Medal for Lifetime Achievement. It had been discovered that Cattell, a towering figure in psychology (who sometimes merits a chapter to himself in Personality textbooks), had written extensively about the importance of finding out which races are genetically fit and which are not, with the proposal that the unfit groups should be eliminated (Saeman, 1997). Instructors might also show students a segment from ABC's news program *Nightline*, entitled "The Secret Shame" (Lamonica, 1997), which describes Sweden's practice between 1935 and 1975 of sterilizing people who were judged to have a mental disorder or an antisocial lifestyle. And lest students assume that such practices could not happen in the United States, instructors can point out that up until the 1970s, most states had sterilization laws targeting people regarded as feebleminded, handicapped, or degenerate (Reilly & Wertz, 1999).

To illustrate the "nurture" side of the nature–nurture controversy, I usually assign some of my own writings on parenting and gender role socialization. This might include a review chapter on the different behaviors that mothers and fathers model, and their differential treatment of girls and boys, across a range of cultures (Bronstein, 2001), or a research report examining parenting behaviors that suggest gender role socialization across cultures (Bronstein, 1984; Brooks & Bronstein, 1996). I also may include research showing that parental receptivity to children's emotions is related to different patterns of emotional expressiveness and social and psychological adjustment for girls and boys in late adolescence (Bronstein, Briones, Brooks, & Cowan, 1996). This kind of evidence suggesting that parents' behaviors are a significant factor in the shaping and reinforcing of gender differences can provide an effective counter to claims that differences in girls' and boys' behaviors are dictated primarily by biology.

The Measurement of Personality

Since most of the personality psychologists students read about in textbooks are male, some gender balance can be provided by informing them of the important (and often unrecognized) roles played by women in the development of personality measures. For example, widely used clinical diagnostic instruments such as the Draw-A-Man, Draw-A-Person, and Bender Visual Motor Gestalt tests were developed by women (Stevens & Gardner, 1982). Henry Murray is generally credited with the development of the Thematic Apperception Test; however, in a letter to the Radcliffe College alumni newsletter, he stated that his colleague Christiana Morgan "had the main role" in developing it, and that the original idea for the test in fact came from a Radcliffe student in abnormal psychology (Murray, 1985, p. 2). Janet Taylor Spence, more currently known for her Personal Attributes Questionnaire (Spence, Helmreich, & Stapp, 1975), which measures gender role attributions, is also the author of the widely used Manifest Anxiety Scale (Taylor, 1953).

In teaching about personality research methodology, I use readings that simultaneously provide information on important social and multicultural issues. For example, as a multimethod approach to personality measurement, I have included selections from Oliner and Oliner's (1988) *The Altruistic Personality*, a study of non-Jews in Nazi-dominated countries who rescued—or did not rescue—Jews during the Holocaust. Using both questionnaire data and personal stories of courage and commitment, this compelling work illuminates factors that appear to contribute to the development of altruism. Along with the reading assignment, I have shown *The Courage to Care* (Rittner & Myers, 1986), a video that presents a number of rescuers telling their stories; the reading and video open the way for powerful class discussions regarding the psychological origins of prejudice and oppression as well as of caring and altruism. I have also assigned selections from *Drylongso: A Self-Portrait of Black America* (Gwaltney, 1981), a series of personal narratives from urban Black communities collected by an African American anthropologist. These elegant and moving stories demonstrate the wider possibilities that alternative methods may offer, both for examining personality development and for understanding the links between culture and personality.

To enhance students' understanding of personality measurement, I have used a range of hands-on approaches. For example, after going over the mechanics of scale construction, I break students into groups of three, and ask that each group create a scale to measure some trait that they think might be related to gender. Throughout the class period, I move among the groups, raising questions and giving feedback. They write out their hypothesis and a brief rationale for their expectations, and hand those in with the scale at the end of class. If there is time, some of the groups may share their work with the class, or I will present particularly interesting examples for discussion in the next class meeting.

Another exercise I have developed fosters students' understanding of scales, projective measures, and interviews, while heightening their awareness of personality dynamics related to prejudice and oppression. I start off by reading aloud segments from recent media reports about sexism, racism, and homophobia in the U.S. military, as a way of alerting them to these issues. They then choose one of those topics, or another entitled "Women's adaptability in a predominantly male environment," and break into groups of three or four according to their choice. I give them a handout that sums up the issues, and asks them to imagine that the class is a psychology consulting firm hired by the Joint Chiefs of the Armed Forces to screen new enlistees as well as officers being considered for promotion. The task of each group is to devise two different kinds of assessment procedures which, depending on the topic they choose, will help either to (a) weed out individuals who show tendencies toward the kinds of cognitions, emotions, and behaviors that could make them prone to the antisocial behaviors manifested as sexism, racism, or homophobia, or (b) assure the success of women in the military by assessing whether female recruits and officer candidates will be likely to handle the psychological, social, and emotional challenges of operating in domains that have only recently been opened to women. The process involves several class periods (during which I provide guidance and feedback), plus some out-of-class meeting time for each group to coordinate their efforts and plan a 15-min class presentation. The results are generally both impressive and engaging; students' questionnaires and interview protocols are usually well conceived, and their uses of such things as magazine illustrations and video segments as projective measures are often highly creative.

Finally, to give students firsthand knowledge of qualitative approaches, and to highlight issues related to gender, culture, and class, I often provide some of my own data for them to analyze. In groups of three or four, they read a small sampling of qualitative material, and attempt to come up with central, personality-related issues to code, which the class as a whole then discusses. For this I have used Mexican children's projective stories, segments from life history interviews of ethnic minority faculty, and segments from interviews with older adolescents looking back on their high school years—although many other topics would be equally meaningful. Working closely with qualitative data gives students an appreciation of the advantages and disadvantages of this approach compared with more structured methods of measurement, as well as a greater understanding of the researcher's role in shaping questions and finding meaning.

Sociocultural Factors in Personality Development

I allocate several weeks specifically to sociocultural and ethnic factors, with readings related to African American, Latino, Asian American, American Indian, and Jewish personality development (e.g., Kagan & Knight, 1979; LaFramboise, Heyle, & Ozer, 1990; Langman, 1995; Wang, 1995; Ward, 1996; Weiner, 1991). There is a rapidly expanding literature on multicultural issues (e.g., Comas-Díaz & Greene, 1994; Landrine, 1995; Siegel & Cole, 1997), and instructors will find many additional personality-relevant articles, collections, and memoirs cited throughout the present volume. At various points in the course I also include readings from literature and anthropology, to provide information about personality development in cultures within and outside the United States (e.g., Mead, 1935/1963; Tan, 1989). As a way of illustrating the effects of social class on personality development, I show the video *28-Up* (Morris & Apted, 1984), which is part of a longitudinal series that focuses on the lives and development of a group of British children beginning at the age of seven, and then every subsequent 7 years, until age 42. I use this particular segment (which covers ages 7–28) because the interviews at ages 21 and 28 touch on life issues that are particularly salient for traditional-age undergraduate students. In addition to providing rich evidence of the role of sociocultural factors in shaping personality and life directions, this video also illustrates individuals' capacity for growth and change.

An exercise I have found effective is to have students participate in a small discussion group with people from the same socioeconomic or ethnic background. Students decide what the groups should be, and which one they will join; thus the composition of the groups depends on the diversity in the class and students' willingness to acknowledge and explore their own backgrounds. Once in their groups, they take turns talking about their own experiences growing up with that particular background; I encourage them to consider what they are proud of, what they found hard, what values and expectations were communicated to them, and what they would like others not of that background to know about them. One person in each group is appointed to take notes, and at the end, the group presents some of its ideas and conclusions to the class and answers questions. Sharing with others from a similar background is often a powerful experience, especially for students who are in a minority at their institution and who may have been trying to downplay or deny their sense of differentness. Similarly, it is eye-opening for the other students to learn, often for the first time, what it may be like to grow up working class, African American, or Jewish in U.S. society.

I also offer a number of paper assignments that relate personality to gender and sociocultural factors. For example, students can choose to write a self-analysis in which they examine ways that gender role socialization and ethnic and socioeconomic background may have affected their personality development. They can choose two characters from *The Joy Luck Club* (Tan, 1989) and two of the people interviewed in *Drylongso* (Gwaltney, 1981), and write a brief analysis of each one's personality development from a sociocultural perspective. In addition, I require students to do an audiotaped, 30-min interview with a person whose background and life experience are different from their own, and to write a paper relating the person's background to her or his current personality, values, and perspective on life. This assignment encourages students to move beyond what may be a limited circle of family and social relations, to get to know a Vietnamese graduate student or the Italian American bakery owner in their hometown—although they may also learn for the first time about their immigrant grandmother's childhood. In preparation for the interview assignments, I provide information on technique (Seidman, 1998) and require that students both get my approval in advance for the questions they will ask and also hand in the tapes with their papers. These steps assure that they that they will ask questions that are meaningful and nonoffensive and that I can check their interviewing technique and the accuracy of their reporting.

Gender, Sexual Identity, and Personality Development

Although gender issues, like sociocultural factors, are woven into every aspect of the course, I also devote a specific segment to them and to sexual identity in relation to personality development. There are many readings that can help students become more aware of gender role messages in the family (e.g., Bronstein, 2001; Rubin, Provenzano, & Luria, 1974), in school (Grant, 1994; Sadker & Sadker, 1994; Thorne, 1986), in the media (Faludi, 1991; Rhode, 1995), and across cultures (e.g., Mead 1935/1963; Whiting & Edwards, 1988). There are also many theorists, researchers, and clinicians who have written about girls' and women's psychological development (e.g., Belenky, Clinchy, Goldberger, & Tarule, 1986; Gilligan, Rogers, & Tolman, 1991; hooks, 1989; Jordan, 1997; Miller, 1976; Pipher, 1994; Stewart & Ostrove, 1998), as well as boys' and men's (e.g., Kimmel & Messner, 1995; Levant & Pollack, 1995; Lewis, 1978; McLean, Carey, & White, 1996; Silverstein & Rashbaum, 1994), and there are interesting collections focusing on gender per se (e.g., Beall & Sternberg, 1993; Clinchy & Norem, 1998). In addition, I assign readings related to sexual identity development (e.g., Savin-Williams, 1996; Troiden, 1993), including a cross-cultural perspective (Williams, 1996).

I have found some useful television programs for illustrating gender issues and stimulating lively class discussion. A *Primetime Live* segment entitled "Boy or Girl" (Sawyer & Snyderman, 1997) reported on the short- and long-term psychological effects of sex reassignment at birth based on ambiguous genital formation or genital injury. Another segment, entitled "He/She" (Sawyer, 1997), provided an engaging and provocative interview with a transgendered college student. *Candid Camera* (Funt, 1997) devoted an entire program to reactions to nontraditional gender role behaviors, with scenarios that were both amusing and thought provoking.

CONCLUSION

The field of personality, perhaps more than any other area in psychology, has suffered from the constraints of gender and cultural bias. Over the years, its quest has been to discover universalities of human nature, yet in ignoring the contributions of gender and culture, its theoretical models and empirical research have in fact provided information about a very small segment of humanity; in focusing intently on a small stand of oaks, personality researchers have missed the enormous variety of the forest. Feminist and multicultural scholars are providing new perspectives and new research tools, but these are just beginning to find their way into undergraduate Personality textbooks. Instructors of Personality need to recognize that the traditional course presents very little meaningful information about the nature and development of human beings, and to utilize new materials and approaches in creating a course that reflects the richness and realities of the world around us.

REFERENCES

Beall, A. E., & Sternberg, R. J. (Eds.). (1993). *The psychology of gender*. New York: Guilford Press.

Belenky, M. F., Clinchy, B. M., Goldberger, N. R., & Tarule, J. M. (1986). *Women's ways of knowing: The development of self, voice, and mind*. New York: Basic Books.

Bernay, T., & Cantor, D. W. (Eds.). (1986). *The psychology of today's woman: New psychoanalytic visions*. Hillsdale, NJ: Analytic Press.

Bleier, R. (1984). *Science and gender: A critique of biology and its theories on women*. New York: Pergamon Press.

Bronstein, P. (1984). Differences in mothers' and fathers' behavior to children: A cross-cultural comparison. *Developmental Psychology, 20*, 995–1003.

Bronstein, P. (2001). Parenting. In J. Worell (Ed.), *Encyclopedia of women and gender* (pp. 795–808). San Diego, CA: Academic Press.

Bronstein, P., Briones, M., Brooks, T., & Cowan, B. (1996). Gender and family factors as predictors of late adolescent emotional expressiveness and adjustment: A longitudinal study. *Sex Roles, 34*, 739–765.

Brooks, T., & Bronstein, P. (1996, March). *Cross-cultural comparison of mothers' and fathers' behaviors toward girls and boys.* Poster presented at the biennial meeting of the Society for Research on Adolescence, Boston.

Butler, K. (1996, November/December). The latest on recovered memory. *Networker,* 36–37.

Chodorow, N. (1974). Family structure and feminine personality. In M. S. Rosaldo & L. Lamphere (Eds.), *Women, culture, and society* (pp. 43–66). Stanford, CA: Stanford University Press.

Clinchy, B. M., & Norem, J. K. (Eds.). (1998). *The gender and psychology reader.* New York: New York University Press.

Comas-Díaz, L., & Greene, B. (Eds.). (1994). *Women of color: Integrating ethnic and gender identities in psychotherapy.* New York: Guilford Press.

Faludi, S. (1991). *Backlash: The undeclared war on American women.* New York: Crown.

Fast, I. (1993). Aspects of early gender development: A psychodynamic perspective. In A. E. Beall & R. J. Sternberg (Eds.), *The psychology of gender* (pp. 173–193). New York: Guilford Press.

Fausto-Sterling, A. (1992). *Myths of gender: Biological theories about women and men* (2nd ed.). New York: Basic Books.

Freud, S. (1937). The girl who couldn't breathe (A. A. Brill, Trans.). In J. Breuer & S. Freud, *Studies on hysteria* (pp. 13–24). New York: Nervous and Mental Disease Publishing. (Original work published 1895)

Freud, S. (1989). The aetiology of hysteria. In P. Gay (Ed.), *The Freud reader* (pp. 96–111). New York: Norton. (Original work published 1896)

Freud, S. (1989). Some psychical consequences of the anatomical distinction between the sexes. In P. Gay (Ed.), *The Freud reader* (pp. 670–678). New York: Norton. (Original work published 1925)

Freyd, J. J., & Quina, K. (2000). Feminist ethics in the practice of science: The contested memory controversy as example. In M. Brabeck (Ed.), *Practicing feminist ethics in psychology* (pp. 101–124). Washington, DC: American Psychological Association.

Funt, A. (Producer). (1997, November 7). Battle of the sexes [Television series episode]. In *Candid camera.* New York: Columbia Broadcasting System. (For information about obtaining materials for classroom use, contact Candid Camera, P.O. Box 827, Monterey, CA 93942 or visit http://www.candidcamera.com)

Gilligan, C., Rogers, A. G., & Tolman, D. L. (Eds.). (1991). *Women, girls, and psychotherapy: Reframing resistance.* New York: Haworth Press.

Grant, L. (1994). Helpers, enforcers, and go-betweens: Black females in elementary school classrooms. In M. Baca Zinn & B. T. Dill (Eds.), *Women of color in U.S. society* (pp. 43–63). Philadelphia: Temple University Press.

Gwaltney, J. L. (1981). *Drylongso: A self-portrait of Black America.* New York: Vintage Books.

Heenan, C. (Ed.). (2002). The reproduction of mothering: A reappraisal [special issue]. *Feminism and Psychology, 12*(1).

hooks, b. (1989). *Talking back: Thinking feminist, thinking black.* Boston: South End Press.

Hrdy, S. B. (1998). Raising Darwin's consciousness: Females and evolutionary theory. In B. M. Clinchy & J. K. Norem (Eds.), *The gender and psychology reader* (pp. 265–271). New York: New York University Press.

Jordan, J. V. (Ed.). (1997). *Women's growth in diversity: More writings from the Stone Center.* New York: Guilford Press.

Jordan, J. V., Kaplan, A. G., Miller, J. B., Stiver, I. P., & Surrey, J. L. (Eds.). (1991). *Women's growth in connection: Writings from the Stone Center.* New York: Guilford Press.

Kagan, S., & Knight, G. P. (1979). Cooperation–competition and self-esteem: A case of cultural relativism. *Journal of Cross-Cultural Psychology, 10,* 457–467.

Katz, P. A., Eagly, A., Remer, P., Silverstein, L., Travis, C., & Yoder, J. (2000, Summer). Open letter. *Psychology of Women Newsletter, 18,* 23.

Kimmel, M. S., & Messner, M. A. (Eds.). (1995). *Men's lives.* Boston: Allyn & Bacon.

LaFramboise, T. D., Heyle, A. M., & Ozer, E. J. (1990). Changing and diverse roles of women in American Indian cultures. *Sex Roles, 22,* 455–476.

Lamonica, J. (Producer). (1997, September 16). The secret shame. In *Nightline* [Television series episode]. New York: American Broadcasting Company. (Available from ABC News, Dept. 108, P. O. Box 807, New Hudson, MI 48165; phone: 800-225-5222.)

Landrine, H. (Ed.). (1995). *Bringing cultural diversity to feminist psychology.* Washington, DC: American Psychological Association.

Langman, P. F. (1995, October). Including Jews in multiculturalism. *Journal of Multicultural Counseling and Development, 23,* 222–236.

Levant, R. F., & Pollack, W. S. (Eds.). (1995). *A new psychology of men.* New York: Basic Books.

Lewis, R. A. (1978). Emotional intimacy among men. *Journal of Social Issues, 34,* 108–121.

Lewontin, R. C., Rose, S., & Kamin, L. J. (1984). *Not in our genes: Biology, ideology, and human nature.* New York: Pantheon Books.

Masson, J. M. (1984). *The assault on truth: Freud's suppression of the seduction theory.* New York: Farrar, Straus & Giroux.

McLean, C., Carey, M., & White, C. (Eds.). (1996). *Men's ways of being.* New York: Westview Press.

Mead, M. (1963). *Sex and temperament in three primitive societies.* New York: Morrow. (Original work published 1935)

Mead, M. (1974). On Freud's view of female psychology. In J. Strouse (Ed.), *Women & analysis: Dialogues on psychoanalytic views of femininity* (pp. 95–106). New York: Grossman.

Miller, J. B. (1976). *Toward a new psychology of women*. Boston: Beacon Press.

Morris, S. (Executive Producer), & Apted, M. (Producer/Director). (1984). *28 up* [Videotape]. (Available for rental from Facets Multimedia, 1517 West Fullerton Ave., Chicago, IL 60614, or for purchase from http://shopping.yahoo.com/)

Munroe, R. L., Munroe, R. H., & Whiting, J. W. M. (1980). Male sex-role resolutions. In R. L. Munroe, R. H. Munroe, & B. B. Whiting (Eds.), *Handbook of cross-cultural human development* (pp. 611–632). New York: Garland.

Murray, H. A. (1985, February). Dr. Henry A. Murray replies [Letter to the editor]. *Second Century: Radcliffe News*, p. 2.

Oliner, S. P., & Oliner, P. M. (1988). *The altruistic personality: Rescuers of Jews in Nazi Europe*. New York: Free Press.

Pipher, M. (1994). *Reviving Ophelia: Saving the selves of adolescent girls*. New York: Ballantine Books.

Reilly, P. R., & Wertz, D. C. (1999, February 1). *Eugenics: 1883–1970*. Retrieved September 10, 2001, from http://www.genesage.com/professionals/archives/eugenics18831970.html

Rhode, D. L. (1995). Media images, feminist issues. *Signs: Journal of Women in Culture and Society, 20*, 685–710.

Rittner, C., & Myers, S. (Producers). (1986). *The courage to care* [Videotape]. New York: Anti-Defamation League of B'nai Brith.

Rose, S. (1998). *Lifelines: Biology beyond determinism*. New York: Oxford University Press.

Rubin, J. Z., Provenzano, F. J., & Luria, Z. (1974). The eye of the beholder: Parents' views on sex of newborns. *American Journal of Orthopsychiatry, 44*, 512–519.

Sadker, M., & Sadker, D. (1994). *Failing at fairness: How America's schools treat girls*. New York: Macmillan.

Saeman, H. (1997, September–October). The Cattell convention. *The National Psychologist, 6*(5), 1–3.

Savin-Williams, R. C. (1996). Memories of childhood and early adolescent sexual feelings among gay and bisexual boys: A narrative approach. In R. C. Savin-Williams & K. M. Cohen (Eds.), *The lives of lesbians, gays, and bisexuals* (pp. 94–109). New York: Harcourt Brace.

Sawyer, D. (1997, October 15). He/she. In T. Berman (Producer), *Primetime live* [Television series episode]. New York: American Broadcasting Company. (Available from ABC News, Dept. 108, P. O. Box 807, New Hudson, MI 48165; phone: 800-225-5222.)

Sawyer, D., & Snyderman, N. (1997, September 3). Boy or girl. In T. Berman (Producer), *Primetime live* [Television series episode]. New York: American Broadcasting Company. (Available from ABC News, Dept. 108, P. O. Box 807, New Hudson, MI 48165; phone: 800-225-5222.)

Segura, D. A., & Pierce, J. L. (1993). Chicana/o family structure and gender personality: Chodorow, familism, and psychoanalytic sociology revisited. *Signs: Journal of Women in Culture and Society, 19*, 62–91.

Seidman, I. E. (1998). *Interviewing as qualitative research: A guide for researchers in education and the social sciences* (2nd ed.). New York: Teachers College Press.

Siegel, R. J., & Cole, E. (Eds.). (1997). *Celebrating the lives of Jewish women: Patterns in a feminist sampler.* New York: Harrington Park Press.

Silverstein, O., & Rashbaum, P. (1994). *The courage to raise good men.* New York: Viking.

Spence, J. T., Helmreich, R., & Stapp, J. (1975). Ratings of self and peers on sex-role attributes and their relation to self-esteem and conceptions of masculinity and femininity. *Journal of Personality and Social Psychology, 32,* 29–39.

Stevens, G., & Gardner, S. (1982). *The women of psychology* (Vols. I and II). Cambridge, MA: Shenkman.

Stewart, A. J., & Ostrove, J. M. (1998). Women's personality in middle age: Gender, history, and midcourse corrections. *American Psychologist, 53,* 1185–1194.

Stiver, I. P. (1991). Beyond the Oedipus complex: Mothers and daughters. In J. V. Jordan, A. G. Kaplan, J. B. Miller, I. P. Stiver, & J. L. Surrey (Eds.), *Women's growth in connection: Writings from the Stone Center* (pp. 97–121). New York: Guilford Press.

Tan, A. (1989). *The joy luck club.* New York: Putnam.

Taylor, J. A. (1953). A personality scale of manifest anxiety. *Journal of Abnormal and Social Psychology, 48,* 285–290.

Thorne, B. (1986). Girls and boys together . . . but mostly apart: Gender arrangements in elementary schools. In W. W. Hartup & Z. Rubin (Eds.), *Relationships and development* (pp. 167–184). Hillsdale, NJ: Erlbaum.

Troiden, R. R. (1993). The formation of homosexual identities. In L. D. Garnetts & D. C. Kimmel (Eds.), *Psychological perspectives on lesbian and gay male experiences* (pp. 191–217). New York: Columbia University Press.

Wang, N. (1995). Born Chinese and a woman in America. In J. Adelman & G. M. Enguidanos (Eds.), *Racism in the lives of women: Testimony, theory, and guides to antiracist practice* (pp. 97–110). New York: Haworth Press.

Ward, J. V. (1996). Raising resisters: The role of truth telling in the psychological development of African American girls. In B. J. R. Leadbeater & N. Way (Eds.), *Urban girls: Resisting stereotypes, creating identities* (pp. 85–99). New York: New York University Press.

Weiner, K. (1991). Anti-semitism in the therapy room. In R. J. Siegel & E. Cole (Eds.), *Jewish women in therapy: Seen but not heard* (pp. 119–126). New York: Harrington Park Press.

Weskott, M. (1989). Female relationality and the idealized self. *American Journal of Psychoanalysis, 49,* 239–250.

Westerlund, E. (1986). Freud on sexual trauma: An historical review of seduction and betrayal. *Psychology of Women Quarterly, 10,* 297–309.

Whiting, B. B., & Edwards, C. P. (1988). *Children of different worlds: The formation of social behavior.* Cambridge, MA: Harvard University Press.

Whiting, J. W. M., Kluckhohn, R., & Anthony, A. (1958). The function of male initiation ceremonies at puberty. In E. E. Maccoby, T. M. Newcomb, & E. L. Hartley (Eds.), *Readings in social psychology* (3rd ed., pp. 359–370). New York: Holt.

Williams, W. L. (1996). Two-spirited persons: Gender nonconformity among Native American and Native Hawaiian youths. In R. C. Savin-Williams & K. M. Cohen (Eds.), *The lives of lesbians, gays, and bisexuals* (pp. 416–435). New York: Harcourt Brace.

Zuckerman, M. (1998). Some dubious premises in research and theory on racial differences: Scientific, social, and ethical issues. In P. B. Organista, K. M. Chun, & G. Marín (Eds.), *Readings in ethnic psychology* (pp. 59–69). New York: Routledge.

6

THE EXPERIMENTAL PSYCHOLOGY COURSE

KATHRYN QUINA AND JANET M. KULBERG

In most psychology departments, a research methods course is a requirement for majors. Thus, the way this course is taught is likely to affect how the next generation of psychologists understands and participates in the research process. A redesigned Experimental Psychology course, in providing students with an understanding of a broad range of methodologies, would also expand psychology's knowledge base as some of them become researchers. In addition, sharpening their skills for detecting and eliminating bias in research and its applications would have far-reaching consequences, by providing all students with a greater ability to evaluate psychological research as it impacts legal decisions, media representations of various groups, and public policy. In this chapter we describe such a course, which, in its consideration of research methodology, takes the sociocultural context into account at every level.

COURSE GOALS AND OBJECTIVES

Our specific objectives in the course are for students to learn how to (a) select an appropriate design and statistical analysis from a wide array of methodological options; (b) recognize and minimize bias both in designing research and interpreting results; (c) work toward achieving external as well as internal validity; (d) implement research and interpret results ethically; and (e) be knowledgeable consumers, able to critique studies that find their way into the public realm. In addition, we regard the course as a place for students to begin to develop professional identities as future psychologists.

Asking and Answering Research Questions: Conceptualization, Design, and Analysis

Instructors can help students understand the importance of assessing human experience in ways that are appropriate to the people being studied (Landrine, 1995; Nielson, 1990). This applies not only to the design and analysis of research but also to the development of the appropriate questions to ask (K. J. Gergen, Gulerce, Lock, & Misra, 1996). Mays and Jackson (1991), noting biases in survey research on minorities and AIDS risk, used a decisional model that guides researchers from conceptualization of the problem to the interpretation of the results, taking into account issues of mistrust of research and researchers. Researchers are also using more exploratory and qualitative approaches to begin to understand understudied populations (Reinharz, 1991; Wilkinson, 1996). Quina et al. (1999) offered a research model blending qualitative focus group and quantitative psychometric approaches to adapt surveys to community-based subjects. To acquaint students with the range of recent methodological developments, instructors can have students, individually or in groups, review a current issue of a journal (including newer ones, e.g., *Cultural Diversity and Ethnic Minority Psychology* or *Feminism and Psychology*) and describe the range of empirical questions, research designs, participants, and statistical approaches used across the studies.

Recognizing and Reducing Bias

For generations, students have been taught that as a science, psychology—and the people who conduct psychological research—are objective and apolitical (Riger, 1992). Yet psychologists have always reflected, and at times directed, public attitudes. Articles in the spring 1998 issue of the *Journal of Social Issues*, "Experts in the Service of Social Reform" (Harris & Nicholson, 1998), reveal both negative and positive uses of psychology in significant policy decisions such as desegregation. Hooker's (1993) powerful reflection on her 40 years of research on homosexuality provides further examples of ways that psychology has been shaped by the mores of the times. Sue (1999) provided a compelling discussion of the ways cultural biases have permeated psychological research, and Wyatt (1994) provided specific examples in her description of ethnic biases in sex research on minority women.

Recognizing the biases in traditional psychology, feminist and multicultural scholars have led the way in offering alternative views of the scientific endeavor, including social constructionism (M. M. Gergen, 1988; Riger, 1992), contextualism (Landrine, 1995), multiculturalism (Pedersen, 1999), and postmodernism (Wilkinson, 1996). Comparing different philosophies of science, and examples of research emanating from them, can lead to lively class discussions; useful resources are M. M. Gergen, Chrisler, and LoCicero (1999); Rogler (1999); and Sherif's (1979/1998) groundbreaking article, "Bias in Psychology," and the commentaries around it.

We help students conceptualize the scientific method with the Process Model developed by Kulberg (Quina & Kulberg, 1988). We draw a circle with clockwise arrows and present points along the circle as representing a unidirectional set of decisions: identifying a theory (at the top of the circle); designing an empirical study to test the theory, using deductive logic; carrying out the statistical test of the theory (at the bottom of the circle); and then using inductive logic to interpret results and ultimately to make inferences about the theory. What appear to be objective steps in this process—constructing the hypotheses, designing an internally consistent study with operationally defined variables, applying statistical tests, and reporting the results—are viewed as methodological decision points for the researcher, each of which may be shaped by earlier decisions or by personal bias. Using this Process Model as a guide, logical as well as antibias skills can be practiced through entertaining in-class exercises. For example, to develop deductive skills, we pose everyday sayings as theories, such as "Success breeds success," and "Spare the rod, spoil the child." Students develop hypotheses and operationally defined independent and dependent variables and then share them with other class members.

This exercise also underlines the fact that the process of narrowing a theory down to a logically deduced hypothesis, in order to subject it to real-world tests, involves arbitrary decisions that are easily influenced by personal or cultural norms. In considering "Success breeds success," some students will define success as wealth, others as achievement, still others as satisfaction. We follow with a discussion of how the "objectivity" requirement—that the independent and dependent variables must be observable or quantitatively measurable—shapes researchers' decisions about what to study and how these decisions in turn have influenced the field of psychology.

In the above example, students quickly realize that one of the few usable measures of "success" is income, even though few believe that the amount of money one makes is equivalent to life success. Another effective example is the operational definition of *aggression*, which often is narrowed to physical acts, such as hitting or kicking, because they can be more reliably observed. However, this choice leads to an exaggeration of sex differences in the published literature; whereas physical aggression is more often observed in boys, other, harder-to-measure behaviors, such as verbal insult, occur as often in girls (Caplan & Caplan, 1999).

Instructors can address the inductive phase of the scientific method in a similar way, offering examples of results whose meanings students can ponder. One typical error in interpreting findings is to discuss group differences without reference to confounding or interacting influences. For example, differences between men and women are presumed to be genetic or hormonal, ignoring the myriad social factors that also differentiate them. Similarly, differences between disabled and nondisabled participants are usually attributed to the disability, rather than to the accompanying life circumstances, such as lower income (see chapter 18, this volume). Another common error is to interpret group differences as categorical, typifying of all members of each group (Yee, Fairchild, Weizmann, & Wyatt, 1993), rather than as mean differences with significant overlap across groups. There is also the question of how meaningful the results may be in terms of the real world. For example, in most comparisons, the amount of statistical variability that can be accounted for by the gender variable is quite small, even in such stereotyped areas as aggression and cognitive ability. Caplan and Caplan's (1999) *Thinking Critically About Research on Sex and Gender* presents examples of these and other biases in current topics in a readable, engaging format. We have used this as a supplemental text in Experimental Psychology and in other courses, such as Psychology of Women, at both graduate and undergraduate levels, always to rave reviews.

Instructors can encourage students to consider ways to be creative in designing research to minimize such errors. One of the most interesting areas where this has been done is in menstrual cycle research. Mansfield, Hood, and Henderson (1989) measured husbands' and wives' moods over a period of weeks and plotted them as a function of both the wives' menstrual cycle and the day of the week. Not surprisingly, the effects of day of the week were the only significant predictor for both partners. In another creative study, Chrisler, Johnston, Champagne, and Preston (1994) demonstrated participants' reactivity to the commonly used "Menstrual Distress Questionnaire" (e.g., Boyle, 1992), which assesses only negative experiences of menstruation. They had women answer questions regarding their attitudes toward their menstrual periods after filling out either this survey or a revised version assessing positive experiences, entitled the "Menstrual Joy Questionnaire." The latter group reported significantly more positive attitudes about their own menstrual periods, demonstrating the power of the particular experimental context as well as the dangers inherent in attitude measurements. Additional useful material on this topic are Chrisler and Levy's (1990) content analysis of popular articles about menstruation and Caplan's (1995) description of how research regarding menstrual problems has been distorted and ignored in psychiatric diagnoses.

It is helpful at this point to discuss biases inherent in the traditional scientific method itself. First, a theory is required at the outset, and in a sense this demands a biased view (Greenwald, Pratkanis, Leippe, & Baumgardner, 1986). Furthermore, in the formation of a definitive "test" of that theory, researchers are forced to deduce hypotheses that predict a difference or an effect—one literally cannot set up an experiment to look for "no difference" between groups. In addition, there is a bias against publishing nonsignificant findings (Cortina & Folger, 1998). As a result, group differences are over-represented in the research literature, while the myriad studies that find no differences are not published. Malgady (2000) identified myths about null hypothesis testing in cross-cultural psychological research and offered alternative views.

Increasingly public uses of psychology, from the courtroom to the boardroom, have demonstrated a need to be aware of, and to respond to, political and social biases (Barrett & Morris, 1993, and related articles in the same issue; Freyd & Quina, 2000). Shields (1982) wrote a very readable and informative historical review of the politics of sex differences in the brain that generalizes well to other claims of inherent "difference." More in-depth courses might also include Gould's (1981) classic *The Mismeasure of Man*, which effectively addresses a variety of ways in which people who are culturally or otherwise less powerful have been harmed by researchers' biased attitudes; Guthrie's (1998) *Even the Rat Was White*, which traces the history of racial biases; and Tavris's (1992) *The Mismeasure of Women*, which provides a powerful critique of the treatment of women in several research areas.

Having revealed these flaws, instructors then need to help students learn to love research and to produce helpful work in the future. Sue (1999) argued that the problem is not science itself, but the ways in which that science is practiced. A special issue of *Psychology of Women Quarterly* on innovative research methods in feminist psychology (Crawford & Kimmel, 1999) and the edited book, *Feminist Social Psychologies: International Perspectives* (Wilkinson, 1996) offer interesting examples.

Understanding the Importance of External Validity

Although the emphasis is shifting in some fields of psychology from the laboratory to the community, research topics are still mainly generated from a White Western viewpoint, and the typical participant is still a White middle-class college student (Kazdin, 1999). Although overall the percentage of participants who are women is about equal to that of men, in some journals the majority of studies do not consider participant gender as a variable (Ader & Johnson, 1994). Padilla and Lindholm (1995) discussed the need for greater detail in descriptions of participants in journal articles, including ethnicity and gender. Furthermore, the proportion of studies in American

Psychological Association (APA) journals focusing on ethnic and social minorities has actually declined in recent years, and in such studies, the topic is often negative (e.g., AIDS), with findings cast as deviations from a White "normative" group (Graham, 1992; Wyche, 1993).

Sue (1999) discussed the funding and publication climates that have fostered this lack of diversity, with their emphasis on internal validity (whether the design is well controlled) at the expense of external validity (whether the findings apply to other individuals and groups). He provided examples of culture as a moderating variable from two of his own research studies, one on sexual aggression by men, and the other on using SAT scores to predict school success. In each, prediction models that were significant for White participants did not hold up for other cultural groups, illustrating that it is risky to make presumptions about external validity—or policy decisions—based on one group. Students should view guidelines for inclusion of women and minorities in federally funded research (National Institutes of Health, 1994) and/or their own Institutional Research Board.

Research on populations that are generally excluded from mainstream psychology, such as women at risk for HIV infection (Goldstein & Manlowe, 1997) and incarcerated women (Fletcher, Shaver, & Moon, 1993), can extend students' understanding of the breadth and depth of human experiences that are both negative (e.g., they have experienced high levels of distress) and positive (e.g., their very survival is a success story). For advanced students, a research placement can be particularly illuminating and, as volunteers working in our (Quina and colleagues) research project in the Rhode Island Women's Correctional Facility found, a very positive learning experience (Efreom, 1999).

Students interested in biological psychology will find a discussion of animal subject selection relevant. Our students have been intrigued by de Waal's (1995) proposal that concepts of normal human behavior might be different if researchers had been working with bonobos rather than chimpanzees or rhesus monkeys. Among bonobos, who are phylogenetically and behaviorally closer to humans, sex differences are minimal, males nurture rather than dominate, and sexual behavior is varied and frequent.

Developing a Sense of Ethical and Social Responsibility

Thinking through the ethical issues should be required of all students who will be collecting data, and we recommend their filling out an Institutional Review Board application regardless of whether it is required by the home institution. A guest lecture by a member of that board can underscore the importance of adhering to ethical standards (Sieber, 1992). However, considerations of ethics should go farther than these formal standards. Some writers have extended the concept of ethics to incorporate considerations of what the process of research means to the participant, how participants and researchers may be affected by it, and how the data may ultimately be used (Brabeck, 2000). A special section of the *American Psychologist* devoted to a consideration of the Head Start program and its evaluation (Takanashi & DeLeon, 1994) offers several useful examples of the ethical considerations and social responsibility of researchers, including a concern that this national program is being evaluated without a great deal of knowledge about normative development for the typically minority client populations involved in it.

Becoming Effective Consumers

Not all psychology students expect—or want—to be researchers. Yet there is an important role for the Experimental Psychology course in their lives, to sharpen "consumer skills" for evaluating the almost daily media use (and misuse) of psychological data. Connor-Greene (1993) offered an exercise comparing media reports with the original research, which allows students to see how the media often distort information. Walsh (1996) paired "pro" and "con" articles on timely topics, such as whether scientists should study gender differences and whether abortion leads to emotional harm, which allow students to see for themselves the differences not only in conclusions but also in how the authors reached those conclusions (often with strikingly different and nonoverlapping methodologies). An especially useful debate in Walsh's book deals with the "math gene" (chapter 10), which shows how the media misrepresented the original data and how that misrepresentation affected mothers' encouragement of their daughters in math. We also provide opportunities for students to consider how they have accepted stereotypes such as "women are not mathematically or statistically inclined," or "math is only for a certain few" (a version to which men can relate), in limiting their own career choices.

Just because a work is authored by someone with the label "scientist," or uses scientific methods, does not mean it necessarily meets the criteria of "good science" (Freyd & Quina, 2000). Students can benefit from examining both sides of well-publicized scientific controversies. For example, Herrnstein and Murray (1994) claimed that research studies reveal genetically based race and social class differences in intelligence and offered proposals for limiting the fertility of "inferior" women. Two reviews—one pro (Bouchard, 1995), one critical (Dorfman, 1995)—of this book, originally published in in *Contemporary Psychology*, show both the political and scientific issues involved in the controversy. Kamin (1995) and Fischer et al. (1996) have offered detailed critiques; Goldberger and Manski (1995) provided an online bibliography.

The role of science in the debate about recovered memories of childhood abuse is particularly illuminating, because it has taken place largely in courtrooms and the media. Freyd and Quina (2000) discussed the scientific–ethical issues, including the politics behind the science. Freyd and DePrince (2001) provided a comprehensive review of the cognitive science literature pertaining to the issue, and Pezdek and Banks (1996) offered perspective on the debate itself.

Finally, students are often amazed to find that differences they had taken for granted may represent more complex social phenomena. Raag (1999) highlighted the relation between social expectations (i.e., does an adult disapprove) and gender differences in children's toy choices. Mulac and Bradac (1995) discussed ways to question whether different language styles often attributed to men and women are instead a function of social power.

An assignment we have found useful for honing students' evaluation skills is to ask them to critique empirical publications according to specific guidelines, which include ways to detect bias (adapted from McHugh, Koeske, & Frieze, 1986). They often report shock and dismay over the extent of gender and racial bias that they find, as well as other logical flaws, such as poorly controlled designs (Caplan & Caplan, 1999). At the same time, they report greater confidence in their own judgment and are pleased with the power to question or reject claims such as gender or racial inferiority. Allowing students a choice of content and encouraging them to explore a range of journals introduce students to a wider definition of psychology. We further encourage them to apply their emerging skills to the public domain. Students can review a current issue of the *APA Monitor* or go to the APA Web site (http://www.apa.org) to identify ways in which psychology is being applied to "hot topics."

Developing a Professional Identity

Professional identity-building has traditionally been considered incidental to the classroom. Because the majority of role models within experimental research continue to be White, nondisabled men (Pion et al., 1996), women and students from underrepresented populations can be deterred from careers in math and science by the lack of a professional identity and sense of belonging (Farmer, Wardrop, & Rotella, 1999). We provide role models of women and minorities by integrating their work (and their names) as illustrations of important concepts and well-designed research. We also take time to discuss issues of professionalism, including potential barriers and ways to overcome them (Collins, Chrisler, & Quina, 1999; Glazer, Bensimon, & Townsend, 1993). Finally, to encourage students to gain research experience, we keep an active roll of ongoing community research projects that accept volunteers and make credit available for student involvement.

CONCLUSIONS

In this chapter, we have laid out a philosophical approach to the Experimental Psychology course that promotes an appreciation for diversity and equity. We have illustrated where and how bias may enter the process of designing, carrying out, and interpreting research. We have suggested instructional approaches that offer students the skills to interpret, evaluate—and, in the future, reshape—psychological research. Teaching Experimental Psychology can be a rewarding experience. It is the place where the "big picture" comes together for many students—the content, statistics, and skills learned in earlier classes start to make sense. The process of active discovery through exercises such as those offered here is exciting to observe and facilitate. Knowing that students will leave the course with a new awareness about the promises and the pitfalls of science, however, is the most exciting outcome of all.

REFERENCES

Ader, D. N., & Johnson, S. B. (1994). Sample description, reporting, and analysis of sex in psychological research: A look at APA and APA division journals in 1990. *American Psychologist, 49,* 216–218.

Barrett, G. V., & Morris, S. B. (1993). The American Psychological Association's amicus curiae brief in *Price Waterhouse v. Hopkins:* The values of science versus the values of the law. *Law and Human Behavior, 17,* 201–215.

Bouchard, T. J., Jr. (1995). Breaking the last taboo. Retrieved January 3, 2003 from http://www.apa.org/journals/bell.html

Boyle, G. J. (1992). Factor structure of the Menstrual Distress Questionnaire (MDQ): Exploratory and LISREL analysis. *Personality & Individual Differences, 13,* 1–15.

Brabeck, M. (2000). *Practicing feminist ethics in psychology.* Washington, DC: American Psychological Association.

Caplan, P. J. (1995). *They say you're crazy: How the world's most powerful psychiatrists decide who's normal.* Reading, MA: Addison-Wesley.

Caplan, P. J., & Caplan, J. (1999). *Thinking critically about research on sex and gender* (2nd ed.). Needham Heights, MA: Allyn Wesley Longman.

Chrisler, J. C., Johnston, I. K., Champagne, N. M., & Preston, K. E. (1994). Menstrual joy: The construct and its consequences. *Psychology of Women Quarterly, 18,* 375–387.

Chrisler, J. C., & Levy, K. B. (1990). The media construct a menstrual monster: A content analysis of PMS articles in the popular press. *Women & Health, 16,* 89–104.

Collins, L. H., Chrisler, J. C., & Quina, K. (Eds.). (1999). *Strategies for women in academia: Arming Athena.* Thousand Oaks, CA: Sage.

Connor-Greene, P. A. (1993). From the laboratory to the headlines: Teaching critical evaluation of press reports of research. *Teaching of Psychology, 20,* 167–169.

Cortina, J. M., & Folger, R. G. (1998). When is it acceptable to accept a null hypothesis: No way, Jose? *Organizational Research Methods, 1,* 334–350.

Crawford, M., & Kimmel, E. (Eds.). (1999). Innovations in feminist research [Special issue]. *Psychology of Women Quarterly, 23*(2).

de Waal, F. B. M. (1995, March). Bonobo sex and society. *Scientific American, 272,* 82–88.

Dorfman, D. D. (1995). Soft science with a neoconservative agenda. Retrieved January 3, 2003 from http://www.apa.org/journals/bell.html

Efreom, Y. (1999). *Volunteer experience in a women's prison.* Unpublished honors thesis, University of Rhode Island.

Farmer, H. S., Wardrop, J. L., & Rotella, S. C. (1999). Antecedent factors differentiating women and men in science/nonscience careers. *Psychology of Women Quarterly, 23,* 763–780.

Fischer, C. S., Hout, M., Jankowski, M., Lucas, S. R., Swidler, A., & Voss, K. (1996). *Inequality by design.* Princeton, NJ: Princeton University Press.

Fletcher, B. R., Shaver, L., & Moon, D. G. (Eds.). (1993). *Women prisoners: A forgotten population.* Westport, CT: Praeger/Greenwood.

Freyd, J. J., & DePrince, A. P. (Eds.). (2001). *Trauma and cognitive science: A meeting of minds, science, and human experience.* Binghamton, NY: Haworth Press.

Freyd, J. J., & Quina, K. (2000). Feminist ethics in the practice of science: The contested memory controversy as an example. In M. Brabeck (Ed.), *Practicing feminist ethics in psychology* (pp. 101–123). Washington, DC: American Psychological Association.

Gergen, K. J., Gulerce, A., Lock, A., & Misra, G. (1996). Psychological science in cultural context. *American Psychologist, 41,* 496–503.

Gergen, M. M. (Ed.). (1988). *Feminist thought and the structure of knowledge.* New York: New York University Press.

Gergen, M. M., Chrisler, J. C., & LoCicero, A. (1999). Innovative methods: Resources for research, publishing and teaching. *Psychology of Women Quarterly, 23,* 431–456.

Glazer, J. S., Bensimon, E. M., & Townsend, B. K. (Eds.). (1993). *Women in higher education: A feminist perspective.* Needham Heights, MA: Ginn Press.

Goldberger, A. S., & Manski, C. F. (1995, June). Review article: *The Bell Curve.* Retrieved September 26, 2002, from http://www.ssc.wisc.edu/irp/featured/bellcurv.htm#refer

Goldstein, N., & Manlowe, J. (Eds.). (1997). *The gender politics of HIV/AIDS in women.* New York: New York University Press.

Gould, S. J. (1981). *The mismeasure of man.* New York: Norton.

Graham, S. (1992). "Most of the subjects were White and middle class": Trends in published research on African Americans in selected APA journals, 1970–1989. *American Psychologist, 47,* 629–639.

Greenwald, A. G., Pratkanis, A. R., Leippe, M. R., & Baumgardner, M. H. (1986). Under what conditions does theory obstruct research progress? *Psychological Review, 93,* 216–229.

Guthrie, R. V. (1998). *Even the rat was white: A historical view of psychology* (2nd ed.). Boston: Allyn & Bacon.

Harris, B., & Nicholson, A. M. (Eds.). (1998). Experts in the service of social reform [special issue]. *Journal of Social Issues, 54*(1).

Herrnstein, R. J., & Murray, C. (1994). *The bell curve.* New York: Free Press.

Hooker, E. (1993). Reflections of a 40-year exploration: A scientific view on homosexuality. *American Psychologist, 48,* 450–453.

Kamin, L. J. (1995). Review of *The Bell Curve. Scientific American, 272,* 99–103.

Kazdin, A. E. (1999). Overview of research design issues in clinical psychology. In P. C. Kendall, J. N. Butcher, & G. N. Holmbeck (Eds.), *Handbook of research methods in clinical psychology* (pp. 3–30). New York: Wiley.

Landrine, H. (1995). Cultural diversity in theory and methodology in feminist psychology. In H. Landrine (Ed.), *Bringing cultural diversity to feminist psychology: Theory, research, and practice* (pp. 21–137). Washington, DC: American Psychological Association.

Malgady, R. G. (2000). Myths about the null hypothesis and the path to reform. In R. H. Dana (Ed.), *Handbook of cross-cultural and multicultural personality assessment: Personality and clinical psychology series* (pp. 49–62). Mahwah, NJ: Erlbaum.

Mansfield, P. K., Hood, K. E., & Henderson, J. (1989). Women and their husbands: Mood and arousal fluctuations across the menstrual cycle and days of the week. *Psychosomatic Medicine, 51,* 66–80.

Mays, V. M., & Jackson, J. S. (1991). AIDS survey methodology with Black Americans. *Social Science and Medicine, 33,* 47–54.

McHugh, M., Koeske, R., & Frieze, I. (1986). Issues to consider in conducting nonsexist research: A guide for researchers. *American Psychologist, 41,* 879–890.

Mulac, A., & Bradac, J. J. (1995). Women's style in problem solving interaction: Powerless, or simply feminine? In P. J. Kalbfleisch & M. J. Cody (Eds.), *Gender, power, and communication in human relationships* (pp. 83–104). Hillsdale, NJ: Erlbaum.

National Institutes of Health. (1994). Guidelines on the inclusion of women and minorities as subjects in clinical research. *NIH Guide, 23*(11).

Nielson, J. M. (1990). Introduction. In J. M. Nielson (Ed.), *Feminist research methods: Exemplary readings in the social sciences* (pp. 1–37). Boulder, CO: Westview Press.

Padilla, A. M., & Lindholm, K. J. (1995). Quantitative educational research with ethnic minorities. In J. A. Banks & C. A. McGee-Banks (Eds.), *Handbook of research on multicultural education* (pp. 97–113). New York: Macmillan.

Pedersen, P. (1999). *Multiculturalism as a fourth force.* Philadelphia: Brunner/Mazel.

Pezdek, K., & Banks, W. P. (Eds.). (1996). *The recovered memory/false memory debate.* San Diego, CA: Academic Press.

Pion, G. M., Mednick, M. T., Astin, H. S., Hall, C. C., Ikenkel, M. B., Keita, G. P., et al. (1996). The shifting gender composition of psychology: Trends and implications for the discipline. *American Psychologist, 51,* 509–528.

Quina, K., & Kulberg, J. (1988). The experimental psychology course. In P. Bronstein & K. Quina (Eds.), *Teaching a psychology of people: Gender and sociocultural awareness in the curriculum* (pp. 69–79). Washington, DC: American Psychological Association.

Quina, K., Morokoff, P. J., Harlow, L. L., Deiter, P. J., Lang, M. A., Rose, J. S., Johnsen, L. W., & Schnoll, R. (1999). Focusing on participants: Feminist process model for survey modification. *Psychology of Women Quarterly, 23,* 459–483.

Raag, T. (1999). Influences of social expectations of gender, gender stereotypes, and situational constraints on children's toy choices. *Sex Roles, 41,* 809–831.

Reinharz, S. (1991). *Feminist methods in social research.* Oxford, England: Oxford University Press.

Riger, S. (1992). Epistemological debates, feminist voices: Science, social values, and the study of women. *American Psychologist, 47,* 730–740.

Rogler, L. H. (1999). Methodological sources of cultural insensitivity in mental health research. *American Psychologist, 54,* 424–433.

Sherif, C. W. (1998). Bias in psychology. *Feminism & Psychology, 8,* 58–76. (Original work published 1979)

Shields, S. A. (1982). The variability hypothesis: The history of a biological model of sex differences in intelligence. *Signs, 7,* 769–797.

Sieber, J. E. (1992). *Planning ethically responsible research: A guide for students and internal review boards.* Newbury Park, CA: Sage.

Sue, S. (1999). Science, ethnicity, and bias: Where have we gone wrong? *American Psychologist, 54,* 1070–1077.

Takanashi, R., & DeLeon, P. H. (1994). A Head Start for the 21st century. *American Psychologist, 49,* 120–122.

Tavris, C. (1992). *The mismeasure of women.* New York: Simon & Schuster.

Walsh, M. R. (Ed.). (1996). *The psychology of women: Ongoing debates.* New Haven, CT: Yale University Press.

Wilkinson, S. (Ed.). (1996). *Feminist social psychologies: International perspectives.* Bristol, PA: Open University Press.

Wyatt, G. E. (1994). The sociocultural relevance of sex research. *American Psychologist, 49,* 748–754.

Wyche, K. F. (1993). Psychology and African-American women: Findings from applied research. *Applied & Preventive Psychology, 2,* 115–121.

Yee, A. H., Fairchild, H. H., Weizmann, F., & Wyatt, G. E. (1993). Addressing psychology's problems with race. *American Psychologist, 48,* 1132–1140.

7

TEACHING BIOPSYCHOLOGY: THE INTERDEPENDENCE OF PSYCHOLOGY AND BIOLOGY

ETHEL TOBACH

Biology is the study of the fundamental biochemical and physiological processes in all living organisms; *psychology* is the study of the mental and behavioral activity of the organism throughout its life. Ignoring the obvious interdependence between the two disciplines leads to a one-dimensional perspective on psychology that either omits physiological and biochemical factors or sees them as the prime causes of behavior. In reality, the interdependence of biological and psychological processes works in both directions (Tobach, 1995). Biological factors operate in psychological processes, and psychological processes have been found to affect hormonal levels (Salvador, Suay, Martinez-Sanchis, Simon, & Brain, 1999; Schultheiss, Campbell, & McClelland, 1999), neurophysiological processes (Stern, 1997), and immune function (Laban, Markovic, Dimitrijevic, & Jankovic, 1995; Lubach, Coe, & Ershler, 1995).

Another key aspect of this interdependence is the setting in which the individual lives—both the inanimate (e.g., air, water) and the animate environments. Especially significant is the organism's relation to other members of its species. Humans are unique among all animals in that their social settings are modulated by societal processes such as laws and customs, which are prescribed by other humans and transmitted from generation to generation. These processes define many critical aspects of an individual's developmental history, particularly societal roles, which formulate the access an individual has to various life-supporting activities.

For example, the societal position of expectant parents may determine their access to pre-and postnatal health care, which in turn may affect their child's behavioral development. An illustration of this is the way that low birthweight, a frequent neonatal problem, is approached. When substance abuse and perinatal processes are not involved, the most common predisposing factor is the mother's socioeconomic status. Women with low incomes are less likely to have an adequate diet, prenatal monitoring and care, and health care for themselves and their infants during and after delivery (Stevens-Simon & Orleans, 1999). Examination of low-birthweight newborns often reveals poor neural development (Susser, 1983), which indicates a need for further attention. In well-run hospitals, where health care for new mothers and their babies is provided routinely, the finding of a birth weight that is less than 2000–2500 g is a signal that further evaluation is necessary. However, racial (Boone, 1985), ethnic (Kieffer et al., 1999), and socioeconomic (Resnick et al., 1999) differences in societal settings result in different levels of caregiving for mothers and their newborns. Expensive tests and procedures are not carried out for every newborn who needs extra attention (U.S. Department of Health & Human Services, 1999; Zeuner et al., 1999).

When dietary and other medical needs resulting from low birthweight are met, faulty neurological development during pre- and postnatal stages may be reversed, thereby avoiding problems in language development, psychomotor function, and performance in school (e.g., Hughes & Simpson, 1995; Ramey & Ramey, 1998). It should be noted, however, that these medical interventions do not address the fact that poor economic conditions can result in a dysfunctional family environment, which can also adversely affect the psychological development of the child (Campbell et al., 1999).

RACE AND GENDER BIAS IN THE DEVELOPMENT OF BIOPSYCHOLOGY

Darwin's (1859) proposal that all life forms were descended from a common ancestor stimulated a great deal of searching for the ways in which the various forms of animals were related to each other, leading to the development of comparative neurology, comparative anatomy, and comparative psychology. In addition, evolutionary theory spurred the development of *anthropology* (the study of "man") and in the process provided racism with a pseudoscientific foundation. *Race* was a term used to describe different kinds of plants and animals produced by selective breeding. Because different breeds, or "races," of animals looked different, it was thought that people who looked different must be different species, or "races" (Gobineau, 1915; Lewontin, 1995, 2000). People of color were considered inferior "races" by the industrialized nations, an assumption then used by those nations as justification for the exploitation of mineral and other resources without compensating the people who lived there. Through the use of a similar kind of justification, women were considered simply weaker and imperfect copies of men (Kleinbaum, 1977); this sexism has continued to haunt various areas of psychological research that attempt to examine biochemical (genetic and hormonal) and physiological processes in relation to behavior (Shields, 1975; Tobach & Rosoff, 1994). Historical–cultural perspectives on the use of the concept of "race" (e.g., Tobach, 1998) and "sex differences" can be eye opening.

Comparative Psychology

As psychology came under the influence of Darwinian evolutionary theory, comparative psychology—the study of the evolution and development of all animals, including people—was established. The similarities among species were seen as providing a scientific basis for studying nonhuman animals in order to understand human behavior. Today, much of the biopsychological literature is based on research with animals other than humans, usually mammals.[1] Experimenters often rely on selectively bred stocks and strains of animals with certain genetic characteristics, which reflects an early and persistent interest in "inherited" behavior and the search for genetic explanations of behavior.

Because there is an evolutionary continuity in biochemistry (genes and hormones) and morphology, animal research came to be seen as beneficial to humankind in that it provided data that suggested guiding principles, such as the plasticity of the central nervous system. For example, today it is known from research on nonhuman animals and humans that the localization of brain function is not permanently fixed (e.g., Valenstein, 1973) and that new neurons are produced in response to experience throughout life in areas of the brain significantly involved with learning and problem solving (e.g., Gould, Tanapat, Hastings, & Shors, 1999). These findings emphasize the role of experience in neuropsychological function and show how researchers were stimulated to investigate the ways that social and societal factors might affect behavior.

---

[1]I recommend that instructors address at the outset students' concerns about the treatment of animals in experimentation (Thomas & Blakemore, 1999). To encourage discussion, it is helpful for instructors to present openly their own views on biopsychological and comparative approaches with a frank recognition of differences in value systems.

Understanding that the comparative method considers differences as well as similarities is essential when one is attempting to generalize research results from other animals to humans. It is also important to be aware that as research continues, previously held ideas require reconsideration and modification. For example, recent research on Bonobos, an egalitarian, non-aggressive, and sexually very active (including same-sex contact) species, has challenged ideas about human sexual activity, sex differences, and social organization that were based on other primate species, such as baboons or chimpanzees (de Waal, 1995).

Genetics and Behavior

The field of biopsychology is becoming increasingly concerned with genetic and *proteomic* (the study of the structure and function of proteins) processes. Because the study of genetics and behavior is marked by controversy, it is important that the instructor of a basic biopsychology course spend a fair amount of time exploring the various theoretical and empirical approaches to the relation between behavior and genomics–proteomics, as well as misunderstandings and misuses of genomics–proteomics (e.g., Fausto-Sterling, Gowaty, & Zuk, 1997; Lewontin, 2000).

Genetic determinism

The terms *genetic control* and *genetic determinism* convey the meaning that the ultimate (final) causes of behavior reside in the genes. However, although genes are necessary for all life processes, they are not sufficient to explain something as complex as human behavior. Nuclear and cytoplasmic genetic coding can only produce proteins, and the relation between those proteins and the development of all structures and functions, including behavior, has not yet been demonstrated (a position now accepted by geneticists). Thus current genetic research findings cannot be used to explain behavior or individual differences in behavior (Lewontin, 1998).

There are four approaches to the study of behavior that are based on an "ultimate" role for genes in behavior: (a) *ethology*, also called the study of instinct, and defined as the objective "study of the causes of innate behaviour" (Tinbergen, 1951, p. 2); (b) *behavior genetics*, which is particularly concerned with "harnessing the power of molecular genetics to identify specific genes for complex behaviors" (Plomin, Owen, & McGuffin, 1994, pp. 1734–1735), such as extraversion, general intelligence, reading disabilities, and vocational interests; (c) *sociobiology*, the systematic study of the biological basis of social behavior (E. O. Wilson, 1975), particularly in relation to population genetics; and (d) *evolutionary psychology*, which has been defined as "the exploration of the naturally selected design features of the mechanisms that control behavior . . . such as altruism towards kin, aggression, mate choice, parental care, reciprocation, and their cumulative consequences on social structure" (Tooby, 1988, pp. 67–68). Many scientists working with these premises deny that their approach inherently lends itself to sexism, racism, or homophobia (e.g., see Caporael & Brewer, 1991, and other articles in the same journal issue). However, the media use the writings of the followers of those ideologies to support the notion that women are "innately . . . better nurturers of small children than . . . men" and that "the population below the poverty line in the United States has a configuration of the relevant genetic makeup that is significantly different from the configuration of the population above the poverty line" (Murray, 2000, p. 48; see also Rothstein, 1996; Wright, 1996).

Molecular genetics

To understand behavior genetic research, students need to learn some basic facts about molecular genetics and what it can or cannot tell one about human behavior (Marks, 1997; Smith & Sapp, 1997). For example, behavior geneticists who work with DNA sequencing laboratories may report that they have found an association between some fraction of a nucleotide configuration (molecular genetics) and a behavioral measure they have chosen because it can be quantified (e.g., IQ test scores; Plomin, McClearn, et al., 1994). However, molecular geneticists have stated that finding such a fraction does not obviate the next steps that are necessary to establish a causal relationship (Blattner et al., 1997). The reality is that finding the pathway from an original protein produced by nuclear and cytoplasmic genetic function (proteomics) to the structure and function of a complex system is a time-consuming, arduous task, whether the nucleotide is related to a morphological (muscle or bone) or a neurological characteristic. Such an analysis has not been completed even for a number of known "genes" associated with neurological and behavioral pathology, such as those related to Huntington's chorea and phenylketonuria. The difficulties of this task are compounded when attempting to associate a "gene" or cluster of genes with a complex human behavioral pattern such as intellectual performance. Claims by behavior geneticists that the discovery of the location of a quantified trait on a gene will enable psychologists to understand complex human behavior (e.g., Plomin, McClearn, et al., 1994) overlook the facts that molecular geneticists have found that the locus of a gene is not always fixed and that the quantifiability of a trait is a difficult problem (Kiberstis & Roberts, 2002; Lewontin, 1998; Strohman, 2002; Willett, 2002). Finally, using a score on an IQ test as a valid trait is itself beset by many difficulties (Kamin, 1974).

Media reports of findings relating genes to psychological processes occur with regularity (e.g., Wade, 1999a, 1999b). The media proclaim connections between some molecular genetic configuration and characteristics of a disease and then make the assumption that equally credible associations must therefore exist between genetic configurations and behavior (e.g., dyslexia; Fagerheim et al., 1999). A "gene for homosexuality" on the X chromosome (Hamer, Hu, Magnuseon, & Pattatucci, 1993; Risch, Squires-Wheeler, & Keats, 1993) is listed by the Human Genome Project among diseases for which the genes have been identified (HUGO Committee Reports, 2001). Instructors can challenge these assumptions by inviting their students to critique this research (and the categorizing of homosexuality as a disease), acknowledging the complexity of the behavior patterns and the limitations of the evidence.

It may also be helpful to discuss the credibility of "genetic" diseases. When a particular molecular genetic configuration is known to be the generator of particular protein deficiencies, resulting in a disease (e.g., phenylketonuria), the relationship is credible. However, in many cases the pathway from molecular configuration to protein to disease has not yet been established—yet theorists continue to generate theories solely on the basis of possible connections. For example, the high rate of hypertension in African American men has been attributed to genes that were carried by slaves who survived the Middle Passage—the forcible transport of African women and men to the western hemisphere by ship. Early research claimed that the slaves who survived carried genes that permitted men to cope with the dehydration resulting from the brutal conditions of the passage. These genes conferred a special tolerance of high sodium levels in the blood (T. W. Wilson & Grim, 1991). This assumption has not been borne out by research on sodium tolerance levels in men in various African countries or in men of African background in the western hemisphere (Cooper, 1997). Scientists who have studied the occurrence of hypertension in African American men have concluded that the stress of living as an African American is a more likely explanation of their higher levels of hypertension than is their level of sodium tolerance. Although there may be some molecular genetic configuration related to sodium tolerance levels, it cannot be assumed that a particular population will express that genetic fault (Jackson, 1991). The class might consider the credibility of this and other genetics–disease relationships and the roles that societal and economic factors may play (e.g., Anderson, 1995; Geschwind, Boone, Miller, & Swerdloff, 2000; Hovatta, 1999).

Population genetics

The Human Genome Project (Smith & Sapp, 1997) demonstrated the population genetics approach to the study of genes and behavior. This approach focuses on gene function, based on the statistical analysis of the frequencies with which particular traits are found in populations with a defined nucleotide configuration (gene). The project, which is designed to map all the genes in humans as well as other animals, is important, because it elaborates a new technology in the "biology" aspect of biopsychology. It has emphasized genetic processes in diseases and physiological dysfunction; encouraged research into behavioral "pathology," such as bipolar disorder (Craddock & Jones, 1999) and schizophrenia (Portin & Alanen (1997); and, as mentioned earlier, listed a gene for homosexuality in the documentation of "Genetic Diseases by Chromosome" (HUGO Committee Reports, 2001). The Human Genome Project does not deal with the contribution of environmental processes to disease, except for a small program investigating environmental factors and genetic function. The research programs of biopsychologists (particularly behavior geneticists and neuroscientists) have increasingly been supported by genomic funding agencies. Backed by governments in the industrialized nations, genomics–proteomics is now a major private industry reaching into every aspect of human life: the food people grow and eat, medical practices, and genetic engineering of nonhuman animals (Human Genome Project, retrieved October 6, 2002, from http://www.ornl.gov/hgmis).

GENDER AND RACIAL ISSUES IN BIOPSYCHOLOGY: SOME CONTEMPORARY EXAMPLES

As mentioned above, biopsychological theories and research have too often reflected biases about gender or race–ethnicity, and findings have reflected sexist and racist beliefs (Kamin, 1974; Tobach & Rosoff, 1994).

Gender Issues

In the early days of biopsychological research, experimenters almost exclusively used male animals, because it was thought that because they did not show hormonal cycles, males would yield more generalizable data. Although researchers now know that variations in hormonal function are present in males across species (e.g., Ancrenaz, Blanvillain, Delhomme, Greth, & Sempere, 1998; McEwen, Alves, Buloch, & Weiland, 1998; Zitzmann & Nieschlag, 2001), much of the research is still conducted with male animals, and the possibility that such fluctuations might affect research results is inadequately considered.

The practice of not including women in many biopsychological studies also reflects the belief that hormones play a more significant role in the behavior of women than of men because of women's regularly changing levels of reproductive hormones. When women have been studied, the focus has been on these reproductive hormones, seeking differences in psychological behavior at different hormonal levels (McEwen et al., 1998) and during different menstrual phases (Hampson, 1990; Postma, Winkel, Tuiten, & van Honk, 1999); however, the data have not yielded robust support for these differences (Gordon & Lee, 1993; Morgan, Rapkin, D'Elia, Reading, &

Goldman, 1996). When reproductive hormones have been studied in men, the focus has been on a presumed relationship between testosterone levels and aggression and social dominance, although it is not unusual for the title or abstract to speak of the study as an investigation of "normal humans" even when no women were included (e.g., Gerra et al., 1996).

However, there has been a renewed interest in the reproductive hormones that has yielded interesting new data. For example, research has begun to include more females and to connect estrogen (Baum, 1998) and testosterone (Silverman, Kastuk, Choi, & Phillips, 1999) to cognitive processes. There are known receptors for estrogen in the brains of both females and males, and estrogen has been implicated in different types of learning—for example, estrogen has been found to stimulate a transient increase in new neurons in adult female rats (Tanapat, Hastings, Reeves, & Gould, 1999). Testosterone, which is metabolized to estradiol (a form of estrogen), is being studied in relation to learning and cognition (Arlt et al., 1999; Barrett-Connor, Goodman-Gruen, & Patay, 1999; Ostatnikova, Dohnanyiova, Putz, Laznibatova, & Hajek, 2000).

Racial Issues

The emphasis on genetic processes is concordant with the belief that there are inherent racial differences among humans, particularly in intelligence and social behavior. Attempts to experimentally demonstrate this has resulted in a plethora of articles and books (e.g., Jensen, 1980; Rushton, 1984), some of which have received considerable positive media attention (notably Herrnstein & Murray, 1994). Instructors can introduce critiques of this research (Ethical, Legal and Social Implications of Human Genome Research Working Group, 1996; Newby & Newby, 1995) and discuss the misuse of population genetics (Lewontin, 1998).

ENHANCING STUDENTS' UNDERSTANDING OF THE RESEARCH PROCESS

Students' ability to evaluate recent findings, claims, and challenges within the field of biological psychology can be greatly enhanced by a solid understanding of the research process. One way to help them develop this understanding is to have them write critiques of assigned articles, to use as a basis for class discussion of the issues and problems involved in biopsychological research. For example, they can read Morgan, Rapkin, D'Elia, Reading, and Goldman's (1996) investigation of the relation between hormones and learning and then address such questions as: Is the theoretical rationale clear and explicit? What is the historical–cultural basis of the research question? What assumptions have been made about the relation between the hormones and the kind of learning chosen for study? Were the participants in the study appropriate (e.g., were both genders included)? How did they become part of the study? What social or societal factors were taken into account in developing the research and interpreting the findings? This kind of analysis and discussion can illustrate the preconceptions and limitations embedded in both the conceptualization and execution of studies linking biochemical and hormonal processes to human behavior.

Hands-on experience in an animal laboratory can also provide important research skills; however, because work with nonhuman species requires expensive research equipment, extensive training, and conformance with governmental and institutional rules and regulations, undergraduate Biopsychology courses often are not able to offer this opportunity. As an alternative, instructors can arrange for students to visit animal research laboratories, so that they can develop a better understanding of such research. In addition, students can learn about imaging techniques that are now used to study human brain activity in nonintrusive ways during different behavioral activity—such as memorizing, speaking, attending, and problem solving—so that much research with animals is obviated (e.g., Joseph, 1999; Roser et al., 1999).

Finally, instructors can encourage students to develop their own research, using anonymous anecdotal reports and surveys. They can collect data about physiological processes that may have psychological significance, such as the relation between stress and physiological functioning, recording reported effects such as vascular responses (flushing or blanching), hormonal functioning (menstrual changes or penile erection), or disturbed sleep patterns. As the students formulate the research questions, select methods, and interpret the data, discussions might focus on definitions of stress and the relation of social factors to its cause, enhancement, or reduction—including issues of gender, ethnicity, race, age, sexual orientation, socioeconomic level, and social–societal status (e.g., teacher or student, boss or employee).

CONCLUDING REMARKS

The collection of scientific data and the reporting of findings are important societal processes; as such, they need to be subjected to sociopolitical and social psychological analysis. Instructors need to teach themselves and their students to ask how a study was conceived, supported financially, and carried out; instructors need to teach students the skills necessary for finding the answers to such questions; and instructors need to examine the implications of those answers for public policy. Some might argue that these considerations do not have a place in teaching an undergraduate Biopsychology course; however, a failure to understand the psychological, social, and societal consequences that may follow from incorrect or misleading information is a failure of biopsychology. For example, some new "finding" of a genetically based difference between women's and men's ability to execute certain types of complex thinking, or of a genetic predisposition for criminality within a particular cultural group, may have serious effects on human welfare. This is not a call for restrictions on research; it is a call for explicit awareness on the part of researchers, science writers, teachers, and students of the historical–cultural meanings and responsibilities inherent in biopsychological research.

REFERENCES

Ancrenaz, M., Blanvillain, C., Delhomme, A., Greth, A., & Sempere, A. J. (1998). Temporal variations of LH and testosterone in Arabian Oryx (*Oryx leucoryx*) from birth to adulthood. *General and Comparative Endocrinology, 111,* 283–289.

Anderson, C. E. (1995). The genetics of disorders of the developing nervous system. In S. Duckett (Ed.), *Pediatric neuropathology* (pp. 41–53). Baltimore: Williams & Wilkins.

Arlt, W., Haas, J., Callies, F., Reincke, M., Hubler, D., Oettel, M., Ernst, M., Schulte, H. M., & Allolio, B. (1999). Biogranformation of oral dehydroepilandrosterone in elderly men: Significant increase in circulating estrogens. *Journal of Clinical Endocrinological Metabolism, 84,* 2170–2176.

Barrett-Connor, E., Goodman-Gruen, D., & Patay, B. (1999). Endogenous sex hormones and cognitive function in older men. *Journal of Clinical Endocrinological Metabolism, 84,* 3681–3685.

Baum, M. J. (Ed.). (1998). Estrogen effects on cognition across the life-span [Special issue]. *Hormones and Behavior, 34*(2).

Blattner, F. R., Plunkett, G., III, Bloch, C. A., Perna, N. T., Burland, V., Riley, M., et al. (September, 1997). The complete genome sequence of *Escherichia coli* K-12. *Science, 277,* 1453–1462.

Boone, M. S. (1985). Social and cultural factors in the etiology of low birthweight among disadvantaged Blacks. *Social Science and Medicine, 20,* 1001–1011.

Campbell, J., Torres, S., Ryan, J., King, C., Campbell, D. W., Stallings, R. Y., et al. (1999). Physical and nonphysical partner abuse and other risk factors for low birthweight among full term and preterm babies: A multi-ethnic case-control study. *American Journal of Epidemiology, 150,* 714–726.

Caporael, L. R., & Brewer, M. E. (1991). The quest for human nature: Social and scientific issues in evolutionary psychology. *Journal of Social Issues, 47*(3), 1–9.

Cooper, R. (1997). The prevalence of hypertension in seven populations of West African origin. *American Journal of Public Health, 87,* 160–167.

Craddock, N., & Jones, I. (1999). Genetics of bipolar disorder. *Journal of Medical Genetics, 36,* 585–594.

Darwin, C. (1859). *The origin of species.* London: John Murray.

de Waal, F. (1995). Bonobo sex and society. *Scientific American, 272*(3), 82–88.

Ethical, Legal and Social Implications of Human Genome Research (ELSI) Working Group. (1996). ELSI Working Group responds to *The Bell Curve*. *Human Genome News, 7*(5), 1–2.

Fagerheim, T., Raeymaekers, P., Tonnessen, F. E., Pedersen, M., Tranebjaerg, L., & Lubs, H. A. (1999). A new gene (DYX3) for dyslexia is located on chromosome 2. *Journal of Medical Genetics, 36*, 664–669.

Fausto-Sterling, A., Gowaty, P. A., & Zuk, M. (1997). Evolutionary psychology and Darwinian feminism. *Feminist Studies, 23*, 403–417.

Gerra, G. P., Avanzini, A., Zaimovic, G., Fertonani, R., Caccavari, R., Delsignore, F., et al. (1996). Neurotransmitter and endocrine modulation of aggressive behavior and its components in normal humans. *Behavior and Brain Research, 81*(1-2), 19–24.

Geschwind, D. H., Boone, K. B., Miller, B. L., & Swerdloff, R. S. (2000). Neurobehavioral phenotype of Klinefelter Syndrome. *Mental Retardation & Developmental Disability Research Review, 6*, 107–116.

Gobineau, A. de (1915). *The inequality of human races* (A. Collins, Trans.). New York: Putnam.

Gordon, H. W., & Lee, P. A. (1993). No difference in cognitive performance between phases of the menstrual cycle. *Psychoendocrinology, 18*, 521–531.

Gould, E., Tanapat, P., Hastings, N. B., & Shors, T. J. (1999). Neurogenesis in adulthood: A possible role in learning. *Trends in Cognitive Sciences, 3*, 186–192.

Hamer, D. H., Hu, S., Magnuseon, V. L., & Pattatucci, A. M. L. (1993). A linkage between DNA markers on the X chromosome and male sexual orientation. *Science, 261*, 321–327.

Hampson, E. (1990). Estrogen-related variations in human spatial and articulatory motor skills. *Psychoendocrinology, 15*, 97–111.

Herrnstein, R. J., & Murray, C. (1994). *The bell curve: Intelligence and class structure in American life*. New York: Free Press.

Hovatta, O. (1999). Pregnancies in women with Turner's syndrome. *Annals of Medicine, 31*, 106–110.

Hughes, D., & Simpson, L. (1995). The role of social change in preventing low birth weight. *Future Child, 5*(1), 87–102.

HUGO Committee Reports. (2001). Genes on Chromosome X: Gene HMS1. Retrieved July 10, 2001, from http://www.gdb.org/gdb-bin/genera/accno?accessionNum=GDB:251827

Jackson, F. (1991). An evolutionary perspective on salt, hypertension and human genetic variability. *Hypertension, 17*(Suppl. 1), 129–132.

Jensen, A. R. (1980). *Bias in mental testing*. New York: Free Press.

Joseph, R. (1999). Frontal lobe psychopathology: Mania, depression, confabulation, catatonia, perseveration, obsessive compulsions and schizophrenia. *Psychiatry, 62*, 138–172.

Kamin, L. J. (1974). *The science and politics of IQ*. Potomac, MD: Erlbaum.

Kiberstis, P., & Roberts, L. (April, 2002). It's not just the genes. *Science, 296*, 685.

Kieffer, E. C., Nolan, G. H., Carman, W. J., Sanborn, C. Z., Guzman, R., & Ventura, A. (1999). Glucose tolerance during pregnancy and birth weight in a Hispanic population. *Obstetrics & Gynecology, 94*(5, Part 1), 741–746.

Kleinbaum, A. R. (1977). Women in the age of light. In R. Bridenthal & C. Koonz (Eds.), *Becoming visible: Women in European history* (pp. 217–235). Boston: Houghton Mifflin.

Laban, O., Markovic, B. M., Dimitrijevic, M., & Jankovic, B. D. (1995). Maternal deprivation and early weaning modulate experimental allergic encephalomyelitis in the rat. *Brain, Behavior and Immunology, 9*, 9–19.

Lewontin, R. C. (1995). *Human diversity*. New York: Freeman.

Lewontin, R. C. (1998). Quantitative genetics. In A. D. J. Griffths, J. H. Miller, D. T. Suzuki, & R. C. Lewontin (Eds.), *Modern genetic analysis* (pp. 817–847). New York: Freeman.

Lewontin, R. C. (2000). *The triple helix: Gene, organism, and environment*. Cambridge, MA: Harvard University Press.

Lubach, G. R., Coe, C. L., & Ershler, W. B. (1995). Effects of early rearing environment on immune responses of infant rhesus monkeys. *Brain, Behavior and Immunology, 9*, 31–46.

Marks, J. (1997). Skepticism about behavioral genetics. In M. S. Frankel (Ed.), *Exploring public policy issues in genetics* (pp. 159–172). Washington, DC: American Association for the Advancement of Science.

McEwen, B. S., Alves, S. E., Buloch, K., & Weiland, N. G. (1998). Clinically relevant basic science studies of gender differences and sex hormone effects. *Psychopharmacological Bulletin, 34*, 251–259.

Morgan, M., Rapkin, J., D'Elia, L., Reading, A., & Goldman, L. (1996). Cognitive functioning in premenstrual syndrome. *Obstetrics & Gynecology, 88*, 961–966.

Murray, C. (2000, January 24). Deeper into the brain. *National Review*, 46–49.

Newby, R. G., & Newby, D. (1995). *The Bell Curve*: Another chapter in the continuing political economy of racism. *American Behavioral Scientist, 39*, 12–24.

Ostatnikova, D., Dohnanyiova, M., Putz, Z., Laznibatova, J., & Hajek, J. (2000). Salivary testosterone and cognitive ability in children. *Bratislava Lek Listy, 101*, 470–473.

Plomin, R., McClearn, G. E., Smith, D. L., Vignetti, S., Chorney, M. J., Chorney, K., et al. (1994). DNA markers associated with high versus low IQ: The IQ Quantitative Trait Loci (QTL) project. *Behavior Genetics, 24*, 107–118.

Plomin, R., Owen, M. J., & McGuffin, P. (June, 1994). The genetic basis of complex human behaviors. *Science, 264*, 1733–1739.

Portin, P., & Alanen, Y. O. (1997). A critical review of genetic studies of schizophrenia: I. Epidemiological and brain studies. *Acta Psychiatrica Scandinavica, 95*(2), 1–5.

Postma, A., Winkel, J., Tuiten, A., & van Honk, J. (1999). Sex differences and menstrual cycle effects in human spatial memory. *Psychoendocrinology, 24,* 175–192.

Ramey, C. T., & Ramey, S. L. (1998). Prevention of intellectual disabilities: Early interventions to improve cognitive development. *Preventive Medicine, 27,* 224–232.

Resnick, M. B., Gueuorguieva, R. V., Carter, R. L., Ariet, M., Sun, Y., Roth, J. B., et al. (1999). The impact of low birthweight, perinatal conditions and sociodemographic factors on educational outcome in kindergarten. *Pediatrics, 104*(6), 74–96.

Risch, N. Y., Squires-Wheeler, E., & Keats, D. J. B. (April, 1993). Male sexual orientation and the genetic evidence. *Science, 262,* 2063–2065.

Roser, W., Bubl, R., Buergin, D., Seelig, J., Radue, E. W., & Rost, B. (1999). Metabolic changes in the brain of patients with anorexia and bullemia nervosa as detected by proton magnetic resonance spectroscopy. *International Journal of Eating Disorders, 26,* 119–136.

Rothstein, E. (1996, June 10). Beyond "The Selfish Gene," where ideas alter the ways in which we think. *The New York Times,* p. D5.

Rushton, J. P. (1984). Sociobiology: Toward a theory of individual and group differences in personality and social behavior (with commentaries and response). In J. R. Royce & L. P. Mos (Eds.), *Annals of theoretical psychology* (Vol. 2, pp. 1–8). New York: Plenum.

Salvador, A., Suay, F., Martinez-Sanchis, S., Simon, V. M., & Brain, P. F. (1999). Correlating testosterone and fighting in male participants in judo contests. *Physiology & Behavior, 68,* 205–209.

Schultheiss, O. C., Campbell, K. L., & McClelland, D. C. (1999). Implicit power motivation moderates men's testosterone responses to imagined and real dominance success. *Hormones and Behavior, 36,* 234–241.

Shields, S. (1975). Functionalism, Darwinism, and the psychology of women: A study in social myth. *American Psychologist, 30,* 739–754.

Silverman, I., Kastuk, D., Choi, J., & Phillips, K. (1999). Testosterone levels and spatial ability in men. *Psychoneuroendocrinology, 24,* 813–822.

Smith, E., & Sapp, W. (Eds.). (1997). *Plain talk about the Human Genome Project.* Tuskegee, AL: Tuskegee University Press.

Stern, J. M. (1997). Trigeminal lesions and maternal behavior in Norway rats: 3. Experience with pups facilitates recovery. *Developmental Psychobiology, 30,* 115–126.

Stevens-Simon, C., & Orleans, M. (1999). Low-birthweight prevention programs: The enigma of failure. *Birth, 26,* 184–191.

Strohman, R. (April, 2002). Maneuvering in the complex path from genotype to phenotype. *Science, 296,* 701–703.

Susser, M. (1983). Prenatal nutrition, birthweight, and psychological development: An overview of experiments, quasi-experiments, and natural experiments in the past decade. *American Journal of Clinical Nutrition, 34*(Suppl. 4), 784–803.

Tanapat, P., Hastings, N. B., Reeves, A. J., & Gould, E. (1999). Estrogen stimulates a transient increase in the number of new neurons in the dentate gyrus of the adult female rat. *Journal of Neuroscience, 19,* 5792–5801.

Thomas, D., & Blakemore, C. (1999, April 24). Is it morally wrong to experiment on animals? *The Guardian,* p. 2.

Tinbergen, N. (1951). *The study of instinct.* London: Oxford University Press.

Tobach, E. (1995). One view of the concept of integrative levels. In K. Hood, G. Greenberg, & E. Tobach (Eds.), *Behavioral development* (pp. 399–414). New York: Garland.

Tobach, E. (1998, September). *Psychology, racist science and the law in post-civil war America.* Keynote address delivered to the Psychological Society of South Africa, Cape Town, South Africa.

Tobach, E., & Rosoff, B. (1994). A critique of genetic determinist research in genetics. In B. Rosoff & E. Tobach (Eds.), *Challenging racism and sexism: Alternatives to genetic determinist explanations* (pp. 22–34). New York: Feminist Press.

Tooby, J. (1988). The emergence of evolutionary psychology. In D. Pines (Ed.), *Syntheses in sciences* (pp. 67–76). Redwood City, CA: Addison-Wesley.

U.S. Department of Health and Human Services. (1999). Evaluating newborn screening program data systems—Georgia, 1998. *Morbidity and Mortality Weekly Reports, 48,* 1101–1104.

Valenstein, E. S. (1973). *Brain control.* New York: Wiley.

Wade, N. (1999a, September 2). Smarter mouse is created in hope of helping people. *The New York Times,* pp. A1, A24.

Wade, N. (1999b, September 7). Of smart mice and even smarter men. *The New York Times,* pp. F1–F2.

Willett, W. C. (April, 2002). Balancing life-style and genomics research for disease prevention. *Science, 296,* 695–698.

Wilson, E. O. (1975). *Sociobiology.* Cambridge, MA: Harvard University Press.

Wilson, T. W., & Grim, C. E. (1991). Biohistory of slavery and blood pressure differences in Blacks today: A hypothesis. *Hypertension, 17*(Suppl. 1), 122–128.

Wright, R. (1996, October 28). Science and original sin. *Time, 148*(20), 76–78.

Zeuner, D., Ades, A. E., Karnon, J., Brown, J., Dezateux, C., & Anionwu, E. N. (1999). Antenatal and neonatal haemoglobinopathy screening in the UK: Review and economic analysis. *Health Technology Assessment, 3*(11), 1–186.

Zitzmann, M., & Nieschlag, E. (2001). Testosterone levels in healthy men and the relation to behavioural and physical characteristics: Facts and constructs. *European Journal of Endocrinology, 144*(3), 183–197.

8

BEYOND GREAT MEN
AND GREAT IDEAS:
HISTORY OF PSYCHOLOGY IN
SOCIOCULTURAL CONTEXT

LAUREL FURUMOTO

Most History of Psychology courses and textbooks present a celebratory, decontextualized narrative of great men and their great ideas from antiquity to the present, from a Western cultural perspective. This approach does little to make psychology students aware of the sociocultural embeddedness of the field they are preparing to enter, or of how much more there is to psychology's past than what is offered by the standard account. An alternative, which I have called the *new history* of psychology, moves beyond traditional textbook history to teach "a history that is more contextual, more critical, more archival, more inclusive, and more pastminded" (Furumoto, 1989, p. 30). Specifically, the new history explores the lives and work of women and others often omitted from the standard account, tries to understand psychology's participation in particular sociocultural settings, and encourages students to question and to go beyond the traditional textbook version of psychology's past.

THE TRADITIONAL HISTORY OF PSYCHOLOGY COURSE:
AN APPRAISAL

Two recent studies of the History of Psychology course provide valuable overviews of how it is currently being taught. Hogan, Goshtasbpour, Laufer, and Haswell (1998) examined 357 undergraduate course syllabi and found that for the majority, the textbook was the only reading material. A few texts devoted pages specifically to women and ethnic minorities, but in the syllabi Hogan et al. analyzed, only about 17% considered women's issues beyond the text, and only about 10% addressed ethnic minority representation in psychology. Furthermore, the syllabi rarely mentioned international or applied psychology.

The downplaying of applied psychology in particular contributes to the underestimation of women's role in the history of the field. After World War I, jobs in the United States in applied areas began to proliferate, and in the 1920s and 1930s female psychologists, who were discriminated against in the academic job market, came to predominate in the applied sectors—for example, as mental testers and clinicians. In fact, between the two world wars, a gendered occupational hierarchy took shape in psychology, with men predominant in the higher status, academic domain of the discipline and women occupying the lower status, practitioner roles (Furumoto, 1987). For a discussion of the migration of women into the applied areas of testing, child welfare, school psychology, and clinical work, see Scarborough's (1992) history of women in the American Psychological Association (especially pp. 312–314). For information on early female industrial and organizational psychologists, see Koppes (1997).

Cicciarelli (1998) reached a conclusion similar to that of Hogan et al. (1998) in his examination of the goals, structure, and content of History and Systems courses at American Psychological Association-accredited graduate programs in clinical psychology. In 41.5% of the 65 syllabi he collected, textbooks were the only required reading, and in 61.5% there were no requirements that students read primary source materials. Courses were generally lecture driven rather than discussion based, and only a small proportion paid any attention to methods and theories of historical research, social context, female psychologists, feminist perspectives, or ethnic minority populations. Cicciarelli's findings indicated that many graduate-level History and Systems courses have been taught from a traditional perspective, relying "primarily on a decontextualized presentation of the 'great men' and intellectual achievements of psychology" (p. 260), which reflects a tendency in such courses to celebrate psychology's history instead of critically analyzing it.

Although in recent years some textbook writers have attempted to depart from the prevailing convention by including material on women, ethnic minorities, and the applied aspects of the discipline, these efforts have been meager and have not altered the standard narrative in any fundamental way. The time has come for a radical pedagogical overhaul of the History of Psychology course, and perhaps a good place to begin is to identify the values undergirding the conventional textbook, which the standard course so closely mirrors in content. Most of the textbooks follow a convention begun by E. G. Boring's (1929) A History of Experimental Psychology—an intellectual history of the discipline portraying great men, their great ideas, and the emergence of psychology as an experimental science. Subsequent generations of textbook writers and teachers of the History of Psychology course have perpetuated Boring's definition of the boundaries and contents of the field, which to this day remains the dominant pedagogical view. Why was it Boring's more scientific portrayal of psychology's past that won out, rather than other views of the field, such as those presented in Walter Pillsbury's (1929) less scholarly textbook and Gardner Murphy's (1929) more pluralistic survey? For historian of American psychology James H. Capshew (1999), the answer is that in the 1920s, as psychology began to expand rapidly in new directions outside of academia, "it seemed more important than ever to reaffirm a fundamental faith in experimental research in order to legitimate various kinds of social applications and personal interventions" (pp. 25–26). Boring's vigorous defense of this kind of research fit the bill perfectly, serving "a useful function for the entire profession by providing a scientific pedigree that was both impressive and plausible, to insiders and outsiders alike" (Capshew, 1999, p. 26).

In Boring's (1929) deterministic approach, developments in the history of psychology that could not be attributed to individual creativity were said to be a result of the Zeitgeist, by which he meant the total body of knowledge and opinion in the culture at a given time. Ross (1969) provided a compelling critique of the notion of the Zeitgeist, concluding that it is not an adequate principle of historical explanation because it does not do justice to the complexity of history. Yet, despite the fact that her caveat was published more than 30 years ago, the Zeitgeist concept is still frequently encountered, casually invoked as an explanatory principle in the history of psychology. Ross's article should be required reading for any teacher or textbook writer who is tempted to resort to its use.

TOWARD A MULTIVOICED HISTORY OF PSYCHOLOGY

An alternative view to Boring's (1929) is that it is much too limiting to define psychology as nothing but a pure science and that it is preferable to use a contextual rather than a deterministic approach to understanding its history. This approach, which allows for the inclusion of many different voices, can ultimately supplant the single-voiced standard historical account. Instructors, in fact, will find that a substantial body of historical scholarship already exists, mostly published within the last 20 years (to which I referred earlier as the *new history* of psychology), that they can use to transform the History of Psychology course (Furumoto, 1989).

An important new source of such contextual, multivoiced scholarship is the quarterly journal *History of Psychology*, official journal of the American Psychological Association's (APA's) Division 26, History of Psychology. In the few years since its inaugural issue, it has published two articles featuring the contributions of American female psychologists—Mary Whiton Calkins (Wentworth, 1999) and Helen Thompson Woolley (Milar, 1999), an article on E. G. Boring and antisemitism in the history of psychology from the 1920s to the 1950s (Winston, 1998), and an article on the life and work of Chen Li, who is regarded as "China's elder psychologist" (Blowers, 1998). Other potentially valuable sources include the official journal of APA's Division 2, the Society for the Teaching of Psychology, *Teaching of Psychology*, which regularly features articles relevant to the history of psychology, and the joint Web site of Division 26 of the APA; Cheiron, the International Society for the History of Behavioral and Social Sciences; and related organizations (http://www.psych.yorku.ca/orgs/resource.htm).

A useful assignment is to ask students to locate and share with their classmates information gleaned from other interesting Web sites, or from paths already laid down in existing sites. For example, Marcos Pereira created a rich "timeline of psychological ideas" from the year 600 to the present, color coded by the continent/country in which they occurred, with links to other resources on the individuals and ideas featured in the timeline (retrieved September 29, 2002, from http://www.geocities.com/Athens/Delphi/6061/en_linha.htm).

Roles and Contributions of Women

There is now a sizeable literature on the experiences and contributions of American women psychologists, which once was a neglected area. The publication of a special issue of the *Psychology of Women Quarterly* (O'Connell & Russo, 1980), devoted to eminent women in the field, was a benchmark in the effort to increase the visibility of women in the history of psychology. Consisting of an overview of women's contributions, several biographies of individual women, and a bibliography of biographical and autobiographical material, it represented "an attempt to begin to ameliorate the neglect of women's achievements" (p. 16). Since that time, O'Connell and Russo have edited several more works that dramatically expanded the published information available on women in psychology. These include two volumes of autobiographical accounts (O'Connell & Russo, 1983, 1988), one volume of biographical accounts (O'Connell & Russo, 1990), and another special issue of *Psychology of Women Quarterly* with articles documenting "women's contributions to, and the impact of feminist critiques on, the discipline of psychology and its organizations" (O'Connell & Russo, 1991, p. 495). In another book, which aimed to show that women had played a role in American psychology since its emergence as a science in the 1890s, Elizabeth Scarborough and I offered an account of the lives of the first generation of women psychologists: 25 who had entered the field by the early years of the 20th century. The book paid attention to gender-specific themes that made these women's experience different from those of the men in the field and documented their careers and contributions (Scarborough & Furumoto, 1987). An additional resource is Linda Woolf's informative Web site on women in the history of psychology and other social science disciplines, which includes photographs and links to additional sites (http://www.webster.edu/~woolflm/women.html).

Gender and the History of Psychology

Instructors who want to include in their courses a look at how psychologists have viewed men, women, children, and the family will find Lewin's (1984) *In the Shadow of the Past: Psychology Portrays the Sexes* a useful resource. Those who want to introduce students to the notion that psychology itself is gendered might look at my essay on how the values associated with the new masculine ideal of the late 19th century came to be embedded in American psychology as it established itself as a discipline in the 20th century (Furumoto, 1998).

An Ethnic Minority Perspective

For an ethnic minority perspective, teachers of the History of Psychology now have available to them the second edition of *Even the Rat Was White: A Historical View of Psychology* (Guthrie, 1998). In this revised and expanded volume, the author continues to articulate an alternative, nontraditional perspective on psychology's past from his standpoint as an African American. He underscored the importance of consulting nontraditional archival sources such as the *Journal of Negro Education*, *Voice of the Negro*, and *Journal of Negro History* in this enterprise. Guthrie examined both the consideration of racial differences within the history of psychology and the experience of Black psychologists in America, and he discusses the implications of the alternative perspective that he offers.

Psychology as a Social Force

Several recent books can help instructors teaching the History of Psychology course give their students an appreciation of how psychology was influenced by, and how it helped shape, American society over the course of the 20th century. Ellen Herman (1995), an American social historian, contends that "few institutions, issues or spheres of existence remain untouched by the progress of psychology" and "more important, the progress of psychology has changed American society" (p. 1). In *The Romance of American Psychology*, she explores how and why this happened in the short span of a few decades following World War II. According to Herman, during the war, psychologists got their first taste of power, as psychological experts came into contact with governmental policymakers for the first time. She sees psychological experts after 1945 as carving out an ever-expanding sphere of social influence, and she explores facets of this in chapters devoted to Cold War military policy; racial matters, from educational segregation to employment; and the women's liberation movement. Herman eschews simple answers and the temptation to celebrate or denounce what psychological experts have wrought, as she thoughtfully addresses the questions of why they were so persuasive and whether they have "spoken the truth or manufactured deception . . . expanded the realm of freedom or perfected the means of control" (p. 10).

Moving from the changing influence of psychology on American society to the changes taking place in the discipline itself during the middle of the 20th century, historian of science James H. Capshew (1999) also targets World War II as a pivotal event. He claims that in mid-century a confluence of social forces and intellectual trends dramatically and enduringly transformed the role of the psychologist. In his book *Psychologists on the March*, Capshew investigates both the causes and the consequences of the rapid growth of the field—a tenfold increase, from 3,000 to 30,000 in just the three decades of the 1940s through the 1960s. He provides a rich historical tapestry of the psychology profession in this singularly important era, demonstrating that psychologists are not independent of societal influence and viewing their behaviors as clues to the larger context of American culture.

Impact of psychotherapy

Because psychotherapy has become an integral part of the everyday world, it is important to examine its function and impact in U.S. society. Cushman's (1995) *Constructing the Self, Constructing America* looks at psychotherapy in sociopolitical context, exploring "the social construction of several schools of American psychotherapy by drawing out and interpreting some of their historical antecedents, economic constituents, and political consequences" (p. 3). For example, Cushman argues that between the two world wars, psychotherapists were confronted with two theoretical pathways: one the American theory of Harry Stack Sullivan, the other the European innovations of psychoanalyst Melanie Klein. The post-World War II era witnessed the triumph of Klein's object-relations theory, which locates social interaction within the self-contained individual, over Sullivan's interpersonal psychiatry, which situates social interaction in the space between people. In Cushman's view, this outcome prepared the way for the coming era of consumerism by making it scientifically legitimate to conceptualize the process of growing up as a type of "consuming" and the goal of human life as a constant filling up of the "empty self."

Cushman's (1995) examination of the moral dimension of psychotherapy, which he claims is usually ignored or disavowed, may be especially valuable to students who are considering entering therapy or becoming therapists. He maintains that psychotherapy is a technology of the self that presumably "helps people live better" and that "better . . . is a qualitative and evaluative term," that is to say, "a moral term" (p. 281). For example, referring to the implicit morality of psychoanalysis, Cushman points to "the valuing of awareness over drivenness, choice over prohibition, and of personal responsibility over the nostalgic wish to be dominated and used" (p. 288). He strongly advocates openly acknowledging that psychotherapy throughout its history has been a moral discourse with political consequences, as a way to help liberate it from the influence of disguised ideologies.

Impact of psychological testing

Another aspect of psychology that has had a major impact on late 20th-century American society and culture is standardized psychological testing, particularly in the realms of education and employment practices (Sokal, 1987). In addition to its role in society, mental testing was also vitally important in placing psychology on the map as a profession (Samelson, 1979). For both of these reasons, the topic warrants fuller treatment than it is usually given in the standard History of Psychology course, with its characteristic minimizing of applied areas.

One source that provides valuable historical perspectives on mental testing, psychology, and society is *Psychological Testing and American Society (1890–1930)* (Sokal, 1987), which goes beyond previously published accounts of the mental testing movement by carefully examining the work of the testers in social and political context. The book does not align itself with either the defenders or the opponents of testing but instead endeavors to demonstrate how testing "emerged and evolved in response to real problems, as American society changed rapidly and the Progressives looked to science for guidance" (pp. 16–17). Another excellent book on this topic is *Measuring Minds: Henry Herbert Goddard and the Origins of American Intelligence Testing* (Zenderland, 1998), which views the institutionalization of intelligence testing as an event that transformed both the profession of psychology and American society.

Historians prior to Zenderland (1998) paid little attention to Goddard or to the early American intelligence testing movement he led. One intriguing question Zenderland raised, which can generate provocative discussion in a History of Psychology course, relates to Goddard's hereditarian stance on intelligence—and more specifically to his 1912 monograph *The Kallikak Family*, which claimed to prove that the inheritance of subnormal intelligence produced devastating social consequences. Zenderland asks how and why this work, which scholars have repeatedly criticized over the past 50 years as deeply flawed, was praised in its own time as a major scientific accomplishment. Seeking explanations that go beyond a simple questioning of the political motives of those involved at the time, she pays attention to changes in the meaning of terms such as *heredity* and *environment*. In addition, she attempts to reconstruct the perspectives of participants in the early intelligence testing debates, and in allowing them "to debate their own issues in their own terms—to frame their own questions, to find their own answers, and to make sense of their findings in their own ways" (p. 13), she offers present-generation students a new understanding of the history of intelligence testing.

Early social activism

It is also important to note that social activism was not absent from American psychology in the 1920s and 1930s but instead was overlooked by historians who focused their studies of that era on the phenomenon of behaviorism. Pandora (1997) explored the work of three social and personality psychologists—Gordon Allport, Gardner Murphy, and Lois Barclay Murphy—each of whom she portrays as a dissenter from the neobehavioristic paradigm that had become orthodoxy in American psychology by the 1930s. Claiming that these three psychologists were social activists as well as social scientists, she maintains that the internationalist and political concerns that they articulated during the 1930s continued to play out within the discipline of psychology over the subsequent decades, with links to the civil rights movement of the 1960s. History of Psychology instructors may find her book useful in pointing out to students that there was more to American psychology of the 1920s and 1930s than triumphal behaviorism. Moreover, it would make students aware that some respected insiders of that era were debating issues that would come to be of vital concern to the discipline in the 1960s— a critique of psychology conceived as a value-free natural science and a call for a rethinking of psychology and its role in a democratic society.

International Roots and Perspectives

Instructors who are seeking to place the origins and development of psychology in international context can consult works by Richards (1997) and Danziger (1990, 1997). In *'Race,' Racism and Psychology: Towards a Reflexive History*, Richards provides a comprehensive history of how the discipline of psychology in the United States, Great Britain, and Europe dealt with issues surrounding race from the mid-19th century to 1970. Topics that he explores include scientific racism at the end of the 19th century; Nazi racist psychology; the emergence of Black psychology in the United States; and the race-and-IQ debate, which he calls an "undead controversy." Richards's "reflexive" approach to history emphasizes the ways in which the discipline of psychology emerges from, reflects, and participates in the social concerns of its surrounding milieu.

In *Constructing the Subject* (Danziger, 1990), which focuses on the latter part of the 19th and first half of the 20th centuries, Danziger gives an account of the historical origins of psychological research, emphasizing both the fundamentally social nature of scientific activity and the socially constructed nature of psychological knowledge. According to Danziger, three models of psychological investigation emerged in the latter part of the 19th century, differing in their goals and social arrangements: (a) the one inaugurated in Wundt's Leipzig laboratory; (b) the "clinical experiment" devised by a group of French investigators who were using hypnosis as a tool of psychological research; and (c) the one created by Francis Galton, who set up a laboratory for testing the mental abilities of members of the public for a fee at an international health exhibition in London in 1884. Yet, although American investigators initially exhibited eclecticism by rapidly adopting all three models, in the course of the first half of the 20th century, a version of the Galtonian model, which was compatible with applied psychology's goals of prediction and control, eventually came to dominate. Danziger analyzes how this came about, presenting a thoughtful examination of the relations the psychological investigators had with each other and with the wider cultures of which they were a part.

In *Naming the Mind*, Danziger (1997) eloquently challenges the view that the psychological categories used in 20th-century American psychology reflect a natural and universal order. He begins the book with a telling anecdote about his experience teaching psychology at an Indonesian university. He and an Indonesian colleague had agreed to offer joint seminars in which they planned to compare the Western psychology in which Danziger had been schooled with the indigenous, Eastern psychology taught by his Indonesian counterpart. However, the seminars never took place because of the discovery, when the two of them sat down to discuss the topics to be included, that there were virtually no topics that their psychologies had in common. Danziger recalls this as an unsettling experience; the vivid, first-hand demonstration that there was more than one possible psychology raised questions for him about the purported objectivity of the categories of Western psychology. Similar subsequent experiences led him eventually to view psychology "as a cultural construction with specific historical roots" (p. 181); *Naming the Mind* is devoted to an exploration of some of these roots. In it, students will encounter a convincing argument that psychological categories are not timeless and universal, but rather the product of a specific time, place, and culture.

Finally, Danziger maintains that after the first third of the 20th century, psychology became essentially an American discipline. This was due to both the enormous size of the discipline in the United States compared to in the rest of the world—and, more significant, to the fact that "it was imported, and sometimes reimported, by the rest of the world as part and parcel of its importation of American values, American educational and business practices, American media, American advertising, American conceptions of mental health, and so on" (pp. 197–198). That historical insight helps make intelligible to students the movements that are now underway in some countries, which have as their goal the reclaiming of indigenous psychologies that American psychology supplanted over the course of the 20th century.

CONCLUSION

Major changes in the way we teach the History of Psychology course are past due—changes more radical than attempting to make Boring more interesting, or supplementing the traditional course with an add-women-and-minorities-and-stir approach. It is time for the History of Psychology course to provide students with knowledge about the complex reciprocal relationships that have existed over time between psychology and the society that it has inhabited. Excellent scholarly resources for teaching a contextualized, inclusive, critical history are already available and will increase as scholars continue to pursue these new lines of inquiry. Instructors now need to move toward creating a course that will prepare students to make decisions and take action in their present and future lives, as psychologists or consumers of psychology, informed by an understanding of relevant aspects of the past.

REFERENCES

Blowers, G. H. (1998). Chen Li: China's elder psychologist. *History of Psychology, 1*, 315–330.

Boring, E. G. (1929). *A history of experimental psychology*. New York: Century.

Capshew, J. H. (1999). *Psychologists on the march: Science, practice, and professional identity in America, 1929–1969*. Cambridge, England: Cambridge University Press.

Cicciarelli, T. (1998). *The history and systems of psychology course: Origins, political consequences, and alternative constructions*. Unpublished doctoral dissertation, California School of Professional Psychology, Alameda.

Cushman, P. (1995). *Constructing the self, constructing America: A cultural history of psychotherapy*. Reading, MA: Addison-Wesley.

Danziger, K. (1990). *Constructing the subject: Historical origins of psychological research*. Cambridge, England: Cambridge University Press.

Danziger, K. (1997). *Naming the mind: How psychology found its language*. London: Sage.

Furumoto, L. (1987). On the margins: Women and the professionalization of psychology in the United States, 1890–1940. In M. G. Ash & W. R. Woodward (Eds.), *Psychology in twentieth century thought and society* (pp. 93–113). Cambridge, England: Cambridge University Press.

Furumoto, L. (1989). The new history of psychology. In I. S. Cohen (Ed.), *The G. Stanley Hall lecture series* (Vol. 9, pp. 5–34). Washington, DC: American Psychological Association.

Furumoto, L. (1998). Gender and the history of psychology. In B. M. Clinchy & J. K. Norem (Eds.), *The gender and psychology reader* (pp. 69–77). New York: New York University Press.

Guthrie, R. V. (1998). *Even the rat was white: A historical view of psychology* (2nd ed.). Boston: Allyn & Bacon.

Herman, E. (1995). *The romance of American psychology: Political culture in the age of experts*. Berkeley: University of California Press.

Hogan, J. D., Goshtasbpour, F., Laufer, M. R., & Haswell, E. (1998). Teaching the history of psychology: What's hot and what's not. *Teaching of Psychology, 25,* 206–208.

Koppes, L. L. (1997). American female pioneers of industrial and organizational psychology during the early years. *Journal of Applied Psychology, 82,* 500–515.

Lewin, M. (Ed.). (1984). *In the shadow of the past: Psychology portrays the sexes. A social and intellectual history*. New York: Columbia University Press.

Milar, K. S. (1999). "A coarse and clumsy tool": Helen Thompson Woolley and the Cincinnati Vocation Bureau. *History of Psychology, 2,* 219–235.

Murphy, G. (1929). *An historical introduction to modern psychology*. New York: Harcourt, Brace.

O'Connell, A. N., & Russo, N. F. (Eds.). (1980). Eminent women in psychology: Models of achievement [Special issue]. *Psychology of Women Quarterly, 5*(1).

O'Connell, A. N., & Russo, N. F. (Eds.). (1983). *Models of achievement: Reflections of eminent women in psychology*. New York: Columbia University Press.

O'Connell, A. N., & Russo, N. F. (Eds.). (1988). *Models of achievement: Reflections of eminent women in psychology* (Vol. 2). Hillsdale, NJ: Erlbaum.

O'Connell, A. N., & Russo, N. F. (Eds.). (1990). *Women in psychology: A bio-bibliographic sourcebook*. New York: Greenwood Press.

O'Connell, A. N., & Russo, N. F. (Eds.). (1991). Women's heritage in psychology: Origins, development, and future directions [Special issue]. *Psychology of Women Quarterly, 15*(4).

Pandora, K. (1997). *Rebels within the ranks: Psychologists' critique of scientific authority and democratic realities in New Deal America*. Cambridge, England: Cambridge University Press.

Pillsbury, W. B. (1929). *The history of psychology*. New York: Norton.

Richards, G. (1997). *"Race," racism and psychology: Towards a reflexive history*. London: Routledge.

Ross, D. (1969). The "Zeitgeist" and American psychology. *Journal of the History of the Behavioral Sciences, 5*, 256–262.

Samelson, F. (1979). Putting psychology on the map: Ideology and intelligence testing. In A. R. Buss (Ed.), *Psychology in social context* (pp. 103–168). New York: Irvington.

Scarborough, E. (1992). Women in the American Psychological Association. In R. B. Evans, V. S. Sexton, & T. C. Cadwallader (Eds.), *The American Psychological Association: A historical perspective* (pp. 303–325). Washington, DC: American Psychological Association.

Scarborough, E., & Furumoto, L. (1987). *Untold lives: The first generation of American women psychologists*. New York: Columbia University Press.

Sokal, M. M. (Ed.). (1987). *Psychological testing and American society, 1890–1930*. New Brunswick, NJ: Rutgers University Press.

Wentworth, P. A. (1999). The moral of her story: Exploring the philosophical and religious commitments in Mary Whiton Calkins' self-psychology. *History of Psychology, 2*, 119–131.

Winston, A. S. (1998). "The defects of his race": E. G. Boring and antisemitism in American psychology. *History of Psychology, 1*, 27–51.

Zenderland, L. (1998). *Measuring minds: Henry Herbart Goddard and the origins of American intelligence testing*. Cambridge, England: Cambridge University Press.

9

DIVERSIFYING HEALTH PSYCHOLOGY: THE SOCIOCULTURAL CONTEXT

HOPE LANDRINE AND ELIZABETH A. KLONOFF

On the whole, health psychology textbooks communicate the following messages to students: There are two types of people in the world, the healthy and the sick. Healthy people are healthy because of their innate physiology (they lack a biological predisposition for diseases such as hypertension) and because of their health-promoting behaviors (they do not smoke, abuse alcohol, or fail to exercise). Sick people and those who die before their time, on the other hand, have biological predispositions for diseases that they themselves precipitate by failing to engage in health-promoting behaviors. The message is that health is primarily a function of individual attitudes and behaviors (i.e., dispositions) that can be understood without reference to the sociocultural context in which they are shaped and maintained (Landrine & Klonoff, 2001a). In addition, texts often highlight that healthy people tend to be Whites of privileged economic status and

This chapter was supported by funds provided by grants from the University of California Tobacco-Related Disease Research Program (6RT-0081, 8RT-0013, and 9RT-0043), the California Department of Health Services Tobacco Control Section, (94-20962 and 96-26617), and the National Institutes of Health (National Cancer Institute Grant 1-u-56-CA 92079-01A1).

125

that sick people tend to be minorities, poor, and women, without reference to the larger sociocultural context of these health disparities (Landrine & Klonoff, 2001b; Sallis & Owen, 1996).

Unfortunately, instructors of Health Psychology find it difficult to challenge this dispositional model of health, because sociocultural variables are largely ignored by health psychology as a discipline. For example, the major health psychology journals (*Health Psychology* and *Journal of Behavioral Medicine*) do not often publish articles on the social or cultural variables related to health (see Klonoff, Landrine, & Lang, 1997, for a review). To find data on social and cultural variables in health, instructors must turn to the literature in public health, preventive medicine, and medical anthropology. Thus, in this chapter we present interdisciplinary data that can be used to assist students in understanding the context of health, along with concrete suggestions for integrating this information into the Health Psychology course. The specific sociocultural-context variables highlighted here are access to alcohol, opportunities to exercise, youth access to tobacco, violence against girls and women, racial and gender discrimination, and racial and ethnic segregation.

THE NEIGHBORHOOD CONTEXT OF HEALTH: ALCOHOL USE AND EXERCISE

Two major foci of Health Psychology textbooks are problems associated (a) with alcohol abuse and (b) with a lack of exercise. These two topics provide clear examples of the role of the surrounding neighborhood in individual behavior.

Alcohol Use and Abuse

Numerous studies have found strong relationships between alcohol use and abuse and negative health outcomes. People who are intoxicated or drunk are significantly more likely than their sober counterparts to get into car accidents and violent confrontations, fail to use a condom, and have the chronic health problems that are caused by excessive drinking (National Center for Health Statistics [NCHS], 1998). Alcohol use and abuse are significantly more frequent among minorities and the poor (NCHS, 1998). Health Psychology texts include these facts, yet they rarely address the larger context in which alcohol use and abuse are elicited and maintained—specifically, the availability of alcohol in one's neighborhood. Studies conducted in communities as diverse as New Orleans, Louisiana, and San Diego, California, all have found that the number of liquor stores in a neighborhood is one of the strongest predictors of alcohol use and abuse by the residents of that neighborhood. In addition, the shorter the distance between each residence and a liquor store, the higher the frequency of alcohol use and abuse and the higher the prevalence of the car accidents, violent crimes, chronic health problems, and high-risk sexual behaviors that are caused by being drunk (Lipton & Gruenewald, 2002; Scribner, Cohen, & Farley, 1998; Tatlow, Clapp, & Hohman, 2000). Studies also have demonstrated that there are significantly more alcohol outlets in low-income communities and in minority communities compared with higher income and White neighborhoods, with the highest density found in low-income, minority neighborhoods (LaVeist & Wallace, 2000; Lipton & Gruenewald, 2002; Scribner, Cohen, & Fisher, 2000). Residents of low-income, minority communities do not desire or control the numerous liquor stores that are present in their neighborhoods (Polednak, 1997). Thus, an ostensibly disposition-based, lifestyle behavior that is implicated in numerous negative health outcomes is largely elicited and maintained by the local context of alcohol availability.

Exercise

One of the strongest predictors of health is exercise. Physical inactivity plays a significant, causal role in acute and chronic disease morbidity and mortality (NCHS, 1998). In addition, studies indicate that minorities, the poor, older people, and women tend to be less physically active than their Anglo, middle-class, younger, and male counterparts (Centers for Disease Control, 1999). Health Psychology textbooks often fail to note that the neighborhood context is a strong predictor of exercise. Specifically, people (women in particular) who reside in dangerous neighborhoods, or in neighborhoods with poor lighting, few sidewalks, high traffic, few play areas, and an absence of hills, are significantly less likely to jog and engage in physical activity or play outdoors than those who reside in safer, exercise-supportive areas (Brownson, Baker, Housemann, Brennan, & Bacak, 2001; Lee & Cubbin, 2002; Wilcox, Castro, King, Housemann, & Brownson, 2000). Physical inactivity among minorities, women, and the poor is better understood as a function of their exercise-prohibiting neighborhoods than as a function of their exercise-related beliefs, attitudes, and other dispositions (Centers for Disease Control, 1999).

To bring the neighborhood context to the foreground, students can conduct neighborhood availability studies. For example, they can compare the number of alcohol or tobacco outlets, bars, sidewalks, parks, fast food outlets, or stores selling fresh fruits and vegetables (as well as data on the price of tobacco, alcohol, and fruits and vegetables) in neighborhoods that differ by ethnicity, social class, or both. Likewise, students can collect similar availability and price data in their own neighborhood and relate them to the number of family members and friends residing in that neighborhood who smoke, consume alcohol frequently, exercise, or eat fatty or healthy foods. They also can be directed to examine census bureau data (available on the

Internet; www.census.gov) on the ethnic composition, income, and violent crime rates of specific census tracts in relation to the number of alcohol outlets and bars in those tracts. Students can present their findings as individual or group papers, as well as convention posters. We have found that students enjoy collecting and analyzing such data and are fascinated by the results, particularly when these involve the behavior of friends and family.

THE SOCIAL CONTEXT OF HEALTH: MINORS' ACCESS TO TOBACCO

All Health Psychology textbooks devote considerable attention to cigarette smoking because it is the single most preventable cause of disease and death, and it is a health behavior amenable to intervention (U.S. Department of Health and Human Services, 1994, 2001). Almost all adult smokers begin smoking in childhood or adolescence and then later find quitting difficult. Textbooks often detail the many psychological variables that play a role in smoking initiation among youth and note that smoking rates are higher among Blacks than among Whites; some also mention that smoking among girls and minority youth has been increasing. No textbook we have examined, however, mentions youth access to tobacco as a predictor of youth smoking.

Studies indicate that being able to acquire cigarettes (i.e., youth access) is the strongest predictor of experimental smoking among youth and indicate that being able to acquire inexpensive cigarettes is the strongest predictor of youth becoming regular smokers (Robinson, Klesges, Zbikowski, & Glaser, 1997; U.S. Department of Health and Human Services, 1994, 2001). This contextual variable—access—is a better predictor of youth experimental and regular smoking than all psychological variables (e.g., peer smoking, parental smoking, weight concerns, rebelliousness) combined. Hence, numerous efforts to prevent youth smoking have focused on reducing youth access to tobacco (Forster & Wolfson, 1998; Harrison, Fulkerson, & Park, 2000), and researchers have highlighted the cost-effectiveness of supply-side interventions (e.g., penalizing merchants for illegally selling cigarettes to children) over demand-side interventions (e.g., school-based prevention programs; DiFranza, Peck, Radecki, & Savageau, 2001). By ignoring the supply side, Health Psychology texts not only omit the best predictor of the behavior but also conceal the role that the social context plays in ethnic and gender differences in smoking among youth.

Specifically, several studies have found that merchants are significantly more likely to sell cigarettes to girls and to ethnic minority youth than to boys and to Anglo youth (e.g., Klonoff, Landrine, & Alcaraz, 1997; Landrine, Klonoff, & Alcaraz, 1998; Landrine, Klonoff, Campbell, & Reina-Patton, 2000; Landrine, Klonoff, & Fritz, 1994). For example, in one study

(Klonoff, Landrine, & Alcaraz, 1997), equal numbers of Black, White, and Latino girls and boys were sent into the same 72 stores, at the same time of day, to buy cigarettes. The children were matched by age and size, and they memorized a script so that each made precisely the same request in the same manner. These youth made 2,592 attempts to purchase cigarettes—the largest investigation to date. Logistic regression revealed that store clerks were nearly twice as likely to sell cigarettes to girls than to boys, and 3.5 to 8 times more likely to sell to minority youth than to Whites. The gender and ethnicity of the clerk also played a role: Men were significantly more likely than women to sell cigarettes to children, and Black clerks were significantly less likely than all others to do so. Our most recent studies reveal the persistence of this discrimination (Landrine & Klonoff, in press).

Thus, access to tobacco—the best predictor of smoking among youth—differs by minors' ethnicity and gender. Clerks do not sell cigarettes to any and all children, but instead, sell most often to girls and minorities, the two groups for whom smoking is on the rise. Furthermore, youth transition from experimental to regular smoking is better predicted by the price of cigarettes (i.e., access to cheap tobacco) than by psychological variables (Robinson et al., 1997). By presenting data on minors' access to tobacco and on discrimination in that access, Health Psychology instructors can assist students in understanding that not only health outcomes, but also health behaviors, occur in a social context that, in this case, encourages smoking in particular among minorities and girls.

THE STRUCTURAL–POLITICAL CONTEXT OF HEALTH: RACE AND GENDER INEQUALITY

Racial and gender inequality, as reflected in violence against women, racial and gender discrimination, and racial–ethnic segregation, are aspects of the larger, structural–political context in which health is shaped.

Violence Against Women

Battered women comprise 20%–30% of all women seeking treatment in emergency rooms and health clinics and 40%–64% of adult female psychiatric patients (Abbott, Johnson, Koziol-McLain, & Lowenstein, 1995). Such violence has been shown to cause a plethora of long-term, negative health outcomes for women, including substance abuse, eating disorders, psychiatric disorders, suicide, high-risk sexual behavior, sexual dysfunction, reproductive problems, chronic pain, and recurrent vaginal infections. When this violence is perpetrated against pregnant women (who are more likely than nonpregnant women to be battered), there are additional negative health consequences (Goodman, Koss, & Russo, 1993a, 1993b; Russo, Denious,

Keita, & Koss, 1997). Gender inequality and male violence also may best explain the increasing rate of AIDS among women insofar as women do not control their male partners' condom use; neither can they prevent rape (Gollub, 1999).

Violence against women also plays a major role in women's health behavior, including cigarette smoking, drug and alcohol abuse, and high-risk sexual behavior (Davis, 1994; Landrine & Klonoff, 2001b). Both early smoking initiation among girls and smoking among adult women during pregnancy are better predicted by a history of physical and sexual abuse than by beliefs or attitudes (Bullock, Mears, Woodcock, & Record, 2001; Ellickson, Tucker, & Klein, 2001; McNutt, Carlson, Persaud, & Postmus, 2002). Violence against women also has implications for the high cost of health care (Abbott et al., 1995; Bergman, Brismal, & Nordin, 1992; Koss, Heise, & Russo, 1994). Women who have been physically or sexually abused visit hospitals twice as often as their nonabused counterparts, at a cost more than double that of nonvictim visits (because of the extent of their injuries)—and their higher level of health care utilization does not predate their victimization (Koss, Koss, & Woodruff, 1991). Although all the Health Psychology textbooks we reviewed highlight the high cost of health care, along with the fact that women utilize health services far more often than do men, the role of violence against women is never taken into account in the discussion of costs and utilization patterns.

Classroom discussion of violence against women can place these data in their larger social context. Discussion questions might include: Why is violence against women generally not considered in discussions of women's higher rate of health care utilization or political debates about the high cost of health insurance? Why does health psychology address preventing youth violence but fail to address preventing violence against women?

Racial and Gender Discrimination

The stress of coping with discrimination is a strong predictor of psychiatric and physical symptoms among women (Klonoff, Landrine, & Campbell, 2000; Landrine, Klonoff, Gibbs, Manning, & Lund, 1995) and among Latinos and African Americans (Finch, Kolody, & Vega, 2000; Klonoff, Landrine, & Ullman, 1999). Likewise, racial discrimination is a stronger predictor of smoking among African Americans than are education and income, and it appears to account for Black–White differences in adult smoking rates, particularly when combined with segregation (Landrine & Klonoff, 2000a, 2000b). Most important, several studies have revealed that the chronic stress of ethnic and gender discrimination also plays a direct, causal role in cardiovascular reactivity and hypertension among women and Blacks (Krieger, 1990; Krieger & Sidney, 1996; Max, Matthews, & Bromberger, 2001). When examining ways in which stress may cause disease by altering immune functions and cardiovascular reactivity, instructors can introduce discrimination as an additional stressor specific to women and minorities that in part accounts for gender and ethnic health disparities.

Racial Segregation

The United States continues to be racially segregated and was more segregated in 1990 than it was in 1860, 1910, and 1940 (Massey & Denton, 1993). This "American apartheid" is neither the unfortunate remnant of a racist past nor the result of a Black preference to live in Black neighborhoods but instead is an outcome of racial discrimination in housing and home loans (Massey & Denton, 1993; Polednak, 1997). Residential segregation predicts Black infant mortality rates, Black male life expectancy, Black-on-Black homicide rates, and mortality rates from all causes for Black females and males ages 15–54 (Polednak, 1997). For example, in low-segregated cities, mortality rates for Blacks from cardiovascular diseases do not differ from those for Whites, whereas in highly segregated cities (i.e., where 70% of Blacks would have to move to achieve city-level integration), Black rates of hypertension and deaths from cardiovascular disease are three times those of Whites (Polednak, 1997). In fact, impoverished Black men living in racially segregated Harlem (New York) are significantly less likely to live to age 65 than equally impoverished men living in rural Bangladesh (McCord & Freeman, 1990). This segregation effect has been attributed to racially separate and unequal health care facilities; poor housing quality; greater crowding, noise, and exposure to environmental toxins; low prevalence of physicians; greater exposure to tobacco and alcohol advertising; and a higher density of alcohol and tobacco outlets (Polednak, 1997; Smith, 1998). Nonetheless, we were unable to find a Health Psychology textbook that mentioned the role of segregation in Blacks' poor health or in the Black–White health disparities they detailed.

UNDERSTANDING THE IMPORTANCE OF SOCIOCULTURAL CONTEXT: CLASSROOM STRATEGIES

The above examples highlight that a wide range of health-related behaviors, such as smoking, exercise, alcohol use and abuse, and high-risk sexual activities, are shaped and maintained by larger social contexts whose influence outweighs that of the dispositions (e.g., health knowledge, beliefs, and intentions) emphasized in Health Psychology textbooks. To assist students in understanding the limitations of the dispositional perspective, instructors might begin with a discussion of the *fundamental attribution error* (FAE), the common mistake of attributing the cause of a person's behavior to that person's internal dispositions, despite the well-established finding that behavior is typically a response to situational contingencies (Gilbert & Malone, 1995; Ross & Nisbett, 1991). Health psychology's view that health behavior is largely a function of dispositions can be framed as an example of the pervasiveness of the FAE in Western cultures.

Students probably unwittingly engage in the FAE several times each day. Analyzing such experiences can help them understand how culturally pervasive the FAE is and how easy it is to underestimate the role of the context in behavior. For example, one common manifestation of the FAE is the *planning fallacy*, the tendency to overestimate the number of tasks that can be completed in a given day or week (and so to overschedule) because of focusing on one's dispositions (intentions, skills, desires) while ignoring the power of situations to subvert one's plans (Buehler, Griffin, & Ross, 1994). Students no doubt have planned to accomplish several tasks in a day, only to find that situations led to them accomplish only one. The FAE then probably led them to attribute their failure to accomplish all of the intended tasks to dispositional factors, such as poor time management or procrastination.

Once students have examined the FAE in their own lives, they can more readily apply contextual analysis to health behaviors. For example, health psychology's two major theories (the theory of planned behavior and the health belief model) posit, respectively, that the best predictor of health behavior is the intention to engage in it, and that health behavior is predicted by perceiving a behavior as a threat to one's health and believing that changing the behavior will reduce that threat. Students can examine personal examples of intentions derailed by situations, and of engaging in behaviors despite knowledge of their health threat, to better understand how contextual contingencies can be more powerful than dispositions. Assignments might entail students tracking their knowledge and intentions regarding a health behavior such as eating a balanced diet or exercising, as well as their actual behavior, and analyzing the situational contingencies that may have controlled the latter. This can be followed by discussion of the contextual contingencies that are likely to subvert knowledge and intentions among others, such as single mothers living in poverty.

SUMMARY AND CONCLUSIONS

Health Psychology textbooks teach students that health and disease are the result of individual behaviors and dispositions and fail to address the larger sociocultural contexts in which these are shaped and maintained. Social, contextual, and economic variables are tied together and play a role in the health of all Americans, but as we have shown, these variables differentially influence the health-damaging behaviors, morbidity, and mortality of ethnic minorities and women. To diversify the Health Psychology course, instructors must highlight the sociocultural context and help students develop the skills to look beyond dispositional attributions. This will not only help students understand the existing limitations within the field but also point the way toward better prevention efforts and healthier behavior for all people.

REFERENCES

Abbott, J., Johnson, R., Koziol-McLain, J., & Lowenstein, S. R. (1995). Domestic violence against women: Incidence and prevalence in an emergency department population. *Journal of the American Medical Association, 273*, 1763–1767.

Bergman, B., Brismal, B., & Nordin, D. (1992). Utilization of medical care by abused women. *British Medical Journal, 305*, 27–28.

Brownson, R. C., Baker, E. A., Housemann, R. A., Brennan, L. K., & Bacak, S. J. (2001). Environmental and policy determinants of physical activity in the United States. American *Journal of Public Health, 91*, 1995–2003.

Buehler, R., Griffin, D. W., & Ross, M. (1994). Exploring the planning fallacy: Why people underestimate their task completion times. *Journal of Personality and Social Psychology, 67*, 366–381.

Bullock, L. F., Mears, J. L., Woodcock, C., & Record, R. (2001). Retrospective study of the association of stress and smoking during pregnancy in rural women. *Addictive Behaviors, 26*, 405–413.

Centers for Disease Control. (1999). Neighborhood safety and the prevalence of physical inactivity—Selected states, 1996. *Morbidity and Mortality Weekly Report, 48*(7), 143–146.

Davis, M. (1994). *Women and violence*. London: Zed Press.

DiFranza, J. R., Peck, R. M., Radecki, T. E., & Savageau, J. A. (2001). What is the potential cost-effectiveness of enforcing the prohibition on the sale of tobacco to minors? *Preventive Medicine, 32*, 168–174.

Ellickson, P. L., Tucker, J. S., & Klein, D. J. (2001). High-risk behaviors associated with early smoking. *Journal of Adolescent Health, 28*, 465–473.

Finch, B. K., Kolody, B., & Vega, W. (2000). Perceived discrimination and depression among Mexican-origin adults in California. *Journal of Health and Social Behavior, 41*, 295–313.

Forster, J. L., & Wolfson, M. (1998). Youth access to tobacco: Policies and politics. *Annual Review of Public Health, 19*, 203–235.

Gilbert, D., & Malone, P. S. (1995). The correspondence bias. *Psychological Bulletin, 117*, 21–38.

Gollub, E. L. (1999). Human rights is a US problem too: The case of women and HIV. *American Journal of Public Health, 80*, 1479–1482.

Goodman, L. A., Koss, M. P., & Russo, N. F. (1993a). Violence against women: Physical and mental health effects. Part II: Conceptualizing posttraumatic stress. *Applied & Preventive Psychology: Current Scientific Perspectives, 2*, 123–130.

Goodman, L. A., Koss, M. P., & Russo, N. F. (1993b). Violence against women:

Physical and mental health effects. Part I: Research findings. *Applied & Preventive Psychology: Current Scientific Perspectives, 2*, 79–89.

Harrison, P. A., Fulkerson, J. A., & Park, E. (2000). The relative importance of social versus commercial sources in youth access to tobacco, alcohol, and other drugs. *Preventive Medicine, 31*, 39–48.

Klonoff, E. A., Landrine, H., & Alcaraz, R. (1997). An experimental analysis of sociocultural variables in sales of cigarettes to minors. *American Journal of Public Health, 87*, 823–826.

Klonoff, E. A., Landrine, H., & Campbell, R. R. (2000). Sexist discrimination may account for well-known gender differences in psychiatric symptoms. *Psychology of Women Quarterly, 24*, 92–98.

Klonoff, E. A., Landrine, H., & Lang, D. L. (1997). Introduction: The state of research on Black women in health psychology and behavioral medicine. *Women's Health, 3*, 165–181.

Klonoff, E. A., Landrine, H., & Ullman, J. B. (1999). Racial discriminiation and psychiatric symptoms among Blacks. *Cultural Diversity and Ethnic Minority Psychology, 5*(4), 329–339.

Koss, M. P., Heise, L., & Russo, N. F. (1994). The global health burden of rape. *Psychology of Women Quarterly, 18*, 509–530.

Koss, M. P., Koss, P. G., & Woodruff, W. (1991). Deleterious effects of criminal victimization on women's health and medical utilization. *Archives of Internal Medicine, 151*, 342–357.

Krieger, N. (1990). Racial and gender discrimination: Risk factors for high blood pressure? *Social Science & Medicine, 30*, 1273–1281.

Krieger, N., & Sidney, S. (1996). Racial discrimination and blood pressure. *American Journal of Public Health, 86*, 1370–1378.

Landrine, H., & Klonoff, E. A. (2000a). Racial discrimination and smoking among Blacks: Findings from two studies. *Ethnicity and Disease, 10*, 195–202.

Landrine, H., & Klonoff, E. A. (2000b). Racial segregation and cigarette smoking among Blacks: Findings at the individual level. *Journal of Health Psychology, 5*, 211–219.

Landrine, H., & Klonoff, E. A. (2001a). Cultural diversity and health psychology. In A. Baum, J. Singer, & T. Revenson (Eds.), *Handbook of health psychology* (pp. 855–895). Mahwah, NJ: Erlbaum.

Landrine, H., & Klonoff, E. A. (2001b). Health and health care: How gender makes women sick. In J. Worell (Ed.), *The encyclopedia of gender* (pp. 577–592). San Diego, CA: Academic Press.

Landrine, H., & Klonoff, E. A. (in press). Validity of assessments of youth access to tobacco: The Familiarity Effect. *American Journal of Public Health*.

Landrine, H., Klonoff, E. A., & Alcaraz, R. (1998). Minors' access to single cigarettes in California. *Preventive Medicine, 27*, 503–505.

Landrine, H., Klonoff, E. A., Campbell, R., & Reina-Patton, A. M. (2000). Sociocultural variables in minors' access to tobacco: Replication 5 years later. *Preventive Medicine, 30*, 433–437.

Landrine, H., Klonoff, E. A., & Fritz, J. M. (1994). Preventing cigarette sales to minors: The need for contextual, sociocultural analyses. *Preventive Medicine, 23,* 322–327.

Landrine, H., Klonoff, E. A., Gibbs, J., Manning, V., & Lund, M. (1995). Physical and psychiatric correlates of gender discrimination: An application of the Schedule of Sexist Events. *Psychology of Women Quarterly, 19,* 473–492.

LaVeist, T. A., & Wallace, J. M., Jr. (2000). Health risk and inequitable distribution of liquor stores in African American neighborhoods. *Social Science & Medicine, 51,* 613–617.

Lee, R. E., & Cubbin, C. (2002). Neighborhood context and youth cardiovascular health behaviors. *American Journal of Public Health, 92,* 428–436.

Lipton, R., & Gruenewald, P. (2002). The spatial dynamics of violence and alcohol outlets. *Journal of Studies on Alcohol, 63,* 187–195.

Massey, D. S., & Denton, N. A. (1993). *American apartheid.* Cambridge, MA: Harvard University Press.

Max, G., Matthews, K. A., & Bromberger, J. T. (2001). Discrimination and unfair treatment: Relationship to cardiovascular reactivity among African American and European American women. *Health Psychology, 20,* 315–325.

McCord, C., & Freeman, H. P. (1990). Excess mortality in Harlem. *New England Journal of Medicine, 322,* 173–177.

McNutt, L. A., Carlson, B. E., Persaud, M., & Postmus, J. (2002). Cumulative abuse experiences, physical health and health behaviors. *Annals of Epidemiology, 12,* 123–130.

National Center for Health Statistics. (1998). *Health, United States, 1998, with socioeconomic status and health chartbook.* Hyattsville, MD: Author.

Polednak, A. (1997). *Segregation, poverty, and mortality in urban African Americans.* New York: Oxford University Press.

Robinson, L. A., Klesges, R. C., Zbikowski, S. M., & Glaser, R. (1997). Predictors of risk for different stages of adolescent smoking in a biracial sample. *Journal of Consulting and Clinical Psychology, 65,* 653–662.

Ross, L., & Nisbett, R. E. (1991). *The person and the situation.* New York: McGraw-Hill.

Russo, N. F., Denious, J. E., Keita, G. P., & Koss, M. P. (1997). Intimate violence and Black women's health. *Women's Health, 3,* 315–348.

Sallis, J. F., & Owen, N. (1996). Ecological models. In K. Glanz, F. M. Lewis, & B. K. Rimer, (Eds.), *Health behavior and health education* (pp. 403–424). San Francisco, CA: Jossey-Bass.

Scribner, R. A., Cohen, D. A., & Farley, T. A. (1998). A geographic relation between alcohol availability and gonorrhea rates. *Sexually Transmitted Disease, 25,* 544–548.

Scribner, R. A., Cohen, D. A., & Fisher, W. (2000). Evidence of a structural effect for alcohol outlet density. *Alcoholism: Clinical and Experimental Research, 24,* 188–195.

Smith, D. B. (1998). The racial segregation of hospital care revisited: Medicare discharge patterns and their implications. *American Journal of Public Health, 88,* 461–463.

Tatlow, J. R., Clapp, J. D., & Hohman, M. M. (2000). The relationship between the geographic density of alcohol outlets and alcohol-related hospital admissions in San Diego County. *Journal of Community Health, 25,* 79–88.

U.S. Department of Health and Human Services. (1994). *Preventing tobacco use among young people: A report of the Surgeon General.* Atlanta, GA: Centers for Disease Control.

U.S. Department of Health and Human Services. (2001). *Health and Human Services fact sheet: Preventing disease and death from tobacco use.* Atlanta, GA: Centers for Disease Control.

Wilcox, S., Castro, C., King, A. C., Housemann, R., & Brownson, R. C. (2000). Determinants of leisure time physical activity in rural compared with urban older and ethnically diverse women in the U.S. *Journal of Epidemiology and Community Health, 54,* 667–672.

10

WHO IS THE WOMAN IN THE PSYCHOLOGY OF WOMEN?

BEVERLY J. GOODWIN, MAUREEN C. MCHUGH,
AND LISA OSACHY TOUSTER

Feminist psychologists have argued that research conducted from a male perspective or on only male participants has resulted in a biased understanding of human behavior (e.g., McHugh, Koeske, & Frieze, 1986; Sherif, 1979). The burgeoning scholarship on the psychology of women over the past 25 years has attempted to correct this bias, resulting in the formulation of new research questions, topics, and modes of inquiry focused on women's lives. Psychology of Women courses are included in most undergraduate curricula; however, a number of feminist scholars have argued that the psychology of women has not moved very far from traditional psychology, in that it is primarily the psychology of White middle-class American women (A. Brown, Goodwin, Hall, & Jackson-Lowman, 1985; Espín, 1997; Landrine, 1995).

LIMITATIONS AND CHALLENGES IN FEMINIST SCHOLARSHIP

The omission of diversity has serious implications both for feminist scholarship and for the field of psychology. Like the exclusion of women in general, the exclusion of particular groups of women results in a limited and distorted conception of human behavior (Williams, McCandies, & Dunlap, 2002). To place the experiences and issues of one group of women at the center is to marginalize other women's experience or to render them invisible (hooks, 1994). Such exclusions have particular implications for the Psychology of Women course, in which many female undergraduates enroll to study the impact of gender on their own lives. The lesbians, women of color, large women, women with physical challenges, and working-class and poor women who take the course hoping to better understand their experiences in a gendered and multicultural world are likely to find themselves remarginalized, with their lives and issues omitted or barely represented in the content. Failure to include marginalized women may make it more difficult for them to connect new knowledge with personal experience and sends a message about whose experiences are "appropriate" for class discussion (LePage-Lees, 1997). The experiences of marginalized women need to become a central part of the Psychology of Women course, not only in response to their needs but also for the education of White middle-class heterosexual students. Such inclusion makes all students cognizant of how important culture, race, ethnicity, class, sexual orientation, and physical and mental ability have been in their own development. In addition, this revision would have positive effects on the discipline as a whole, reshaping the questions future psychologists will seek to answer.

Instructors who seek to include empirical research on marginalized women will find that few such studies exist. An earlier review of the contents of the journal *Psychology of Women Quarterly* (Fine, 1985) found that most of the participants in the studies appeared to be White, with only 9% of the studies mentioning non-White respondents. A subsequent study of the empirical articles published in *Psychology of Women Quarterly* and *Sex Roles* found that only 15% of the articles analyzed the impact of race or ethnicity (Reid & Kelly, 1994). Recently, Saris and Johnston-Robledo (2000) reported that less than 3% of the abstracts included in PsycLIT for the years 1991–1997 pertained to poor or working-class women.

Underlying these practices is a persistent tendency to frame questions from the perspective of the dominant culture (Reid, 1993). Race and class biases are evident in the fact that when authors refer to women, they commonly mean White, middle-class, heterosexual women; race, class, and sexual orientation are indicated only when the participants are non-White, not middle class, and not heterosexual (Reid & Kelly, 1994; Williams et al., 2002). Research on samples of White middle-class women is more likely to be presented as theoretical, whereas research on minority, poor, and working-class women is usually viewed as applied—and therefore, presumably, of less scientific value (Graham, 1992; Reid & Kelly, 1994).

Feminists have criticized research that compares women to men, focusing on the differences. They have pointed out that it frequently leads to labeling women as deficient (Hare-Mustin & Marecek, 1990; Kimball, 1995; McHugh & Cosgrove, 2002), overgeneralizes about both men and women (Baca Zinn, Hondagneu-Sotelo, & Messner, 2000; Rhode, 1990), and essentializes gender—that is, it views men and women as possessing inherent gendered characteristics (Bohan, 1993; McHugh & Cosgrove, 2002). Likewise, studying the experiences of nondominant women only in comparison to what is viewed as the established, normative (i.e., White, middle-class, heterosexual) female experience has similar drawbacks. Such dichotomous approaches are overly simplistic and inaccurate and serve existing societal power structures by reinforcing the notion of "us" and "them," the deserving and the not deserving (Hare-Mustin & Marecek, 1990; Kimball, 1995; McHugh & Cosgrove, 2002; Rhode, 1990).

In addition, even when women of color are taken into account, the term *women of color* itself—which refers to women from non-European cultures and backgrounds—suggests the perspective of outsiders (Collins, 1990) and can be viewed as perpetuating the White–non-White distinctions made by the dominant group. Furthermore, it is important to develop a theoretical framework for understanding the variations in culture and life experiences among women of color (Landrine, 1995), instead of continuing to lump them into this all-encompassing category. Women of color in the United States are diverse with regard to many variables, including cultural heritage, immigration history, skin color, language, gender roles, access to education and employment, and relationship to the dominant group (Williams et al., 2002).

CREATING A MORE INCLUSIVE PSYCHOLOGY OF WOMEN COURSE

A better approach in psychology of women research and courses would be to focus on the experience of excluded groups individually, without comparing them implicitly or explicitly to the dominant group, with the goal of examining gender as it is experienced in different sociocultural contexts (Landrine, 1995; Reid & Kelly, 1994). This is the goal we have for Psychology of Women courses. In this chapter, we present some of the strategies we have used to create a more inclusive Psychology of Women course. Here, we have focused in particular on African American women, poor and working-class women, and fat women, as examples of inclusiveness that can be applied to other marginalized groups as well. We review the textbook coverage of these groups and provide suggestions for readings, discussion topics, and classroom activities. We hope that this model will be useful to instructors in transforming their courses to include a wide multicultural representation of women.

African American Women

Textbook review

A. Brown and her colleagues (1985) systematically reviewed textbooks of the psychology of women published between 1944 and 1981 and concluded that race and class biases resulted in the exclusion, limited inclusion, and biased treatment of African American women. Since that time, psychology of women textbook authors have attempted to add more material on African American women and other women of color (Goodwin, Brown, & Jackson-Lowman, 1989; Hyde, Matlin, & Walsh, 1990); however, a recent textbook review (Goodwin & Delazar, 2000) raised concerns about their continuing invisibility in Psychology of Women curricula and perfunctory treatment in feminist psychology. Furthermore, critics have noted that the lives of African American women have not been considered within a sociohistorical context (Landrine, 1995); that relevant sociocultural information about them has been omitted in recommendations of videos or class projects; that they are still not well represented in illustrations and photographs; and that their experiences are not analyzed in relationship to other identities, such as class, region, religion, or sexual orientation (Goodwin & Delazar, 2000). Content about African American women has usually been added to textbooks that have been organized around issues most important to White women (or even men) but that may not be relevant to women of color. It is also important that African American women not be portrayed as victimized or as uniform in their experiences and perspectives (hooks, 1992).

Suggestions for teaching

Comas-Díaz (1991) identified some feminist principles of importance to women of color that can provide a framework for research and teaching about African American women. Like Landrine (1995), she emphasized the sociocultural and historical context of their lives as affecting their experiences and has recommended addressing historical and contemporary social action as a means of coping and empowerment for women of color (e.g., see Giddings, 1984). Students can learn about positive adaptations and resiliency in African American women by considering acts of resistance (e.g., Collins, 1990; Giddings, 1984); there are countless examples of African American women who challenged injustice (e.g., Sojourner Truth, Rosa Parks, Ida B. Wells-Barnett, Angela Davis, Anita Hill). As examples of social action, instructors can highlight the role of African American women in historical movements, such as the civil rights and women's movements (Giddings, 1984).

In addition, instructors can help students analyze the ways that systematic societal forces such as racism, discrimination, and economic oppression may affect African American women's mental and physical health (Cutrona,

Russell, Hessling, Brown, & Murry, 2000; Villarosa, 1994). They can also invite students to consider the role of religion and spirituality in African American women's psychological well-being (Wade-Gayles, 1995) and cover such relevant topics as standards of beauty, internalized oppression, and representations of African American women in the media (hooks, 1992; Wade, 1996; West, 2000) Students may then begin to understand the concept of multiracial feminism as a theoretical framework, within which race is viewed as a power system interacting with other structured inequalities to shape gender (Baca Zinn & Dill, 2000; Comas-Díaz, 1991).

Speaking Up: Working-Class and Poor Women

Class distinctions and class-based perspectives affect most people's experiences in contemporary U.S. culture (hooks, 2000), yet the field of psychology has largely failed to acknowledge their existence (Baker, 1996; Reid, 1993). Franzblau (1991) concluded that psychology, like the media, considers the affluent, the middle class, the powerful, and the intellectual to be the only people of interest or significance. Because women academics for the most part do not represent the poor or working class (Reid, 1993), they have been unlikely to conceive of women's experience from those perspectives. Students and professors from poor or working-class families may not want to speak about their background for fear of exposing their own deficiencies or exposing their families as not educated or not sharing the values and perspectives implicitly and explicitly accepted within the academy (LePage-Lees, 1997). They have learned—and at times have been explicitly warned—to avoid language, activities, behaviors, and values that are "déclassé."

In addition, for a working-class person to become educated is to refute the working-class value system, in effect accepting a system that erases or invalidates one's life experience. Furthermore, silence about one's disadvantaged background may contribute to feelings of shame, alienation, and lack of competence (LePage-Lees, 1997; Palmer, 1996; Raey, 1997). On the other hand, for working-class women, speaking about their lives can transform their gendered class-based experience into a resource; this feminist work can produce both new knowledge and social change (Cohen, 1998; Raey, 1997; Zandy, 2001).

Certain class-based assumptions have had a hidden but pervasive influence on psychological research and theory. One assumption is that people's behavior is guided by their own disposition or volition (Orza & Torrey, 1995). When applied to people living in poverty, it suggests a tacit acceptance of the cultural premise that poverty is a voluntary condition (Allison, 1994) that any competent and determined individual can rise above or avoid. The failure of psychologists to view women's behavior—in particular, poor women's behavior—as influenced by the context of their lives is equivalent to holding them responsible for their own subordination

(Orza & Torrey, 1995). It is important to note that the lower sense of mastery and control that poor women often experience is a reflection of the realities of their daily lives (Lachman & Weaver, 1998). Franzblau (1991) challenged another assumption in the field, suggesting that theories of early development (e.g., attachment theory) that emphasize full-time mothering and the development of independence are class biased. Zandy (2001) asked readers to imagine what it would be like if the experiences of working-class people were at the center of the academy. For example, would the textbooks continue to emphasize dual-career families and the glass ceiling as issues for working women?

Textbook and journal review

Poor and working-class women, as is the case in most psychology research (Franzblau, 1991; Reid, 1993; Saris & Johnston-Robledo, 2000), are seldom found in the psychology of women literature. In a 1985 analysis, Fine found that 50% of the studies in *Psychology of Women Quarterly* had been conducted on college students, and 14% had been conducted on professional couples. A quick review that we conducted of *Psychology of Women Quarterly* for 1999 indicated that college students were still the participants in 38% of the empirical studies reported, although the college samples were sometimes racially diverse. Also, often when a community sample was reported, or when a special population was studied (e.g., battered women), the class background of the participants was not easily identified.

Similarly, Psychology of Women textbooks have traditionally not included poor and working-class women. Earlier textbooks (with the exception of Lott, 1987) made no reference to class issues (McHugh & Goodwin, 1991). Current textbooks have just begun to consider both poverty and class; for example, Crawford and Unger's (2000) most recent edition now includes information about class in discussions of the adolescence experience and images of women, and Donelson's (1999) textbook, which contains the most extensive indexed references to class of the eight texts we reviewed, has 15 listings under *poverty* and 33 under *socioeconomic status*. In most textbooks, when working-class women are included, comparisons between middle-class and working-class or poor women are made, and as is usually the case with the difference model, such comparisons are generally not neutral—to the detriment of the latter. Full integration of class diversity would entail more than an extended series of comparisons. Like members of other nondominant groups, poor and working-class women come from diverse backgrounds, with a great variety of daily experiences (Baker, 1996; Reid, 1993). Including them in the Psychology of Women course will require the addition of new themes and topics but, more important, it will involve a re-visioning of the field. Lott and Bullock (2001) provided a valuable resource for beginning this process.

Suggestions for teaching

Although feminist psychologists have generally not addressed the issues of poor and working-class women, other women's studies scholars have done so (e.g., Mahony & Zmroczek, 1997; Zandy, 1990), providing good sources both for analyses and autobiographical poetry and prose. The experiences of poor and working-class women have also been included in multicultural readers (e.g., Baca Zinn et al., 2000; Ballentine & Inclan, 1995; Disch, 2000; Kirk & Okazawa-Rey, 1998). These collections reveal a number of themes that are relevant to working-class women's lives; they include, for example, essays on money, work, unions, physical health and safety, religion, sexuality, violence, harassment, oppression, social activism, and survival. Other working-class experiences instructors might address include gossip, meal preparation, holidays, and motherhood. For example, before a holiday break, we sometimes ask members of the class to share their expectations for what will happen in their families during the break, encouraging them to analyze how their experiences are affected not only by gender but also by ethnicity, region, religion, and class. Holiday celebrations are one instance in which working-class and poor students are sometimes seen as advantaged because of their close family ties, home cooking, and ethnic traditions.

In addition, we have often used the short film *Clothesline* (Cantow, 1981) to open the discussion of social class. The video examines women's experiences with hanging out laundry. Discussion of the film usually raises the issues of diversity (not all women do laundry or have the same feelings about the laundry) and challenges the societal (de)valuation of women's work. Members of the class can usually see that women who perform de-valued work are themselves devalued. Most important, students can see class differences in the backgrounds of their classmates, based on what they choose to reveal about the laundry in their own homes. Middle-class and affluent women do not hang out their laundry. This simple observation can help students understand the impact of social class on women's experiences and to see the problem of universalizing the experience of middle-class and affluent women.

Strom (1994) detailed an approach she uses in her writing course. She asks the (mostly working-class) students to write about their own and their families' work histories and share them with the class.

> Individually and collectively they create an impressive story of working class life within the community . . . . Writing and hearing the stories helps students identify themselves as members of the same economic class while also showing them how differences such as race, gender, sexual orientation and income level can complicate that identity. (p. 134)

We have used a similar approach, asking students to talk about their job experiences to date. They often see gender harassment and other problems they experience as having been related to the types of work they were doing. What they sometimes need prodding to recognize is that many women remain in these jobs for a lifetime.

Sometimes the cultural valuation and privilege of middle-class women are explicitly expressed by students in our classes, who acknowledge that they do not want to talk or learn about poor or working-class women. Lott (2000) described the resistance of middle-class students in her classes to learn about poverty and their inability to empathize with poor women. These are the same values that have helped to shape the theory and content of the psychology of women. It is important to recognize and challenge such values, even if poor and working-class women remain silent.

Fat Yet Invisible: Sizism in Feminist Psychology

Fat women, who are a marginalized group both in the popular media and the academy, have been rendered invisible in the psychology of women literature. Despite increasing social activism against fat oppression, in feminist analyses size is ignored or viewed as a false difference. For example, in their analysis of the importance of race and class as primary organizing principles of society, Baca Zinn and Dill (2000) dismissed fat as a category of oppression, reducing it to an individual characteristic. Although our intent is not to argue about the hierarchy of oppressions (Lorde, 2000), we propose that size is a source of identity and oppression and that relations in families, school, and the work world are strongly influenced by sizism. Students need to understand that rejection, disgrace, shame, and guilt are attached to the experience of being fat in today's culture. Research has documented that fat women are discriminated against in educational and employment settings and are treated differently in medical and mental health settings. For example, in a survey of mental health workers, Young and Powell (1985) found that obese clients were seen as having more psychopathology and were rated more negatively. This is information that should be included in a Psychology of Women course, along with the research on the ineffectiveness and risks of diets, lack of health risk in being fat, lack of controllability of weight, and fat oppression in U.S. society.

Textbook review

Touster (2000) examined the representation of fat women in the photographs and text of current Psychology of Women textbooks. Only one book had a detailed discussion of fat oppression, and fewer than 8% of the photographs included fat women, even though fat women are estimated to comprise 25%–30% of the adult population. In fact, fat women were generally better represented in Introductory Psychology textbooks than they were in Psychology of Women textbooks, and Introductory textbooks were also more likely to include information on the ineffectiveness of diets and to correct myths about fat people's eating behaviors. L. S. Brown and Rothblum (1989) advocated "overcoming within ourselves and our colleagues long and firmly held prejudices about the value of being thin. We must deal with our own fears of our female bodies, of being ample, taking space, carrying weight" (p. 3). The failure to include coverage of fat women in Psychology of Women courses and texts has implications for women of all sizes. Whereas fat women suffer from discrimination, nonfat women live in fear of becoming fat, which leads many to obsess over weight, hate their bodies, avoid physical and social activities, and engage in self-destructive dieting or purging behaviors.

Suggestions for addressing sizism

Instructors can assign narrative accounts of fat women's experiences, such as those found in *FAT!SO!* (Wann, 1998), *Shadow on a Tightrope: Writings by Women on Fat Oppression* (Schoenfielder & Weiser, 1983), and *Overcoming Fear of Fat* (L. S. Brown & Rothblum, 1989). Fat women's stories of harassment, ridicule, and humiliation are not isolated incidents but common experiences (Packer, 1989; Schoenfielder & Weiser, 1983; Stunkard, 1976), including being yelled at on the street, being physically assaulted, being the target of cruel jokes, and being socially isolated (Wadden & Stunkard, 1993).

Instructors can design and teach units on sizism within the health or diversity section of a course or as a free-standing workshop. They can design and conduct a mini-experiment investigating bias against fat women—for example, having participants rate applicants for a job, with photos attached to the applicant files. They can also have students monitor the media for representation of large women and consider the effects of the mass media on the formation of eating and body-image disturbances.

It is important to help students see that fat people represent a subordinate, stigmatized group. Instructors can point out the ways that attitudes toward gays and lesbians have changed within the field of psychology and examine fat oppression in this context. They can make students aware of the way "eating disorders" are conceptualized—for example, that the diagnosis of anorexia nervosa includes many criteria, but the diagnosis of obesity is made just by a number on a scale. They can challenge why being thinner than the norm isn't medicalized or pathologized in the same way that being fatter is and question the political and economic incentives behind maintaining this medical model. Class discussions might consider current events, such as antidiscrimination laws regarding weight discrimination and diet disclosure (http://www.cswd.org/disclaws.html; http://www.naofa.org/info/legal/court.html). Instructors can encourage students to design creative ways to prevent eating disorders, end dieting, and promote healthy body image.

Instructors who find the issue of sizism too challenging personally can cover the issues by means of films, such as *Margaret Cho—I'm the One That I Want* (Coleman, 2000), or speakers, whom they may be able to find through a local chapter of the National Association to Advance Fat Acceptance (http://www.naafa.org). They can also introduce students to resources such as Fat!So? (http://www.fatso.com) and the Council on Size and Weight Discrimination (http://www.cswd.org).

Additional Classroom Strategies and Techniques

There are a number of additional things instructors can do to create a more inclusive Psychology of Women course. One very basic tactic is to change the language and examples they use in lectures, to include not only women of color but also other marginalized groups, such as lesbians and bisexuals and physically challenged, fat, older, poor, and working-class women. Visually representing these groups through slides, overheads, and videos is an important antidote to the homogenized images of women typically presented. It is also important not to represent these various groups in stereotypic ways, solely as oppressed victims or as deficient in comparison with young, thin, White, able-bodied, middle-class women.

One strategy we use to contradict stereotypes is to include marginalized groups under topics where students may not be expecting to encounter them. For example, we cover disabled women under the topic of relationships by showing the video *Towards Intimacy* (McGee & Hubert, 1992), an account of the intimate relationships of five women with varied disabilities. We start the course with images of women from other countries, or with the video *The Way Home* (Butler, 1998), which features "councils" of women from varied racial and ethnic backgrounds. We introduce issues of diversity early on in a unit on images and beauty. We discuss why eating disorders and body image problems are experienced differently and less frequently by African Americans and Latinas, as a way of helping students to understand the cultural and heterosexual context of women's self-images.

Another good starting place is to raise students' consciousness about bias in education (Orza & Torrey, 1995). We encourage them to reflect on their own education: Who decided what was important to know? What counts as knowledge? Whose life and work are considered important? In our course, students read Rich's (1979) essay "Claiming an Education" and do an in-class writing assignment that they later expand into a formal essay in which they analyze their own education. We also teach students how to analyze journals and textbooks for content about women and diversity, and we ask them to count the number of women of color or older women on television or in various popular magazines. We ask them to keep track of who in their classes talks and who does not.

Creating a sense of community in the classroom is an important component of diversity training (hooks, 1994). We raise the issue of diversity early, encouraging students to consider their own identity through exercises such as talking about their name and what it reflects about who they are. Another way to help students share their perspectives and experiences is to have them bring in photos of themselves as children, to spark a discussion of gender in childhood.

Instructors might also encourage students to become involved with diversity issues in the wider community. They might facilitate a read-aloud of poems and narratives in class and then on campus. They can encourage students to attend diversity-related events on campus or in the community; they can ask students to monitor the local press and campus newspaper for coverage of diversity issues and include a short time at the start of class when news or current events are addressed briefly.

A basic tactic is to supplement the textbook with outside readings on the lives and experiences of diverse women, and a growing number of multicultural anthologies are available from which to choose (e.g., Baca Zinn et al., 2000; Ballentine & Inclan, 1995; Disch, 2000; Kirk & Okazawa-Rey, 1998). We have recently adopted a new approach to class readings, assigning four or five texts, some of which are single-author textbooks and some of which are anthologies. We encourage students to buy at least two of them and to work with another student who owns a different set. We assign readings from all the texts and try to incorporate references to many of the readings in our lectures and discussions. It generally does not matter which set of readings a student has done, as long as he or she has read something on the topic. We find that students tend to take more responsibility for their education when we allow them to select readings that appeal to them and to pursue a topic of interest more intently by reading about it in several texts. Finally, this approach incorporates the understanding that there is not a single correct perspective on a topic, but a variety of ways of viewing it (McHugh & Cosgrove, 2002).

Another approach we have found useful is to expose students more directly to the perspectives and life experiences of women from groups other than their own. In addition to having students read narratives of women who are different from them, instructors can invite guest presenters from underrepresented groups, or they can show films or videos about the lives of women from different backgrounds, such as 5 Girls (Finitzo, 2001). In our experience, focusing on any form of diversity can open the discussion and help nonmajority students feel comfortable. Covering groups other than African Americans, such as Jews or immigrants, sometimes helps African Americans to feel more comfortable in the class. For example, we have used Krause's (1985) *Grandmothers, Mothers, and Daughters*, which presents interviews with three generations of ethnic immigrant women from Pittsburgh.

CONCLUSION

In this chapter, we have endorsed the inclusion of research and narratives about groups of women who were previously invisible or silenced in the Psychology of Women. We see this approach as a temporary phase on the way to transformation of the field. A fully inclusive psychology of women will require not only the acquisition of more data on diverse groups but also the coverage of new topics and the investigation of new questions; most important, it will require a transformation in conceptualizing and doing research that recognizes culture, ethnicity, class, and other aspects of diversity as part of the context of women's lives. Baca Zinn et al. (2000) suggested seeing gender through the prism of difference; they called for a theoretical analysis that "emphasizes differences and inequalities not as discrete areas of separation, but as interrelated bands of color that together make up a spectrum" (p. 7). In our work, we hope to contribute to the transformation of psychology, to generate new knowledge and understanding of the experiences of women, and to ensure that the newest ideas and approaches are shared with our students in a fully inclusive Psychology of Women course.

REFERENCES

Allison, D. (1994). *Skin: Talking about sex, class, and literature*. Ithaca, NY: Firebrand Books.

Baca Zinn, M. B., & Dill, B. T. (2000). Theorizing differences from multiracial feminism. In M. B. Baca Zinn, P. Hondagneu-Sotelo, & M. A. Messner (Eds.), *Through the prism of difference: Readings on sex and gender* (pp. 23–30). Needham Heights, MA: Allyn & Bacon.

Baca Zinn, M. B., Hondagneu-Sotelo, P., & Messner, M. A. (2000). Introduction: Sex and gender through the prism of difference. In M. B. Baca Zinn, P. Hondagneu-Sotelo, & M. A. Messner (Eds.), *Through the prism of difference: Readings on sex and gender* (pp. 1–12). Needham Heights, MA: Allyn & Bacon.

Baker, N. L. (1996). Class as a construct in a classless society. *Women & Therapy, 18*(3–4), 13–23.

Ballentine, S. F., & Inclan, J. B. (1995). *Diverse voices of women*. Mountain View, CA: Mayfield.

Bohan, J. (1993). Regarding gender: Essentialism, constructionism and feminist psychology. *Psychology of Women Quarterly, 17*, 5–21.

Brown, A., Goodwin, B. J., Hall, B. A., & Jackson-Lowman, H. (1985). A review of psychology of women textbooks: Focus on the Afro-American woman. *Psychology of Women Quarterly, 9*, 29–38.

Brown, L. S., & Rothblum, E. D. (Eds.). (1989). *Overcoming fear of fat*. Binghamton, NY: Harrington Park Press.

Butler, S. (Producer and Director). (1998). *The way home* [Videotape]. Oakland, CA: World Trust.

Cantow, R. (Producer and Director). (1981). *Clothesline* [Videotape]. Minneapolis, MN: New Front Programming Services.

Cohen, R. M. (1998). Class consciousness and its consequences: The impact of an elite education on mature working class women. *American Educational Research Journal, 35,* 353–376.

Coleman, L. (Director). (2000). *Margaret Cho—I'm the one that I want* [DVD]. Fox Lorber.

Collins, P. H. (1990). *Black feminist thought: Knowledge, consciousness, and the politics of empowerment.* New York: Routledge.

Comas-Díaz, L. (1991). Feminism and diversity in psychology: The case of women of color. *Psychology of Women Quarterly, 15,* 597–609.

Crawford, M., & Unger, R. (2000). *Women and gender: A feminist psychology* (3rd ed.). New York: McGraw-Hill.

Cutrona, C. E., Russell, D. W., Hessling, R. M., Brown, P. A., & Murry, V. (2000). Direct and moderating effects of community context on the psychological well-being of African American women. *Journal of Personality and Social Psychology, 79,* 1088–1101.

Disch, E. (2000). *Reconstructing gender: A multicultural anthology* (2nd ed.). Mountain View, CA: Mayfield.

Donelson, F. E. (1999). *Women's experiences: A psychological perspective.* Mountain View, CA: Mayfield.

Espín, O. M. (1997). *Latina realities: Essays on healing, migration, and sexuality.* Boulder, CO: Westview Press.

Fine, M. (1985). Reflections on a feminist psychology of women. *Psychology of Women Quarterly, 9,* 167–173.

Finitzo, M. (Producer and Director). (2001). *5 girls.* [Videotape]. Chicago: Kartemquin Educational Films.

Franzblau. S. (1991, March). *Struggling against women's oppression: The need for a working class analysis.* Paper presented at the annual meeting of the Association for Women in Psychology, New Haven, CT.

Giddings, P. (1984). *When and where I enter: The impact of Black women on race and sex in America.* New York: Morrow.

Goodwin, B. J., Brown, A. B., & Jackson-Lowman, H. (1989, April). *A review of psychology of women textbooks from 1979–89: Focus on African American women.* Paper presented at the annual meeting of the Mid-Atlantic Region National Women's Studies Association, East Stroudsburg, PA.

Goodwin, B. J., & Delazar, M. E. (2000, March). *A review of psychology of women textbooks: Focus on African American women.* Paper presented at the annual meeting of the Association for Women in Psychology, Salt Lake City, UT.

Graham, S. (1992). Most of the subjects were white and middle class: Trends in published research on African Americans in selected APA journals, 1970–1989. *American Psychologist, 47,* 629–639.

Hare-Mustin, R. T., & Marecek, J. (Eds.). (1990). *Making a difference: Psychology and the construction of gender*. New Haven, CT: Yale University Press.

hooks, b. (1992). *Black looks: Race and representation*. Boston: South End Press.

hooks, b. (1994). *Teaching to transgress: Education as the practice of freedom*. New York: Routledge.

hooks, b. (2000). *Where we stand: Class matters*. New York: Routledge.

Hyde, J. S., Matlin, M. W., & Walsh, M. R. (1990, August). Teaching the psychology of women. Pre-conference workshop presented at the 98th Annual Convention of the American Psychological Association, Boston, MA.

Kimball, M. M. (1995). *Double visions: Feminist visions of gender similarities and differences*. Binghamton, NY: Harrington Park Press.

Kirk, G., & Okazawa-Rey, M. (Eds.). (1998). *Women's lives: Multicultural perspectives*. Mountain View, CA: Mayfield.

Krause, C. A. (1985). *Grandmothers, mothers, and daughters: Oral histories of three generations of ethnic-American women*. Boston: Twayne.

Lachman, M. E., & Weaver, S. (1998). The sense of control as a moderator of social class in health and well being. *Journal of Personality and Social Psychology, 74*, 763–773.

Landrine, H. (Ed.). (1995). *Bringing cultural diversity to feminist psychology: Theory, research and practice*. Washington, DC: American Psychological Association.

LePage-Lees, P. (1997). Struggling with a nontraditional past: Academically successful women from disadvantaged backgrounds discuss their relationship with "disadvantage." *Psychology of Women Quarterly, 21*, 365–385.

Lorde, A. (2000). There is no hierarchy of oppressions. In V. Cyrus (Ed.), *Experiencing race, class, and gender in the United States* (3rd ed., pp. 302–303). Mountain View: CA: Mayfield.

Lott, B. (1987). *Women's lives: Themes and variations in gender learning*. Belmont, CA: Brooks/Cole.

Lott, B. (2000). Global connections: The significance of women's poverty. In J. C. Chrisler, C. Golden, & P. D. Rozee (Eds.), *Lectures on the psychology of women* (2nd ed., pp. 17–27). New York: McGraw-Hill.

Lott, B., & Bullock, H. E. (Eds.). (2001). Listening to the voices of poor women [Special issue]. *Journal of Social Issues, 57*(2).

Mahony, P., & Zmroczek, C. (Eds.). (1997). *Class matters: "Working-class" women's perspectives on social class*. New York: Taylor & Francis.

McGee, D. (Director), & Hubert, N. (Producer). (1992). *Toward intimacy* [videotape]. New York: Filmakers Library.

McHugh, M. C., & Cosgrove, L. (2002). Gendered subjects in psychology: Dialectic and satirical perspectives. In M. Dunlap, L. Collins, & J. Chrisler (Eds.), *Charting a new course for feminist psychology* (pp. 3–19). New York: Praeger.

McHugh, M. C., & Goodwin, B. J. (1991, March). *Who is the woman in the psychology of women?* Paper presented at the annual meeting of the Association for Women in Psychology, Hartford, CT.

McHugh, M. C., Koeske, R. D., & Frieze, I. H. (1986). Issues to consider in conducting nonsexist psychological research: A guide for researchers. *American Psychologist, 41*, 879–890.

Orza, A., & Torrey, J. W. (1995). Teaching the psychology of women. In J. C. Chrisler & A. H. Helmstreet (Eds.), *Variations on a theme: Diversity and the psychology of women* (pp. 201–226). Albany: State University of New York Press.

Packer, J. (1989). The role of stigmatization in fat people's avoidance of physical exercise. In L. S. Brown & E. D. Rothblum (Eds.), *Overcoming fear of fat* (pp. 52–65). Binghamton, NY: Harrington Park Press.

Palmer, P. (1996). Pain and possibilities: What therapists need to know about working class women's issues. *Feminism & Psychology, 6*, 457–462.

Raey, D. (1997). The double bind of the working class feminist academic: The success of failure or the failure of success. In P. Mahony & C. Zmroczek (Eds.), *Class matters: "Working-class" women's perspectives on social class* (pp. 18–29). New York: Taylor & Francis.

Reid, P. T. (1993). Poor women in psychological research: Shut up and shut out. *Psychology of Women Quarterly, 17*, 133–150.

Reid, P. T., & Kelly, E. (1994). Research on women of color: From ignorance to awareness. *Psychology of Women Quarterly, 18*, 477–486.

Rhode, D. L. (Ed.). (1990). *Theoretical perspectives on sexual difference.* Binghamton, NY: Vail-Ballou Press.

Rich, A. (1979). *On lies, secrets and silence: Selected prose: 1966–1978.* New York: Norton.

Saris, R. N., & Johnston-Robledo, I. (2000). Poor women are still shut out of mainstream psychology. *Psychology of Women Quarterly, 24*, 233–235.

Schoenfielder, L., & Weiser, B. (Eds.). (1983). *Shadow on a tightrope: Writings by women on fat oppression.* San Francisco: Aunt Lute Books.

Sherif, C. W. (1979). Bias in psychology. In J. A. Sherman & E. T. Beck (Eds.), *The prisms of sex: Essays in the sociology of knowledge* (pp. 93–133). Madison: University of Wisconsin Press.

Strom, L. (1994). Reclaiming our working class identities: Teaching class studies in a blue collar community. In N. Porter (Ed.), *Women's studies quarterly* (pp. 131–141). New York: Feminist Press.

Stunkard, A. J. (1976). *The pain of obesity.* Palo Alto, CA: Bull.

Touster, L. O. (2000). *Fat oppression: The complicity of psychology.* Unpublished doctoral dissertation, Indiana University of Pennsylvania.

Villarosa, L. (Ed.). (1994). *Body & soul: The Black women's guide to physical health and emotional well-being.* New York: Harper Perennial.

Wadden, T. A., & Stunkard, A. J. (1993). Psychosocial consequences of obesity and dieting: Research and clinical findings. In A. Stunkard & T. A. Wadden (Eds.), *Obesity theory and therapy* (pp. 163–177). New York: Raven Press.

Wade, T. J. (1996). The relationship between skin color and self-perceived global, physical, and sexual attractiveness, and self-esteem for African Americans. *Journal of Black Psychology, 22*, 358–373.

Wade-Gayles, G. (1995). *My soul is a witness: African-American women's spirituality.* Boston: Beacon Press.

Wann, M. (1998). *FAT!SO?* Berkeley, CA: Ten Speed Press.

West, C. M. (2000). Developing an "oppositional gaze" toward the images of Black women. In J. C. Chrisler, C. Golden, & P. D. Rozee (Eds.), *Lectures on the psychology of women* (2nd ed., pp. 221–233). New York: McGraw-Hill.

Williams, M. K., McCandies, T., & Dunlap, M. R. (2002). Women of color and feminist psychology: Moving from criticism and critique to integration and application. In L. H. Collins, M. R. Dunlap, & J. C. Chrisler (Eds). *Charting a new course for feminist psychology* (pp. 65–89). Westport, CT: Praeger.

Young, L. M., & Powell, B. (1985). The effects of obesity on the clinical judgments of mental health professionals. *Journal of Health and Social Behavior, 26,* 233–246.

Zandy, J. (Ed.). (1990). *Calling home: Working class women's writing.* New Brunswick, NJ: Rutgers University Press.

Zandy, J. (2001). *What we hold in common: An introduction to working-class studies.* New York: Feminist Press.

II

GENDER, ETHNIC, AND SOCIOCULTURAL PERSPECTIVES: SPECIALIZED COURSES AND CONTENT AREAS

11

TEACHING ABOUT CULTURE, ETHNICITY, AND MENTAL HEALTH

NNAMDI POLE, JENNIFER J. TREUTING, AND ROBERT W. LEVENSON

In this chapter we describe and evaluate the Berkeley Culture, Ethnicity, and Mental Health (CEMH) Project, a graduate student initiated effort to increase pluralistic thinking, train culturally responsive psychologists, recruit excellent scholars of color for future faculty positions, and provide role models and mentorship for Berkeley's ethnic minority students. The idea grew out of a series of regular meetings between a few minority graduate students (Juanita Dimas, Sybil Madison, and Joe Harris) and the director of the Clinical Psychology Program at the University of California, Berkeley (Robert W. Levenson). These meetings were devoted to examining ways that the Clinical Psychology Program could better meet the needs of students of color. As a result of these meetings, Dr. Levenson and this core group of graduate students enlisted the help of four additional graduate students of color (Nnamdi Pole, Jeanne Tsai, Teron Park, and Richard Renfro) and formed a steering committee to plan the CEMH Project in the fall of 1993.

A draft of this chapter received first prize in the 1996 American Psychological Association Division 29 Student of Color Paper Competition, awarded to Nnamdi Pole and Jennifer J. Treuting.

The steering committee conceived and implemented a comprehensive educational package made up of four interwoven modules: (a) a graduate seminar, (b) two undergraduate discussion sections, (c) a colloquium series, and (d) five colloquium-linked professional development dinners, all of which ran in parallel over the course of one semester.[1] These components addressed issues relevant to the mental health of Asian Americans, African Americans, American Indians, and Latinos and featured presentations by some of the most eminent scholars in the area of minority mental health.[2] The curriculum was organized around five content areas: (a) history of the field, (b) research, (c) intervention, (d) assessment, and (e) training.[3]

In this chapter, we describe the project from the perspective of the students who participated in it, based on anonymous, narrative evaluations that were obtained at regular intervals throughout by Nnamdi Pole and Jennifer J. Treuting, a European American graduate student participant. These comments are reproduced here with permission. One advantage of obtaining feedback multiple times over the semester rather than only at the usual end-of-semester evaluation is that we were able to capture the participants' emotional reactions as they unfolded over time. In fact, we found that reactions changed dramatically over the course of the semester, which provides an important lesson for those who may wish to implement such a course in their own academic setting. Initial negative reactions to this emotionally charged material may not necessarily predict how the students will feel about such a course in retrospect.

GRADUATE SEMINAR

Like many others, the Berkeley psychology department lacked a full-time, in-house faculty member with an active program of scholarly work in minority mental health. This was particularly ironic because of Berkeley's strong tradition of recruiting of graduate students of color and a history that

---

[1]Although a very similar project was initiated in our department by Professor Stephen Glickman and a group of graduate students almost a decade earlier (Abernethy et al., 1988), amazingly, the present project was designed without any knowledge of the previous course.

[2]Six noted ethnocultural scholars were featured: Stanley Sue (University of California, Los Angeles), Claude Steele (Stanford University), Maribel Taussig (University of Southern California), Eduardo Duran (Family and Child Guidance Center, Oakland, CA), Sergio Aguilar-Gaxiola (California State University, Fresno), and Joe White (University of California, Irvine).

[3]We acknowledge the generous financial support of the following funding sources at the University of California at Berkeley: Department of Psychology ($5,000), Graduate Division ($2,500), Instructional Mini-Grant from the Office of Educational Development ($1,000), the Affirmative Action Office ($2,000), and the Wright Institute ($1,000). The project cost $11,500 during the first semester. These monies paid for airfare, lodging, and honoraria for the various scholars; professional development dinners; salary for the graduate course lecturer; and course development expenses for the undergraduate seminars.

included having one of the first training grants from the National Institute of Mental Health devoted to minority mental health. One of the first tasks of the steering committee was to search for an outside instructor who had experience teaching such a course, familiarity with the relevant literature, and dedication to the overall mission of the project. They were delighted to find Dr. Veronique Thompson, who agreed not only to teach the graduate seminar but also to design one that covered the five content areas, complemented the colloquium series, and provided a safe context in which to explore feelings arising from the course material. Her seminar was a 3-hr, once-weekly class. On the days when visiting scholars were on campus, their colloquium presentations were substituted for the first half of the graduate seminar. Twenty-one graduate students enrolled in the seminar, representing all years of the clinical graduate program, both genders, and several ethnic backgrounds: African Americans (21%), Asian Americans (21%), Latinos (16%), and European Americans (42%).

The first meeting of the seminar was devoted to providing an overview of the course and defining basic terms in ethnocultural psychology (e.g., *third world psychology*, *people of color*, *multiculturalism*, and *pluralism*). Almost immediately, this material met with a palpable resistance. Many of the minority students vigorously challenged the instructor's use of these terms. The European American students, although notably silent, were nonetheless emotionally stirred by the discussion as evidenced by their feedback (obtained shortly after the first class):

- "I felt frustrated and annoyed . . . the climate was hostile (the assumption was that one should know the terminology and that ignorance was politically incorrect)."
- "I wanted to walk out."
- "I felt as though my opinions and comments were less valued because I am not of color—I felt threatened and contemplated dropping the course."
- "I felt frustrated at the focus on terminology—I felt as if White students didn't have a valued place in the discussion."

The first class meeting was perhaps best summarized by one student: "It is going to be more complicated than I thought."

During the next several weeks, the graduate students participated in an exercise designed to encourage exploration of how race and culture had influenced their senses of identity. With all students gathered in a large group, the instructor raised a series of questions about ethnocultural heritage. The first order of business was for the students to "define themselves ethnoculturally." The students were challenged by the complexity of trying to agree on the scope of the terms *ethnicity* and *culture*. Did gender or sexual orientation belong in this discussion? Did subcultures within the larger European American culture (e.g., Irish, Jewish) count? The actual variety of cultural and ethnic identities presented far exceeded what one might have guessed from a cursory glance around the room. It became readily apparent that although these issues were seldom explicitly discussed, they were of central importance to each person's sense of self.

The exercise continued in small groups, usually four or five students, exploring even more personal issues and addressing questions such as the following (Boyd-Franklin, 1989; Massachusetts School of Professional Psychology, 1991; Thompson, 1994):

- Who in your family influenced your sense of ethnic identity?
- What characteristics of your ethnic group(s) do you like best and least?
- How are gender roles defined in your culture?
- What are the dominant religions of the culture?
- What role do religion and spirituality play in the everyday lives of the members of the culture?
- Describe a time in your life where you felt different from others and where this difference led you to feel excluded.
- When you were growing up, how many racial, ethnic, and religious groups were represented in your neighborhood and school?
- Which group(s) did your friends and your family's friends come from?
- How old were you when you first got to know someone of a different racial or ethnic background than your own? Who was/were the person(s) in your life? How did she/he/they fit as well as challenge any stereotypes you had learned?
- As a child and adolescent, how were you encouraged to or discouraged from playing or socializing with or dating people from different backgrounds (race, ethnicity, religion, class, etc.)?
- What ethnic group(s), other than your own, do you think that you understand best?
- What cultural group(s) do you think you will have the easiest and most difficult time working with clinically?
- What issues divide members within your ethnic group?
- What incorrect assumptions do people make about your group?
- If you were about to leave this country forever, what object, symbolic of your cultural identity, would you take with you to a new homeland?

Discussions were sometimes touching and fairly revealing, at other times comical, and for many people, one of the most personally significant experiences of the course, as evidenced by retrospective accounts given at the end of the semester:

- "These were the best classes. They made the entire class worthwhile.
- "It was very useful and succeeded in removing more of the tension previously present."

By the time this group process exercise was over, the tone of the class had shifted from being uncomfortably heavy and tense to feeling cautiously safe. Having gotten over a major initial struggle, students appeared more enthusiastic and more trusting. When asked during midsemester how their feelings had changed, many students mentioned the change in atmosphere.

As the weeks passed, the class time shifted from experiential to didactic work. Dr. Thompson began each class with a brief lecture before leading the students in lively discussions of the assigned readings. The students read articles on ethnic minority perspectives on research (e.g., Betancourt & Lopez, 1993; S. Sue, Ito, & Bradshaw, 1982), assessment (e.g., Dana, 1993; Lopez & Hernandez, 1986; Okazaki & Sue, 1995; Westermeyer, 1987), intervention (e.g., Atkinson, Casas, & Abreu, 1992; Greene, 1985; Homma-True, Greene, Lopez, & Trimble, 1993), and training (e.g., Brown, 1993; Mio & Morris, 1990; D. W. Sue, 1991; see the Appendix for complete list of topics and readings). As a result of these readings and discussions, the importance of achieving multicultural competence became more apparent. Students also began to understand one reason that these issues are so often neglected in the academic setting: This is difficult work! In casual conversations on leaving class, students often described how the seeming intractability of these issues left them feeling emotionally drained and professionally challenged.

COLLOQUIUM SERIES

Because the colloquium series was designed to be the backbone of the CEMH Project, the steering committee went to great lengths to ensure that it was treated as a special event by (a) inviting undergraduate participants to what was typically a graduate student and faculty event (thereby increasing the enthusiasm level and audience size); (b) videotaping each talk (thereby emphasizing the rareness of this opportunity); and (c) assigning a steering committee member to invite the speaker, organize travel logistics, and serve as the local host and introduce the speaker (thereby highlighting the prominent role played by the graduate students in the CEMH Project). Speakers were selected on the basis of their expertise in at least one of our five major content areas and their membership in one of our four targeted minority groups. Each speaker delivered a 60-min colloquium presentation followed by a 30-min question-and-answer period. After a short break, the graduate seminar students had an additional hour of discussion with the speaker in a small-group format.

The talks taught several key lessons, including the following:

- challenging the application of traditional psychiatric diagnoses and treatments to members of ethnic minority groups, especially when their apparent symptoms are better explained by racism, discrimination, or stereotyping—as in diagnosing "depression" when the appropriate diagnosis is "oppression" (e.g., Duran, 1990);
- identifying barriers to the delivery of mental health services to ethnic minority clients, such as inadequate cultural sensitivity of services offered to Chinese Americans (S. Sue & Zane, 1987);
- inspiring students to conduct research on politically controversial yet socially important topics, such as the effects of stereotyping and stereotype threat on the performance of women and African Americans (e.g., Steele & Aronson, 1995);
- understanding the importance of considering language match in the assessment of populations for whom English is not the primary language (Taussig, Mack, & Henderson, 1996; Vega, Kolody, Aguilar-Gaxiola, & Alderete, 1998); and
- considering the influence of Black enslavement on the current mental health status of African Americans (White, 1991).

Students responded favorably to every speaker, although there were tense moments. For example, fresh from the painful discussions of the first week, some students objected to a speaker's exclusion of European Americans as "ethnic." He gently explained that there were "no perfect terms," which not only satisfied the students but also helped relieve some of the tensions from the previous discussion. The speakers also contributed greatly to the important goal of providing multicultural role models. Students came to recognize that they could learn much from presenters who differed in ethnicity, gender, presentation style, professional background, and areas of interest.

Feedback from the students about the presenters was consistently favorable:

- "I was impressed by his ability to address a very charged issue without alienating anyone or seeming angry."
- "I could only dream of touching people the way he touched me."
- "[The speaker] seemed too angry initially. However, I found

him extremely inspirational and honest . . . . He challenged us to think in non-traditional ways."

UNDERGRADUATE DISCUSSION SECTIONS

As mentioned earlier, undergraduates were an integral part of the project. Twenty-one students were selected by members of the steering committee from a large group of applicants, with the following resulting ethnic breakdown: African Americans (5%), Asian Americans (37%), Latinos (37%), and European Americans (11%). The remaining 10% defined themselves in complex multiracial ways. The undergraduate students were assigned to one of two discussion sections that were taught by pairs of graduate students who were concurrently taking the graduate seminar. The discussion sections were conducted as process groups, devoted to exploring personal feelings related to race and racism. They also served as a place to clarify questions raised in the colloquium talks. Before attending the colloquium talks, the undergraduates read articles by each speaker (e.g., Duran, 1990; Steele & Aronson, 1995; S. Sue, 1983) and prepared questions based on their readings for both seminar and postcolloquium discussions.

Whereas the story of the graduate course was complex, the story of the undergraduate seminars was one of unqualified success. They seemed to bypass the growing pains that the graduate students went through, perhaps because these sections were composed almost entirely of students of color. The general feeling was that "we're all in this together," and the students reported that everyone involved seemed to feel safe. These were typical undergraduate reactions to the project:

> I can unhesitatingly say that the class gave me what all classes should give their students. By this I mean that the class provided intellectual stimulation that will last beyond my time in school. The issues discussed challenged and expanded how I view the world. Not only did I learn from some great speakers, but also from my fellow students in discussions where everyone had something valuable to contribute.
>
> It was one of the most interesting and invigorating classes that I have ever taken . . . the course has affected me so much that I wish to pursue something like this as a career.

PROFESSIONAL DEVELOPMENT DINNERS

Graduate and undergraduate students who wished to have further contact with and mentoring from the guest speakers attended professional development dinners in which more personal questions about career paths and ethnoculturally related obstacles were discussed. Speakers talked about the compromises they had made, the fears they had experienced, and the race-related challenges they had faced and continue to face. In addition, speakers gave invaluable advice to students about pursuing lives as clinical psychologists and offered predictions about what was to come in the next decade of work on culture, ethnicity, and mental health.

FINAL EVALUATIONS OF THE PROJECT

In addition to gathering the narrative accounts that have been excerpted here, we had both the graduate and undergraduate participants provide overall quantitative ratings of the three modules at the end of the project. Evaluations were made on a scale that ranged from 1 (very poor) to 7 (excellent). The graduate seminar received an average rating of 6.1, the colloquium series received an average rating of 6.6, and the undergraduate section received an average rating of 6.9. Seminars at Berkeley typically receive ratings closer to 5.5.

We were delighted by this positive response to the CEMH Project. We believe that the project made good progress toward the goals of increasing pluralistic thinking in psychological work, training culturally responsive psychologists, and exposing the department to first-rate ethnocultural clinicians and scholars. Overall, it was an important first step in the enormous task of preparing psychologists for an increasingly multicultural society in the 21st century. Thanks to funding from the university, the project has continued for two more iterations over the past 6 years.[4] Overall, it has had a lasting legacy. The empowerment that has resulted for students of color in the clinical graduate program has been palpable, and it has spilled over to include the European American graduate students as well.

It is clear, however, that there is more work to be done. For the faculty, it became increasingly apparent that even although many of them conduct research and teaching in which cultural variation plays an important role, this is not the same as having a colleague whose central focus is on issues related to minority status and minority mental health. The dialogue stimulated by the CEMH Project clarified for many the importance of having more

---

[4]A number of individuals deserve credit for securing funding for the additional trials of the project, including Chang-Lin Tien (former Chancellor), William Simmons (former Dean of Social Sciences), Sheldon Zedeck (former Chair of the Psychology Department), Bob Levenson (former Chair of the clinical area), and Nnamdi Pole (former graduate student in the clinical area). However, special thanks are extended to Anatasia Seung-Shin Kim (current doctoral candidate in clinical psychology at the University of California, Los Angeles), who at the time was a graduating senior at Berkeley and participant in the undergraduate seminar. Anastasia tried for months to seek audience with the Chancellor to request additional financial support for the course but could not get an appointment. Eventually, she posed as a freshman and participated in convocation exercises to get the Chancellor's attention. It was this action that led to our initial negotiations with the Chancellor for additional funding.

ethnic minority faculty. Unfortunately, this realization came simultaneously with changing policies in California against affirmative action, and progress in this particular area has been slow.

On a more positive note, in the years since this project was initiated, the topics of culture and minority status have become increasingly interwoven into the discourse of the Berkeley psychology department as a whole and of the clinical area in particular. Culture has played a major role in a colloquium series in either the clinical or the social–personality area almost every year for the past five years. The Institute for Personality and Social Research declared culture as one of its focal areas of interest, and recently sponsored a training grant proposal to the National Institute of Mental Health devoted to fostering research on the bidirectional influences between culture and psychological processes. A number of departmental faculty have sought and obtained extramural research funding for projects in which culture plays a central role. The clinical interns also recently dedicated a series of their case conference meetings to cultural competency training. They began with the evocative documentary *The Color of Fear* (Wah, 1994) and continued with a process-oriented workshop led by an outside facilitator. As expected, the process was powerful and at times quite difficult. Not surprisingly, however, the students reported that the experience was invaluable in fostering their growth as clinicians.

We have articulated a model for giving culture and ethnicity a central voice in mental health training that we believe is transportable to other university departments that do not have the resources "in house" to do justice to these issues. Both hardships and rewards accompany such an undertaking. Despite the challenges, the endeavor has been well worth the effort. In the continuing striving to institutionalize ethnocultural scholarship in our department, the first priority is to advocate for the hiring of a faculty member with a primary interest in studying ethnic minority issues. Eventually, this person will teach the graduate and undergraduate courses related to these issues. The second priority is to push for an integration of an ethnocultural perspective into our core curriculum. When this goal is reached, special funding for the kind of grassroots effort described here will no longer be necessary.

APPENDIX

Course Topics and Readings

I. *Culture, Ethnicity and Mental Health: An Overview of the Issues:* No assigned readings.

II. *Ethnocultural Development: The Psychologist's Use of Self:* Boyd-Franklin (1989, pp. 95–120); Matsumoto, Kitayama, and Markus (1994); Tatum (1992); Yamato (1992).

III. *Ethnocultural Issues and Psychological Research:* Betancourt and Lopez (1993), Mio and Iwamasa (1993), S. Sue et al. (1982).

IV. *Ethnocultural Issues and Psychological Assessment:* Dana (1993, pp. 110–139); Jones and Thorne (1987); Lopez and Hernandez (1986); Pavkov, Lewis, and Lyons (1989); Westermeyer (1987).

V. *Ethnocultural Issues and Psychological Intervention:* Atkinson et al. (1992); Greene (1985); Homma-True et al. (1993); La Fromboise and Dixon (1981); Rogler, Malgady, Costantino, and Blumenthal (1987); Trimble (1991); Tsui and Schultz (1985); Zane, Sue, Hu, and Kwon (1991).

VI. *Ethnocultural Issues & Psychological Education/Training:* Brown (1993); Davis-Russell, Bascuas, Duran, and Forbes (1991); Mio and Morris (1990); Stricker (1993); D. W. Sue (1991).

VII. *Closing: Future Steps and Celebrating Ethnocultural Diversity:* Matsumoto (1994).

REFERENCES

Abernethy, A. D., Cowan, P. A., Gurza, R., Huang, K. H., Kim, N. A. Y., King, N., et al. (1988). Psychology tomorrow: A unified ethnic psychology course. In P. Bronstein & K. Quina (Eds.), *Teaching a psychology of people: Resources for gender and sociocultural awareness* (pp. 115–119). Washington, DC: American Psychological Association.

Atkinson, D. R., Casas, A., & Abreu, J. (1992). Mexican-American acculturation, counselor ethnicity, cultural sensitivity, and perceived counselor competence. *Journal of Counseling Psychology, 39*, 515–520.

Betancourt, H., & Lopez, S. (1993). The study of culture, ethnicity, and race in American psychology. *American Psychologist, 48*, 629–637.

Boyd-Franklin, N. (1989). *Black families in therapy: A multisystems approach.* New York: Guilford Press.

Brown, L. (1993). Antidomination training as a central component of diversity in clinical psychology education. *The Clinical Psychologist, 46*, 83–87.

Dana, R. H. (1993). *Multicultural perspectives for professional psychology.* Boston: Allyn & Bacon.

Davis-Russell, E., Bascuas, J., Duran, E., & Forbes, W. T. (1991). Ethnic diversity and the core curriculum. In R. L. Peterson, J. D. McHolland, R. J. Bent, E. Davis-Russell, G. E. Edwall, K. Polite, et al. (Eds.), *The core curriculum in professional psychology* (pp. 126–137). Washington, DC: American Psychological Association.

Duran, E. (1990). *Transforming the soul wound: A theoretical/clinical approach to American Indian psychology.* Berkeley, CA: Folklore Institute.

Greene, B. A. (1985). Considerations in the treatment of Black patients by White therapists. *Psychotherapy, 22*, 389–392.

Homma-True, R., Greene B., Lopez, S., & Trimble, J. E. (1993). Ethnocultural diversity in clinical psychology. *The Clinical Psychologist, 46*, 50–63.

Jones, E. E., & Thorne, A. (1987). Rediscovery of the subject: Intercultural approaches to clinical assessment. *Journal of Consulting and Clinical Psychology, 55*, 488–495.

La Fromboise, T. D., & Dixon, D. N. (1981). American Indian perception of trustworthiness in a counseling interview. *Journal of Counseling Psychology, 28*, 135–139.

Lopez, S., & Hernandez, P. (1986). How culture is considered in evaluations of psychopathology. *Journal of Nervous and Mental Disease, 176*, 598–606.

Massachusetts School of Professional Psychology. (1991). *Prework questionnaire for student cultural diversity meeting.* Unpublished survey.

Matsumoto, D. (1994). Conclusion. In D. Matsumoto (Ed.), *People: Psychology from a cultural perspective* (pp. 175–180). Pacific Grove, CA: Brooks/Cole.

Matsumoto, D., Kitayama, S., & Markus, H. R. (1994). Culture and self: How cultures influence the way we view ourselves. In D. Matsumoto (Ed.), *People:*

Psychology from a cultural perspective (pp. 17–37). Pacific Grove, CA: Brooks/ Cole.

Mio, J. S., & Iwamasa, G. (1993). To do, or not to do: That is the question for White cross-cultural researchers. *The Counseling Psychologist, 21,* 197–212.

Mio, J. S., & Morris D. R. (1990). Cross-cultural issues in psychology training programs: An invitation for discussion. *Professional Psychology: Research and Practice, 21,* 434–441.

Okazaki, S., & Sue, S. (1995). Methodological issues in assessment research with ethnic minorities. *Psychological Assessment, 7,* 367–375.

Pavkov, T. W., Lewis, D. A., & Lyons, J. S. (1989). Psychiatric diagnoses and racial bias: An empirical investigation. *Professional Psychology: Research and Practice, 20,* 364–368.

Rogler, L. H., Malgady, R. G., Costantino, G., & Blumenthal, R. (1987). What do culturally sensitive mental health services mean? The case of Hispanics. *American Psychologist, 42,* 565–570.

Steele, C. M., & Aronson, J. (1995). Stereotype threat and the intellectual test performance of African Americans. *Journal of Personality and Social Psychology, 69,* 797–811.

Stricker, G. (1993). Diversity in clinical psychology. *The Clinical Psychologist, 46,* 88–89.

Sue, D. W. (1991). A model for cultural diversity training. *Journal of Counseling and Development, 70,* 99–105.

Sue, S. (1983). Ethnic minority issues in psychology: A reexamination. *American Psychologist, 38,* 583–592.

Sue, S., Ito, J., & Bradshaw, C. (1982). Ethnic minority research trends and directions. In E. E. Jones & S. J. Korchin (Eds.), *Minority mental health* (pp. 37–58). New York: Praeger.

Sue, S., & Zane, N. (1987). The role of culture and cultural techniques in psychotherapy: A critique and reformulation. *American Psychologist, 42,* 37–45.

Tatum, B. D. (1992). Talking about race, learning about racism: The application of racial identity developmental theory in the classroom. *Harvard Educational Review, 62,* 1–23.

Taussig, I. M., Mack, W. J., & Henderson, V. W. (1996). Concurrent validity of Spanish-language versions of the Mini-Mental State Examination, Mental Status Questionnaire, Information–Memory–Concentration Test, and Orientation–Memory–Concentration Test. *Journal of the International Neuropsychological Society, 2,* 286–298.

Thompson, V. (1994). *Sociocultural issues in psychology.* Berkeley, CA: Wright Institute.

Trimble, J. E. (1991). *The mental health service and training needs of American Indians: Ethnic minority perspectives on clinical training and services in psychology.* Washington, DC: American Psychological Association.

Tsui, P., & Schultz, G. L. (1985). Failure of rapport: Why psychotherapeutic engagement fails in the treatment of Asian clients. *American Journal of Orthopsychiatry*, *55*, 561–569.

Vega, W. A., Kolody, B., Aguilar-Gaxiola, S., & Alderete, E. (1998). Lifetime prevalence of *DSM–III–R* psychiatric disorders among urban and rural Mexican Americans in California. *Archives of General Psychiatry*, *55*, 771–778.

Wah, L. M. (Director and Producer). (1994). *The color of fear* [Videotape]. Oakland, CA: Stir-Fry Productions.

Westermeyer, J. (1987). Cultural factors in clinical assessment. *Journal of Consulting and Clinical Psychology*, *55*, 471–478.

White, J. L. (1991). Toward a Black psychology. In R. L. Jones (Ed.), *Black psychology* (3rd ed., pp. 5–13). Berkeley, CA: Cobb & Henry.

Yamato, J. (1992). Something about the subject makes it hard to name. In P. S. Rothenberg (Ed.), *Race, class, and gender in the United States: An integrated study* (2nd ed., pp. 58–62). New York: St. Martin's Press.

Zane, N. W. S., Sue, S., Hu, L., & Kwon, J. (1991). Asian American assertion: A social learning analysis of cultural differences. *Journal of Counseling Psychology*, *38*, 63–70.

12

TEACHING CROSS-CULTURAL PSYCHOLOGY

WALTER J. LONNER

Although modern scientific psychology originated in Europe, with Wilhelm Wundt's establishment of the first psychology laboratory at the University of Leipzig in 1879 serving as a catalyst, before long it crossed the Atlantic and took firm root in the United States. Further nurtured in the 1930s by the arrival of major European figures in the field who were fleeing Hitler's persecution, American psychology eventually came to dominate the world scene. In numerous colleges and universities throughout the United States, psychologists have over many decades continued to generate an impressive volume of theory, research, and applications. However, the "subjects" of this research have generally been European-American college students, a fact that has led many psychologists to question how the many findings would fare if carried across cultural boundaries. Because generalizability is a necessary attribute of science, this is a serious concern.

CULTURE BOUNDNESS AND CULTURE BLINDNESS WITHIN PSYCHOLOGY

As it is usually taught in the United States, psychology has been accused of being both culture bound and culture blind. The accusation of culture boundness stems from an overall omission of research that has been conducted outside of the United States and other English-speaking countries (Berry, Poortinga, Segall, & Dasen, 2002). Charges regarding its culture blindness derive from the fact that U.S. psychology has generally not taken into account non-Western social structures, family types (e.g., see Kagitcibasi, 1996), or views on virtually all areas of psychological functioning. In short, the majority of psychology faculty have either assumed that cognitions and behaviors described in the United States and other Western-based literature are valid everywhere, or that cognition and behavior as they occur elsewhere are of no consequence to the science they teach—or, they are simply so unfamiliar with research conducted in or about other cultures that they do not even consider including it in their teaching and research.

In the first edition of this book, Albert (1988) listed a number of factors that have contributed to the neglect of cultural variables by most psychologists. She mentioned psychology's focus on the individual rather than on normative patterns, the methodological difficulties in cross-cultural research, and the difficulty in finding funds for this type of inquiry. Other inhibiting factors may reside within individual teachers of psychology. Instructors who have had little or no direct contact with other cultures and no competencies with other languages may simply not view behavior that occurs elsewhere as being salient to themselves or to their students. They may also feel that there is insufficient time in most introductory-level courses to give any significant attention to culture, arguing that it is challenging enough to try and explain thought and behavior in their own world. Moreover, in some psychology departments there may be little incentive to deal with what many may describe as "exotic" or "peripheral" material, because information about other cultures often does not conform to traditional views of scientific orthodoxy. In addition, some instructors may compartmentalize disciplines, arguing that culture and ethnicity should be left in the domain of anthropology and sociology, and not psychology.

Another possibility for such oversight is that some psychology instructors may have social or political perspectives that lead them to exclude culture and ethnicity from their courses. They may fear that inquiry into cultural and ethnic variations in behavior will create or reinforce stereotypes and that a discussion of findings of between-group differences may contribute to further prejudice and discrimination. They may even fear that not "getting it right" because of unfamiliarity with the cross-cultural literature could be professionally risky or embarrassing, possibly causing them to appear as if they have little command of a topic about which they are supposed to be an expert. Or, they may view a focus on cultural differences as inconsistent with the U.S. ideals of egalitarianism and assimilation. There is also the possibility, given the dominant political and economic position of this country and its long history of ethnocentrism, that some instructors may be lulled into believing that there is nothing important to be learned or gained from other cultures. This kind of attitude can only reinforce the scientific isolationism within the field.

CONCEPTUAL AND METHODOLOGICAL PERSPECTIVES ON THE STUDY OF OTHER CULTURES

There are two key questions one might pose about cross-cultural research: (a) "Should there be an emphasis on the cultural context of human behavior?" and (b) "Are there commonalities in human thought and behavior?" Answering each question with a simple "no" or "yes" results in four different philosophical positions. One position—that there are no commonalities in human thought and behavior and that culture should not be considered a factor—not only denies the validity of cross-cultural studies but also invalidates a guiding principle of the entire discipline. The other three positions, however, epitomize the main approaches to the consideration of culture within the field of psychology.

The *absolutist* position assumes that there is an underlying commonality to all human thought and activity and that culture is at most a thin veneer covering the essence and core of invariant human nature. This is, in fact, the position of many individuals in "mainstream" psychology—the assumption that almost everything one reads in a psychology text is true for all humans, regardless of culture. Absolutists prefer not to be bothered by culture, which they believe is unimportant and irrelevant in their quest for basic principles of human nature. Basic introductory psychology texts published in the United States from the turn of the 20th century up to the mid-1980s have reflected this perspective, giving culture only simplistic, perfunctory, and essentially token attention (Lonner, 1990). However, a significant change has occurred over the last 10 years, with a number of recent introductory texts giving greater coverage to cultural and ethnic factors than ever before.

The *relativist* position asserts that it is futile to search for absolute or fixed truths in human thought and behavior. Relativists maintain instead that it is more appropriate to focus on human thought and activity as they occur in specific sociocultural contexts. Eschewing cultural comparisons or contrasts, researchers who take this position believe in *social constructionism*, which is the view that all cultures, and even all individuals within all cultures, seek and construct their own meanings. Those who identify with an approach known as *cultural psychology* (e.g., Boesch, 1991; Cole; 1996; Shweder & Sullivan, 1993) tend to align themselves with this position. In the view of cultural psychologists, thought and behavior can never be separated from specific historical and cultural contexts. It is within this arena that a complex confluence of perceptions, languages, beliefs, religions, myths, longings, and other attributes of the human condition exhibit their deeply intense and quixotic dramas. This is why cultural psychology is often aligned with cognitive anthropology, semiotics, and hermeneutics. It is also why, as cultural psychologist Ernest Boesch (1996) wisely argued, good *cross-cultural* psychological research should be preceded by good *cultural* psychological research.

The *universalist* position (Lonner & Adamopoulos, 1994) represents a combining of the absolutist and relativist perspectives. It assumes that there is a dynamic interaction between human beings and their environment and that

> it should, in theory, be possible to establish broad commonalities in human nature that reflect a deeper reality than the scientists' own conceptual categories. At the same time, advocates of this perspective agree with the relativists about the importance of culture. (Lonner & Adamopoulos, 1994, p. 131)

GOALS OF CROSS-CULTURAL PSYCHOLOGY

The overarching aspiration of cross-cultural psychology is to examine the extent to which the theories and principles that form the foundation of psychology are universally valid (Lonner, 1980). Any number of questions may be asked in this quest. For instance, are laws of learning, memory, perception, and other basic processes universal? If they are not, what accounts for variations? Can psychologists be certain that conformity is the same everywhere, that there are no variations in the causes and etiology of depression and that the structure of personality is invariant? There is substantial research evidence to suggest that there is at least some variation across cultures and ethnic groups in just about any psychological topic that one elects to study. Whether the focus is on values, moral reasoning, child development, depression, concepts of self, rules of social interaction, or countless other topics, cultural beliefs, traditions, and socialization practices play a significant role in shaping human behavior. The documentation of cultural variation in thought and behavior across cultures is the main objective in the impressive accumulation of studies done under the umbrella of cross-cultural psychological research (e.g., Brislin, 2000; Matsumoto, 2000, 2001; Segall, Dasen, Berry, & Poortinga, 1999).

There are three specific goals in this quest to establish possible psychological universals (Berry et al., 2002). The first, called the *transport and test goal*, seeks to *carry specific theories, findings, or hypotheses that work well in one particular culture into one or more other cultures, to test the extent to which they are valid in those cultures.* However, as Berry et al. (2002) pointed out, because researchers obviously start with what is known to be the case in their own culture, their research questions may not be very sensitive means for discovering important psychological phenomena in the other (target) culture. For instance, if a certain type of moral reasoning, or child rearing, or problem solving, is not found in target cultures, its absence does not necessarily mean that some form of these phenomena do not exist. Typical orthodox models or paradigms may not be flexible enough to accommodate new information.

To remedy this problem, cross-cultural psychologists endorse a second goal in most of their research: to *explore other cultures in an effort to discover psychological variations that are not evident in their own culture.* Phenomena found elsewhere may help establish how a particular aspect of psychological functioning operates—an understanding that could not be achieved without examining other cultures. For instance, it may eventually be found that reading from right to left (as is the case with Arabic and other languages) instead of left to right affects the way in which the brain processes information. Or it may be found, as it has been in Japan (Kleinknecht, Dinnel, Tanouye-Wilson, & Lonner, 1994; Tseng, Asai, Kitanishi, McLaughlin, & Kyomen, 1992), that certain aspects of anxiety differ across cultures and indeed that various psychological disorders are largely culture bound (Simons & Hughes, 1985). Information about such variations can provide valuable insights about the etiology of psychopathological problems.

These two goals lead to a third goal of *integrating knowledge in an attempt to generate a more nearly universal psychology.* This third goal is necessary

> because of the distinct possibility that, in pursuing our first goal, we will find limits to the generality of our existing psychological knowledge, and that in pursuing our second goal, we will discover some novel psychological phenomena that need to be taken into account in a more general psychological theory. (Berry et al., 2002, p. 4)

Findings from psychological research done in other cultures should ideally be "folded back" into the basic pool of psychological knowledge, thus enriching the entire field and enhancing generalizability.

Fulfillment of each of these goals obviously requires the use of appropriate methodology if the results of research are to be considered credible. A major challenge in cross-cultural research is to assure that equivalent measures and equivalent, comparable samples are used in each culture involved in a particular study. Translation is especially important; if the same word or phrase does not have essentially the same meaning across cultures, the data analysis and results will be meaningless at worst or misleading at best (van de Vijver & Hambleton, 1996). Instructors who present an overview of cross-cultural psychology will want to include a segment on the perils and complexities of cross-cultural research methodology so that students can understand the special requirements of such research and develop a critical eye in reading the research literature (see Brislin, Lonner, & Thorndike, 1973; Lonner & Berry, 1986; Triandis & Berry, 1980; van de Vijver & Leung, 1997).

ENGAGING STUDENTS IN THE STUDY OF OTHER CULTURES: RESOURCES AND ACTIVITIES

Instructors can familiarize themselves with the breadth and scope of research in cross-cultural psychology by examining some of the many books in the area. The original six-volume *Handbook of Cross-Cultural Psychology* (Triandis et al., 1980) and the three-volume revision by Berry et al. (1997) give comprehensive overviews. The *Handbook of Culture and Psychology* (Matsumoto, 2001) has a similar comprehensive scope. These volumes are primarily intended for use by researchers and graduate students, but psychology instructors may find them useful in that they provide details of studies in a wide range of areas. There are also number of relatively inexpensive texts, generally available in paperback, that can be used either by themselves or as supplements in various undergraduate courses. They include general overviews of cross-cultural psychology (Brislin, 2000; Lonner & Malpass, 1994; Matsumoto, 2000; Segall et al., 1999) and cross-cultural perspectives on developmental psychology (Gardiner & Kosmitzki, 2001; Kagitcibasi, 1996) and social psychology (Adamopoulos & Kashima, 1999; Smith & Bond, 1999; Triandis, 1994). A briefer historical and theoretical overview of cross-cultural psychology can be found in Adamopoulos and Lonner (2001).

In addition, in teaching about cultural variations in thought and behavior, instructors may find it beneficial to use examples and exercises in class. Two recent books that have provided ways to engage students in active consideration of cross-cultural issues are *Teaching About Culture, Ethnicity, and Diversity* (Singelis, 1998), which consists of many exercises and planned activities, and a workbook entitled *Cross-Cultural Explorations: Activities in Culture and Psychology* (Goldstein, 2000). These books cover a wide range of topics, and either would provide valuable additions to courses dealing with cultural and ethnic variations.

Professional associations and journals in the field are another source of valuable information about cross-cultural psychological research and about activities such as conferences and workshops. The bimonthly *Journal of Cross-Cultural Psychology* is the basic outlet for this type of research and is the flagship journal in this area; it is closely associated with the International Association for Cross-Cultural Psychology (IACCP), as is the quarterly *Cross-Cultural Psychology Bulletin*. Instructors can find detailed information about these sources of information at the IACCP Web site (http://www.fit.edu/CampusLife/clubs-org/iaccp). IACCP has held international conferences since its inception in 1972; instructors can consult the latest published proceedings for information concerning its efforts (Lonner, Dinnel, Forgays, & Hayes, 1999). The International Academy of Intercultural Research sponsors the *International Journal of Intercultural Relations*, which has a heavily applied orientation. Another relatively new professional journal is *Culture and Psychology*, which is primarily of interest to individuals who identify with cultural psychology. Yet another periodical is the quarterly *Cross-Cultural Research*, an interdisciplinary journal that publishes material of interest to anthropologists, sociologists, psychologists, and others who appreciate an expanded spectrum of approaches. The International Council of Psychologists is concerned about psychology in international scope, and the Interamerican Society of Psychologists is important to psychologists whose research and scholarship involve people and organizations from Mexico and Central and South America.

Another source of extensive and helpful information is a large collection of short chapters concerning the interface between psychology and culture. This material is contained in a new and ongoing project entitled "Online Readings in Psychology and Culture" (Lonner, Dinnel, Hayes, & Sattler, 2002). Prepared by many scholars from throughout the world in the spirit of unselfish scholarship, these chapters are free and instantly available. Instructors can use these chapters either to supplement standard texts or as comprehensive readings in an entire course that focuses on culture from a global perspective.

Once familiar with the basic books, readings collections, journals, and associations, interested students will have access to a widening circle of related publications and groups of individuals with similar interests. They will, in their consideration of psychological principles and issues, be able to leave the confines of one particular culture and examine human thought and behavior from a multicultural, multi-ethnic, and multilingual perspective. Until all the world's cultures are examined as carefully as those from the affluent Western world have been, psychology will offer only a tentative and incomplete picture of the range of human thought and behavior. One can, however, be somewhat confident that the role played by culture and ethnicity in psychological science is increasingly being taken seriously. Indeed, the flowering of cross-cultural psychological research has been one of the more important contributions to the discipline during the last 25 years (Segall, Lonner, & Berry, 1998), and its importance and influence will continue into the indefinite future.

REFERENCES

Adamopoulos, J., & Kashima, Y. (Eds.). (1999). *Social psychology and cultural context*. Thousand Oaks, CA: Sage.

Adamopoulos, J., & Lonner, W. J. (2001). Culture and psychology at a crossroad: Historical perspective and theoretical analysis. In D. Matsumoto (Ed.) *The handbook of culture and psychology* (pp. 11–34). Oxford: Oxford University Press.

Albert, R. D. (1988). The place of culture in modern psychology. In P. Bronstein & K. Quina (Eds.), *Teaching a psychology of people: Resources for gender and sociocultural awareness* (pp. 12–18). Washington, DC: American Psychological Association.

Berry, J. W., Poortinga, Y. H., Pandey, J., Dasen, P. R., Saraswathi, T. S., Segall, M. H., et al. (Eds.). (1997). *Handbook of cross-cultural psychology* (2nd ed., Vols. 1–3). Needham Heights, MA: Allyn & Bacon.

Berry, J. W., Poortinga, Y. H., Segall, M. H., & Dasen, P. R. (2002). *Cross-cultural psychology: Research and applications* (2nd ed.). New York: Cambridge University Press.

Boesch, E. E. (1991). *Symbolic action theory and cultural psychology.* Berlin: Springer-Verlag.

Boesch, E. E. (1996). The seven flaws of cross-cultural psychology: The story of a conversion. *Mind, Culture, and Activity, 1*(3), 2–10.

Brislin, R. (2000). *Understanding culture's influence on behavior* (2nd ed.). Fort Worth, TX: Harcourt Brace.

Brislin, R. W., Lonner, W. J., & Thorndike, R. M. (1973). *Cross-cultural research methods.* New York: Wiley.

Cole, M. (1996). *Cultural psychology: A once and future discipline.* Cambridge, MA: Belknap/Harvard.

Gardiner, H. W., & Kosmitzki, C. (2001). *Lives across cultures: Cross-cultural human development.* Needham Heights, MA: Allyn & Bacon.

Goldstein, S. (2000). *Cross-cultural explorations: Activities in culture and psychology.* Boston: Allyn & Bacon.

Kagitcibasi, C. (1996). *Family and human development: A view from the other side.* Mahwah, NJ: Erlbaum.

Kleinknecht, R. A., Dinnel, D. L., Tanouye-Wilson, S., & Lonner, W. J. (1994). Cultural variations in social anxiety and phobia: A study of Taijin-Kyofusho. *The Behavior Therapist, 17,* 175–178.

Lonner, W. J. (1980). The search for psychological universals. In H. C. Triandis & W. W. Lambert (Eds.), *Handbook of cross-cultural psychology: Vol. 1. Perspectives* (pp. 143–204). Boston: Allyn & Bacon.

Lonner, W. J. (1990). The introductory psychology text and cross-cultural psychology: Beyond Ekman, Whorf, and biased I.Q. tests. In D. Keats, D. Munro, & L. Mann (Eds.), *Heterogeneity in cross-cultural psychology: Selected papers from the ninth International Conference of the International Association for Cross-Cultural Psychology* (pp. 4–22). Lisse, The Netherlands: Swets & Zeitlinger.

Lonner, W. J., & Adamopoulos, J. (1994). Absolutism, relativism, and universalism in the study of human behavior. In W. J. Lonner & R. S. Malpass (Eds.), *Psychology and culture* (pp. 129–134). Needham Heights, MA: Allyn & Bacon.

Lonner, W. J., & Berry, J. W. (Eds.). (1986). *Field methods in cross-cultural research.* Beverly Hills, CA: Sage.

Lonner, W. J., Dinnel, D. L., Forgays, D. K., & Hayes, S. A. (Eds.). (1999). *Merging past, present, and future in cross-cultural psychology: Selected proceedings of the 14th International Congress of the International Association for Cross-Cultural Psychology.* Lisse, The Netherlands: Swets & Zeitlinger.

Lonner, W. J., Dinnel, D. L., Hayes, S. A., & Sattler, D. N. (Eds.). (2002). *Online readings in psychology and culture*. Retrieved May 27, 2002, from http://www.wwu.edu/~culture

Lonner, W. J., & Malpass, R. S. (Eds.). (1994). *Psychology and culture*. Needham Heights, MA: Allyn & Bacon.

Matsumoto, D. (2000). *Culture and psychology* (2nd ed.). Pacific Grove, CA: Brooks/Cole.

Matsumoto, D. (Ed.). (2001). *Handbook of culture and psychology*. New York: Oxford University Press.

Segall, M. H., Dasen, P. R., Berry, J. W., & Poortinga, Y. H. (1999). *Human behavior in global perspective* (2nd ed.). Boston: Allyn & Bacon.

Segall, M. H., Lonner, W. J., & Berry, J. W. (1998). Cross-cultural psychology as a scholarly discipline: On the flowering of culture in behavioral research. *American Psychologist, 53*, 1101–1110.

Shweder, R., & Sullivan, M. A. (1993). Cultural psychology: Who needs it? *Annual Review of Psychology, 44*, 497–527.

Simons, R., & Hughes, C. C. (Eds.). (1985). *The culture-bound syndromes*. Dordrecht, The Netherlands: Reidel.

Singelis, T. M. (Ed.). (1998). *Teaching about culture, ethnicity, and diversity*. Thousand Oaks, CA: Sage.

Smith, P. B., & Bond, M. H. (1999). *Social psychology across cultures* (2nd ed.). Needham Heights, MA: Allyn & Bacon.

Triandis, H. C. (1994). *Culture and social behavior*. New York: McGraw-Hill.

Triandis, H. C., & Berry, J. W. (Eds.). (1980). *Handbook of cross-cultural psychology: Volume 2. Methodology*. Boston: Allyn & Bacon.

Triandis, H. C., Lambert, W. W., Berry, J. W., Lonner, W. J., Heron, A., Brislin, R. W., et al. (Eds.). (1980). *Handbook of cross-cultural psychology* (Vols. 1–6). Boston: Allyn & Bacon.

Tseng, W., Asai, M., Kitanishi, K., McLaughlin, D., & Kyomen, H. (1992). Diagnostic patterns of social phobia: Comparisons in Tokyo and Hawaii. *Journal of Nervous and Mental Disease, 180*, 380–385.

van de Vijver, F. J. R., & Hambleton, R. K. (1996). Translating tests: Some practical guidelines. *European Psychologist, 1*, 89–99.

van de Vijver, F. J. R., & Leung, K. (1997). *Methods and data analysis for cross-cultural research*. Thousand Oaks, CA: Sage.

13

PSYCHOLOGICAL ISSUES OF ASIAN AMERICANS

CONNIE S. CHAN

This chapter focuses on the history, identity, and psychology of Asian Americans and suggests curriculum materials and teaching strategies to bring this information into the psychology classroom. The terms *Asian American* and *Asian Pacific American* refer to individuals from at least 40 separate and distinct ethnic groups, speaking 40 different languages, from more than 20 countries (Zhan, 1999). Although these groups are often categorized together—because of their common ethnic origins in Asia or the Pacific, because they have some similarities in physical appearance, and because they are presumed to share common values—they actually comprise a very diverse and heterogeneous population. Each ethnic group has its own language(s), values, customs, and unique experiences of migration to the United States. There are, in addition, many individual and group differences even within what would be considered the same ethnic group.

On the other hand, although Asian American cultural values and behaviors have rarely been studied empirically, many writings and anecdotal reports do in fact describe similarities among Asian American groups (Uba, 1994). Some of these can be traced to the common values shared by their cultures of origin, loosely based on Confucian, Taoist, and Buddhist philosophies, which stress harmony with others, putting family and group needs ahead of individual needs, and fulfilling expected familial and societal roles. In addition, many Asian immigrants and Americans of Asian descent have experienced similar group histories of oppression in this country, as well as similar effects of racism, which remains a deeply embedded aspect of U.S. society. There are also new perspectives on Asian American psychological issues, offered in several recent books: Uba (2002) challenged existing paradigms of knowledge as they relate to Asian American psychology, Hall and Okazaki (2002) provided a framework for the conceptual and methodological development of Asian American psychology, and Chin (2000) looked at Asian American women's relationships in cultural context.

A BRIEF IMMIGRATION HISTORY OF ASIAN GROUPS IN THE UNITED STATES

A brief history of Asian ethnic groups in the United States can provide students with a background for understanding Asian Americans' psychological issues. There have been several different waves of immigration (L. C. Lee, 1997; Takaki, 1989), each producing cultural and political forces that continue to resonate today in the lives of Asian Americans.

The First Immigrations: 1840–1924

Historian Sucheng Chan (1991) pointed out that by the time the Chinese were recruited to immigrate to the United States, in the 1840s as laborers and in the 1860s as railroad workers, "color prejudice had become . . . a habit of heart and mind" (p. 45) for European Americans, who had already pushed aside, enslaved, and subjugated indigenous peoples, Africans, and Mexicans. Considered too "foreign" in their physical appearance, their customs, and their language to be accepted as Americans, the Chinese were the first nationality in U.S. history to be barred from immigration. Other discriminatory legislation allowed only Chinese men and not women to immigrate (an attempt to ensure that the Chinese did not produce families and settle in the United States), forbade marriage between Chinese and Whites, forced Chinese to live in Chinatown ghettos, and excluded Chinese and other Asians from becoming naturalized American citizens (L. C. Lee, 1997; Takaki, 1989).

In the 1880s, the Japanese settled in Hawaii and the West coast region of the United States mainland to work on plantations and farms. Anti-Japanese sentiment, similar to that directed at the Chinese, led to acts of physical violence against the Japanese (S. Chan, 1991). In 1907, the Gentlemen's Agreement, signed with Japan, restricted the numbers of Japanese allowed to immigrate. However, many Japanese immigrant men married quickly before the door shut, often arranging "picture-bride" marriages by mail, and by 1920 there were more than 130,000 individuals of Japanese ancestry living in the United States, primarily on the West coast and in Hawaii. These immigration patterns—of recruiting men from an Asian ethnic group to come to the United States as laborers, prohibiting women and family members from joining them, and excluding them from obtaining legal immigration status—were repeated, in smaller numbers, for Koreans and Filipinos during the period between 1903 and 1920 (S. Chan, 1991).

Immigration and Restrictions, 1924–1965

The 1924 Immigration Act severely limited immigration from all Asian countries until 1965 (S. Chan, 1991). After the Japanese bombing of Pearl Harbor in 1941, there was a period of strong anti-Asian sentiment, focused on the Japanese but also touching many individuals from Asian backgrounds. Although some Asians had lived in the United States for as long as 50 years, they were still regarded by other Americans as potential enemies—unlike European immigrants whose countries of origin were also at war with the United States. More than 110,000 Americans of Japanese ancestry were forced from their homes and confined for up to 3 years in "internment camps," which were little more than tent cities with subsistence barely provided. When World War II ended, they were released from the internment camps and dispersed across the United States; many who tried to return to their homes found their property had been appropriated, especially on the West coast (Takaki, 1989). There are personal accounts of the internment camp experience (e.g., Houston & Houston, 1973; Okada, 1976; Weglyn, 1976), and several films offer a moving lesson about institutionalized prejudice on a large scale, including the feature movie *Snow Falling on Cedars* (Bass & Baum, 2000) and the documentaries *Children of the Camps* (Ina, 1999) and *Unfinished Business: The Japanese Internment Cases* (Okazaki, 1986). In addition, some of the Japanese American writers, filmmakers, and activists who lived through the internment experience are still alive, and guest lectures on these topics can be particularly compelling.

In 1952, with the end of the Korean War, the McCarran-Walter Act was passed, allowing Asians to become naturalized citizens—and thus reversing more than 100 years of exclusion from the American political process. Japanese, Korean, and Filipina wives of American soldiers were allowed to enter the United States as nonquota immigrants, although only a very small quota of other Asians were afforded the same privilege (S. Chan, 1991). However, in 1965, spurred by the moral imperative of the civil rights movement in the United States, Congress finally passed the Immigration and Naturalization Act, abolishing national origins quotas. As a result, between 1965 and 1975 the Asian American population increased dramatically; in particular, many Koreans, Indians, Chinese and Filipinos settled in the United States.

New Immigrants and Refugees: 1975 to Present

Over the last 25 years, nearly 1 million Asian refugees have arrived in the United States, mostly from Vietnam, and the rest from the neighboring countries of Laos and Kampuchea (formerly Cambodia). The Vietnam war played a large role in creating this refugee exodus. After waging a ground and air war (including dropping well over 2 million tons of bombs on Laos, Cambodia, and Vietnam), the United States withdrew from Vietnam in 1973, leaving many South Vietnamese supporters of the United States in great danger. When Vietnam, Cambodia, and Laos fell to Communist control in 1975, those who managed to escape did so amid terror and horrendous violence and endured arduous stays in refugee camps. First-person Vietnamese accounts of the war and refugee experience are provided in *When Heaven and Earth Changed Places* (Hayslip, 1989) and *South Wind Changing* (Huynh, 1994). Other military conflicts, and a genocidal campaign by Pol Pot, the leader of the Khmer Rouge in Cambodia, created another exodus of refugees. The feature film *The Killing Fields* (Puttnam & Smith, 1984) tells the stories of Cambodian refugees who escaped after torture and imprisonment.

Asians currently are the fastest growing immigrant group in the United States; the Asian population nearly doubled in size during the 1980s and 1990s. The 2000 U.S. Census reports that people of Asian heritage number almost 12 million, or about 4.2% of the total U.S. population (U.S. Bureau of the Census, 2000).

TEACHING ABOUT ASIAN AMERICAN PSYCHOLOGICAL ISSUES

There are many aspects of the Asian immigrant and Asian American experience that would be appropriate to include in a course on Asian American Psychology or that could be integrated into developmental, social, personality, clinical, or psychology of women courses. I next discuss three important topics—cultural influences, minority group status, and refugee adaptation—that would suit either purpose.

Cultural Influences in Asian American Psychology

Whereas it is important to make students aware of the great diversity within and among the many Asian American ethnic groups, some generalizations can be made about common values, beliefs, and customs that they may share. These cultural ways may help shape personality, behaviors, communication style, interpersonal relationships, sexuality, and gender role expectations.

Importance of the family

Perhaps the most obvious difference between Asian and American cultures is the importance of the family (Liu & Chan, 1996). Whereas the traditional U.S. marriage is based on romantic interest between a couple, with continuing intimacy and open communication, Asian marriage is based on the desirability of the union to both families. The Confucian ideal for families is to be tightly knit, with close, ongoing contact with extended family members, including cousins, aunts, uncles, and grandparents. The ideal family is led by two heterosexual parents who care for their own elderly parents and who have established clear rules and discipline for their children. Women are expected to take care of domestic needs and to be nurturing, family oriented, and home centered. Men are expected to be dominant, strong, stoic, and family oriented, but also worldly. Parents generally are not openly affectionate, either physically or emotionally, with each other, or with their children, but demonstrate the strength of their relationship through their sense of responsibility to each other and to their children. Respect, order, hierarchical authority, and duty (Dion & Dion, 1993; Liu & Chan, 1996), in which communication is indirect or inferred through behavior, is the norm within the family. Family expectations form the foundation for Asian cultural values of proper behavior.

Whereas non-Asian American parents work toward supporting their children's growth and eventual independence, with the expectation that adult children will create their own separate families and lives, many Asian parents expect their children to be living with them or nearby, as part of their lives, until the parents die. Obedience to parents' wishes, even if individual desires run counter to them, and respect for elders and for authority figures, are strong cultural expectations (Chiu, 1987; Uba, 1994). These rules may govern career decisions, geographic location of residence, and even choice of mate. Non-Asian advisors and counselors are often surprised when Asian or Asian American college students are willing to choose a major to satisfy their parents, often in an area viewed as good for employment, such as accounting, or engineering—even if they are passionate about another discipline. A recent example I encountered was a male college student, originally from Korea, who sought counseling from me because his father expected him to go to Korea after graduation to find a bride. He already had a girlfriend here in the United States and was torn between his desire to fulfill his family's cultural expectations and his desire to keep the relationship with his non-Korean girlfriend. He was also expected to live with or near his parents once his education was completed.

Levels of acculturation

To understand the psychology of Asian Americans, it is important to know something about their level of acculturation, which is not necessarily correlated with length of time in they have been in the United States. Some Asian Americans who represent their families' third or fourth generation in this country may still hold very traditional Asian cultural values, whereas more recent immigrants may be acculturated quickly into American culture and life. It is ironic that more recent immigrants may hold traditional values less strongly and be more "Westernized" in styles and customs, because of the almost universal exposure to Western goods and ideas through English-speaking media and the globalization of industry into previously isolated Asian countries (C. S. Chan, 1995).

On the other hand, wide variations can exist within the same family. One sibling, often the eldest, may retain a more traditional cultural role than the others, and levels of acculturation can even vary greatly between parents, particularly if only one is working outside the home. The parent or child(ren) who has greater contact with American society may serve the role of introducing other family members to mainstream American customs and behaviors; however, they may also conflict with relatives who maintain Asian cultural customs and behaviors closely.

Behavior and communication style

Asian Americans are often unaware of particular cultural character-istics in their personality, behavior, or communication style, attributing differences they may have from non-Asian peers to individual or family characteristics rather than to Asian cultural influences. These cultural dif-ferences may in fact be so subtle that they are not recognized as such even by therapists working with Asian American clients.

An important cultural value of Asian Americans is the precedence of group needs over individual interests. Because interpersonal harmony is considered to be essential, Asian American individuals will often take a con-ciliatory role in group discussions. They may appear to be accommodating, conforming, and well mannered rather than being confrontational or draw-ing attention to themselves. Whereas this behavior usually reflects a desire to avoid conflict, it is often mistaken as unassertiveness or submissiveness—and in the classroom, it may be viewed as a sign that a student does not know or understand the material or is less competent. This communication style can be even more pronounced among Asian American women, who may have absorbed voice-muting messages from both Asian and American cultures.

The ability to communicate indirectly by getting a message across with-out having to directly confront or embarrass the other person is highly val-ued. If a subject is difficult to talk about openly, such as sexuality, then Asian Americans may communicate in an indirect manner so that it is understood by both parties but never needs to be openly stated. For example, if an Asian American woman wanted to know if her brother knew that she was a lesbian and in a relationship with another woman, she might not discuss it openly but might hint at it. She might tell her brother that she would be spending a weekend with her partner. Then he might mention that he had heard that it was a romantic place and a good weekend getaway location. That way, he would be communicating his understanding of the relationship to his sister without having to openly address the issue in conversation.

Another example of indirect communication involves allowing a friend the opportunity to create social boundaries that are comfortable for both parties. If an Asian American woman wanted to find out if she would be welcome to stay at a friend's home for the weekend in another city, she would not ask the friend directly. A direct request could put the friend in the awkward position of having to decline if a stay were not convenient or desired. Instead, an Asian American might ask, "I am coming to your town next month. Can you suggest some reasonably priced hotels?" This would allow the potential host the options of offering her home or offering suggestions for hotel accommodations. In this manner, both guest and host maintain interpersonal harmony, avoid conflict, and are both able to save face (Bond, 1991).

The desire to avoid conflict and interpersonal discomfort often results in constrained expression of emotions and avoidance of conversational topics about which disagreement might arise. Many Asian Americans are reluctant to reveal feelings or personal problems, even to a therapist. This avoidance is especially pronounced in family discussions, where there is commonly little open and honest communication between generations because of an understood desire for the appearance of harmony among all.

Public displays of emotion are particularly discouraged; Asian Americans consider it a virtue to be able to contain their feelings, hiding them until they are alone, and thus avoiding embarrassment to themselves or others (Carlin & Sokoloff, 1985). They generally consider it best to convey emotions through a written message. That way, both the sender and the recipient can experience and express their feelings in private and avoid any risk of public exposure.

To respect the importance placed on avoiding conflict and embarrassment, and allowing all parties to save face, Asian Americans are often taught to be observant of subtle social cues, both verbal and nonverbal. A great deal can be communicated through nonverbal means, including a quick look of disapproval from parents to children, or a lingering look in which one person might hold the contact of another eyes for just a second longer. This very subtle form of nonverbal communication can often indicate emotional or sexual interest and can be easily missed by the casual observer (C. S. Chan, 1995).

Effects of Minority Group Status

The psychology of Asian Americans is influenced not only by their own historical and cultural backgrounds but also by their minority group status in the United States. As an ethnic minority group, they may experience marginality, because their values, customs, and behaviors differ from those of the majority culture. They are also likely to be affected, psychologically, by non-Asians' perceptions of them and by the stereotyping and racism that exist within the dominant culture, which occur in a variety of forms.

The struggle to be American

One form of racism Asian Americans encounter is to be persistently regarded as foreigners, no matter how long their families may have lived in the United States, and how assimilated they may be. Many Asian Americans, while acknowledging some cultural influences from their Asian background, identify primarily with mainstream U.S. culture. Thus it is a shock when the outside world, seeing their racial characteristics, perceives them as other than American. It is not uncommon to be asked where they are from, how long they have lived in this country, and to be told that they speak very good, unaccented English—when indeed, English is their native language and their families have lived in the United States for decades. Asian language, customs, religions, foods, family structure, and culture are all perceived to be foreign and distinct from the European-based U.S. culture. Although the United States prides itself on being a melting pot of many cultures, Asian Americans are perceived as still not blending into the mix.

The myth of the model minority

The most prevalent forms of racism targeting Asian Americans today are more subtle than the laws of the past that restricted immigration, housing, and employment. Nowadays, their perceived success may, ironically, be used as a justification for discrimination. Often labeled the "model minority," they are viewed as having "made it" in the United States, because of the purportedly low rates of mental disorders and high levels of education, household income, and occupational status among some Asian Americans. However, a low rate of mental health services use may not indicate a low need for mental health services (Uba, 1994), and a higher average family income may be due to the fact that more Asian American family members are in the workforce than in the overall population. In college admissions, the perception that Asian American students are an ethnic minority group that does not require special consideration has sometimes led to lower rates of acceptance of Asian American students at prestigious universities. Between 1983 and 1986, several leading universities acknowledged discriminating against Asian American applicants and using quotas and ceilings to limit the enrollment of Asian Americans (Takagi, 1992).

Moreover, the model-minority argument is based on an assumption of homogeneity among Asian American groups (Uba, 1994) and does not take into account the disparities between those who have been in the country for decades compared to those who have arrived recently. Although some Asian American ethnic groups, particularly those who have been in this country for longer periods of time, have a strong record of academic achievement in the United States, there are others who have far lower levels of achievement than their non-Asian peers.

Furthermore, even when educational achievement has led to occupational success, there is often a glass ceiling beyond which Asian Americans are not promoted or perceived as leaders, whether in business and industry or higher education. For example, despite the large number of Asian Americans in colleges and universities, a 1989 survey found that they occupied only 1% of executive or managerial positions in American higher education (Escueta & O'Brien, 1991). Income levels for both immigrant and U.S.-born Asian Americans are not as high as would be expected given their educational levels, indicating discrimination in promotion and salary compensation (Barringer, Takeuchi, & Xenos, 1990; Uba, 1994).

Stereotypes and racial slurs

Subtle racism and stereotyping are often sources of stress for Asian Americans because even a high socioeconomic level or education cannot protect them. Upper middle class Asian American professionals may find that although they are viewed as competent technicians or researchers, they are perceived as quiet and lacking leadership qualities and thus not promoted to managerial positions. Stereotypes of Asian Americans as hardworking and uncomplaining may lead to exploitation—more work without compensation or promotion. In schools and university settings, Asian American students are frequently perceived as quiet but diligent students who "raise the curve" in math and science classes. Such stereotypes not only arouse resentment among non-Asian peers but also perpetuate the notion that whereas Asian American students are good technicians, they are not verbal or creative, which may narrow their opportunities (Takagi, 1992). An accumulation of experiences with racial discrimination, whether overt or subtle, can over time create a sense of bewilderment and frustration. Individuals who are aware of these subtle slights may be able to develop a wide range of adaptive responses, but others may develop feelings of helplessness and lowered self-esteem (Uba, 1994).

Asian American women have had to endure several forms of stereotyping on the basis of their race and gender. One, which characterizes them as diligent, unassertive, and submissive, derives from the historical lower status and subservience of women in China and Japan (True, 1990). Another, which implies that Asian women have an exotic sexiness or sexuality, is based on the Japanese geisha model as well as the similar, but more diabolical model of the manipulative "dragon lady" (Tajima, 1989). Still another, of the hardworking, quietly efficient laborer, reflects the limited employment opportunities that were historically available to Asian American women as garment workers, domestics and, more recently, as technicians and researchers. The last stereotype is that of the "lotus blossom baby"—the fragile, attractive "Suzie Wong" prostitute type—who has also become the subject of pornography (Tajima, 1989). This stereotype developed primarily as a consequence of the most recent American wars fought in Asia, where American soldiers' primary contact with Asian women was with prostitutes, and later as a consequence of the mail-order bride business, in which men from America and other western countries paid large sums of money to be matched with an Asian woman pictured in a catalog (Brownmiller, 1975; C. S. Chan, 1987). Such stereotypes of sexuality may lead some men to assume that Asian American women are more available and will not complain or reject them, thus making the women more vulnerable to unwanted advances and sexual harassment (Uba, 1994). The documentary *Slaying the Dragon* (Gee, 1988), a historical perspective of the media's portrayal of Asian American women in film, provides an excellent illustration of these stereotypes.

Refugee Experiences: Stress and Adaptation

It is particularly useful for students in clinical and counseling psychology to learn about the experiences of the southeast Asians who have immigrated to the United States in recent decades, many of whom were refugees from political violence or military conflict. Their issues are complex. For many, in addition to handling the usual economic, cognitive, and emotional challenges involved in adapting to a new language and culture, as well as the racism that targets people of color in the United States, they have had to deal with the psychological effects of the traumas they experienced before leaving their homeland. These traumas have included seeing family members killed, having bombs dropped literally in their own backyards, and living with daily terror, as well as enduring stays in refugee camps and coping with the uncertainties of resettlement in the United States (Kinzie et al., 1990). Researchers have found that Cambodian refugees have been affected to the greatest extent because of the genocide and executions by the Khmer Rouge, which killed up to one third of the population (Mollica et al., 1990). Posttraumatic stress disorder is high among the Cambodian population in the United States, as many refugees continue to experience delayed psychological effects of their war trauma, including survivor guilt, nightmares, and depression.

Thus, unlike other immigrant groups, southeast Asians refugees have often relocated to the United States because they had no other choice, facing torture, rape, starvation, or imprisonment in their home countries. In addition to their many losses, they have faced many stressors in this country, including difficulty learning English, culture shock, unemployment, racism from Americans who harbor negative feelings about the Vietnam war, and a variety of health problems resulting from conditions during the war years and in the refugee camps (Mollica, Wyshak, & Lavelle, 1987). Given their experiences, many southeast Asian refugees and their families are at higher risk for mental and physical problems.

Underutilization of Mental Health Services

Although Asian Americans in general are vulnerable to psychosocial stresses because of their cultural differences and minority group status, psychological problems appear to be more prevalent among foreign-born immigrants (particularly refugees) than among people of Asian descent born in this country (Uba, 1994). However, despite the need for mental health services within both groups, research has shown that Asian Americans have generally not used such services in proportion to their numbers in the population (Sue, 1977). Asian cultural values, which emphasize stoicism and discourage expression of feelings, contribute to this underutilization. In addition, the absence of linguistically and culturally appropriate services in many areas limits outreach to Asian American communities. Ng (1998) and Hong and Ham (2000) have provided useful resources that recognize these challenges and offer information and suggestions for understanding and counseling Asian Americans.

TEACHING STRATEGIES WITH ASIAN AMERICAN STUDENTS

The cultural values discussed in this chapter have implications for Asian Americans in classroom settings. First, because the course instructor is likely to be a stranger with no relationship to the students and no sense of trust yet established, Asian American students may be extremely wary about expressing personal feelings. Thus, they may not participate in discussions involving personal disclosure, even of what may seem to be minor information to the instructor—or they may do so with great discomfort and then drop the course. The fear of shaming the family and losing individual and family honor may also hinder Asian Americans from disclosing any personal information in a classroom setting. In addition, group exercises may be uncomfortable for them, because they are likely to feel responsible for group harmony at the expense of their own input or control over the final product.

Given the importance of privacy and saving face, Asian American students may also opt to remain silent about difficulties with class materials or personal problems that are interfering with their performance. Or, problems and concerns may be expressed as psychosomatic difficulties, such as insomnia and stomach pains. Within Asian cultures, it is more acceptable to seek relief if one has physical ailments than if one has psychological problems such as anxiety or depression (E. Lee, 1988; Owan, 1985; Uba, 1994). For many Asian Americans, there is also a belief that feelings, particularly negative ones such as sadness, anger, guilt, or shame, should be controlled by the individual and that expressing them to others is a sign of weakness of character. Developing insight into one's psychological well-being and evaluating one's feelings are not viewed as admirable or even helpful.

Instructors can create more effective and culturally sensitive classrooms if they allow time for Asian American students to become comfortable; make an effort to establish a trusting relationship with them; avoid exercises that demand public discussion of emotional or personal issues; and provide some structure in discussions, perhaps by being more directive in their questions. Other structured options that can facilitate effective communication include journal entries, to which the instructor writes responses that students can review in private, and homework assignments that give students explicit permission or instruction to pay attention to their emotional or personal reactions to material and to record these feelings on paper. However, such journals or assignments should not be shared with others without permission of the student.

Another useful assignment is for students to interview their parents and other elders, to learn the story of their family's immigration to the United States, thus providing a sociohistorical context for understanding their own development. This assignment can be used with all students, to enable them to learn about their family's background; if they are from a family that immigrated long ago, they can compare their family's experience with that of a newer Asian immigrant's family. Another assignment might involve going to an Asian American community organization and interviewing individuals about their immigration experiences. The objective of these assignments is to provide some hands-on experience, to make the material on Asian American cultural issues and immigration relevant and alive for all students regardless of cultural background. A further approach is to use some of the many memoirs, novels, and films that address Asian themes, such as *The Woman Warrior: Memoirs of a Childhood Among Ghosts* (Kingston, 1976), *The Joy Luck Club* (novel by Tan, 1989; video produced by Wang, 1994), *The Wedding Banquet* (Hope, Schamus, & Lee, 1994), and *Picture Bride* (Mark & Onodera, 1995).

CONCLUSION

Although the number and diversity of Americans of Asian descent continue to grow, there is little available psychological research on Asian Americans overall, and even less on specific ethnic groups. Most of the research has been conducted on Japanese and Chinese Americans, although there is beginning to be a focus on southeast Asians, Pacific Islanders, and south Asians. There is a great need to understand both the diversity and the commonalties among and within the Asian American ethnic groups and to integrate this understanding into the psychology curriculum. It is important to provide an educational environment in which students from Asian backgrounds feel acknowledged and accepted and in which students from other backgrounds can come to understand and value the diversity of Asian American experiences in their historical and societal contexts.

REFERENCES

Barringer, H. R., Takeuchi, D., & Xenos, P. (1990). Education, occupational prestige, and income of Asian Americans. *Sociology of Education, 63,* 27–43.

Bass, R., & Baum, C. (Producers). (2000). *Snow falling on cedars* [Motion picture]. Universal Studios, CA: Universal Pictures.

Bond, M. H. (1991). *Beyond the Chinese face: Insights from psychology.* Hong Kong: Oxford University Press.

Brownmiller, S. (1975). *Against our will: Men, women, and rape.* New York: Basic Books.

Carlin, J., & Sokoloff, B. (1985). Mental health treatment issues for Southeast Asian refugee children. In T. Owan (Ed.), *Southeast Asian mental health: Treatment, prevention, services, training, and research* (pp. 91–112). Washington, DC: U.S. Department of Health and Human Services.

Chan, C. S. (1987). Asian American women: Psychological responses to sexual exploitation and cultural stereotypes. *Women and Therapy, 6,* 33–38.

Chan, C. S. (1995). Issues of sexual identity in an ethnic minority: The case of Chinese American lesbians, gay men, and bisexual people. In A. D'Augelli & C. Patterson (Eds.), *Lesbian, gay, and bisexual identities over the lifespan* (pp. 87–101). New York: Oxford University Press.

Chan, S. (1991). *Asian Americans: An interpretive history.* Boston: Twayne.

Chin, J. (Ed.). (2000). *Relationships among Asian American women.* Washington, DC: American Psychological Association.

Chiu, L. (1987). Child-rearing attitudes of Chinese, Chinese-American, and Anglo-American mothers. *International Journal of Psychology, 22,* 409–419.

Dion, K. K., & Dion, K. L. (1993). Individualistic and collectivistic perspectives on gender and the cultural context of love and intimacy. *Journal of Social Issues, 49*(3), 53–69.

Escueta, E., & O'Brien, E. (1991). Asian Americans in higher education: Trends and issues. In *Research briefs* (Vol. 2, No. 4). Washington, DC: American Council on Education.

Gee, D. (Producer and Director). (1988). *Slaying the dragon.* [Videotape]. New York: Women Make Movies. Available from National Asian American Telecommunications Association, 346 Ninth Street, 2nd floor, San Francisco, CA 94103.

Hall, G., & Okazaki, S. (Eds.). (2002). *Asian American psychology: The science of lives in context.* Washington, DC: American Psychological Association.

Hayslip, L. (1989). *When heaven and earth changed places*. New York: Doubleday.

Hong, G., & Ham, M. D. (2000). *Psychotherapy and counseling with Asian Americans: A practical guide*. Thousand Oaks, CA: Sage.

Hope, T., & Schamus, J. (Producers), & Lee, A. (Producer and Director). (1993). *The wedding banquet* [Videotape]. Beverly Hills, CA: Fox Video.

Houston, J. W., & Houston, J. D. (1973). *Farewell to Manzanar*. San Francisco: Houghton-Mifflin.

Huynh, J. (1994). *South wind changing*. St. Paul, MN: Graywolf Press.

Ina, S. (Producer and Director). (1999). *Children of the camps* [Videotape]. (Available from National Asian American Telecommunications Association, 346 Ninth Street, 2nd Floor, San Francisco, CA 94103.)

Kingston, M. H. (1976). *The woman warrior: Memoirs of a childhood among ghosts*. New York: Knopf.

Kinzie, J. D., Boehnlein, J., Leung, P., Moore, L., Riley, C., & Smith, D. (1990). The prevalence of post-traumatic stress disorder and its clinical significance among Southeast Asian refugees. *American Journal of Psychiatry, 147*, 913–917.

Lee, E. (1988). Cultural factors in working with Southeast Asian refugee adolescents. *Journal of Adolescence, 11*, 167–179.

Lee, L. C. (1997). An overview. In L. C. Lee & N. Zane (Eds.), *Handbook of Asian American psychology* (pp. 1–19). Thousand Oaks, CA: Sage.

Liu, P. M., & Chan, C. S. (1996). Lesbian, gay, and bisexual Asian Americans and their families. In J. Chrisler & R. J. Green (Eds.), *Lesbians and gays in couples and families* (pp. 137–152). San Francisco: Jossey-Bass.

Mark, D., & Onodera, L. (Producers). (1995). *Picture bride* [Motion picture]. Burbank, CA: Miramax Pictures.

Mollica, R., Wyshak, G., & Lavelle, J. (1987). The psychological impact of war trauma and torture on Southeast Asian refugees. *American Journal of Psychiatry, 144*, 1567–1571.

Mollica, R., Wyshak, G., Lavelle, J., Truong, T., Tor, S., & Yang, T. (1990). Assessing symptom change in Southeast Asian refugee survivors of mass violence and torture. *American Journal of Psychiatry, 147*, 83–88.

Ng, K. (1998). *Counseling Asian Americans from a systems perspective: The family psychology and counseling series*. Washington, DC: American Counseling Association.

Okada, J. (1976). *No-no boy*. Seattle: University of Washington Press.

Okazaki, S. (Producer and Director). (1986). *Unfinished business* [Videotape]. (Available from National Asian American Telecommunications Association, 346 Ninth Street, 2nd floor, San Francisco, CA 94103.)

Owan, T. (1985). Southeast Asian mental health: Transition from treatment to prevention—A new direction. In T. Owan (Ed.), *Southeast Asian mental health: Treatment, prevention, services, training, and research* (pp. 141–167). Washington, DC: U.S. Department of Health and Human Services.

Puttnam, R., & Smith, I. (Producers), & Joffe, R. (Director). (1984). *The killing fields* [Videotape]. Burbank, CA: Warner Studios Home Video.

Sue, S. (1977). Community mental health services to minority groups: Some optimism, some pessimism. *American Psychologist, 32,* 616–624.

Tajima, R. E. (1989). Lotus blossoms don't bleed: Images of Asian women. In Asian Women United of California (Eds.), *Making waves: An anthology of writings by and about Asian American women* (pp. 308–317). Boston: Beacon Press.

Takagi, D. (1992). *The retreat from race: Asian American admissions and racial politics.* New Brunswick, NJ: Rutgers University Press.

Takaki, R. (1989). *Strangers from a different shore.* Boston: Little, Brown.

Tan, A. (1989). *The joy luck club.* New York: Random House.

True, R. H. (1990). Psychotherapeutic issues with Asian American women. *Sex Roles, 22,* 477–486.

Uba, L. (1994). *Asian Americans: Personality patterns, identity, and mental health.* New York: Guilford Press.

Uba, L. (2002). *A postmodern psychology of Asian Americans: Creating knowledge of a racial minority.* Albany: State University of New York Press.

U.S. Bureau of the Census. (2000). *Summary file–1.* Retrieved January 22, 2003 from http://www.census.gov/Press-Release/www/2001/sumfile1.html

Wang, W. (Producer and Director). (1994). *The joy luck club* [Videotape]. Burbank, CA: Buena Vista Home Videos.

Weglyn, M. (1976). *Years of infamy.* New York: Morrow.

Zhan, L. (1999). *Asian voices: Asian and Asian-American health educators speak out.* Sudbury, MA: Jones and Bartlett.

14

TEACHING AFRICAN AMERICAN PSYCHOLOGY: RESOURCES AND STRATEGIES

HALFORD H. FAIRCHILD, LISA WHITTEN,
AND HARRIETTE W. RICHARD

African American psychology was virtually unknown 35 years ago. By the end of the 1990s, however, it had earned a solid place in U.S. college curricula. In this chapter, we provide a definition and description of the field, offer resources for instructors teaching African American Psychology, and describe specific strategies for classroom interaction.

WHAT IS AFRICAN AMERICAN PSYCHOLOGY?

Defining African American or Black psychology is difficult, because it is a constantly growing and changing field (see Jones, 1999a, 2003). It may be distinguished from European American or White psychology in a number of ways (Fairchild, 2000). Specifically, it tends to: (a) emphasize the collective, with the group and not the individual as the unit of analysis; (b) consider current behavior within a historical context (vs. the ahistorical tendency of

195

European American psychology); (c) focus on both the material and the immaterial or spiritual (vs. emphasizing only that which can be seen, measured, and manipulated); (d) consider introspection ("knowledge from within") as a valid means of data collection (vs. an external orientation characterized by observations, surveys, or experiments); (e) see harmony in nature (vs. seeking to control nature); (f) counter racism and sexism (vs. ignoring or even promoting those ideologies); and (g) be grounded in a set of values that seeks African liberation on the continent and throughout the African diaspora (vs. the "value-free," "neutral" or "objective" approach of European American psychology).

However, it should be noted that this list is idealized. African American psychologists are trained in European American schools and traditions and embrace many of the values of that training. Thus, these distinguishing features are not alternatives to European American psychology, but different emphases.

TEACHING AFRICAN AMERICAN PSYCHOLOGY

The teaching of African American psychology began in the 1920s and 1930s, with the efforts of African American psychologists Francis Cecil Sumner, Charles Henry Thompson, Inez Beverly Prosser, and others (Guthrie, 1998). However, broader scholarly attention to teaching this material began with the publication of the *Sourcebook on the Teaching of Black Psychology* (Jones, 1978). Still available from the publisher, this early manual offers a wealth of concrete suggestions, although its list of curricular resources is out of date.

Courses and Specialty Areas

The field of African American psychology has become so extensive that an entire curriculum could (and should) be developed. Such a curriculum would parallel, to an extent, the curriculum in White psychology by offering courses in developmental, abnormal, counseling, and social psychology, and in other core areas. In addition, specialty courses unique to African American psychology might focus on such areas as Black or African identity, traditional healing methodologies, or male–female relationships. The following suggested topics and resources are germane to introductory or specialty courses within African American psychology—as well as courses within the general psychology curriculum. Useful general resources, particularly at the introductory level, are Jones (2003); Parham, White, and Ajamu (1999); and Guthrie (1998), who provide critiques detailing the omission of African Americans from mainstream psychology as well as mainstream psychology's preoccupation with dehumanizing African people.

Developmental psychology

Developmental courses can include the entire life span or focus on a particular period along the continuum. Hill (1999) and McAdoo (2002) are useful resources on African American children. Jones (1999b) provides an excellent compilation on children, youth and parenting. Course topics in child development might include the debate over the pedagogical uses of Ebonics, or African American dialects (see Fairchild & Edwards-Evans, 1990; Seymour, Abdulkarim, & Johnson, 1999); cross-ethnic issues in cognitive and psychological assessment (Cunningham, Henggeler, & Pickrel, 1996); and the continuing controversy surrounding transracial adoption (Abdullah, 1996; Baden, 2002). Gibbs (1998) is an excellent resource on Black adolescence. Course topics on this period might include the development of racial or ethnic identity (Resnicow, Soler, Braithwaite, Selassie, & Smith, 1999); cross-ethnic comparisons of sexual norms and behaviors (Miller, Forehand, & Kotchick, 1999); and the factors that contribute to the development of youth gangs, particularly in urban areas (Quamina, 1999). Resources are also available for the adult and elderly periods, particularly regarding factors affecting mental and physical health (Bowles & Kington, 1998; Brunswick & Messeri, 1999; Joseph, 1997; Mills & Henretta, 2001; Ramseur, 1998).

Gender and the family

Sufficient material exists to develop courses that focus on African American women, men, the family, or some combination of these. Courses focusing on women might include topics such as work (Turner, 1997), health (Lawson, Rodgers-Rose, & Rajaram, 1999), identity (Collins, 2001), male–female relationships (Bethea, 1998), and mother–daughter relationships (Wharton & Thorne, 1997). White and Cones (1999) provided a good general resource on African American men; special topic areas might include fathering (Bowman & Forman, 1997), career development (Chung, Baskin, & Case, 1999), and mental health (Franklin & Boyd-Franklin, 2000; Hopp & Herring, 1999). Another important topic is family issues for African American lesbians and gay men (Greene & Herek, 1997; Mays, Chatters, Cochran, & Mackness, 1998). McAdoo's (1996) book remains an excellent source of general information on Black families, whereas more recent works focus on parenting (Anderson, 1999), historical perspectives (Gadsden, 1999), family structure (Jarrett & Burton, 1999), marriage (Orbuch, Veroff, & Hunter, 1999), and social support (McCabe, Clark, & Barnett, 1999).

Educational psychology

African American educational psychology is of central importance in understanding adult outcomes. Specific topics include the aforementioned role of language (Hoover, 1998), assessment (Jones, 1996), the relationships between academic achievement and identity (Spradin, Welsh, & Hinson,

2000), and debates about race and IQ (Helms, 1997). Students may examine intelligence testing by reading a racist perspective (e.g., Rushton, 1996) as well as arguments that debunk scientific racism (e.g., Fairchild, 1991; Helms, 1997). Recent work on stereotype vulnerability—the idea that African American youth perform more poorly when there is the possibility of confirming negative stereotypes about academic achievement—is also worth exploring (Steele, 1998; Steele & Aronson, 1995).

Employment and economics

Employment and economics are key areas of investigation within African American psychology. Much of the literature on the economics of being African American have focused on welfare and other forms of public assistance (Vartanian, 1999). Because the rate of unemployment is much higher for African Americans than for other ethnic groups, it is important to investigate its effects on physical and mental health (Rodriguez, Allen, Frongillo, & Chandra, 1999). It is also essential to examine the role of racial discrimination in the workplace, including the effects on health outcomes (Mays, Coleman, & Jackson, 1996) of differential access to jobs (Broman, 1997) and earnings (Tam, 1997). Additional important topics in this area are career development for men (Chung et al., 1999) and women (Turner, 1997), Black professionals (Holder & Vaux, 1998), and racism in the workplace (Kirby & Jackson, 1999).

Personality

One of the most exciting areas of investigation in African American psychology is personality, particularly with respect to identity issues (Cross, Parham, & Helms, 1998). This work has focused on the challenges to a healthy sense-of-self within a sociocultural milieu that degrades Black people (Jones, 1998a). Other research has focused on African American masculinity (Bush, 1999); African self-consciousness and commitment (McCowan & Alston, 1998); and acculturation into the majority (rejecting) culture (Snowden & Hines, 1999), with implications for mental health (Williams & Williams-Morris, 2000). Racial attitudes are also part of the processes and products of personality development (Hudson & Hines-Hudson, 1999).

Clinical and counseling psychology

An extensive body of theory and research exists on clinical and counseling issues regarding African Americans. Instructors will find Jones's (1998b) edited collection on African American mental health a useful general resource. Topics for study might include the etiology, prevalence, or treatment of specific disorders or behavioral problems, such as Alzheimer's disease (Auchus, 1997); anxiety (Neal-Barnett & Crowther, 2000); psychiatric disorders associated with HIV/AIDS (Myers & Durvasula, 1999);

coping with HIV/AIDS (Ball, Tannenbaum, Armistead, & Maguen, 2002); anger (Franklin, 1998); eating and body image disorders (Demarest & Allen, 2000; Harris & Kuba, 1997); drug and alcohol abuse (Brunswick, 1999; Burlew, Neely, & Johnson, 2000; Obot, Hubbard, & Anthony, 1999); or suicide (Burr, Hartman, & Matteson, 1999). A key issue to understand is that the mental and social functioning of African Americans are affected by their second- (or third-) class status in a racist social order. This affects the way that problems originate, express themselves, and are treated (Thompson, 2002). Failure to take this into consideration can lead to misdiagnoses, inappropriate treatment strategies, and the inability to ameliorate the presenting problems. Instructors might introduce important new work on "African centered" therapeutic approaches (Okpaku, 1999; Phillips, 1998), including traditional African approaches to medicine and healing (Ashanti, 1998; Grills & Rowe, 1998). Another essential topic for students to consider is the race of therapist. African American clients, depending on their own racial identity, may or may not need an African American therapist (Carter & Boyd-Jackson, 1998). In addition, racial attitudes of the therapist may affect initial clinical impressions (Abreu, 1999), therapeutic progress (Leary, 1995), and ultimate therapeutic success (Sterling, Gottheil, Weinstein, & Serota, 1998).

Teaching Strategies

We have found a number of specific strategies to be useful in teaching African American psychology. Interactive techniques (vs. relying solely on lectures) are usually more effective in helping students to grapple with challenging material (Richard, 1996). We also recommend the videotaped lectures by eminent psychologists that are available from The Association of Black Psychologists (P.O. Box 55999, Washington, DC 20040-5999), featuring a wide range of dynamic speakers so that students can see and hear about cutting-edge thinking and research in the field.

Assignments and discussion

We have found several approaches useful for engaging students in active consideration of the course content. One involves requiring them to write brief thumbnail sketches of the readings and more lengthy reaction statements, which allow them to offer any personal reaction, positive or negative, that they have to the reading material. The class then sits in a circle, and after the instructor makes brief introductory remarks, the students are asked to share those reactions. This assures that students come to class well prepared and produces a stimulating interchange of ideas, with the instructor helping to clarify or amplify key points. Another useful approach is to have students work on separate components of an assignment and then come together to share their insights and knowledge. This can involve the critical analysis of readings or a review of one another's papers. The instructor organizes the students into heterogeneous groups, which fosters cross-fertilization of ideas and exposure to varied learning and thinking styles (Whitten, 1993). Students generally respond well to collaborative exercises when cultural and racial issues are addressed (Whittlesey, 2001).

Movies and movie clips

The presence of African American themes in popular motion pictures has grown over the last 10 years or so. Instructors may find many opportunities to show movies—or, preferably, movie clips—in order to generate discussion around pertinent issues in the course. Movies produced and directed by Spike Lee are particularly helpful. For example, *She's Gotta Have It* (S. J. Lee & Lee, 1986) explores sexuality; *Jungle Fever* (S. Lee, 1991) examines color consciousness, marriage, and interracial relationships; *Do The Right Thing* (S. Lee, 1989) explores race relations; and *Bamboozled* (S. Lee, 1999) focuses on color consciousness and identity. *Sankofa*, an excellent movie by the independent filmmaker Haile Gerima (1993), portrays slavery and examines African American identity issues. Another independent movie, *One Week* (Seaton, 2001), ignites discussions about relationships and HIV/AIDS. Useful documentaries include *Ethnic Notions* (Riggs, 1996), which examines media images; *Nappy* (Douglas, 1997), which focuses on hair and racial identity; and *A Question of Color* (Sandler, 1992), which explores color consciousness in the African American community.

CONCLUSION

Theory and research in African American psychology have progressed enormously over the last 30 years. A curriculum reflecting this body of knowledge could easily include a dozen or more courses. One of the challenges within the field of psychology in the years to come will be to expand its parameters and diversify its content so that this broadened vision becomes a reality.

REFERENCES

Abdullah, S. B. (1996). Transracial adoption is not the solution to America's problems of child welfare. *Journal of Black Psychology, 22*, 254–261.

Abreu, J. M. (1999). Conscious and nonconscious African American stereotypes: Impact on first impression and diagnostic ratings by therapists. *Journal of Consulting and Clinical Psychology, 67*, 387–393.

Anderson, L. P. (1999). Parentification in the context of the African American family. In N. D. Chase (Ed.), *Burdened children: Theory, research, and treatment of parentification* (pp. 154–170). Thousand Oaks, CA: Sage.

Ashanti, K. C. (1998). Rootwork and voodoo in the diagnosis and treatment of African American patients. In R. L. Jones (Ed.), *African American mental health: Theory, research, and intervention* (pp. 511–541). Hampton, VA: Cobb & Henry.

Auchus, A. P. (1997). Demographic and clinical features of Alzheimer disease in Black Americans: Preliminary observations on an outpatient sample in Atlanta, Georgia. *Alzheimer Disease and Associated Disorders, 11,* 38–46.

Baden, A. L. (2002). The psychological adjustment of transracial adoptees: An application of the cultural–racial identity model. *Journal of Social Distress and the Homeless, 11,* 167–191.

Ball, J., Tannenbaum, L., Armistead, L., & Maguen, S. (2002). Coping and HIV infection in African-American women. *Women and Health, 35,* 17–37.

Bethea, P. D. (1998). African-American women and the male–female relationship dilemma: A counseling perspective. In D. R. Atkinson & G. Morton (Eds.), *Counseling American minorities* (5th ed., pp. 87–94). Boston: McGraw-Hill.

Bowles, J., & Kington, R. S. (1998). The impact of family function on health of African American elderly. *Journal of Comparative Family Studies, 29,* 337–347.

Bowman, P. J., & Forman, T. A. (1997). Instrumental and expressive family roles among African American fathers. In R. J. Taylor & J. S. Jackson (Eds.), *Family life in Black America* (pp. 216–247). Thousand Oaks, CA: Sage.

Broman, C. L. (1997). Families, unemployment, and well-being. In R. J. Taylor & J. S. Jackson (Eds.), *Family life in Black America* (pp. 157–166). Thousand Oaks, CA: Sage.

Brunswick, A. F. (1999). Structural strain: An ecological paradigm for studying African American drug use. *Drugs and Society, 14*(1–2), 5–19.

Brunswick, A. F., & Messeri, P. A. (1999). Life stage, substance use and health decline in a community cohort of urban African Americans. *Journal of Addictive Diseases, 18,* 53–71.

Burlew, K., Neely, D., & Johnson, C. (2000). Drug attitudes, racial identity, and alcohol use among African-American adolescents. *Journal of Black Psychology, 26,* 402–420.

Burr, J. A., Hartman, J. T., & Matteson, D. W. (1999). Black suicide in U.S. metropolitan areas: An examination of the racial inequality and social integration-regulation hypotheses. *Social Forces, 77,* 1049–1080.

Bush, L. V. (1999). Am I a man? A literature review engaging the sociohistorical dynamics of Black manhood in the United States. *Western Journal of Black Studies, 23,* 49–57.

Carter, R. T., & Boyd-Jackson, S. (1998). Racial identity and psychotherapy. In R. L. Jones (Ed.), *African American identity development* (pp. 99–119). Hampton, VA: Cobb & Henry.

Chung, Y. B., Baskin, M. L., & Case, A. B. (1999). Career development of Black males: Case studies. *Journal of Career Development, 25,* 161–171.

Collins, P. H. (2001). Like one of the family: Race, ethnicity, and the paradox of US national identity. *Ethnic and Racial Studies, 24,* 3–29.

Cross, W. E., Parham, T. A., & Helms, J. E. (1998). Nigrescence revisited: Theory and research. In R. L. Jones (Ed.), *African American identity development* (pp. 3–71). Hampton, VA: Cobb & Henry.

Cunningham, P. B., Henggeler, S. W., & Pickrel, S. G. (1996). The cross-ethnic equivalence of measures commonly used in mental health services research with children. *Journal of Emotional and Behavioral Disorders, 4,* 231–239.

Demarest, J., & Allen, R. (2000). Body image: Gender, ethnic, and age differences. *Journal of Social Psychology, 40,* 465–473.

Douglas, L. (Producer and Director). (1997). *Nappy* [Motion picture]. (Available from Peazey Head Productions, 238 Park Avenue, No. 2, Takoma Park, MD 20912.)

Fairchild, H. H. (1991). Scientific racism: The cloak of objectivity. *Journal of Social Issues, 47,* 101–115.

Fairchild, H. H. (2000). African American psychology. In A. E. Kazdan (Ed.), *Encyclopedia of psychology* (Vol. 1, pp. 92–99). New York: Oxford University Press.

Fairchild, H. H., & Edwards-Evans, S. (1990). African American dialects and schooling: A review. In A. Padilla, H. Fairchild, & C. Valadez (Eds.), *Bilingual education: Issues and strategies* (pp. 75–86). Newbury Park, CA: Sage.

Franklin, A. J. (1998). Treating anger in African American men. In W. S. Pollack & R. F. Levant (Eds.), *New psychotherapy for men* (pp. 239–258). New York: Wiley.

Franklin, A. J., & Boyd-Franklin, N. (2000). Invisibility syndrome: A clinical model of the effects of racism on African-American males. *American Journal of Orthopsychiatry, 70,* 33–42.

Gadsden, V. L. (1999). Black families in intergenerational and cultural perspective. In M. E. Lamb (Ed.), *Parenting and child development in "nontraditional" families* (pp. 221–246). Mahwah, NJ: Erlbaum.

Gerima, H. (Producer and Director). (1993). *Sankofa* [Motion picture]. (Available from Mypheduh Films, 2714 Georgia Avenue, NW, Washington, DC 20001.)

Gibbs, J. T. (1998). African American adolescents. In J. T. Gibbs & L. N. Huang (Eds.), *Children of color: Psychological interventions with culturally diverse youth* (rev. ed., pp. 171–214). San Francisco: Jossey-Bass.

Greene, B., & Herek, M. (Eds.). (1997). *Ethnic and cultural diversity among lesbians and gay men.* Thousand Oaks, CA: Sage.

Grills, C., & Rowe, D. (1998). African traditional medicine: Implications for African-centered approaches to healing. In R. L. Jones (Ed.), *African American mental health: Theory, research, and intervention* (pp. 71–100). Hampton, VA: Cobb & Henry.

Guthrie, R. V. (1998). *Even the rat was white: A historical view of psychology.* Boston: Allyn & Bacon.

Harris, D. J., & Kuba, S. A. (1997). Ethnocultural identity and eating disorders in women of color. *Professional Psychology: Research and Practice, 28*, 341–347.

Helms, J. E. (1997). The triple quandary of race, culture, and social class in standardized cognitive ability testing. In D. P. Flanagan & J. L. Genshaft (Eds.), *Contemporary intellectual assessment: Theories, tests, and issues* (pp. 517–532). New York: Guilford Press.

Hill, S. A. (1999). *African American children: Socialization and development in families.* Thousand Oaks, CA: Sage.

Holder, J. C., & Vaux, A. (1998). African American professionals: Coping with occupational stress in predominantly White work environments. *Journal of Vocational Behavior, 53*, 315–333.

Hoover, M. R. (1998). A recommended reading list for teachers of students who speak Ebonics. *Journal of Negro Education, 67*, 43–47.

Hopp, J. W., & Herring, P. (1999). Promoting health among Black American populations: An overview. In R. M. Huff & M. V. Kline (Eds.), *Promoting health in multicultural populations: A handbook for practitioners* (pp. 201–221). Thousand Oaks, CA: Sage.

Hudson, J. B., & Hines-Hudson, B. M. (1999). A study of the contemporary racial attitudes of Whites and African Americans. *Western Journal of Black Studies, 23*, 22–34.

Jarrett, R. L., & Burton, L. M. (1999). Dynamic dimensions of family structure in low-income African American families: Emergent themes in qualitative research. *Journal of Comparative Family Studies, 30*, 177–187.

Jones, R. L. (Ed.). (1978). *Sourcebook on the teaching of Black psychology.* Washington, DC: Association of Black Psychologists.

Jones, R. L. (Ed.). (1996). *Handbook of tests and measurements for Black populations* (Vols. 1 & 2). Hampton, VA: Cobb & Henry.

Jones, R. L. (Ed.). (1998a). *African American identity development.* Hampton, VA: Cobb & Henry.

Jones, R. L. (Ed.). (1998b). *African American mental health.* Hampton, VA: Cobb & Henry.

Jones, R. L. (Ed.). (1999a). *Advances in African American psychology.* Hampton, VA: Cobb & Henry.

Jones, R. L. (Ed.). (1999b). *African American children, youth and parenting.* Hampton, VA: Cobb & Henry.

Jones, R. L. (Ed.). (2003). *Black psychology* (4th ed.). Hampton, VA: Cobb & Henry.

Joseph, J. (1997). Fear of crime among Black elderly. *Journal of Black Studies, 27*, 698–717.

Kirby, D., & Jackson, J. S. (1999). Mitigating perceptions of racism: The importance of work group composition and supervisor's race. In A. J. Murrell & F. J. Crosby (Eds.), *Mentoring dilemmas: Developmental relationships within multicultural organizations. Applied social research* (pp. 143–155). Mahwah, NJ: Erlbaum.

Lawson, E. J., Rodgers-Rose, L. F., & Rajaram, S. (1999). The psychosocial context of Black women's health. *Health Care for Women International, 20*, 279–289.

Leary, K. (1995). Interpreting in the dark: Race and ethnicity in psychoanalytic psychotherapy. *Psychoanalytic Psychology, 12*, 127–140.

Lee, S. (Producer and Director). (1989). *Do the right thing* [Motion picture]. Universal City, CA: MCA Home Video.

Lee, S. (Producer and Director). (1991). *Jungle fever* [Motion picture]. Universal City, CA: Universal Home Video.

Lee, S. (Producer and Director). (1999). *Bamboozled* [Motion picture]. Los Angeles: New Line Cinema.

Lee, S. J. (Producer), & Lee, S. (Director). (1986). *She's gotta have it* [Motion picture]. New York: Polygram Video.

Mays, V. M., Chatters, L. M., Cochran, S. D., & Mackness, J. (1998). African American families in diversity: Gay men and lesbians as participants in family networks. *Journal of Comparative Family Studies, 29*, 73–87.

Mays, V. M., Coleman, L. M., & Jackson, J. S. (1996). Perceived race-based discrimination, employment status, and job stress in a national sample of Black women: Implications for health outcomes. *Journal of Occupational Health Psychology, 1*, 319–329.

McAdoo, H. P. (Ed.). (1996). *Black families* (3rd ed.). Beverly Hills, CA: Sage.

McAdoo, H. P. (Ed.). (2002). *Black children: Social, educational, and parental environments* (2nd ed.). Thousand Oaks, CA: Sage Publications.

McCabe, K. M., Clark, R., & Barnett, D. (1999). Family protective factors among urban African American youth. *Journal of Clinical Child Psychology, 28*, 137–150.

McCowan, C. J., & Alston, R. J. (1998). Racial identity, African self-consciousness, and career decision making in African American college women. *Journal of Multicultural Counseling and Development, 26*, 28–38.

Miller, K. S., Forehand, R., & Kotchick, B. A. (1999). Adolescent sexual behavior in two ethnic minority samples: The role of family variables. *Journal of Marriage and the Family, 61*, 85–98.

Mills, T. L., & Henretta, J. C. (2001). Racial, ethnic, and sociodemographic differences in the level of psychosocial distress among older Americans. *Research on Aging, 23*, 131–153.

Myers, H. F., & Durvasula, R. S. (1999). Psychiatric disorders in African American men and women living with HIV/AIDS. *Cultural Diversity and Ethnic Minority Psychology, 5*, 249–262.

Neal-Barnett, A. M., & Crowther, J. H. (2000). To be female, middle class, anxious, and Black. *Psychology of Women Quarterly, 24*, 129–137.

Obot, I. S., Hubbard, S., & Anthony, J. C. (1999). Level of education and injecting drug use among African Americans. *Drug and Alcohol Dependence, 55*, 177–182.

Okpaku, S. O. (1999). Prescribing for Africans: Some transcultural guidelines. In J. M. Herrera & W. B. Lawson (Eds.), *Cross cultural psychiatry* (pp. 53–62). Chichester, England: Wiley.

Orbuch, T. L., Veroff, J., & Hunter, A. G. (1999). Black couples, White couples: The early years of marriage. In E. M. Hetherington (Ed.), *Coping with divorce, single parenting, and remarriage: A risk and resiliency perspective* (pp. 23–43). Mahwah, NJ: Erlbaum.

Parham, T. A., White, J. L., & Ajamu, A. (1999). *The psychology of Blacks: An African centered perspective.* Upper Saddle River, NJ: Prentice Hall.

Phillips, F. B. (1998). Spirit-energy and NTU psychotherapy. In R. L. Jones (Ed.), *African American mental health: Theory, research, and intervention* (pp. 357–377). Hampton, VA: Cobb & Henry.

Quamina, A. (1999). Adolescent gangs: A practitioner's perspective. In C. W. Branch (Ed.), *Adolescent gangs: Old issues, new approaches* (pp. 39–56). Philadelphia: Brunner/Mazel.

Ramseur, H. P. (1998). Psychologically healthy African American adults. In R. L. Jones (Ed.), *African American mental health: Theory, research, and intervention* (pp. 3–31). Hampton, VA: Cobb & Henry.

Resnicow, K., Soler, R. E., Braithwaite, R. L., Selassie, M. B., & Smith, M. (1999). Development of a racial and ethnic identity scale for African American adolescents: The Survey of Black Life. *Journal of Black Psychology, 25,* 171–188.

Richard, H. (1996). Filmed in black and white: Teaching the concept of racial identity at a predominantly White university. *Teaching of Psychology, 23,* 159–161.

Riggs, M. (Producer and Director). (1986). *Ethnic notions* [Videotape]. (Available from California Newsreel, 149 Ninth Street, San Francisco, CA 94103.)

Rodriguez, E., Allen, J. A., Frongillo, E. A., Jr., & Chandra, P. (1999). Unemployment, depression and health: A look at the African-American community. *Journal of Epidemiology and Community Health, 53,* 335–342.

Rushton, J. P. (1996). Race, genetics, and human reproductive strategies. *Genetic, Social, and General Psychology Monographs, 122,* 21–53.

Sandler, K. (Producer and Director). (1992). *A question of color* [Videotape]. (Available from California Newsreel, 149 Ninth Street, San Francisco, CA 94103.)

Seaton, C. (Director). (2001). *One week.* [Motion Picture]. Available from Film Life, Inc., 100 Avenue of the Americas, New York, NY 10013).

Seymour, H. N., Abdulkarim, L., & Johnson, V. (1999). The Ebonics controversy: An educational and clinical dilemma. *Topics in Language Disorders, 19*(4), 66–77.

Snowden, L. R., & Hines, A. M. (1999). A scale to assess African American acculturation. *Journal of Black Psychology, 25,* 36–47.

Spradin, L. K., Welsh, L. A., & Hinson, S. L. (2000). Exploring African American academic achievement: Ogbu and Brookover perspectives. *Journal of African American Men, 5,* 17–33.

Steele, C. M. (1998). A threat in the air: How stereotypes shape intellectual identity and performance. In J. L. Eberhardt & S. T. Fiske (Eds.), *Confronting racism: The problem and the response* (pp. 202–233). Thousand Oaks, CA: Sage.

Steele, C. M., & Aronson, J. (1995). Stereotype threat and the intellectual test performance of African Americans (pp. 369–389). In C. Stangor (Ed.), *Stereotypes and prejudice: Essential readings*. New York: Psychology Press.

Sterling, R. C., Gottheil, E., Weinstein, S. D., & Serota, R. (1998). Therapist/patient race and sex matching: Treatment retention and 9-month follow-up outcome. *Addiction, 93*, 1043–1050.

Tam, T. (1997). Sex segregation and occupational gender inequality in the United States: Devaluation or specialized training? *American Journal of Sociology, 102*, 1652–1692.

Thompson, V. L. S. (2002). Racism: Perceptions of distress among African Americans. *Community Mental Health Journal, 38*, 111–119.

Turner, C. W. (1997). Psychosocial barriers to Black women's career development. In J. V. Jordan (Ed.), *Women's growth in diversity: More writings from the Stone Center* (pp. 162–175). New York: Guilford Press.

Vartanian, T. P. (1999). Childhood conditions and adult welfare use: Examining neighborhood and family factors. *Journal of Marriage and the Family, 61*, 225–237.

Wharton, A. S., & Thorne, D. K. (1997). When mothers matter: The effects of social class and family arrangements on African American and White women's perceived relations with their mothers. *Gender and Society, 11*, 656–681.

White, J. L., & Cones, I. (1999). *Black man emerging: Facing the past and seizing a future in America*. New York: Freeman.

Whitten, L. A. (1993). Infusing Black psychology into the introductory psychology course. *Teaching of Psychology, 20*, 13–21.

Whittlesey, V. (2001). *Diversity activities in psychology*. Boston: Allyn & Bacon.

Williams, D. R., & Williams-Morris, R. (2000). Racism and mental health: The African American experience. *Ethnicity and Health, 5*, 243–269.

15

TEACHING LATINO PSYCHOLOGY

CYNTHIA DE LAS FUENTES, AUGUSTÍNE BARÓN, JR.,
AND MELBA J. T. VÁSQUEZ

The history of Latinos[1] in North, Central, and South America, and the Caribbean, includes conquests by foreign cultures and the persistent sequelae of social, economic, and political persecution, oppression, and discrimination. This history, however, also includes brave struggles for liberation and an impressive resilience manifested by oppressed peoples' outstanding cultural accomplishments. Most Latinos living in the United States are *mestizos*—descendants of both oppressive European cultures and oppressed indigenous peoples.

The purpose of this chapter is to introduce theoretical, research, and applied information that we believe is critical in teaching a course on Latino psychology or infusing Latino issues into traditional courses. Among the topics to be covered are demographics; immigration history; educational attainment data; and a variety of social, psychological, and cultural concepts.

---

[1]We have chosen to use the term *Latino* as the inclusive term for all subgroups that comprise the larger population. *Latina* refers to women only; *Latino* refers to men and women.

THE LATINO POPULATION IN THE UNITED STATES:
A DEMOGRAPHIC SURVEY

The Latino population in the United States has grown 38% since 1990—to 31 million—while the overall U.S. population has grown just 9%. Currently, Latinos constitute approximately 11% of the total population and 36% of all ethnic subgroups. By 2005, Latinos are projected to be the largest minority in the country, and by 2050, nearly one quarter of the population will be Latino. Within the U.S. Latino population, Mexicans represent 66.1%, Puerto Ricans 9%, Cubans 4%, and Central and South Americans 14.5% (U.S. Bureau of the Census, 2001). Latinos come from 22 different countries of origin; some are White, and some are Black or Asian, but most are mestizos.

Immigration

Although many indigenous Mexicans lived in the southwestern region of the present-day United States long before the first Puritans settled in Plymouth (Shorris, 1992), most Latinos immigrated after World War II; they include refugees of war, intellectuals persecuted for their politics, affluent individuals with resources, and impoverished people seeking economic opportunities. To understand the psychological significance of immigration, it is helpful to understand the experiences of the people who migrate, because immigration, even when willingly chosen, results in a variety of significant sequelae for the individual and his or her family (de las Fuentes & Vásquez, 1999). Immigration usually involves major changes in physical, cultural, and social environments (Strier, 1996). These changes result in a complexity of feelings, including the pain of a lack of shared experiences with peers; stress and weariness from the effort to acculturate to, and cope with, cultural differences; rejection from the new and dominant culture, which may affect mood and self-worth; confusion in terms of role expectations, values, and identity; and a sense of powerlessness from being unable to function as effectively in the new culture as one did in the home culture (Espín, 1997).

A course in Latino Psychology should include an overview of the unique social and political histories of the countries of origin and of the immigration patterns of the different groups of Latinos living in the United States (e.g., McGoldrick, Giordano, & Pearce, 1996). For example, because of the common United States–Mexico border of more than 2,000 miles, and the closeness of families, many Mexican immigrants and Mexican Americans preserve a strong ethnic identity that is reinforced by steady contact between the societies and cultures across the borders. Some Mexicans may view their stay as time limited, guided by financial considerations, until they are able to return to their homes south of the border. As a result, expectations about the duration of their stay curtail some Mexicans' involvement in entrepreneurship (Roberts, 1995). Because of low socioeconomic status, many Mexicans do not have enough influence to confront the desperate conditions in the neighborhoods where they live or the political climate that discriminates against them.

Another group with a highly varied immigration history is Cubans. The initial wave of Cuban immigrants, who arrived during the later 1800s, was largely composed of tobacco farm owners. A second large wave occurred between 1959 and 1980 after Fidel Castro's rise to power. During this period, six stages of immigration can be distinguished, each resulting in demographically different Cuban subgroups (Gonzalez, 1991).

Educational and Economic Status

According to the American Council on Education (1995, cited in Commission on Ethnic Minority Recruitment, Retention, and Training in Psychology, 1997), high school completion rates among 18- to 24-year-old Latino youth are lower than for any other ethnic group; in 1993, the rate was 60%. Among Whites, rates remained stable, at approximately 83%, during the same 20-year period. College enrollment figures indicate that by 1993 Latinos had increased their proportional representation at colleges to 7.4%, due mainly to the enrollment of women and older students (American Council on Education, 1995, cited in Commission on Ethnic Minority Recruitment, Retention, and Training in Psychology, 1997).

Educational attainment varies across different Latino subgroups (Rumbaut, 1994). For example, many upper class South Americans tend to come to the United States specifically for educational opportunities and return afterward to their countries of origin. Although they are unable to return to Cuba, many Cubans who immigrated in the 1950s, especially those who were in the professional class, are also academically successful. However, many Mexicans and refugees of the war in Central America came from communities where educational attainment was precluded by the need for economic and physical survival (McCloskey, Southwick, Fernandez-Esquer, & Locke, 1995). As a result, their assimilation into the U.S. marketplace has been segmented, resulting in a high concentration in the labor class (Rumbaut, 1994)—and the need for economic survival often prohibits their pursuit of an education. Thus, Central American immigrant families have the highest unemployment and lowest level occupational status of all Latinos in the United States (McCloskey et al., 1995). Having fled war and torture, many immigrated without proper documentation, which unfortunately has made them more vulnerable to the exploitation of employers who pay low wages under the table for service jobs, often in the domestic, garment, and construction industries.

Further illustration of the economic disparities between U.S. Latinos and non-Hispanic Whites is provided by a U.S. Bureau of the Census (1999) comparison of median household incomes for the years 1972–1998. While the income of Hispanics remained relatively stable over the 26 years, at around $28,000, the income for non-Hispanic Whites rose during that same period, from $38,000 to $42,000.

FAMILY AND CULTURAL VALUES

One of the characteristics shared among all Latino groups involves the importance of strong family values and unity. Large extended families have been a source of vitality and resilience for Latinos, along with close friends (*compadres*) who are often considered part of the extended family network (Ginorio, Gutierrez, Cauce, & Acosta, 1995). Vásquez (1994) suggested that the strong, persistent familistic and collectivistic orientation is a source of strength and resilience for Latinos and that the White western values of independence, individuality, and competition may not be as applicable to Latinos.

Gender Issues and the Family

Traditional gender role socialization for Latinos includes strict norms prescribing specific behaviors, attitudes, and beliefs for girls and boys. For example, a preferred role for Latinas includes showing the virtuous and maternal characteristics that are attributed to the Virgin Mary, which are referred to as *marianismo*. Adherence to this role is not without cost. For example, *aguantarse* ("to tolerate") is often used as an imperative to compel women to endure adversity and human suffering (e.g., husbands who are unfaithful and children who are disrespectful). Implicit in the *marianista* identity is also the suppression of sexuality, given that sex is considered an act of obligation for the purpose of procreation (Vásquez & de las Fuentes, 1999). If a woman engages in sexual behavior prior to marriage she is considered valueless and a whore. This tension in the Madonna–whore continuum leaves a void between the two positions and is used not only to protect a girl's marital prospects but also to preserve her family's honor and pride. Such attitudes and beliefs vary greatly as a function of acculturation.

Latino boys and men are traditionally given far more social and familial freedoms. For Latino men, the continuum is that of *caballero–macho*. The *caballero* identity encompasses values of being a gentleman, a respectable family leader and role model, and a primary wage earner, thereby deserving of the respectful title of *Don*. On the other end of the continuum, the macho identity focuses on sexual and physical virility. A *machista* is proud of his sexual prowess, may have one or more mistresses, and is sometimes abusive physically toward women and children, and toward himself through the abuse of alcohol. In Latino families, the identity of the caballero is upheld as ideal, and any deviation from that is considered shameful. Instructors might explore the effects of economic marginalization on this identity and ask the class to consider what it might mean for a man whose ethnic culture requires him to provide well for his family but who is generally undereducated and discriminated against by a U.S. culture and marketplace.

Acculturation to the dominant White culture in the United States may create dilemmas between first-generation children and their parents (de las Fuentes & Vásquez, 1999). Children tend to learn the English language faster than their parents, diminishing the prominence of a traditionally patriarchal family structure. These children often become the family's "culture brokers," with parents becoming dependent on them to negotiate with the outside world (Hernandez, 1996). In their attempts to develop an identity that fits their American peer group, daughters especially may present an immense challenge for their parents, whose traditions may include prescribed attitudes and behaviors for "proper" girls (de las Fuentes & Vásquez, 1999). Additional Latino mental health issues and needs relevant to gender have been addressed by Chacon, Cohen, and Strover (1986) and Vásquez (1994).

Because strong gender norms are established and maintained in the family and the culture, it is very difficult for lesbian and gay Latinos to be "out" and to identify with their lesbian and gay communities. Both the cultural value of saving face, and respect for the family who might feel shamed by this public declaration, leads many gay and lesbian Latinos to avoid this identity (Comas-Díaz, 1993, cited in Greene, 1994). Furthermore, Espín (1987) suggested that in identifying themselves as lesbian, Latina lesbians compel their cultures to confront their rigid gender norms.

Most of the psychological research on or about lesbians and gays uses samples in which White, middle-class (too often college students) are over-represented (Greene, 1994). Similarly, research on people of color rarely addresses gays and lesbians of color. Instructors of Latino Psychology should address this lack of intersecting research, asking the class questions such as: How can ethnic and gender development and identity affect each other? How can the prejudices of racism, sexism, and heterosexism affect self-perceptions, self esteem, general well-being, and adherence to familial and cultural values and beliefs?

Simpatia and Respeto

Simpatia involves being polite and avoiding ill-mannered behavior in all situations, to prevent interpersonal discord (Triandis, Marín, Lisansky, & Betancourt, 1984). Along with deference to authority, *simpatia* is an aspect of *respeto* (respect) shown to persons in positions of authority. For example, children are expected to use the formal, second-person pronoun of *usted* (you) when addressing adults until permission is granted to do otherwise.

Similarly, it is considered disrespectful and condescending to use first names before familiarity is established among adults.

These values have implications for the faculty–student relationship. For example, a Latina visiting her professor during office hours may seem to agree with her professor's instructions, all the while not understanding them. She might assume that if she were to ask for clarification she would be implying that the instructions were delivered unclearly—and she would rather risk her grade than risk insulting or angering her professor.

Familismo and Personalismo

Familismo is the primary organizing principle of the Latino family, indicating that the needs of the family and the group are primary, superseding the needs of the individual (Zea, García, Begrave, & Quezada, 1997). Large and geographically close families have traditionally been an important source of financial, emotional, and spiritual support for Latino families. Children are encouraged to remain in their parent's home until they marry—and even longer if needed, until the couple achieves financial stability. Unrelated families in a neighborhood will pull together in times of need, for child rearing and disciplining, and for social events. In contrast, the U.S. dominant culture values individualism as an organizing principle: Families are smaller; parents look forward to their children's independence; and neighbors, who are often strangers, would never discipline another's child (McGoldrick et al., 1996)

Personalismo in Latino cultures focuses on the unique qualities in the individual that make a family and community proud. It is not separateness; rather, it is a recognition of the pride a family and community has in the gifts and talents of its individual members. For example, musical and oratorical talents are highly valued and often showcased in neighborhood parties and talent shows, bringing much pride to the individual's family.

Instructors might ask non-Latino students to describe their concepts of normal family functioning and to compare their descriptions with descriptions given by Latino students. Differences in assumptions of normality may lead to a discussion of biases that could appear in the counseling setting, where Latino clients might receive a more pathological diagnosis based on "unresolved dependency needs."

Religion and Spirituality

Although there were many pre-historical religions practiced in the New World, since the colonization by Spain, Catholicism has been a pervasive force in the lives of many Latinos (Cervantes & Ramírez, 1992). Adherence to traditional Catholic values, specifically the religious value discussed above regarding *marianismo* and the practice of *aguantar*, may prevent some Latinas from seeking psychological treatment (Acosta, Yamamoto, & Evans, 1982), favoring instead the support of religious and layperson in their churches.

Perhaps as a legacy of the hybridizing of native religions with European Christianity, *curanderia* (folk healing) is practiced by many Latinos. *Curanderismo* has been described as a set of folk and medical beliefs, rituals, and practices that address the psychosocial and spiritual concerns of some Latinos, especially Mexicans and Mexican Americans (Cervantes & Ramírez, 1992). For many Latinos, Catholicism and curanderia coexist in their lives and are manifested in such ways as candle lighting on religious feast days and devout church attendance while also using specific poultices to ward off troublesome spirits.

There are numerous native and European-based religions and spiritual faiths practiced by Latinos today, ranging from Christianity and Judaism to *santeria* and voodoo. An interesting assignment would be for students to explore the evolution of this blending of European with native beliefs and practices. Guest lectures by *curanderos* and field trips to local herbalogists can also provide interesting educational opportunities.

ACCULTURATION

Acculturation is a central explanatory variable in the study of ethnic minorities (Bernal & Knight, 1993). Instructors should include some discussion of this construct, particularly given the fact that so much cross-cultural research in the past has failed to control for acculturational status. Rogler, Malgady, and Rodriguez (1989) defined *acculturation* as a process through which the attitudes, values, beliefs, customs, and behaviors of a minority group change toward those of a dominant society, through continual exposure and contact. Acculturational processes are complex, in that the rate of acculturation can be halted, slowed down, accelerated, or reversed depending on a variety of factors (Barón & Constantine, 1997; Cásas & Vásquez, 1989).

There are a number of paper-and-pencil measures of acculturation that instructors can administer to students as a class exercise, providing them with an opportunity to apply and discuss acculturation theory. Among the more notable instruments are the Measure of Acculturation for Chicano Adolescents (Olmedo, Martínez, & Martínez, 1978), the Bilingualism/Multiculturalism Experience Inventory (Ramírez, 1991), the Acculturation Rating Scale for Mexican Americans (Cuellar, Harris, & Jasso, 1980), and the Behavioral Acculturation Scale (Szapocznik, Scopetta, & Tillman, 1979). Such measures are typically designed to assess degree of acculturation along a dimension ranging from traditional (unacculturated) to balanced (bicultural) to acculturated (assimilated).

ETHNIC AND RACIAL IDENTITY DEVELOPMENT

It is important to differentiate between acculturation and ethnic and racial identity development but also to note that there is a degree of overlap. Whereas acculturation is broadly concerned with the degree to which dominant cultural norms are accepted, rejected, and transformed by the minority person, *ethnic and racial identity development* refers to attitudes, beliefs, and feelings one has about one's own group in comparison to the dominant culture (Barón & Constantine, 1997; Keefe & Padilla, 1987; Phinney, 1990). It is a measure of how ethnic minority individuals perceive their group relative to that of the dominant culture.

Over the last 20 years, a number of theoretical models have attempted to conceptualize ethnic and racial identity development (e.g., Atkinson, Morten, & Sue, 1979; Christensen, 1986; Cross, 1971; Helms, 1985, 1990; C. W. Thomas, 1971). Commonalties across most of the models include hypothesized stages that ethnic minority individuals pass through as they manage issues of diversity. Usually this entails confronting negative stereotypes about one's own ethnic and racial group; moving through a phase of immersion into the positive aspects of one's own group; and achieving a healthy state of self-esteem, pride, and multicultural sensitivity.

Identity development models have given therapists useful road maps for understanding the developmental pathways for ethnic and racial minorities. Rather than relying only on pathological perspectives, such models provide ways of interpreting thoughts, feelings, and actions that can empower individuals. In addition, in stressing the importance of the broader social context, they provide a fuller appreciation of the interplay between internal and external forces that minority individuals must deal with on a daily basis. Instructors can point out that for ethnic minority individuals, ethnicity, race, and general minority status are highlighted in many overt and covert ways by the dominant society and that identity development status plays a role in successful client–therapist matching (Parham & Helms, 1981); degree of self-regard, self-esteem, and self-actualization (Parham & Helms, 1985a, 1985b); and degree of felt anxiety (Parham & Helms, 1985b).

AUDIOVISUAL AND LITERARY RESOURCES AND CLASSROOM ACTIVITIES

There are now a variety of films, videos, and novels related to Latino life and culture that instructors may wish to incorporate into their courses. These resources can make certain psychosocial concepts come alive, especially when opportunities for real life applications in practica or field placements are limited. The following examples illustrate ways films and literature can be used to help students apply and understand concepts such as family and cultural values, acculturation, and ethnic identity development.

Two excellent and widely available films are *El Norte* (The North; A. Thomas & Nava, 1984) and *Mi Familia* (My Family; A. Thomas & Nava, 1995). The former is the story of a brother and sister from Guatemala, who seek a better life in Los Angeles after their father is killed by military junta members and their mother is taken away to prison. Their struggles as illegal aliens are graphically depicted as their dreams are shattered by the realities of poverty and discrimination. *Mi Familia* is a three-generation saga of the Sanchez family as told by the eldest son. The movie covers a span of time from the father's journey from Mexico to California in the 1920s to the family's present-day struggles to capture the American dream. The constellation of family and other characters, as well as the time period covered, make this film an especially rich and enjoyable resource for exploration and discussion.

The range of available novels is much more extensive. An especially popular one is *Bless Me, Ultima* (Anaya, 1972), about a young man's remembrance of growing up with his mystical grandmother (Ultima), a noted folk healer in northern New Mexico. This work introduces readers to the mysterious and magical world of that rural part of the United States and provides insights into values, customs, and beliefs still alive today in many Latino families. A teaching guide has recently been published (Baeza, 1997) to help readers understand the overall structure of the novel and its characters. *Carry Me Like Water* (Saenz, 1995) chronicles the story of a disparate group of Latinos and Whites, both gay and straight, who come to recognize each other from former lives, with hope, forgiveness, confrontations with their pasts, and a redefinition of the notion of family.

These resources can be used to develop an analysis of gender and acculturation, focusing on one or more of the characters. For example, as an individual or group project, instructors can ask students to select characters from *Mi Familia* and assess their acculturational status using one of the acculturation measures at various points in the family's history. Other possibilities include asking students to compare the changing gender norms and roles across the generations or to apply one or more ethnic identity development models. Instructors can also invite students to compare the Sanchez family to their own through the use of genograms, which are excellent tools for teaching about intergenerational dynamics and the development of family-based cultural norms (McGoldrick & Gerson, 1985).

INCORPORATING LATINO PSYCHOLOGY INTO GRADUATE CLINICAL AND COUNSELING COURSES

A graduate-level course syllabus would need to include in-depth information about specific clinical and research topics. For example, the assessment of acculturation can assist in decisions about client assignment to a psychotherapist as well as in determining appropriate treatment goals and interventions. Research has shown that unacculturated individuals may often prefer ethnically similar therapists, bicultural individuals may not have a strong preference, and acculturated individuals may tend to favor therapists of the dominant culture (Atkinson, Casas, & Abreu, 1992). Less acculturated individuals are likely to expect a few sessions of therapy (fewer than three) provided by a directive, active therapist, to produce clear, concrete outcomes. Acculturated individuals are more likely to expect and appreciate longer treatment by a less directive therapist, with goals focused on broad personal and developmental issues (Atkinson et al., 1992). Acculturation is also a critical variable in issues related to psychotherapy such as client dropout rates (Miranda, Andujo, Caballero, Guerrero, & Ramos, 1976), content and extent of self-disclosure (Castro, 1977), overall success of therapy (Miranda & Castro, 1977), preferences for an ethnically similar therapist (Sanchez & Atkinson, 1983), and likelihood of seeking particular mental health services (Atkinson et al., 1992).

More generally, graduate courses on psychological assessment can incorporate major psychodiagnostic and intellectual assessment instruments in both English and Spanish. Supervised opportunities for administering, scoring, and interpreting the measures would add much depth to such a class. A course on psychopathology should incorporate culturally influenced mental disorders and how to assess and treat them (e.g., López & Guarnaccia, 2000). A therapy techniques course should include relevant literature on therapy strategies and therapeutic issues with Latinos. A practicum placement at a site that serves Latino clients would certainly enhance students' knowledge and skill development.

A FINAL NOTE

Although the topics described in this chapter are not exhaustive, we have presented those that we believe are particularly important in the teaching of Latino Psychology. We have looked at general issues of immigration, acculturation, identity, and cultural and familial values held by many people of Latino heritage. We have also suggested specific exercises and resources that can facilitate and enhance the understanding of the issues and concepts. We hope that the information we have provided will contribute to an enhanced awareness of Latino culture, issues, and life experiences for psychology instructors—and for their students, who will live out their lives in an increasingly multicultural society.

REFERENCES

Acosta, F. X., Yamamoto, J., & Evans, L. A. (1982). *Effective psychotherapy for low income and minority patients*. New York: Plenum.

Anaya, R. A. (1972). *Bless me, Ultima: A novel*. Berkeley, CA: Tonatiuh International.

Atkinson, D. R., Casas, J. M., & Abreu, J. (1992). Mexican American acculturation, counselor ethnicity and cultural sensitivity, and perceived counselor competence. *Journal of Counseling Psychology, 39,* 515–520.

Atkinson, D. R., Morten, G., & Sue, D. W. (1979). *Counseling American minorities: A cross-cultural perspective*. Dubuque, IA: W. C. Brown.

Baeza, A. (1997). *Keep blessing us, Ultima: A teaching guide for* Bless Me, Ultima *by Rudolfo Anaya*. Austin, TX: Easkin Press.

Barón, A., & Constantine, M. G. (1997). A conceptual framework for conducting psychotherapy with Mexican American college students. In. M. C. Zea & J. Garcia (Eds.), *Psychological interventions with Latino populations* (pp. 108–124). Needham Heights, MA: Allyn & Bacon.

Bernal, M. E., & Knight, G. P. (Eds.). (1993). *Ethnic identity: Formation and transmission among Hispanics and other minorities*. Albany: State University of New York Press.

Casas, J. M., & Vásquez, M. J. T. (1989). Counseling the Hispanic client: A theoretical and applied perspective. In P. Pedersen, J. G. Draguns, W. J. Lonner, & J. E. Trimble (Eds.), *Counseling across cultures* (3rd ed., pp, 153–175). Honolulu: University of Hawaii Press.

Castro, F. G. (1977). *Level of acculturation and related considerations in psychotherapy with Spanish speaking/surnamed clients* (Occasional Paper No. 3). Spanish Speaking Mental Health Research Center, University of California, Los Angeles.

Cervantes, J. M., & Ramírez, O. (1992). Spirituality and family dynamics in psychotherapy with Latino children. In L. A. Vargas & J. D. Koss-Chioino (Eds.), *Working with culture: Psychotherapeutic interventions with ethnic minority children and adolescents* (pp. 103–128). San Francisco: Jossey-Bass.

Chacon, M., Cohen, E., & Strover, S. (1986). Chicanas and Chicanos: Barriers to progress in higher education. In M. A. Olivas (Ed.), *Latino college students* (pp. 296–324). New York: Columbia University Press.

Christensen, C. (1986). *Cultural boundaries*. Toronto, Ontario, Canada: University of Toronto Press.

Commission on Ethnic Minority Recruitment, Retention, and Training in Psychology. (1997). *Visions and transformations . . . the final report*. Washington, DC: American Psychological Association.

Cross, W. E. (1971). The Negro-to-Black conversion experience: Toward a psychology of Black liberation. *Black World, 20,* 13–27.

Cuellar, I., Harris, L. C., & Jasso, R. (1980). An acculturation rating scale for Mexican-American normal and clinical populations. *Hispanic Journal of Behavioral Sciences, 2,* 199–217.

de las Fuentes, C., & Vásquez, M. J. T. (1999). Immigrant adolescent girls of color: Facing American challenges. In N. G. Johnson, M. C. Roberts, & J. Worell (Eds.), *Beyond appearance: A new look at adolescent girls* (pp. 131–150). Washington, DC: American Psychological Association.

Espín, O. M. (1987). Issues of identity in the psychology of Latina lesbians. In Boston Lesbian Psychologies Collective (Eds.), *Lesbian psychologies: Explorations and challenges* (pp. 35–51). Urbana: University of Illinois Press.

Espín, O. M. (1997). Crossing borders and boundaries: The life narratives of immigrant lesbians. In B. Greene (Ed.), *Ethnic and cultural diversity among lesbians and gay men* (pp. 191–215). Thousand Oaks, CA: Sage.

Ginorio, A. G., Gutierrez, L., Cauce, A. M., & Acosta, M. (1995). Psychological issues for Latinas. In H. Landrine (Ed.), *Bringing cultural diversity to feminist psychology: Theory, research and practice* (pp. 241–264). Washington, DC: American Psychological Association.

Gonzalez, G. M. (1991). Cuban Americans: Counseling and human development issues, problems, and approaches. In C. C. Lee & B. L. Richardson (Eds.), *Multicultural issues in counseling: New approaches to diversity* (pp. 157–169). Alexandria, VA: American Association for Counseling and Development.

Greene, B. (1994). Lesbian women of color: Triple jeopardy. In L. Comas-Díaz & B. Greene (Eds.), *Women of color: Integrating ethnic and gender identities in psychotherapy* (pp. 389–428). New York: Guilford Press.

Helms, J. E. (1985). Toward a theoretical explanation of the effects of race on counseling: A Black and White model. *The Counseling Psychologist, 12*, 153–165.

Helms, J. E. (Ed.). (1990). *Black and White racial identity: Theory, research, and practice*. New York: Greenwood Press.

Hernandez, M. (1996). Central American families. In M. McGoldrick, J. Giordano, & J. K. Pearce (Eds.), *Ethnicity and family therapy* (2nd ed., pp. 214–224). New York: Guilford Press.

Keefe, S. E., & Padilla, A. M. (1987). *Chicano ethnicity*. Albuquerque: University of New Mexico Press.

López, S. R., & Guarnaccia, P. J. (2000). Cultural psychopathology: Uncovering the social world of mental illness. *Annual Review of Psychology, 51*, 571–598.

McCloskey, L. A., Southwick, K., Fernandez-Esquer, M. E., & Locke, C. (1995). The psychological effects of political and domestic violence on Central American and Mexican immigrant mothers and children. *Journal of Community Psychology, 23*, 95–116.

McGoldrick, M., & Gerson, R. (1985). *Genograms in family assessment*. New York: Norton.

McGoldrick, M., Giordano, J., & Pearce, J. K. (Eds.). (1996). *Ethnicity and family therapy* (2nd ed.). New York: Guilford Press.

Miranda, M. R., Andujo, E., Caballero, I. L., Guerrero, C., & Ramos, R. A. (1976). Mexican American dropouts in psychotherapy as related to level of acculturation. In M. R. Miranda (Ed.), *Psychotherapy with the Spanish-speaking: Issues in research and service delivery* (pp. 35–50). Los Angeles: Spanish Speaking Mental Health Research Center, University of California.

Miranda, M. R., & Castro, F. G. (1977). Culture distance and success in psychotherapy with Spanish-speaking clients. In J. L. Martinez (Ed.), *Chicano psychology* (pp. 249–262). New York: Academic Press.

Olmedo, E. L., Martínez, J. L., & Martínez, S. R. (1978). Measure of acculturation for Chicano adolescents. *Psychological Reports, 42*, 159–170.

Parham, T. A., & Helms, J. E. (1981). The influence of Black students' racial attitudes on preferences for counselor's race. *Journal of Counseling Psychology, 28*, 250–257.

Parham, T. A., & Helms, J. E. (1985a). Attitudes of racial identity and self-esteem of Black students: An exploratory investigation. *Journal of College Student Personnel, 26*, 143–147.

Parham, T. A., & Helms, J. E. (1985b). Relation of racial identity attitudes to self-actualization and affective states of Black students. *Journal of Counseling Psychology, 32*, 431–440.

Phinney, J. S. (1990). Ethnic identity in adolescents and adults: A review of research. *Psychological Bulletin, 3*, 499–514.

Ramírez, M. (1991). *Psychology of the Americas: Multicultural perspectives in personality and mental health*. New York: Pergamon.

Roberts, B. (1995). *The effect of socially expected durations on Mexican migration. The economic sociology of immigration: Essays on networks, ethnicity, and entrepreneurship*. New York: Russell Sage Foundation.

Rogler, L. H., Malgady, R. G., & Rodriguez, O. (1989). *Hispanics and mental health: A framework for research*. Malabar, FL: Krieger.

Rumbaut, R. G. (1994). The crucible within: Ethnic identity, self-esteem, and segmented assimilation among children of immigrants. *International Migration Review, 28*, 748–794.

Saenz, B. A. (1995). *Carry me like water: A novel*. New York: Hyperion.

Sanchez, A. R., & Atkinson, D. R. (1983). Mexican-American cultural commitment preference for counselor ethnicity, and willingness to use counseling. *Journal of Counseling Psychology, 30*, 215–220.

Shorris, E. (1992). *Latinos: A biography of the people*. New York: Norton.

Strier, D. R. (1996). Coping strategies of immigrant parents: Directions for family therapy. *Family Process, 35*, 363–376.

Szapocznik, J., Scopetta, M. A., & Tillman, W. (1979). What changes, what stays the same and what affects acculturative change? In J. Szapocznik & M. C. Herrera (Eds.), *Cuban Americans: Acculturation adjustment and the family* (pp. 82–95). Washington, DC: National Coalition of Hispanic Health and Human Services Organizations.

Thomas, A. (Producer), & Nava, G. (Director). (1984). *El norte* [The north; Motion picture]. Farmington Hills, MN: CBS/Fox.

Thomas, A. (Producer), & Nava, G. (Director). (1995). *Mi familia* [My family; Motion picture]. Atlanta, GA: Turner Home Entertainment.

Thomas, C. W. (1971). *Boys no more*. Beverly Hills, CA: Glencoe Press.

Triandis, H. C., Marín, G., Lisansky, J., & Betancourt, H. (1984). Simpatia as a cultural script of Hispanics. *Journal of Personality and Social Psychology, 47*, 1363–1375.

U.S. Bureau of the Census. (1999). *Median household income by race and Hispanic origin: 1972–1998*. Retrieved December 17, 2000, from http://www.census.gov/hhes/income/income98/incxrace.html

U.S. Bureau of the Census. (2001). *The Hispanic Population in the United States*. Retrieved January 7, 2003 from www.census.gov/population/socdemo/hispanic/p20-535/p20-535.pdf

Vásquez, M. J. T. (1994). Latinas. In L. Comas-Díaz & B. Greene (Eds.), *Women of color: Integrating ethnic and gender identities in psychotherapy* (pp. 114–138). New York: Guilford Press.

Vásquez, M. J. T., & de las Fuentes, C. (1999). American-born Asian, African, Latina, and American Indian adolescent girls: Challenges and strengths. In N. G. Johnson, M. C. Roberts, & J. Worell (Eds.), *Beyond appearance: A new look at adolescent girls* (pp. 151–173). Washington, DC: American Psychological Association.

Zea, M. C., García, J. G., Begrave, F. Z., & Quezada, T. (1997). Socioeconomic and cultural factors in rehabilitation of Latinos with disabilities. In J. G. García & M. C. Zea (Eds.), *Psychological interventions and research with Latino populations* (pp. 217–234). Needham Heights, MA: Allyn & Bacon.

16

INFUSING AMERICAN INDIAN AND ALASKA NATIVE TOPICS INTO THE PSYCHOLOGY CURRICULUM

JOSEPH E. TRIMBLE

Substantial psychological and sociocultural information is now available about American Indians and Alaska Natives. The goal of this chapter is to provide guidelines and resources for infusing some of this information into psychology courses. In it, I first present general cultural and demographic information about these groups, and then, in more detail, discuss topics that are particularly relevant to the psychological study of Indian and Native lifeways and thoughtways.

DEFINITIONS AND DEMOGRAPHICS

In the United States, the terms *Native American* or *Native American Indian* often are used interchangeably with *American Indian* and *Alaska Native,*

I express my sincere and heartfelt gratitude to the following friends and colleagues who provided me with guidance, support, and assistance in the preparation of this chapter: Arthur Blue, Mary Clearing-Sky, William Demmert, Dan First Scout Rowe, Joseph Gone, Teresa La Fromboise, Catherine Swan Reimer, Pamela Jumper-Thurman, Peggy Ting Lim, Maiga Miranda, and Lyle Noisy Hawk. I also thank the Radcliffe Institute for Advanced Study, Harvard University, for providing resources and support that facilitated the preparation and writing of this chapter.

to refer to the indigenous, aboriginal peoples of North America. These first two terms are not preferred by most American Indians and Alaska Natives, as they are not considered to be an accurate description of the indigenous people of the United States. Organizations such as the National Congress of American Indians, the National Indian Education Association, and the Society of Indian Psychologists consider the term *Native American* to be too encompassing of ethnic groups in the United States. In actuality, many American Indians and Alaska Natives prefer to be referred by their specific tribal names, such as Dine (Navajo); Lakota, Dakota, and Nakota (Sioux); and Tohono O'odham (Papago).

Thus, the term *American Indian* is an "ethnic gloss" (Trimble, 1991)—an imposed category referring to close to 2 million people who represent more than 550 federally recognized tribes, an additional 225 or so nonfederally recognized tribes, and residents of about 220 Alaska Native villages (Snipp, 1996). The extraordinary diversity contributed by tribal background confounds any attempt to describe a modal American Indian psychology or personality. Students should therefore be cautioned against generalizing from material on one tribal group to another group or to Indians or Natives in general.

Who belongs in this category is another interesting issue. Although tribes, states, and the Bureau of Indian Affairs require that an individual document any tribal membership claim, the U.S. Bureau of the Census uses only a self-identification procedure to establish American Indian identity. On the basis of data from 2000, the U.S. Bureau of the Census (2001) declared that 2,475,956 citizens are American Indians and Alaska Natives—compared with a census report of 552,000 American Indians in 1960 (the census bureau did not include an Alaska Native category at that time, so this figure may be an undercount); thus, between 1960 and 2000 the American Indian population apparently grew by 349%. Clifton (1989) noted a similar phenomenon between 1950 and 1990, when the increase for Indians was more than 400%, whereas the overall U.S. count increased by only 61% during the same period. Given that immigration does not generally occur among American Indians and Alaska Natives, such remarkable increases must be attributed to the growing inclination of Americans to declare their "Indianness."

In addition, in the 2000 U.S. Census, individuals had the option of marking more than one race category, enabling them to declare identification with more than one group—and more than 4,119,000 individuals marked "American Indian and Alaska Native" along with one or more other groups. Thus the "race alone or in combination" count is much higher then the "race alone" count of 2,475,956, which raises the question of which count is more representative of the true Indian population. It is quite possible that many who chose the "race in combination" category are enrolled members of federally recognized tribes—or, conversely, many may not be enrolled in any tribe. Most likely, the true population is somewhere between the two counts.

Another point of confusion is that more than half of the American Indians in the 1990 census resided in urban areas, where they would be less likely to report tribal affiliation, speak or understand their tribal language, participate in tribal cultural activities, or marry Indians than those who reside in rural areas, villages, or reservation communities (Snipp, 1996). Furthermore, the rapid increase in mixed ethnic and intertribal marriages is creating a subpopulation of American Indians who do not identify with any specific tribe, creating a broad pan-Indian ethnocultural category grounded in borrowed and internalized bits and pieces of different tribal traditions, out of which many younger Indians and Natives are creating an identity. Thornton (1996) pointed out that this phenomenon is leading to a time when one will speak of "Native Americans as people of Native American ancestry or heritage" (p. 110) rather than as members of specific tribes.

TEACHING AMERICAN INDIAN PSYCHOLOGY

American Indian psychology is a legitimate field that integrates a number of other academic disciplines, brings together different modes of inquiry, and offers unique theoretical and empirical findings. As such, it merits inclusion in psychology courses across the curriculum. It is a broad area of inquiry, covering an ethnic group that is considerably more diverse than the European groups that immigrated to North America. For example, in the 17th century, a period of accelerated European colonialization of North American, there were at least 150 tribal groups with unique worldviews and approximately 30 different languages residing in the United States east of the Mississippi River.

General Resources

A number of comprehensive bibliographies have been published in the last 20 years, which can provide valuable resources for incorporating American Indian issues into psychology courses. Kelso and Attneave (1981) focused on studies of North American Indian mental health, across many academic disciplines; Trimble and Bagwell (1995) covered psychological and behavioral articles from 1967 to 1994; Lobb and Watts (1989) focused on alcohol use and abuse among American Indian youth. Additional supplemental material includes Bataille's (1993) bibliographic dictionary of 231 American Indian women born between 1595 and 1960; Martin and O'Leary's (1990) bibliography of more than 25,000 books and articles that describe the traditional culture and lifeways of North American Indians; and Sandefur, Rindfuss, and Cohen's (1996) edited volume on demographic and public health characteristics of American Indians. Journals dedicated exclusively to American Indians and Alaska Natives include the *Journal of the National Center for American Indian and Alaska Native Mental Health Research* and the *American Indian Culture and Research Journal*.

Historical and Cultural Considerations in the Course Organization

The field of psychology tends to decontextualize the individual (Cole, 1996). In classroom discussions of Indian and Native experiences, it is particularly important to present psychological topics within a social, political, and historical context. I typically devote some time to a discussion of the history of Indian and European relations and the problems that colonialism presented for both populations (see Duran & Duran, 1995). From the moment of European contact with the western hemisphere's indigenous population, the native people were viewed as an impediment to European immigration and settlement and thus the source of considerable intergroup conflict. Coser (1956) defined *conflict* as a struggle between groups and their factions over values and over claims to scarce status, power, and resources. America's indigenous people initially had the resources and claims to large tracts of territory and the power to maintain and control them; the colonialists wanted native lands for settlement. Early in the history of the Americas, many native groups were willing to share their resources. However, as wave after wave of Europeans immigrated to the new lands, the demands for resources and land increased, which eventually led to intense dissension and fighting.

The history of the relations between American Indians, if not all of the indigenous peoples of the western hemisphere, closely follows Park's (1950) model of race relations, with one exception. Specifically, Park maintained that "the race relations cycle takes the form . . . of contact, competition, accommodation and eventual assimilation (and this is) progressive and irreversible" (p. 150). The exception is that many American Indian and Alaska Native groups never reached Park's final stage of full assimilation into the mainstream of American life. Useful historical sources are Berkhofer (1978), V. Deloria (1974), McNickle (1973), and Thornton (1987).

In addition, in the psychology courses I teach at the graduate and undergraduate levels, I use cultural and ethnic material throughout the semester to provide alternative perspectives to conventional findings. For example, in an Introductory Psychology course, for the unit on psychopathology, I include ethnographic descriptions of different tribes' views on extreme forms of behavioral and affective expressions (Reimer, 1999; Trimble, Manson, Dinges, & Medicine, 1984), including tribal-specific concepts such as "ghost sickness," soul loss and soul gain, spirit intrusion, and taboo breaking (see Clement, 1932, and the contents of the Human Relations Area Files available in many university and college libraries). This often provokes lively discussions about the implications and meaning of the concepts across tribal groups, particularly in light of contemporary approaches to psychiatric diagnoses. For example, what constitutes abnormal behavior in one culture may not be considered deviant in another, or there may be no concept of abnormality in some cultural groups. Kiev (1964) and Kleinman (1980) have presented informative summaries of the cultural issues surrounding the concept of abnormality.

In addition, I have found that students tend to respond most favorably to material concerning Indians and Natives when it is presented in the context of a more familiar topic. For example, when I cover the conventional topic of prejudice and discrimination, my addition of related material about American Indians and Alaska Natives encourages students to apply principles they have learned to groups with which they are unfamiliar.

Suggested Topics for Inclusion

The following topics are particularly relevant to the psychology of American Indians and Alaska Natives and can be incorporated into a wide variety of courses across the psychology curriculum.

Research design and methodology

Conducting field-based research with Indians and Natives presents special challenges to the scientific method and all that conventional laboratory science represents (Berry, 1980). The setting of the community, local lifeways and thoughtways, and the degree to which one can create valid research protocols can influence study outcomes in unpredictable ways. Cross-cultural psychological researchers, having often experienced field-based problems, have thus developed culturally sensitive approaches for designing studies and protocols.

Although there has been little published on the topic of research strategies that relate directly to Indians and Natives, the methodological writings in the field of cross-cultural psychology are useful resources. In Kim and Berry's (1993) *Indigenous Psychologies: Research and Experience in Cultural Context*, many of the chapters describe specific research approaches needed to effectively capture information with unique ethnocultural groups (also see Manson, 1997).

Cultural equivalence is an important topic to discuss with students, because it is pivotal to the reliability and validity of study outcomes. In essence, conceptual or measurement equivalence requires the researcher to make certain that the constructs under investigation mean the same thing, or measure the same characteristic, across cultural groups (Johnson, 1998). Equivalence is an especially useful concept to present to students, because it reinforces the notion that not all cultures conceive of behavior, cognition, and affect in the same ways. As a demonstration, I typically provide students with 5–10 survey items and ask them to obtain translations of the items from international students—and then ask other students from the countries represented in the first translation to translate the items back into English. Often the exercise takes place in class, which helps get the concept of equivalence across more directly as students witness it unfold. Also, I encourage discussion about metric equivalence, beginning with a question concerning the universal applicability of the forced-choice response scales used in conventional surveys. Additional material on cross-cultural research problems and strategies can be found in Berry, Poortinga, Segall, and Dasen (1992); Johnson (1998); Manson (1997); and Trimble, Lonner, and Boucher (1983); and material specifically on conducting research in Indian and Native settings can be found in Manson (1997); Santiago-Rivera, Morse, Hunt, and Lickers (1998); Trimble (1977); and Weaver (1997).

Personality, identity, and self-image

To begin a discussion of personality issues, I ask students to draw a picture of an American Indian. Not surprisingly, in almost all the drawings, the image is of a person wearing a feather or a blanket and displaying some sort of blank look on her or his face. Results from the exercise provide a good stimulus for class consideration of perceived image versus reality. I ask them why most drew the "feathered" or stereotypic image and what influenced their perceptions and attributions, and I follow up by asking them to describe the personality of the image they drew, again probing as to origins of their descriptions. I then engage them in a discussion of the presumed relationship between ethnic identity and self-image and problems such as poverty, alcoholism, and suicide (Trimble, 1987b, 2000). Often, students believe that people from oppressed cultures or impoverished backgrounds cannot possibly have positive self-images or stable personalities. I spend considerable classroom time providing empirical evidence to challenge this perspective, using especially Rosenberg's (1989) work on Black and White adolescent self-esteem.

In addition, I present a few summary case studies from classic anthropology, in which ethnographers have portrayed American Indian or Alaska Native tribes as collective, single-minded personality types (P. J. Deloria, 1998). The works of Ruth Benedict, Margaret Mead, and John Honigmann represent a few of the more distinguished anthropologists who advocated this now somewhat outmoded culture and personality school of anthropology. For example, Honigmann (1954) used broad, sweeping statements to describe the personality of the Kaska Indians of northern British Columbia and the Yukon Territory, such as "unaccustomed and unwilling to respond to any leader," "flexible rather than rigid in his behavior," and showing a "tendency to suppress in his behavior all strong emotion" (pp. 9–10). Often I ask students to comment and debate the statement made by Honigmann (1963) that

A social personality is a type which no specific individual will match perfectly. Still it is likely that everyone, except possibly the most subnormal and marginal members of a social system, will in some degree reveal many of the traits that compose the type. (p. 285)

In classroom discussions, I push students to consider how such broad, shorthanded descriptors influence stereotypes and generalizations about groups of people that can fan the flames of intergroup conflict.

Counseling and psychotherapy

Theories and approaches in counseling and clinical psychology are often at odds with the traditional lifeways and thoughtways of nonacculturated Indians and Natives (Trimble & Thurman, 2002). I point out to students that conventional counseling and clinical practices tend to emphasize individualism; assertiveness; status (involving conventional indicators of success); the open discussion of problems with strangers; and achievement of insights that may lead to cognitive, affective, and behavioral changes. I then present tribal-specific conceptualizations of illness, shamanism, and traditional healing, based on ethnographic information from anthropology, psychology, and transcultural psychiatry (Hawk Wing, 1997; Trimble, Manson, et al., 1984; Voss, Douville, Little Soldier, & Twiss, 1999). I also emphasize that among indigenous peoples, complicated procedures have evolved to deal with individual problems. Many of the tribal-specific therapeutic and healing approaches are embedded in dances such as the winter or Spirit Dances of the Coast Salish and the Gourd Dance of the Kiowa (Jilek, 1989). In addition, I point out that most Native-oriented approaches and diagnostic categories center on the spiritual domain. For example, Powers (1982) stated that the Yuwipi man among the Lakota "is particularly suited and trained by the spirits to diagnose and treat 'Indian sickness,' illnesses that generally were common to the people before the white man arrived" (p. 35; also see Mohatt & Eagle Elk, 2000).

Useful information about providing effective counseling and psychotherapy services for American Indian clients and communities can be found in Trimble and Thurman (2002) and Herring (1999). Reimer (1999) described culturally sensitive counseling approaches that should be used in working with Inupiat village groups.

There are a number of interesting and informative films and videos available for use in this area. *White Shamans, Plastic Medicine Men* (Macy & Hart, 1995) documents the commercialization of American Indian spiritual traditions by non-Indians. *Pomo Shaman* (Heick, Mueller, & Heick, 1964) demonstrates the curing technique used by the Kashia group of the southwestern Pomo Indians, involving hand trembling, trance behavior, and music to draw undesirable spirits from the patient's body. *Denial, Healing and Hope: The Nishnawbe-Aski Nation Youth Forum on Suicide* (Northern Insights,

1994) provides a close look at how First Nation communities in northwestern Ontario are seeking healing solutions to the suicide epidemic among young people, not just at a personal level, but spiritually, as communities.

Alcohol and drug use

The topic of alcohol and drug use is a difficult one to present in a short time period, as there is considerable published information dealing with everything from etiology and epidemiology to treatment and aftercare. Moreover, it is an area rife with myth, stereotypic imagery, and inaccuracy. It is, however, an important area for instructors to include, particularly because alcohol use and misuse are considered by most indigenous people of the United States to be their most serious and significant health problem, one that affects almost every facet of their lives (May, 1992). For more than 25 years, substance use and abuse have been identified as significant problems for large numbers of Indian youth residing on reservations (Oetting, Edwards, & Beauvais, 1988). Nonreservation Indian youth been found to have levels of drug use lower than Indian youth living on reservations but higher than their non-Indian counterparts; Indian boarding school students and high school dropouts report higher drug use than Indian youth in general (Beauvais, 1992). These findings lead to the speculation that although reservation life has many positive aspects, there may be environmental variables (e.g., pervasive poverty and unemployment) that promote higher levels of substance use.

After much of the summary information on the causes and incidence of Indian and Native alcoholism and drug use has been presented, a few students can be expected to bring up the subject of genetics and alcoholism and its relationship to American Indians. My response to the question is an incomplete one, as there is little empirical research bearing directly on the topic and thus there is no substantive evidence to support the genetic hypothesis. Indeed, conversation on this topic tends to be lively, and I usually strive to get students to explore all aspects including research methodological issues.

Another important topic is fetal alcohol syndrome (FAS), which has an unusually high incidence among Indians and Natives, although there is not much available literature about it. Instructors can review May's (1992) research and Dorris's (1990) *The Broken Cord*, a poignant, deeply moving account of the author's struggles in raising an adopted Indian child with FAS at a time when little was known about FAS and its effects.

There are a number of instructive and provocative videos that illustrate the effects of alcohol use and abuse among American Indians. *Children of Wind River* (Hitchcock & Bussian, 1989) documents the problems facing the Arapaho and Shoshone tribes on the Wind River reservation in Wyoming. *The Broken Cord* (Moyers & Vitigliano, 1990) contains Bill Moyers's interviews with writers Louise Erdrich and Michael Dorris about their work, their American Indian heritage, and the problems of parenting a child with FAS. *Bitter Wind* (Whittaker, 1963) dramatizes the breakdown of an American Indian family because of alcoholism. *Now That the Buffalo's Gone* (Afriat & Fash, 1992) traces American Indians' history as victims of massacres, broken promises, worthless treaties, and land-grabbing, and shows that most Indians in the United States live in barren reservations where infant mortality, suicide, and alcoholism are common problems.

Stereotypes and prejudice

There is very little written in the behavioral and social science literature about American Indian and Alaska Native stereotypes and prejudice. However, some useful information can be found in the popular press and in historical literature, beginning with the colonialization and settlement of the western hemisphere and continuing to the present (V. Deloria, 1974, 1997). In covering this topic, I begin by reviewing some of the historical facts, and I then attempt to illustrate how many of the facts were distorted by non-Indians (Berkhofer, 1978; Weatherford, 1988).

Next, I examine contemporary conditions and issues that fuel prejudice and discrimination. For example, I spend some time discussing the use of "Indian mascots" by schools and sports teams. A good video to stimulate classroom discussion is the interview with University of Illinois graduate student Charlene Teters, who is featured in the video, *In Whose Honor? American Indian Mascots in Sports* (Rosenstein, 1997). In it, she discusses the effects of her school's mascot, "Chief Illiniwek," on her family as well as on other Native Americans. Interwoven in the narrative are interviews with students, alumni, current and former "Chiefs," members of the Board of Regents, and members of the community. Another engaging approach I use is to present a brief review of commercial Hollywood-type films involving American Indians, which illustrates how much of the imagery of the first Americans has been reduced to stereotypes (Hilger, 1995; Kilpatrick, 1999). I also present a series of slide and overhead transparencies adapted from Stedman (1982) that illustrate how images of Indians have been distorted to present a stereotypic image to the public. Useful reviews of the literature on American Indian stereotypes have been provided by Berkhofer (1978), Bird (1999), V. Deloria (1974), and myself (Trimble, 1987a, 1988). An interesting theoretical discussion of contemporary Indian problems and issues related to stereotyping and prejudice, from the perspective of American Indian psychologists, can be found in Duran and Duran (1995).

Several excellent videos and films also examine these issues. *House Made of Dawn* (Devine & Larner, 1996), adapted from a book by same title (Momaday, 1968) explores the life of a young American Indian boy caught between two worlds. *Without Reservations: Notes on Racism in Montana*

(Hyppa & Monaco, 1995) shows how an entire culture can be degraded through the casual and insidious use of racist imagery, and it challenges the viewer to examine racism between Whites and Indians.

Suggested Assignments and Activities

The following are strategies, activities, and demonstrations that I have found to be most effective in advancing student learning and interest regarding American Indian and Alaska Native content.

Literature review

Using the cross-cultural counseling protohypotheses developed by Sue and Sundberg (1996) as a guide, I ask students to select one hypothesis and prepare a literature review to substantiate its validity. In addition, I require them to propose and design a research strategy for testing the hypothesis with a specific tribal group. A rationale based on a tribe's lifeways and thought-ways must be included in the proposed research design. In a related activity, I ask students to identify a social psychological principle or hypothesis from the field of conflict and conflict resolution theory and to write an essay illustrating how the principle or hypothesis could be applied to explain an event in the history of Indian–White relations (see Trimble, 1987a).

Classroom demonstration

In senior and graduate-level seminars, I present material describing value orientations of different cultural groups (Trimble, 1976), during which I challenge students to evaluate the different perspectives of collective- and individual-oriented cultures. To demonstrate the value of sharing—and the nature of the Potlatch system of the northwest coast tribes in Canada and the United States—I ask students to bring something of value to the next class meeting and inform them that they may have to give it to someone else. At the beginning of that class, I arrange the students in a circle, and one by one I have them place their valued possession in the circle's center. Students then are asked to pick out their valued possession and give it to someone else in the circle, someone whom they respect and wish to honor for their value to the group (the instructor does not participate in the distribution process). Outcomes differ from class to another. On some occasions, a few students do not receive recognition or gifts, and discussion can become spirited as they attempt to deal with being overlooked. Discussions invariably gravitate to the difference between the reciprocity norm and sharing one's possessions without expecting to receive anything in return.

Journal article review

In senior-level and graduate seminars I require that every 2 weeks, students prepare and submit a 2- to 3-page summary and evaluation of a journal article dealing with American Indian and Alaska Native psychological topics. These include a detailed overview of the contents and a critique of the research problem statement, research design, data analysis strategy, and discussion of results. in addition, I require them to provide and justify an alternative research design for each study. On the day the reviews are due, I ask two or three students to summarize their reviews and follow that with a discussion. This activity helps them to stay on track toward the completion of a term paper (on a topic they selected at the beginning of the term) and provides me with ongoing information about their critical-thinking abilities.

Classroom debate

Toward the end of the term, I require students to participate in a debate about a controversial topic concerning Indian and Native issues. Sometimes students select the topic; however, in most instances I provide them with a specific issue and selected readings. About midway through the term, students are randomly assigned to a "pro" group, a "con" group, or an evaluation team; this last group serves as the judges.

I have recently chosen the issue of isolationism and assimilation as the topic for debate; that is, should indigenous populations be left alone to govern themselves, or should they be brought into the flow of the modern world through use of assimilation and modernization tactics and pressures? To start the debate in motion, I show them the haunting and inquiring film, *The Tribe That Hides From Man: The Kreen-Akrore* (Cowell, 1973), and provide them with excerpts from a book by the same name (Cowell, 1973/1996). The film documents the 2-year search by the Villas Boas brothers for the Kreen-Akore Indians, who lived in a remote area in the Amazon basin region of northern Brazil, in an effort to prevent the inevitable disease, destruction, and death soon to be brought on by outside influences. One of the problems facing the brothers was the fact that no one from the outside had ever made contact with the Kreen-Akrore, in part because of their fierce reputation.

CONCLUSION

Psychological research about American Indians and Alaska Natives has grown considerably in the past 30 years. Much of the focus, however, is limited to mental health and substance abuse issues, in part because these areas represent the problems of major concern to Indian and Native communities. Given this limitation, it would be difficult to organize a general course devoted exclusively to Indian and Native psychology, which might end up using anecdotal and impressionistic material and thus lead to misunderstanding and inaccurate generalizations. At present, I recommend that instructors infuse their existing courses with the work of appropriate researchers and scholars, such as those cited in this chapter, many of whom are of American Indian and Alaska Native background. This approach can provide students with the opportunity to compare and contrast the information with conventional presentations of psychological topics, much of which is European American-centric and individual-focused and therefore culturally encapsulated. The infusion of American Indian and Alaska Native topics can expand students' understanding of diverse cultures and enhance their worldview to include an acceptance of alternative perspectives on human and social behavior.

REFERENCES

Afriat, A. (Editor), & Fash, M. (Photographer). (1992). *Now that the buffalo's gone: A report on the past and present of the American Indian* [Videotape]. Princeton, NJ: Films for the Humanities.

Bataille, G. (1993). *Native American women: A bibliographical dictionary.* New York: Garland.

Beauvais, F. (Ed.). (1992). Indian adolescent drug and alcohol use: Recent patterns and consequences [Special issue]. *American Indian and Alaska Native Mental Health Research, 5*(1).

Berkhofer, R. (1978). *The White man's Indian.* New York: Vintage.

Berry, J. (1980). Introduction to methodology. In H. Triandis & J. Berry (Eds.), *Handbook of cross-cultural psychology* (Vol. 2, pp. 1–28). Boston: Allyn & Bacon.

Berry, J. W., Poortinga, Y. H., Segall, M. H., & Dasen, P. R. (1992). *Crosscultural psychology: Research and applications.* New York: Cambridge University Press.

Bird, E. S. (1999). Gendered construction of the American Indian in popular media. *Journal of Communication, 49*(3), 61–83.

Clement, F. E. (1932). Primitive concepts of disease. *University of California Archaeology and Ethnology, 32,* 185–232.

Clifton, J. A. (1989). Alternate identities and cultural frontiers. In J. A. Clifton (Ed.), *Being and becoming Indian: Biographical studies of North American frontiers* (pp. 1–37). Chicago: Dorsey Press.

Cole, M. (1996). *Cultural psychology: A once and future discipline.* Cambridge, MA: Harvard University Press.

Coser, L. (1956). *The functions of social conflict.* New York: Free Press.

Cowell, A. (Producer). (1973). *The tribe that hides from man: The Kreen-Akrore* [Film]. Philadelphia: Institute for the Study of Human Issues.

Cowell, A. (1996). *The tribe that hides from man.* London: Pimlico (Original work published 1973)

Deloria, P. J. (1998). *Playing Indian.* New Haven, CT: Yale University Press.

Deloria, V. (1974). *Behind the trail of broken treaties: An Indian declaration of independence.* New York: Delacourte.

Deloria, V. (1997). *Red earth, white lies: Native Americans and the myth of scientific fact*. New York: Fulcrum.

Devine, M. (Producer), & Larner, S. (Director). (1996). *House made of dawn* [Videotape]. New York: New Line Home Video, Turner Home Entertainment.

Dorris, M. (1990). *The broken cord*. New York: Harper & Row.

Duran, E., & Duran, B. (1995). *Native American postcolonial psychology*. Albany: State University of New York Press.

Hawk Wing, P. (1997). Lakota teachings: Inipi, Humbleciya, and Yuwipi ceremonies. In D. Sandner & S. Wong (Eds.), *The sacred heritage: The influence of shamanism on analytical psychology* (pp. 193–202). New York: Routledge.

Heick, G. (Editor), Mueller, G. (Producer), & Heick, W. (Photographer). (1964). *Pomo shaman* [Videotape]. Berkeley: University of California Extension Media Center.

Herring, R. D. (1999). *Counseling with Native American Indians and Alaska Natives: Strategies for helping professionals*. Thousand Oaks, CA: Sage.

Hilger, M. (1995). *From savage to nobleman: Images of Native Americans in film*. Lanham, MD: Scarecrow Press.

Hitchcock, V. (Editor), & Bussain, D. (1989). *Children of Wind River* [Videotape]. Boulder, CO: Chariot Productions.

Honigmann, J. (1954). *Culture and personality*. New York: Harper & Row.

Honigmann, J. (1963). *Understanding culture*. New York: Harper & Row.

Hyppa, J. (Producer), & Monaco, P. (Producer). (1995). *Without reservations: Notes on racism in Montana* [Videotape]. Bozeman, MT: Native Voices Public Television.

Jilek, W. (1989). Therapeutic use of altered states of consciousness in contemporary North American dance ceremonials. In C. Ward (Ed.), *Altered states of consciousness and mental health* (pp. 167–185). Newbury Park, CA: Sage.

Johnson, T. P. (1998). Approaches to equivalence in cross-cultural and cross-national survey research. In J. A. Harkness (Ed.), *Cross-cultural survey equivalence* (Nachrichten Spezial, No. 3, pp. 1–40). Mannheim, Denmark: Zentrum fur Umfragen, Methoden und Analysen.

Kelso, D., & Attneave, C. (Eds.). (1981). *Bibliography of North American Indian mental health*. Westport, CT: Greenwood Press.

Kiev, A. (1964). *Magic, faith, and healing*. New York: Free Press.

Kilpatrick, J. (1999). *Celluloid Indians: Native Americans and film*. Lincoln: University of Nebraska Press.

Kim, U., & Berry, J. W. (Eds.). (1993). *Indigenous psychologies: Research and experience in cultural context*. Newbury Park, CA: Sage.

Kleinman, A. (1980). *Patients and healers in the context of culture*. Berkeley: University of California Press.

Lobb, M. L., & Watts, T. W. (1989). *Native American youth and alcohol: An annotated bibliography*. Westport, CT: Greenwood Press.

Macy, T. (Producer), & Hart, D. (Producer). (1995). *White shamans, plastic medicine: A documentary* [Videotape]. Bozeman, MT: Native Voices Public Television.

Manson, S. M. (1997). Ethnographic methods, cultural context, and mental illness: Bridging different ways of knowing and experience. *Ethnos, 25,* 249–258.

Martin, M., & O'Leary, T. (1990). *Ethnographic bibliography of North America* (4th ed. suppl., 1973–1987). New Haven, CT: Human Relations Area Files.

May, P. (1992). Fetal alcohol syndrome and American Indians: A positive challenge in public health and prevention. In E. Haller & L. Aitken (Eds.), *Mashkiki: Old medicine nourishing the new* (pp. 61–68). Lanham, MD: University Press of America.

McNickle, D. (1973). *Native American tribalism: Indian survivals and renewals.* New York: Oxford University Press.

Mohatt, G., & Eagle Elk, J. (2000). *The price of a gift: A Lakota healer's story.* Lincoln: University of Nebraska Press.

Momaday, N. S. (1968). *House made of dawn.* New York: Harper & Row.

Moyers, B. (Producer), & Vitigliano, J. (Director). (1990). *The broken cord, with Louise Erdlich and Michael Dorris* [Videotape]. Princeton, NJ: Films for the Humanities.

Northern Insights (Producer). (1994). *Denial, healing and hope: The Nishnawbe-Aski Nation Youth Forum on Suicide* [Videotape]. Thunder Bay, Ontario, Canada: Author.

Oetting, E., Edwards, R., & Beauvais, F. (1988). Drugs and Native-American youth. *Drugs & Society, 3*(1–2), 1–34.

Park, R. E. (1950). *Race and culture.* New York: Free Press.

Powers, W. (1982). *Yuwipi: Vision and experience in Oglala ritual.* Lincoln: University of Nebraska Press.

Reimer, C. S. (1999). *Counseling the Inupiat Eskimo.* Westport, CT: Greenwood Press.

Rosenberg, M. (1989). Old myths die hard: The case of Black self-esteem. *Revue Internationale de Psychologie Sociale, 2,* 355–365.

Rosenstein, J. (Producer and Director). (1997). *In whose honor? American Indian mascots in sports* [Videotape]. Ho-ho-kus, NJ: New Day Films.

Sandefur, G., Rindfuss, R., & Cohen, B. (Eds.). (1996). *Changing numbers, changing needs: American Indian demography and public health.* Washington, DC: National Academy Press.

Santiago-Rivera, A., Morse, G., Hunt, A., & Lickers, H. (1998). Building a community-based research partnership: Lessons from the Mohawk Nation of Akwesasne. *Journal of Community Psychology, 26,* 163–174.

Snipp, C. M. (1996). The size and distribution of the American Indian population: Fertility, mortality, residence, and migration. In G. Sandefur, R. Rindfuss, & B. Cohen (Eds.), *Changing numbers, changing needs: American Indian demography and public health* (pp. 17–52). Washington, DC: National Academy Press.

Stedman, R. W. (1982). *Shadows of the Indian: Stereotypes in American culture*. Norman: University of Oklahoma Press.

Sue, D., & Sundberg, N. (1996). Research and research hypotheses about effectiveness in intercultural counseling. In P. Pedersen, J. Draguns, W. Lonner, & J. Trimble (Eds.), *Counseling across cultures* (4th ed., pp. 323–352). Thousand Oaks, CA: Sage.

Thornton, R. (1987). *American Indian holocaust and survival: A population history since 1492*. Norman: University of Oklahoma Press.

Thornton, R. (1996). Tribal membership requirements and the demography of "old" and "new" Native Americans. In G. Sandefur, R. Rindfuss, & B. Cohen (Eds.), *Changing numbers, changing needs: American Indian demography and public health* (pp. 103–112). Washington, DC: National Academy Press.

Trimble, J. E. (1976). Value differentials and their importance in counseling American Indians. In P. Pedersen, J. Draguns, W. Lonner, & J. Trimble (Eds.), *Counseling across cultures* (rev. and expanded ed., pp. 203–226). Honolulu: University Press of Hawaii.

Trimble, J. E. (1977). The sojourner in the American Indian community: Methodological concerns and issues. *Journal of Social Issues, 33,* 159–174.

Trimble, J. E. (1987a). American Indians and interethnic conflict: A theoretical and historical overview. In J. Boucher, D. Landis, & K. Arnold (Eds.), *Ethnic conflict: International perspectives* (pp. 208–229). Beverly Hills, CA: Sage.

Trimble, J. E. (1987b). Self-understanding and perceived alienation among American Indians. *Journal of Community Psychology, 15,* 316–333.

Trimble, J. E. (1988). Stereotypic images, American Indians and prejudice. In P. Katz & D. Taylor (Eds.), *Toward the elimination of racism: Profiles in controversy* (pp. 181–202). New York: Pergamon.

Trimble, J. E. (1991). Ethnic specification, validation prospects, and the future of drug abuse research. *International Journal of the Addictions, 25,* 149–169.

Trimble, J. E. (2000). Social psychological perspectives on changing self-identification among American Indians and Alaska Natives. In R. H. Dana (Ed.), *Handbook of cross-cultural/multicultural personality assessment* (pp. 197–222). Mahwah, NJ: Erlbaum.

Trimble, J., & Bagwell, W. (Eds.). (1995). *North American Indians and Alaska Natives: Abstracts of psychological and behavioral literature, 1967–1995*. Washington, DC: American Psychological Association.

Trimble, J. E., Lonner, W., & Boucher, J. (1983). Stalking the wily emic: Alternatives to cross-cultural measurement. In S. Irvine & J. Berry (Eds.), *Human assessment and cultural factors* (pp. 259–273). New York: Plenum.

Trimble, J. E., Manson, S., Dinges, N., & Medicine, B. (1984). Towards an understanding of American Indian concepts of mental health: Some reflections and directions. In A. Marsella, N. Sartorius, & P. Pedersen (Eds.), *Mental health services: The cross-cultural context* (pp. 199–220). Beverly Hills, CA: Sage.

Trimble, J., & Thurman, P. (2002). Ethnocultural considerations and strategies for providing counseling services for Native American Indians. In P. Pedersen,

J. Draguns, W. Lonner, & J. Trimble (Eds.), *Counseling across cultures* (5th ed., pp. 53–91). Thousand Oaks, CA: Sage.

U.S. Bureau of the Census. (2001). *Census of the population: General population characteristics, American Indians and Alaska Natives areas, 2000.* Washington, DC: U.S. Government Printing Office.

Voss, R., Douville, V., Little Soldier, A., & Twiss, G. (1999). Tribal and shamanic-based social work practice: A Lakota perspective. *Social Work, 44,* 228–241.

Weatherford, J. (1988). *Indian givers: How the Indians of the Americas transformed the world.* New York: Fawcett-Columbine.

Weaver, H. (1997). The challenge of research in Native American communities: Incorporating principles of cultural competence. *Journal of Social Service Research, 23*(2), 1–15.

Whittaker, S. (Director). (1963). *Bitter wind* [Videotape]. Ogden, UT: Department of Education, Brigham Young University.

17

INTEGRATING JEWISH ISSUES INTO THE TEACHING OF PSYCHOLOGY

EVELYN TORTON BECK, JULIE L. GOLDBERG, AND
L. LEE KNEFELKAMP

Although in recent years there have been efforts to include diversity in the psychology curriculum, taking into account factors such as gender, race, sexual identity, socioeconomic status, age, and physical (dis)ability, Jewish identity as a marker of difference has continued to be ignored or made invisible altogether—a fact that is particularly striking given the large number of Jews working in the field (Beck, 1991a; Siegel & Cole, 1991). This omission is a reflection of a pervasive attitude within the larger society, that Jewish identity and anti-Jewish oppression are nonissues in the world today.

Jews represent only one third of 1% of the world's population and less than 3% within the United States (American Jewish Committee, 2000). Ashkenazi Jews (Jews of European descent), who comprise the great majority within the United States, have been so identified with the White Christian majority that U.S. society as a whole has tended to trivialize and dismiss as insignificant the effects of centuries of historical and current anti-Semitism on Jews today and to ignore the importance of Jewish identity as a foundation for Jews' psychological well-being. Such issues are even more pronounced for Sephardic Jews, whose ancestors lived in Spain or Portugal before their expulsion in 1492. Although they represent only about 3% of U.S. Jews, they comprise the majority of Jews in the Middle East—yet their existence is often ignored not only by the dominant U.S. culture but also by Ashkenazi Jews (Langman, 1999).

BEING A JEW: DIVERSE MEANINGS

In the United States today, Jews are primarily regarded as a religious group. However, Jewish identity also includes a sense of belonging to the Jewish people (in addition to whatever national citizenship one might have); thus there is a Jewish historical and cultural identity or ethnicity even for those who reject religion altogether. In addition, most Jews, whatever their religious identification, strongly support the existence of the State of Israel (which was created as a refuge for Jews after their near annihilation during the Nazi Holocaust), even if they are critical of its policies and political practices (Lipset & Raab, 1995).

Since the fall of the second temple in 70 C.E., Jews have been dispersed throughout the world in what is called the *Jewish diaspora*. Jews of color can be found in the Middle East, Africa, Asia, Mexico, South America, and the Caribbean, and are a growing population within the United States (*Bridges*, 2001). Although in the United States Jews have entered the middle-class in large numbers, contrary to the myths and stereotypes that still abound, they do not as a group hold significant wealth or positions of power (Lipset & Raab, 1995).

ANTI-SEMITISM AND PERSECUTION

Institutionalized persecutions of Jews have persisted over many centuries, dramatically illustrated by the long history of pogroms and the Nazi Holocaust in Europe. Recent events around the world—for example, in Russia (Bohlen, 1999) and Japan (Goodman & Miyazawa, 1995)—provide evidence of ongoing global hatred toward Jews. In addition, anti-Semitism has intensified throughout the world in response to the terrorist acts of September 11, 2001, for which many blame Israel—and, by extension, the Jews (Anti-Defamation League, 2002, June 27; J. Rosen, 2001). Although it is true that institutionalized anti-Semitism in the United States is at an all-time low, anti-Semitism itself within society is not, as evidenced by the proliferation of extremist anti-Semitic tracts and activity (Dees, 2000) and recent incidents of violence against Jews (Anti-Defamation League, 2002, June 11; Dedman, 1999; Sterngold, 1999). Gerson and Sedlacek (1992) surveyed U.S. college students and found overt, negative attitudes toward Jews, especially women, and Curtis (1990), in an overview of anti-Semitism in the United States, concluded that some negative attitudes toward Jews had in fact increased since 1970. More recently, the Anti-Defamation League (2002, June 11) documented that levels of anti-Semitism in the United States are continuing to rise.

Awareness of these attitudes is reflected in the large percentage of Jews who in a 1999 survey ranked anti-Semitism as the greatest threat to Jews (American Jewish Committee, 1999). Furthermore, this long, continuing history of persecution has had significant impact on Jewish identity (Hammer, 1995). One powerful effect is the internalizing of anti-Semitism—a psychological process in which the vilifying, menacing messages of anti-Jewish oppression are absorbed and converted into self-hatred, shame, and fear of being identified with Jews (Gilman, 1992).

CURRICULAR EXCLUSION

Omitting Jews from the psychology curriculum leaves intact the pervasive negative images that are embedded in popular culture—stereotypes such as the "Jewish mother," the "Jewish American Princess" (JAP), and the ineffectual and effete Jewish male. In the few instances when Jews have been included in the curriculum, as in some social psychology texts, it has usually been only in terms of negative stereotyping and historical victim status, while the more subtle everyday fears of anti-Semitism that so many Jews carry silently (Beck, 1991a, 1991b) have remained unaddressed.

When Jews have attempted to introduce their issues into discussions of multiculturalism, they have often encountered overt or covert resistance. We have witnessed such responses in psychology classes and at professional conferences, including (a) repetition of age-old stereotypes (among the most common are the irrational beliefs that all Jews are rich and exploit the poor, that Jews are Christ killers, that Jews exercise undue control, that Jews are disloyal citizens and are not to be trusted); (b) outright rejection of the idea that Jewish issues belong in the multicultural curriculum; (c) dismissal of the significance of identity issues for Jews (e.g., clinical case presentations where the fact that the patient is a Jew is not considered important); and (d) silence or abrupt change of subject—for example, in response to the observation that whereas many U.S. Jews share in "White privilege," they do not experience the "Christian privilege" of the dominant culture.

Graduate programs often discourage doctoral research that would focus on Jewish themes, on the grounds that it would make the candidate less marketable. In addition, the myth of a Jewish "takeover" creates a shift from invisibility to "overvisibility" and makes it risky for Jews in academia to raise the issue of exclusion. Many, like Jews in the larger society, feel that their position is a precarious one and that acceptance by colleagues and the institution requires that they downplay their Jewish identity (Brody, 1997) and don't "make trouble." A Jew who is willing to raise Jewish concerns (again and again if she or he receives no response) often begins to be viewed as a "problem," thus becoming remarginalized.

STRATEGIES FOR CURRICULAR INCLUSION

To prevent such situations from arising in the classroom, we recommend that psychology instructors familiarize themselves with the psychosocial history of Jews (Wistrich, 1991) and the psychological issues that many Jews share (Klein, 1980; E. J. Rosen & Weltman, 1996). A recent handbook addressing Jewish issues in multiculturalism (Langman, 1999) provides an excellent overview and bibliography. Other resources focus on the ways in which gendered Jewish experiences are both the same and yet different from those of other minorities (Beck, 1989; Siegel & Cole, 1991; Weiner & Moon, 1995).

Bringing Jewish issues into the classroom can have a number of important effects. At a very basic level, an acknowledgment of Jewish cultural facts and traditions can make the class seem more welcoming to Jewish students. For example, the instructor can avoid scheduling exams or assignment due dates on Jewish holy days which all begin at sundown the day before, when Jewish students are likely to be absent, and can also be inclusive in language, such as using *house of worship* as a generic term rather than *church*. Furthermore, the inclusion of Jewish issues enables students to understand better the multiculturalism among them while also fostering an awareness of anti-Semitism and the need to challenge it. In addition, Jewish values of intellectual inquiry and social justice, and the determination for survival in the face of adversity and oppression, can provide positive models for all students (Breitman, 1995; Knefelkamp, 1992). Jewish issues can be relevant to the content of many courses; in the sections that follow, we have provided suggestions for integrating them into different areas of the psychology curriculum.

History and Theory

If instructors and textbooks presented theories in historical context, and provided information about the theorists' cultural backgrounds, Jewish influences on the development of major theories in psychology would be very evident. It is quite startling that Atwood and Stolorow (1979), in their groundbreaking work exploring the ways in which theories of personality are influenced by the subjective world of the theorist, do not once mention Freud's Jewish identity or consider its significance. In fact, Freud's experiences as a Jew living in the virulently anti-Semitic society of Vienna may have shaped his theoretical thinking to a remarkable degree (Gilman, 1993). For example, Freud's core concept of defense mechanisms, which he deemed necessary to protect the ego not only from internal id forces but also from attacks by the external world, can very likely be linked to his own experiences of anti-Semitism. His acute awareness of anti-Semitism may have also influenced his focus on the irrational forces in group processes. Gilman (1993) further speculated that Freud projected the negative characteristics that were associated with the feminized Jewish male onto his theories about women's character and development.

In addition to Freud, there are numerous other Jewish figures who have had a major impact on the field, shaping many of the theories and strategies of psychotherapy (Langman, 1999). These include, for example, Albert Ellis (rational–emotive), Kurt Lewin and Irvin Yalom (group), Jacob Moreno (psychodrama), Victor Frankl (existential), Fritz Perls (Gestalt), and Nathan Ackerman (family). To this list could be added Anna Freud (ego psychology), Melanie Klein and Nancy Chodorow (psychoanalytic/object relations), Laura Brown (lesbian feminist theory and ethics), and Olga Silverstein (feminist family therapy). In addition, Abraham Maslow's notions of a hierarchy of needs, peak experiences, and being-psychology may well have their roots in the writings of Spinoza, a radical Jewish philosopher who had been deeply influenced by Maimonides's five basic faculties of the soul (Hoffman, 1988).

Developmental Psychology

Contemporary developmental psychology proposes that individual identity formation is influenced by societal expectations by both the dominant culture and by particular communities of affinity (such as being Jewish or gay/lesbian). As members of the U.S. mainstream culture, Jews are at the very least bicultural, and additional factors (such as being biracial, lesbian, or working class) result in a multicultural identity. Jewish identity development, then, can be characterized by the necessity to negotiate multiple roles in response to cultural expectations that are often in tension, particularly during the transition to adulthood.

Adolescence

Adolescents typically are confronted with issues of physical attractiveness and body image, as well as questions surrounding dating, friendship groups, and pressure from peers, and these basic experiences of growing up are made more complex by the biculturality of being Jewish in U.S. society (S. W. Schneider, 1984). For example, teens who date across religious lines often face disapproval from both sets of parents. The negative legacies of the Holocaust and the continuing rise of intermarriage contribute to Jewish fears of becoming extinct; more than 50% of Jews marry out, and the overwhelming majority of children born to mixed marriages are raised in the Christian religion (Lipset & Raab, 1995). Thus, Jewish parents may be particularly concerned if their son or daughter wishes to date non-Jews.

At the same time, pressure on Jews to become part of the American mainstream has led many to assimilate and to distance themselves from Jewish traditions and values. Such Jews often focus on upward economic mobility, material comforts, and appearance (as a buffer against anti-Semitism which, as these behaviors suggest, they may have already been internalized). During adolescence, the children of such Jews may be especially vulnerable to pressures to conform. This is probably the reason that nose jobs (i.e., rhinoplasty)—which can be viewed as attempts to erase indications of cultural difference from the Gentile ideal of female beauty—are a common option for adolescent Jewish girls from assimilated families (Schwartz, 1995).

Negative images of "the Jew" that prevail in the larger culture are always present for Jewish teenagers as they attempt to negotiate parental expectations and peer pressures in their own search for an affirming self. Indeed, the internalization of these images can cause difficulties as Jewish teens make judgments about the attractiveness or desirability of potential dating partners. Adolescents who suspect they are gay, lesbian, bisexual, or transsexual may face particular difficulties within the Jewish family, especially if they are religiously observant, because of the religion's strong taboo against nonheterosexual practices (Beck, 1989).

Young adulthood

The issues of adolescence often intensify during young adulthood. Individuals beginning careers may experience subtle anti-Semitism in the workplace or when they seek to partner. For example, Jews may find that there are invisible ceilings beyond which they will not be promoted in the corporate world (Korman, 1988). Moreover, for young adults grappling with Jewish identity issues, dating may require confronting stereotypes—for example, that Jewish women are demanding and that Jewish men are sexually inept (Beck, 1991a). In addition, Jewish young adults often face strong familial pressures to marry and procreate; in fact, Jewish families give such priority to producing grandchildren that when a same-sex couple brings home a child, their partnership may be fully accepted for the first time, despite prejudices against same-sex relationships that are rife in the culture (E. J. Rosen & Weltman, 1996). Mixed-religion heterosexual or homosexual young couples are faced with questions of religious conversion and whether to raise children in one religious tradition or in a "mixed" set of traditions—which can be difficult, as Christian and Jewish traditions differ significantly with respect to conceptualizations of a higher being, an afterlife, and immortality (Medding, Tobin, Fishman, & Rimor, 1992).

Social Psychology

Discussions of social liberation movements (e.g., the civil rights movement) might acknowledge the active role Jews have often played. This pattern of activism can be attributed to *tikkun olam*, a concept deep at the heart of Jewish ethics, which makes it an individual and communal responsibility for Jews to participate in the "repair and restoration of the world" (Greenberg, 1988). As a core Jewish value, it is familiar to Jews regardless of whether they have had formal Jewish education, and it is reflected in the disproportionate number of Jews who have been active in social liberation movements in the United States and abroad (Sorin, 1985).

The Psychology of Women

The last 10 years have seen a proliferation of courses focusing on women and gender, which offer multicultural paradigms for examining ways in which gender, race, ethnicity, socioeconomic status, sexual orientation, and other factors of difference shape the psychological development of women. However, the ways in which culture and religion shape the developmental tasks and psychotherapeutic experiences of Jewish women have often been overlooked. Fortunately, there are now a number of textbooks that focus on the intersection of feminism, psychology, and Judaism (e.g., Siegel & Cole, 1991, 1997; Weiner & Moon, 1995) and illuminate the challenges that Jewish women face at various points in their development. The following is a brief overview of the ways in which Jewish themes could be integrated into a Psychology of Women course.

Appearance and self-esteem

The development of self-esteem in relation to body image and appearance is often a primary focus in such courses. Although all U.S. women are bombarded with racist images of ideal female beauty (White, blonde, blue eyed, small featured, thin), the detrimental effects of such images on some Jewish women, whose Semitic ancestry may have given them dark hair and eyes, large noses, or full figures, is usually ignored. Low self-esteem among Jewish women may be the result of an attempt to resolve the pressures of assimilation—wanting to look and be "American" and at the same time to maintain a connection to one's Jewish roots. Anticipated fears of rejection because of "Jewish looks" may lead some women to deny any sense of Jewish identity and to avoid the company of other Jews—yet the loss associated with splitting from one's Jewishness may result in depression (Siegel, 1995). A related point of which students (including Jewish ones) need to be aware is that most U.S. Jews do not fit the prototype of Semitic appearance and that it would be difficult, in a roomful of European American strangers, to identify which of them were Jewish. Attempts to identify Jews by their looks, or to ascribe "Jewish" features to someone known to be Jewish, are often veiled forms of anti-Semitism in that they reify and perpetuate a stereotype.

Eating disorders

The propensity for Jewish women to feel shame about the image of the *zaftig* (full-figured) Jewish woman has also left them vulnerable to eating disorders, including anorexia, bulimia, and bulimarexia (Schwartz, 1995). Understanding the complexity of eating disorders for Jewish women requires sensitivity to the significance of food in Jewish culture. Historically, people who had food to eat were less vulnerable to the ever-present threat of starvation because of poverty or pogroms. For many post-Holocaust parents, the images of emaciated concentration camp prisoners are assuaged only by the notion that their children have enough food to eat and a full, healthy body (Schwartz, 1995). Thus, Jewish women often grapple with conflicting messages: strong encouragement to eat coupled with praise for fitting the image of the thin, Gentile, female body (Siegel, 1995). For Jewish girls and adolescents, eating and their feelings about their bodies may be entangled in their family relationships, and their bodies can become an arena for conflict as they attempt to negotiate important developmental transitions (S. W. Schneider, 1984).

Jewish mothers

Any attempt to understand the psychology of Jewish women must include an examination of the role of the Jewish mother, both mythic and real. Special attention should be given to the mother–daughter relationship, which has been characterized by the image of the mother as self-sacrificing, overbearing, and intrusive, supposedly undermining her daughter's sense of autonomy, sexual self-expression, and ability to mother well (Moskowitz, 1994). She has also been blamed for the contradictory qualities of Jewish men's supposed "wimpiness" and aggressivity. It is important to understand that the negative stereotype of the Jewish mother is a corruption of the image of the real-life, strong immigrant woman who, in the Old World, had been responsible for providing for her family while her husband devoted himself to prayer and study. In the New World, however, these coping skills were no longer valued, particularly not by her aspiring American children—most notably her sons, who were often educated at the expense of their sisters (Siegel, 1986). Weiner (1990) contended that the pathologizing of Jewish mothers and family interaction patterns as enmeshed overlooks the historical threat of persecution, does not acknowledge the gender patterns in Jewish families, and ignores the impact of assimilation on Jewish women. Reading about the authentic experiences of Jewish mothers (Siegel, Cole, & Steinberg-Oren, 2000) can help to break down the old stereotypes.

Personality and voice

The model of the strong, assertive Jewish woman, carried over from the Old World, has been translated in the New World into other negative characterizations as well. In a society in which the dominant (Gentile) ideal is a "lady"—polite, quiet, undemanding, and accommodating—Jewish women are criticized and marginalized for violating that expectation. Within the professional sphere, they are often punished for showing their intelligence, speaking out about what they know, complaining about inequity, and advocating for change; in academia, the form such punishment may take is an attempt to deny them tenure, for being "noncollegial" and "difficult." Outside the professional world, the widespread stereotype of the "Jewish American Princess," which caricatures personality, values, speech patterns, and behaviors in particularly vicious ways, makes Jewish women vulnerable to self-hatred and shame for being considered too materialistic, demanding, ambitious, and overly sexual—or not sexual enough (Beck, 1991a; Siegel, 1986).

Violence against women

In the last 10 years there has been more attention paid to the realities of violence (often coupled with alcoholism) within Jewish families. This had previously been a silenced subject among Jews, for whom the deeply ingrained notion of *shalom bayit* (a peaceful Jewish home) was the ideal (Walker, 1997), whereas speaking up would bring shame to the whole community. Recent grassroots efforts have increased the number of rabbis (many of whom are now women) trained to deal with domestic violence and have fostered the development of resources such as hotlines, shelters, and prevention task forces within Jewish communities (Giller, 1991; Walker, 1997).

Clinical and Counseling Psychology

Because it is important for therapists to be aware of relevant cultural issues when working with Jewish clients, clinical and counseling programs need to incorporate this information into their training. In addition to the material already discussed, clinical and counseling students should be made aware of the following aspects of being Jewish that can contribute to problems in living for their clients.

Seasonal dissonance

Seasonal dissonance is experienced by most Jews, regardless of whether they are observant of the Jewish holy days. Although those days are now often marked on calendars, there is very little societal support for Jews to prepare for and celebrate them—which means that every year at these times, Jews are confronted with their marginality in the dominant culture. Perhaps even more marginalizing for Jews is the omnipresence of Christmas, and the societal frenzy surrounding its celebration, as evidenced in schools, offices, store windows, lawn displays, and town centers throughout the nation, and in a monthlong media promotion (Pogrebin, 1995). Clinicians in training need to understand the tensions—and, frequently, the depression—that may arise at this time of the year for their Jewish clients, to prevent misdiagnosis and further marginalization as they are attempting to cope with identity issues.

Internalized oppression

Clinical and counseling students need to learn that it is important to explore signs of low self-esteem or negative self-image in Jewish clients as likely indicators of internalized oppression. Thus, feelings of being unattractive, undesirable, or disliked, or of behaving "inappropriately," should be considered as possible reflections of messages about Jews that clients have absorbed from the dominant culture (Brody, 1997; Weiner, 1990). If students are knowledgeable about the dynamics and effects of internalized oppression, they will be able to provide accurate information for Jewish clients who have mistaken negative historical propaganda about Jews for the reality about themselves.

Chronic terror

Another important thing for students to understand is that, because of their history of persecution, Jews may live in a state of what Schwartz (1995) called *chronic terror*. Many may feel that being visible as a Jew brings increased risk of threat and harm and that it is not outside the realm of possibility that they will be killed. Although such feelings may not be conscious most of the time, they can be seen in patterns of behavior that suggest ongoing efforts to "survive." For example, perfectionism, overcontrol, and obsessive attention to detail carry the implication that one's life depends on hypervigilence about every aspect. Overwork and overachievement can be viewed as desperate efforts by Jews to maintain a place in organizations or professions that are all too ready to exclude them. The controlling and intrusive parenting behaviors often attributed to Jewish mothers can be recognized as originating from this chronic terror, which becomes focused on protecting their children from perceived imminent dangers. Clinicians in training need also to be aware that more serious psychological problems, such as anxiety disorders, paranoia, and self-mutilation, may have this terror at their source (Schwartz, 1995).

Suggested Activities

We have found the following activities to be useful learning tools in clinical and counseling psychology courses. Most of them can provide meaningful opportunities in other courses as well for increasing students' awareness of Jewish issues in psychology.

Personal glimpses

Instructors can provide personal glimpses of Jewish lives through readings and films. There are engaging historical and contemporary narratives, such as those by Gluckl (1690/1977), Pogrebin (1995), and Hoffman (1985). In terms of films, *When Shirley Met Florence* (Merrit, Koenig, & Bezalel, 1994) traces the 50-year friendship of two older Canadian Jewish women who become activists; it also documents the impact of the Holocaust. *Number Our Days* (Littman, 1983), based on Barbara Meyrhoff's groundbreaking research, is the study of the rise and decline of a community of old Ashkenazi Jewish men and women; *Half the Kingdom* (Kol Isha & Perles, 1989) offers conversations with six religious and secular Jewish feminists. Several films focus on family issues: *Return to Oulad Moumen* (Lubtchansky & Genini, 1994) follows several generations of a Jewish American family as they embrace their Moroccan roots; *My Knees Were Jumping* (Hacker, 1997) is both the story of a mother–daughter relationship and the documentation of the children who escaped death in the Holocaust by being sent away from their parents on the *Kindertransports*; *Chicks in White Satin* (J. Schneider & Holliman, 1993) documents a Jewish lesbian wedding and raises issues central to Jewish families. To foster a deeper understanding of Jewish culture, identity, and history, we assign students to small groups and ask them to develop discussion questions that raise attention to the Jewish themes of the book or film. Each group is then asked to distribute their questions to the rest of the class and to facilitate a short discussion. As a means of fostering cultural understanding, we have also asked students to create a cultural genogram that marks their family members' cultural attributes (race, ethnicity, religion, education level, and language) and allows them to identify some overall cultural values that have been transmitted to them through their family.

Marginality and mattering

One of us (L. Lee Knefelkamp) has developed an exercise based on Schlossberg's (1989) formulation of degrees of marginality and mattering. The instructor asks students to write down, either at home or in class, a time when they felt marginal in a group and a time when they felt they mattered. They are also asked to consider how they knew they were marginal or mattered, how they felt at the time, and how they behaved in response. They then discuss in small groups what they have written and share the results with the class as a whole. Invariably, everyone has had at least one experience of marginality (i.e., feeling ignored, excluded, and alienated, leading to withdrawal) and of mattering (feeling heard, included and affirmed, leading to participation), which enables people with very different backgrounds and experiences to empathize with one another. The class can then be asked to consider the specificity of a particular marginality in greater depth (in this case, Jewish identity in a predominantly Christian culture), which can be followed by discussions of other religious, ethnic, or sexual minorities, or students from other parts of the world living in the United States. This exercise helps students understand the marginality that Jews often experience and its effect on their development and adjustment. In addition, it helps to make clear that no one group or person experiences marginality or mattering in all circumstances.

Anti-Semitism and Jewish identity

Because anti-Semitism is often not taken seriously in the United States, even Jews sometimes have difficulty recognizing and acknowledging it. Kaye/Kantrowitz, Klepfisz, and Mennis (1989) developed a number of exercises to identify anti-Semitism, counteract negative stereotypes, and help build positive Jewish identity. They further recommended assigning stories by Anzia Yezierska (1985), as a means of generating discussion about the impact of Christian assumptions on Jews as well as the psychological impact of Jewish invisibility.

CONCLUSION

If psychologists are serious in their efforts to further multiculturalism in the field (in research, teaching, and clinical applications), then they must educate the next generation of psychologists to be culturally competent. This means that they must be willing to challenge the practice by even multicultural psychologists to exclude Jews qua Jews and to subsume them into the White Christian paradigm. Such persistent exclusion permits the negative stereotypes of Jews to go unchallenged, and it makes invisible Jewish contributions to both psychology and the society at large. It is our hope that the inclusion of Jewish materials in the teaching of psychology will create a safe environment for Jewish students to explore their own identities and for non-Jewish students to understand the rich diversity of Jewish experiences and recognize and challenge the anti-Semitic elements in society that have perpetuated the marginalization of Jews and their culture.

REFERENCES

American Jewish Committee. (1999). *Survey questionnaire: Annual survey of American Jewish opinion, March 29–April 18, 1999.* New York: Author.

American Jewish Committee. (2000). *American Jewish year book. Volume 100.* New York: Author.

Anti-Defamation League. (2002, June 11). *Anti-Semitism on the rise in America.* Retrieved July 15, 2002, from http://www.adl.org/PresRele/ASUS_12/4109_12asp

Anti-Defamation League. (2002, June 27). *ADL European survey findings: "A potent and dangerous mix."* Retrieved July 15, 2002, from http://www.adl.org/PresRele/ASInt_13/1118_13asp

Atwood, G. E., & Stolorow, R. D. (1979). *Faces in a cloud: Intersubjectivity in personality theory.* Northvale, NJ: Jason Aronson.

Beck, E. T. (Ed.). (1989). *Nice Jewish girls: A lesbian anthology.* Boston: Beacon Press.

Beck, E. T. (1991a). Therapy's double dilemma: Anti-Semitism and misogyny. In R. J. Siegel & E. Cole (Eds.), *Jewish women in therapy: Seen but not heard* (pp. 19–30). New York: Harrington Park Press.

Beck, E. T. (1991b). The politics of Jewish invisibility in women's studies. In J. Butler & J. Walter (Eds.), *Transforming the curriculum: Ethnic studies and women's studies* (pp. 187–197). Albany: State University of New York Press.

Bohlen, C. (1999, March 2). Russia's stubborn strains of anti-Semitism. *The New York Times,* pp. A1, A11.

Breitman, B. E. (1995). Untangling strands of identity: Gender, culture and ethnicity. In K. Weiner & A. Moon (Eds.), *Jewish women speak out: Expanding the boundaries of psychology* (pp. 149–168). Seattle: Canopy Press.

Bridges: A Journal for Jewish Feminists and our Friends. (2001). Writing and art by Jewish women of color [Special issue], 9(1).

Brody, L. (1997). "She looks Jewish: How wonderful!" In L. Brody (Ed.), *Daughters of kings: Growing up as a Jewish woman in America* (pp. 3–35). Boston: Faber and Faber.

Curtis, M. (1990, January). Anti-Semitism in the United States. *Midstream,* pp. 20–26.

Dedman, B. (1999, July 6). Midwest gunman had engaged in racist acts at 2 universities. *The New York Times,* pp. A1, A14.

Dees, M. (2000, January). *Social justice and liberal education.* Paper presented at the meeting of the American Association of Colleges and Universities in conjunction with the American Conference of Academic Deans, Washington, DC.

Gerson, S. S., & Sedlacek, W. E. (1992). Student attitudes toward "Jewish American Princesses": The new anti-Semitism. *College Student Affairs Journal, 11*(3), 44–53.

Giller, B. (1991). All in the family: Violence in the Jewish home. In R. J. Siegel & E. Cole (Eds.), *Jewish women in therapy: Seen but not heard* (pp. 101–110). New York: Harrington Park. Press.

Gilman, S. L. (1992). *Jewish self-hatred: Anti-semitism and the hidden language of the Jews.* Baltimore: Johns Hopkins University Press.

Gilman, S. L. (1993). *Freud, race, and gender.* Princeton, NJ: Princeton University Press.

Gluckl. (1977). *The memoirs of Gluckl of Hameln* (M. Lowenthal, Trans.). New York: Schocken Books. (Original work published 1690)

Goodman, D. G., & Miyazawa, M. (1995). *Jews in the Japanese mind: The history and uses of a cultural stereotype.* New York: Free Press.

Greenberg, I. (1988). *The Jewish way: Living the holidays.* New York: Simon & Schuster.

Hacker, M. (Producer and Director). (1997). *My knees were jumping: Remembering the* Kindertransports [Videotape]. Waltham, MA: National Center for Jewish Film.

Hammer, B. U. (1995). Anti-Semitism as trauma: A theory of Jewish communal trauma response. In K. Weiner & A. Moon (Eds.), *Jewish women speak out: Expanding the boundaries of psychology* (pp. 199–220). Seattle: Canopy Press.

Hoffman, E. (1985). *Lost in translation: Life in a new language.* New York: Penguin Books.

Hoffman, E. (1988). *The right to be human: A biography of Abraham Maslow.* Los Angeles: Jeremy P. Tarcher.

Kaye/Kantrowitz, M., Klepfisz, I., & Mennis, B. (1989). In *gerangl*/in struggle: A handbook for recognizing and resisting anti-Semitism and for building Jewish identity and pride. In M. Kaye/Kantrowitz & I. Klepfisz (Eds.), *Tribe of Dina: A Jewish women's anthology* (pp. 334–346). Boston: Beacon Press.

Klein, J. W. (1980). *Jewish identity and self-esteem: Healing wounds through ethnotherapy.* New York: Institute on Pluralism and Group Identity, American Jewish Committee.

Knefelkamp, L. L. (1992). The multicultural curriculum and communities of peace. *Liberal Education, 78*(2), 26–35.

Kol Isha (Producer), & Perles, B. (Cinematographer). (1989). *Half the kingdom* [Motion picture]. Santa Monica, CA: Direct Cinema.

Korman, A. K. (1988). *The outsiders: Jews in corporate America.* Lexington, MA: Lexington Books.

Langman, P. (1999). *Jewish issues in multiculturalism: A handbook for educators and clinicians.* Northvale, NJ: Jason Aronson.

Lipset, S. M., & Raab, E. (1995). *Jews and the new American scene.* Cambridge, MA: Harvard University Press.

Littman, L. (Producer and Director). (1983). *Number our days* [Videotape]. Santa Monica, CA: Direct Cinema.

Lubtchansky, J. (Producer), & Genini, I. (Director). (1994). *Return to Oulad Moumen* [Videotape]. Waltham, MA: National Center for Jewish Film.

Medding, P. Y., Tobin, G. A., Fishman, S. B., & Rimor, M. (1992). *Jewish identity in conversionary and mixed marriages*. New York: American Jewish Committee.

Merrit, J., & Koenig, W. (Producers), & Bezalel, R. (Director). (1994). *When Shirley met Florence* [Videotape]. Ottowa, Ontario, Canada: National Film Board of Canada.

Moskowitz, F. (Ed.). (1994). *Her face in the mirror: Jewish women on mothers and daughters*. Boston: Beacon Press.

Pogrebin, L. C. (1995). *Deborah, Golda and me: Being female and Jewish in America*. New York: Crown Books.

Rosen, E. J., & Weltman, S. F. (1996). Jewish families: An overview. In M. McGoldrick, J. Giordano, & J. K. Pearce (Eds.), *Ethnicity and family therapy* (2nd ed., pp. 611–630). New York: Guilford Press.

Rosen, J. (2001, November 4). The uncomfortable question of anti-Semitism. *The New York Times Magazine*, pp. 48–51.

Schlossberg, N. K. (1989). Marginality and mattering: Key issues in building community. In D. C. Roberts (Ed.), *Designing campus activities to foster a sense of community*. Jossey-Bass higher education series: New Directions for Student Services, No. 48 (pp. 5–15). San Francisco: Jossey-Bass.

Schneider, J. (Producer), & Holliman, E. (Director). (1993). *Chicks in white satin* [Videotape]. Santa Monica, CA: Holliman Productions.

Schneider, S. W. (1984). *Jewish and female: Choices and changes in our lives today. A guide and sourcebook for today's Jewish woman*. New York: Simon & Schuster.

Schwartz, M. (1995). Truth beneath the symptoms: Issues of Jewish women in therapy. In K. Weiner & A. Moon (Eds.), *Jewish women speak out: Expanding the boundaries of psychology* (pp. 133–148). Seattle: Canopy Press.

Siegel, R. J. (1986). Antisemitism and sexism in stereotypes of Jewish women. *Women and Therapy, 5*, 249–257.

Siegel, R. J. (1995). Jewish women's bodies: Sexuality, body image and self-esteem. In K. Weiner & A. Moon (Eds.), *Jewish women speak out: Expanding the boundaries of psychology* (pp. 41–54). Seattle: Canopy Press.

Siegel, R. J., & Cole, E. (Eds.). (1991). *Jewish women in therapy: Seen but not heard*. New York: Harrington Park Press.

Siegel, R. J., & Cole, E. (Eds.). (1997). *Celebrating the lives of Jewish women: Patterns in a feminist sampler*. New York: Harrington Park Press.

Siegel, R. J., Cole, E., & Steinberg-Oren, S. (2000). *Jewish mothers tell their stories: Acts of love and courage*. New York: Haworth Press.

Sorin, G. (1985). *The prophetic minority: American Jewish immigrant radicals, 1880–1920*. Bloomington: Indiana University Press.

Sterngold, J. (1999, August 12). Man with a past of racial hate surrenders in day camp attack. *The New York Times*, pp. A1, A16.

Walker, L. (1997). Jewish battered women: *Shalom bayit* or a *shonde?* In R. J. Siegel & E. Cole (Eds.), *Celebrating the lives of Jewish women: Patterns in a feminist sampler* (pp. 261–277). New York: Harrington Park Press.

Weiner, K. (1990). Anti-semitism in the therapy room. In R. J. Siegel & E. Cole (Eds.), *Jewish women in therapy: Seen but not heard* (pp. 119–126). New York: Harrington Park Press.

Weiner, K., & Moon, A. (Eds.). (1995). *Jewish women speak out: Expanding the boundaries of psychology.* Seattle, WA: Canopy Press.

Wistrich, R. (1991). *Antisemitism: The longest hatred.* New York: Pantheon Books.

Yezierska, A. (1985). *Hungry hearts and other stories.* New York: Persea Books.

18

INFUSING DISABILITY ISSUES INTO THE PSYCHOLOGY CURRICULUM

ADRIENNE ASCH AND HENRY MCCARTHY

Disability is a part of ordinary human experience—a characteristic much like race or gender, which may subject individuals to stigma, prejudice, and discrimination. Yet research and teaching within psychology have paid relatively little attention to the issues of people with disabilities, even though disability will impinge on virtually everyone's life. Although clinical, counseling, and rehabilitation psychology do provide help with physical, cognitive, and emotional impairments, there is little understanding of the experiences of people with disabilities in a society that does not always accept them and, indeed, is unaware of the systemic nature of its discrimination.

In incorporating disability issues into their courses, instructors can help students shift from thinking of disabilities as flaws to be rehabilitated to viewing people with disabilities as a minority group with civil rights (Americans

Adrienne Asch thanks Carrie Griffin, for excellent research and critical reading, and Taran Jefferies and Lili Schwan-Rosenwald for their as-ever, superb work in making this chapter useful to today's students. Henry McCarthy thanks four outstanding rehabilitation psychologists for their mentoring: Beatrice Wright, Frank Shontz, Chuck Hallenbeck, and Lenny Diller.

with Disabilities Act [ADA] of 1990; Fine & Asch, 1988a). Instructors can also identify and challenge psychological barriers, which are as obstructive as physical barriers, to full equality and participation for people with disabilities (Bickenbach, 1993). In addition, the study of disability issues can offer insights into a wide range of more general psychological phenomena, such as attribution processes, stereotyping, and identity formation (Fine & Asch, 1988a). In this chapter, we introduce key themes in recent literature on people with disabilities. We offer ideas for integrating this material into psychology courses; suggest exercises to increase awareness and sensitivity; and provide resources for helping students and their teachers delve more deeply into the wealth of literature on disability from a social, as opposed to a clinical or medical, perspective.

WHO IS DISABLED, AND WHAT IS DISABILITY?

The continuing challenges and controversies in the mere attempt to define *disability* and to measure its prevalence underscore that disability is a social construct (Roth, 1983). In 1995, nearly 54 million people—20.6% of the total population of noninstitutionalized Americans—reported having a disability (McNeil, 1997). In reality, these data may underestimate the size of the disabled population, because national surveys ask about conditions that limit or prevent a person from fulfilling a major social role—such as attending school, maintaining a home, or working at a job (Haber & McNeil, 1983); people who do not view their impairments as preventing them from carrying out such roles may, therefore, not describe themselves as having a disability. Although people often think of the disabled population as those who are deaf, blind, orthopedically impaired, or mentally retarded, many relatively hidden conditions, such as arthritis, diabetes, heart disease, back problems, cancer, bipolar disorder, schizophrenia, HIV/AIDS, and chronic fatigue syndrome, are also covered by the legal definitions (ADA, 1990). In addition, people with treatment records from past conditions that are in remission or that are otherwise no longer experienced (e.g., cancer, epilepsy, learning disability) are also included in the definition, even though they currently have no functional limitation. Some people, such as those who are cosmetically disfigured or obese, may not have any physical characteristics that affect their performance of tasks, but they are protected by antidiscrimination laws such as the ADA because they are regarded as disabled by others.

Contemporary discussions of disability reserve the word *impairment* to refer to an organic deviation or defect in an individual; use the term *disability* to talk about the functional limitation that results; and use the term *handicap* for the social phenomena of stigma, discrimination, and problems in interacting with the physical and social environment. A 9-year-old girl with fused or missing fingers has a biological impairment; and her difficulty in grasping a pen or in turning the pages of a book is a functional limitation or disability; yet with the proper alternatives, such as using her other hand or using an adapted computer and page-turner, she has no handicap to her educational progress. If, however, teachers expect little from her, or other classmates exclude her from their play because of this characteristic, her biological condition becomes an occasion for stigma, discrimination, and such possible psychological consequences as lowered self-esteem, shame, and depression (Beuf, 1990).

The chief tenet of the social or minority-group perspective on disability is that it is the attitudes and institutions of the nondisabled, even more than the biological characteristics of those who have disabilities, that turn impairments into handicaps. Although atypical biology or difficulties in meeting societal expectations for cognitive or emotional functioning do matter, the social–minority-group perspective stresses that how and when they matter, and what facets of life they affect, depend on the physical and social environment. According to this view, there is no inherent reason why a biological characteristic such as deafness or a heart condition must limit earnings, social participation, or employment. If these consequences occur, as they often do, they are a result of social responses to the characteristic, and not necessarily of the characteristic itself. Employers' fears keep out of the workforce people who are deaf and might require accommodations such as sign language interpreters or written communication; uncertain health coverage for people with pre-existing disabilities such as heart conditions causes people themselves to refrain from seeking postdisability employment. Although the knowledge that someone has a physical impairment should not lead to assumptions about roles and relationships, it often does—in ways that may bear little actual connection to the individual but that may become part of that person's psychic and social reality.

Disability is often seen only within a frame of dependency and inability and without disentangling the biological impairment and functional disability from the social handicap. For example, in the 2000 U.S. census, respondents were asked, "Because of a physical, mental, or emotional condition lasting 6 months or more, do you have any difficulty in doing any of the following activities: a. Learning, remembering, or concentrating?, b. Dressing, bathing, or getting around outside the home?" (U.S. Bureau of the Census 2000). In fact, the inability to get around outside might stem from the lack of a wheelchair or accessible transportation for someone with multiple sclerosis or arthritis, or it might arise because someone with deteriorating vision has not been taught how to use a cane or guide dog.

People with disabilities participate in the labor force far less than those who are nondisabled (Trupin, Sebesta, Yelin, & LaPlante, 1997). Based on a model of disability as individual pathology, these low levels of employment routinely get explained simply as the inability of people with physical, sensory, or mental impairments to hold jobs. However, recent surveys of Americans with disabilities have shown that of the two thirds of them between the ages of 16 and 64 who were out of work, more than three quarters wanted to be employed, and almost half considered themselves employable, if given the opportunity (LaPlante, Kennedy, Kaye, & Wenger, 1996). This report also documents that people with disabilities are much more likely than nondisabled people to live at or below the poverty level. Although having more education substantially narrows the income gap between individuals with and without disabilities, people with disabilities at all educational levels still experience lower incomes and lower rates of workforce participation than their nondisabled counterparts, with effects being most severe for African American women (Asch, Rousso, & Jefferies, 2001). This latter fact illustrates that the ways that disability impinges on individuals and families are influenced by a host of other social and psychological characteristics.

INTEGRATING DISABILITY ISSUES INTO MAINSTREAM COURSES

Disability issues can be integrated into all psychology courses, with appropriate examples to fit the specific content. People who have disabilities should not be presented in a separate section on "abnormal" or "exceptional" people, because such placement perpetuates myths and stereotypes. Rather, instructors should include disability as a fact of many lives or an aspect of diversity, for example, including data on disabilities in population statistics where race, gender, or other distinctions are provided. Instructors can also help students understand the broad range of conditions that fall within the purview of disability and encourage them to apply this knowledge to their families, their friends, and themselves (e.g., a grandparent who has had a stroke, a classmate with diabetes or epilepsy). We now describe some specific ways to integrate disability issues into a variety of courses.

Cultural Psychology

An excellent way to examine the social–minority model of disability is to discuss how that minority status resembles and differs from other groups that have been powerless and stigmatized. Although many people who have disabilities have difficulties in claiming that portion of their identity (Scotch, 1988), approximately half of those responding to a survey by the National Organization on Disability (2001) did perceive disability as a minority status and affirmed a connection with others who had the same or different impairments. The disability-rights movement is, in fact, significant in many people's lives, contributing to their increased psychological well-being and to impressive social change (Fine & Asch, 1988a; Scotch, 1988).

Some people with impairments, like many people of color, can be readily identified, whereas others cannot. Questions of creating identity, "passing," disclosing, and combating prejudice and discrimination all apply to the disabled minority. Unlike racial and ethnic minority status, however, disability can occur at any point in life and usually is not part of family lineage. Thus, disability shares characteristics with sexual orientation as an invisible, nongenerationally transmitted, and changeable status. Hahn (1988) discussed how others' responses to disability are affected by its visibility and considered how differences in visibility influence people with disabilities in developing a sense of identification with the group.

Courses focusing on cultural minorities can look at how their members with disabilities fare in life and how cultural views of health, family, and community influence the way people experience disability (Belgrave, 1998; National Council on Disability, 1999; Zea, Belgrave, Townsend, Jarama, & Banks, 1996). In addition, such courses can consider the challenges involved in incorporating multiple identities into one's self-understanding (Brewer, 1991; Deaux, 1993; Gainer, 1992).

Social Psychology

The psychological literature on disability has perpetuated many erroneous assumptions (Fine & Asch, 1988a) that instructors should avoid passing on. It is often assumed that the disabled person is a "victim," that when a disabled person faces problems, it is the impairment that caused them, and that having a disability is synonymous with needing help and social support. Furthermore, it is generally assumed that disability is central to the disabled person's self-concept, self-definition, social comparisons, and reference groups. In addition, because it is often assumed that disability is located solely in biology, it is accepted uncritically as an independent variable in research. With these assumptions in mind, instructors could ask their class to consider more recent perspectives on disability when they explore some of the following topics.

Stereotypes

Why are stereotypes of people with disabilities predominantly negative? Where do they come from, how can they be changed, and are the issues similar to or different from those faced by people of other social categories? Makas (1988) and Wright (1988) have offered useful discussions of attitudes toward people with disabilities as well as some proposals for attitude change. Class exercises or papers could compare media portrayals in film and television with findings from social science or personal accounts of people with disabilities.

Prejudice, discrimination, and stigma

Ever since the work of Goffman (1963), stigma has been a key concept in explaining the social situation of people described as differing from the majority. Katz (1981) found experimental support for this concept in the lives of people with disabilities; on the other hand, Susman (1994) argued that the concept explains much, but not all, of the story. It is also worth noting that stigma attends people who voluntarily associate with people who have disabilities—as Goldstein and Johnson (1997) found regarding college students' perceptions of nondisabled dating partners of people with disabilities. Fine and Asch (1988a) and Scotch (1988) have argued that the emergence of the disability-rights movement, like the formation of other social movements, brings in a spirit of social activism to combat stigma and discrimination. Instructors can invite comparisons and contrasts with other minority groups, particularly with respect to sources of negative attitudes, their effects on the groups themselves, and the success of strategies for attitude and social change.

"Blaming the victim"

Nondisabled people may on some level blame individuals with a disability for their condition, for example, regarding a disability as punishment for sins of the past. Attributions rooted in a *Just world* psychology (Lerner, 1980), in which people end up blaming victims of rape, accidents, or illnesses for their misfortunes, are often applied to individuals with disabilities (Rubin & Peplau, 1975); these kinds of attributions may serve as a mechanism for people to distance themselves from an awareness of their own weakness or the possibility of becoming disabled themselves (Asch & Rousso, 1985). Instructors can use an examination of these attitudes as a way to help students understand attitude formation in a broader sense (Makas, 1988; Wright, 1988). They can engage students in discussions about tendencies to attribute social and economic disadvantages experienced by people with disabilities to an inferred biological inferiority and draw parallels to attributions about racial minorities and women.

Social interaction

Studies of the behavior of nondisabled people toward people with disabilities demonstrate a variety of responses that, at the very least, hinder ordinary social interaction. These interaction problems include the avoidance of social contact; distorted verbal behavior; and nonverbal behaviors such as turning away, avoiding eye contact, and ignoring a person's presence (Fine & Asch, 1988a; Gliedman & Roth, 1980; Wright, 1983). In an experimental study, Houser (1997) found that disability overwhelmed all other characteristics, so that the disabled individual was perceived as less influential than others in group tasks, despite others' attributions of competence to the disabled group member. In addition, certain impairments can prevent people who have them from using expected communication cues such as articulation, eye contact, or hand movements. Students might consider how those impairments might affect others' perceptions of the individuals who have them, as well as their interactions with them. It is also useful to point out that in real life, people with disabilities may find ways to minimize the problems evidenced in brief encounters in experimental settings (Fine & Asch, 1988a). Despite increased participation of people with disabilities in school, college, work, and recreation, the literature still tells little about coworker or intimate relationships between people with and without disabilities, or between people with disabilities.

Developmental Psychology

Issues related to disability are relevant to many areas of developmental psychology and can be integrated effectively through discussion and debate into various topic areas, as described below.

Developmental stages

Most of what is known about developmental theory has evolved from studies of nondisabled children. Thus, much can be learned about both developmental stages and disability, by examining how major stage theories apply or do not apply to the lives of children with disabilities (Gliedman & Roth, 1980). Students can be invited to consider how particular biological characteristics (impairments) interact with the familial, physical, and social environments to influence the acquisition of cognitive, motor, communication, or relationship skills. They can also discuss what factors might help development proceed positively and smoothly for a person who manages a disability.

Social learning

One of the tenets of social learning theory maintains that young people learn adult roles by observing the models around them. However, most youngsters with disabilities have very limited opportunities to observe, in person or even in the media, how adults manage a disability, physically and socially. Some contend that young people with disabilities need contact with role models or mentors who also have disabilities, in order to develop healthy self-esteem and high aspirations (Rousso, 2001). By discussing the value of disability, race, or gender similarity in role models, students can consider what qualities may be essential for modeling to take place. Students might reflect on people who have served as role models for them and explore reasons they have appreciated specific mentors.

Adolescence

During the adolescent years, substance abuse, athletic injury, traffic accidents, street violence, unsafe sex, and eating disorders are all more likely to occur, and along with them comes an increase in the numbers of people with lifelong physical and psychological impairments. Instructors can ask students to consider how any disability might complicate the search for a comfortable body image, sexual identity, and peer group, which are key aspects of adolescent development, and to discuss what factors might promote or impede the social, psychological, and cognitive development of youth with disabilities.

Life span development

Although approximately 10% of people under age 21 may have impairments, most disability occurs during adulthood. As psychology professionals increase their research and teaching of adult life issues, it is appropriate to incorporate discussions of disability into the treatment of such major topics as work, family, adult friendships, and aging. Often the discussion of disability in adult life mistakenly focuses only on people with newly acquired impairments through illness, injury, or the aging process and frames discussions in terms of role loss for the person acquiring a disability and burdens of adjustment and caregiving for nondisabled family members. Although the literature on stress and coping, adaptation, and rehabilitation (e.g., Brodwin, Tellez, & Brodwin, 2002; Rolland, 1994) give important insights into these experiences, it is crucial to look also at personal accounts and the disability-rights literature to learn how people live with disability as workers, parents, spouses, and citizens after rehabilitation. We strongly urge instructors to become familiar with the literature that demonstrates the satisfactions that people of all ages who have disabilities take in their lives as well as the disbelief of medical and psychological professionals in these findings (Albrecht & DeVlieger, 1999). Recommended resources include Brightman (1984) and Couser (1997) for autobiographies written by people with a range of conditions; Fine and Asch (1988b) for material on the lives of women with disabilities; Vash and McCarthy (1995) for perspectives on the nexus between spirituality and disability; and Shakespeare, Gillespie-Sells, and Davies (1996) for discussions of disability and sexuality.

Family psychology

For any courses on family life, it would be valuable to incorporate material on parenting with a disability (Barker & Maralani, 1997; Wates, 1997; Wates & Jade, 1999), parenting children with disabilities (Ferguson, Gartner, & Lipsky, 2000; Seligman, 1999), sibling relationships (Stoneman & Berman, 1993), and intimate relationships (gay and lesbian as well as heterosexual) of people with disabilities (Brownworth & Raffo, 1999; Fries,

1997; Shakespeare et al., 1996). Instructors can raise questions about role expectations that may make it difficult to imagine people with disabilities as partners and caretakers of others, or as satisfying children to their parents, or as siblings to their nondisabled sisters and brothers. Students can be asked to write a paper about family members' experiences with disability—in their own family or in a family they know—interviewing two or three people about how they view their lives as affected by another's impairment and how they think the family member who has the disability views her or his life.

Personality, Clinical, and Abnormal Psychology

Personality, clinical, and abnormal psychology have suffered from two erroneous assumptions about people with disabilities: (a) that physical disabilities create psychological disorders and (b) that people with disabilities are psychologically "abnormal." Instructors can encourage students to examine both the misperceptions and the actual data (or absence of data) relating to disability and psychopathology. People with disabilities have been viewed, particularly in the psychoanalytic literature, as having a variety of problems, including excessive guilt, unmastered and undischarged aggression, and strong primitive defense mechanisms. Asch and Rousso (1985) and Gliedman and Roth (1980) have described psychoanalytic arguments that a defective body leads to a defective body ego and that a distorted self-image leads to a distorted image of the world. Students need to be made aware that these beliefs are based on small numbers of distressed patients, without a corresponding examination of individuals with disabilities who have not sought help. Providing data on the actual incidence of psychological disorders among the disabled population helps dispel the myth that disability causes psychopathology (Olkin, 1999). It would also be useful for future practitioners to read about clients' perceptions of the lack of awareness and insensitivity reflected in some of the common practices of well-meaning helping professionals (e.g., Buchanan, 1999; McCarthy, 2002; Walsh, 1999).

Many authors overlook the impact of familial and societal treatment on the psychological development of people with disabling conditions. Hostility and rejection in social and occupational settings may eventually cause a person with a disability to internalize society's deprecating attitudes (Asch & Rousso, 1985; Smart, 2001), as can occur for members of other minority groups. Examining the effects of such social experiences on mental health promotes a shift in emphasis away from internal attributions about psychopathology.

The frightened and hostile responses many nondisabled people experience toward disability are also valid topics in the study of personality and psychopathology. These responses may be rooted in unconscious anxieties regarding wholeness, loss, and weakness (Hahn, 1988); castration anxiety; or fears about one's own destructiveness (see Asch & Rousso, 1985, and Olkin, 1999, for additional discussions).

Courses in clinical, abnormal, or personality psychology might benefit from a presentation by a panel of people with physical and mental disabilities who have used psychological services, to discuss the quality of the services, the attitudes of professionals toward their life prospects, and recommendations for improvement. Similarly, providers of psychological services who themselves have disabilities could discuss how their conditions affect their work with disabled and nondisabled clients as well as their reception by the mental health profession (Asch & Rousso, 1985). A 1994 special issue of the *American Journal of Psychotherapy* (Vol. 48, issue 2) provides data on the impact of a patient's or therapist's impairment on the therapeutic process, and Olkin (1999) authored a valuable guide for therapists on disability issues.

Psychology of Women

Fine and Asch's (1988b) edited volume, and Asch et al.'s (2001) chapter can guide instructors to much of the available scholarly and autobiographical literature on gender–disability interaction. Krotoski, Nosek, and Turk (1996) and a 1997 issue of the *Journal of Disability Policy Studies* (Vol. 8, issues 1 and 2) offer empirical data and policy recommendations relevant to the health, sexuality, education, employment, relationships, and service needs of women with disabilities.

It is sadly still true that in virtually all areas of life, women with disabilities face a harsher reality than do nondisabled women or men who have disabilities. The class could discuss questions that recent data reveal: why relatively few college-educated women with disabilities are in the workforce as compared with similarly educated men who have disabilities, and why fewer women than men with disabilities attend college—even though women outnumber men in colleges and universities today (U.S. Bureau of the Census, 1999). The class could also examine the hypothesis, advanced by Asch and Fine (1988), that women with disabilities are rejected as partners by nondisabled people because they are assumed to be unacceptable as nurturers by nondisabled men or women seeking intimate relationships.

Industrial/Organizational Psychology

Participation in the workforce is a central issue in disability studies. As mentioned earlier, people with disabilities continue to find it much harder than their nondisabled cohorts to break into the world of work, with a labor force participation rate that is about 30 percentage points lower than that of the general population (Trupin et al., 1997). Instructors can introduce practical psychological issues for discussion regarding factors that influence the motivation and decision to work. For example, some impairments are expensive to manage because of costly medications, the need for personal attendant assistance (for transportation, eating, or toileting), or the need for readers or interpreters. The federal and state systems of disability benefits, which can include health insurance coverage (usually through Medicare or Medicaid), historically have paid these costs only for people who stayed out of the workforce. Instructors and students should learn about the more flexible benefits options available through the Work Incentive Improvement Act (Social Security Legislative Bulletin, 1999) and their impact on what have been powerful disincentives to labor force participation. In addition, it is important to introduce to students the concept of *reasonable accommodation*, a fundamental principle in both ADA and rehabilitation practice, and to be aware of the multiple dimensions of accessibility. Just as any "environment" can be analyzed in terms of its physical, social, and regulatory dimensions, so too the goal of accessibility has physical, attitudinal, and programmatic aspects that need to be examined and addressed.

PROMOTING AWARENESS AND COMMITMENT TO ACCOMMODATION

Many instructors are unnecessarily fearful of having students with disabilities in their classes. Although they may know that students' rights to equal educational opportunity are protected by legislation, they may not be familiar with the parameters of the law and how to operate within the law. Section 504 of the Rehabilitation Act and Title II of the ADA, which provide official guidelines and technical assistance, should be available from the campus office for services to students with disabilities, or they can be obtained from the Association on Higher Education and Disability, the professional association for these programs and issues (visit http://www.ahead.org, or telephone 617-287-3881). Instructors and psychology departments can also consult the American Psychological Association's Board of Educational Affairs and Committee on Disability Issues in Psychology for guidance in ensuring that courses and classrooms are truly accessible to students with disabilities, and they can review the report of the American Psychological Association Task Force on Diversity Issues at the Precollege and Undergraduate Levels of Education in Psychology (1998). As a simple, proactive strategy, instructors can include a statement in the course syllabus that expresses their willingness to offer reasonable accommodation to legitimate disability-based needs. This would empower the affected students to validate and explain their situations early in the course, in anticipation of needs, and would communicate a message of inclusivity to all students in the course.

Course Assignments on Psychosocial Aspects of Disability

Interviews

Structured interviews of two or three people with disabilities can help students gain an understanding of how those individuals view the social and psychological ramifications of their disability. Students would also see first-hand how interviewees manage certain functions affected by the disability, such as communication, mobility, or learning. Questions might focus on how the individuals' disabilities have influenced, if at all, their lives in such areas as education, work, transportation, housing, friendships, romantic relationships, and parenting. In their write-ups, students could discuss the responses in terms of whether they were surprising, why or why not they were surprising, and the implications for personal or societal change.

We recommend having students interview more than one person, to help students recognize that not everyone with a disability has the same story or responds to disability, or to life, in identical ways. If only one person is interviewed by each student, then the assignment should be followed by a group discussion so that class members can compare their experiences. The class could then discuss the differences in responses in terms of such variables as the gender, age, race, social class, and ethnicity of the interviewee; the nature of the impairment; the age at disability onset; and personality or psychosocial factors. As an alternative to conducting interviews, students could be assigned a report based on reading several narrative accounts from periodicals with insider perspectives on disability, such as *Disability Studies Quarterly* and the magazines *New Mobility: Disability Culture and Lifestyle* and *The Ragged Edge*.

Experiential assignments

We oppose disability-simulation exercises, such as students' spending a day using a wheelchair or wearing earplugs or occluding glasses. Although intended to increase awareness, these exercises end up equating the functional and emotional experience of a very newly disabled person with that of someone who has mastered coping skills. Thus, they are likely to arouse only pity and fear rather than sensitivity and understanding. Instead, we recommend that students be encouraged to spend the time engaged in an experiential assignment that lasts several weeks and that includes a variety of interactions with one or more persons with disabilities. Part of such an assignment might be reflections on prior fears or obstacles that prevented or minimized meaningful contact with people who have disabilities. In designing such experiences, two principal guidelines should be observed: (a) aim at building a relationship based on contact that is either equal status or one in which the student is the primary recipient of help; (b) include interactions that explore the person's varied interests and experiences, rather than focusing exclusively on the disability and its consequences. These parameters are likely to generate a much more meaningful and realistic basis for an outsider to capture the experience of both "the grievances and gratifications in everyday life with a disability" (Wright, 1983, p. 291). The following are two specific examples of worthwhile experiential assignments:

1. Become involved in working on a systems advocacy project that will provide you with the opportunity to: (a) learn about the origins and implications of a disability-rights issue from disability activists and advocates and (b) experience the strategies and realities of creating bureaucratic, legislative, or social change. Write a report of the substantive and experiential outcomes of your work.
2. Serve as a "buddy" or citizen advocate or personal assistant for someone with a significant disability. Record and submit a journal of reflections on the experiences, both enlightening and challenging, that the two of you had together in a variety of home, school, and community settings.

Encouraging students to identify relevant persons and issues for these assignments by networking in the community, rather than giving them prescreened contacts and topics, will further enhance their awareness of disability-related resources and concerns.

CONCLUSIONS AND CAREER OPTIONS

Experiences such as the above assignments, coupled with information provided in readings and class discussions, will not only enrich students' lives but may also provide ideas about career options in psychology. There are a number of vocational possibilities—such as case manager, rehabilitation counselor, and rehabilitation psychologist—for those with psychology training who are interested in working directly with people who have disabilities. Interested students can obtain information from several Web sites; for example: the American Psychological Association's Division of Rehabilitation Psychology (http://www.apa.org/divisions/div22), the American Rehabilitation Counseling Association (http://www.nchrtm.okstate.edu/ARCA), the National Rehabilitation Association (http://www.NationalRehab.org), the National Rehabilitation Information Center (http://www.naric.com), and the Case Management Society of America (http://www.cmsa.org).

REFERENCES

Albrecht, G. L., & DeVlieger, P. (1999). The disability paradox: High quality of life against all odds. *Social Science and Medicine, 48,* 977–988.

American Psychological Association Task Force on Diversity Issues at the Precollege and Undergraduate Levels of Education in Psychology. (1998). Disability as diversity: A guide for class discussion. *APA Monitor, 29*(2), 1–3.

Americans with Disabilities Act of 1990, P.L. 101-336, 42 U.S.C. 12111, 12112.

Asch, A., & Fine, M. (1988). Introduction: Beyond pedestals. In M. Fine & A. Asch (Eds.), *Women with disabilities: Essays in psychology, culture and politics* (pp. 1–37). Philadelphia: Temple University Press.

Asch, A., & Rousso, H. (1985). Therapists with disabilities: Theoretical and clinical issues. *Psychiatry, 48,* 1–12.

Asch, A., Rousso, H., & Jefferies, T. (2001). Beyond pedestals: The lives of girls and women with disabilities. In H. Rousso & M. Wehmeyer (Eds.), *Double jeopardy: Addressing gender equity in special education* (pp. 13–48). Albany: State University of New York Press.

Barker, L. T., & Maralani, V. (1997). *Challenges and strategies of disabled parents: Findings from a national survey of parents with disabilities.* Oakland, CA: Berkeley Planning Associates.

Belgrave, F. Z. (1998). *Psychosocial aspects of chronic illness and disability among African Americans.* Westport, CT: Auburn House.

Beuf, A. H. (1990). *Beauty is the beast: Appearance-impaired children in America.* Philadelphia: University of Pennsylvania Press.

Bickenbach, J. E. (1993). *Physical disability and social policy.* Toronto, Ontario, Canada: University of Toronto Press.

Brewer, M. B. (1991). The social self: On being the same and different at the same time. *Personality and Social Psychology Bulletin, 16,* 475–482.

Brightman, A. J. (Ed.). (1984). *Ordinary moments: The disabled experience.* Baltimore: University Park Press.

Brodwin, M., Tellez, F., & Brodwin, S. (2002). *Medical, psychosocial and vocational aspects of disability* (2nd ed.). Athens, GA: Elliott & Fitzpatrick.

Brownworth, V. A., & Raffo, S. (Eds.). (1999). *Restricted access: Lesbians on disability.* Seattle, WA: Seal Press.

Buchanan, S. (1999). No blood, it doesn't count. In R. Marinelli & A. Dell Orto (Eds.), *The psychological and social impact of disability* (4th ed., pp. 187–190). New York: Springer.

Couser, G. T. (1997). *Recovering bodies: Illness, disability, and life writing.* Madison: University of Wisconsin Press.

Deaux, K. (1993). Reconstructing social identity. *Personality and Social Psychology Bulletin, 19,* 4–12.

Ferguson, P., Gartner, A., & Lipsky, D. (2000). The experience of disability in families: A synthesis of research and parent narratives. In E. Parens & A. Asch (Eds.), *Prenatal testing and disability rights* (pp. 72–94). Washington, DC: Georgetown University Press.

Fine, M., & Asch, A. (1988a). Disability beyond stigma: Social interaction, discrimination, and activism. *Journal of Social Issues, 44,* 3–21.

Fine, M., & Asch, A. (Eds.). (1988b). *Women with disabilities: Essays in psychology, culture and politics*. Philadelphia: Temple University Press.

Fries, K. (1997). *Body, remember: A memoir*. New York: Dutton.

Gainer, K. (1992, September–October). I was born colored and crippled. Now I am Black and disabled. *Mouth: The Voice of Disability Rights, 31*.

Gliedman, J., & Roth, P. (1980). *The unexpected minority: Handicapped children in America*. New York: Harcourt Brace Jovanovich.

Goffman, E. (1963). *Stigma: Notes on the management of spoiled identity*. Englewood Cliffs, NJ: Prentice Hall.

Goldstein, S., & Johnson, V. (1997). Stigma by association: Perceptions of the dating partners of college students with physical disabilities. *Basic and Applied Social Psychology, 19*, 495–504.

Haber, L., & McNeil, J. (1983). *Methodological questions in the estimation of disability prevalence*. Washington, DC: U.S. Bureau of the Census, Population Division.

Hahn, H. (1988). The politics of physical differences: Disability and discrimination. *Journal of Social Issues, 44*, 39–48.

Houser, J. A. (1997). Stigma, spread and status: The impact of physical disability on social interaction (Doctoral dissertation, University of Iowa, 1997). *Dissertation Abstracts International, 58* (5-A), 1940.

Katz, I. (1981). *Stigma: A social-psychological analysis*. Hillsdale, NJ: Erlbaum.

Krotoski, D., Nosek, M., & Turk, M. (Eds.). (1996). *Women with physical disabilities: Achieving and maintaining health and well-being*. Baltimore: Paul H. Brookes.

Langer, K. G. (Ed.). (1994). Psychotherapy and physical disability [Special section, p. 129f]. *American Journal of Psychotherapy, 48*(2).

LaPlante, M., Kennedy, J., Kaye, S., & Wenger, B. (1996). *Disability and employment* [Abstract 11]. Retrieved June 10, 2002, from http://dsc.ucsf.edu/UCSF/pub.taf?_UserReference=9DD3EF4517CDF9FDC0AED7EC&_function=search&recid=57&grow=1

Lerner, M. J. (1980). *The belief in a just world: A fundamental delusion*. New York: Plenum.

Makas, E. (1988). Positive attitudes toward disabled people: Disabled and nondisabled persons' perspectives. *Journal of Social Issues, 44*, 49–62.

McCarthy, H. (2002). On crossing borders and building bridges over troubled waters. *Rehabilitation Counseling Bulletin, 45*, 114–117.

McNeil, J. (1997). *Current population reports: Americans with disabilities, 1994–1995* (Series P70-61). Washington, DC: U.S. Department of Commerce, Bureau of the Census.

National Council on Disability. (1999). *Lift every voice: Modernizing disability policies and programs to serve a diverse nation*. Retrieved June 10, 2002, from http://www.ncd.gov/newsroom/publications/lift_report.html

National Organization on Disability. (2001). *N.O.D./Harris 2000 survey of Americans with disabilities*. Retrieved June 10, 2002, from http://www.nod.org.

Olkin, R. (1999). *What psychotherapists should know about disability.* New York: Guilford Press.

Rolland, J. S. (1994). *Families, illness, and disability: An integrative treatment model.* New York: Basic Books.

Roth, W. (1983). Handicap as a social construct. *Society, 20*(3), 56–61.

Rousso, H. (2001). What do Frida Kahlo, Wilma Mankiller and Harriet Tubman have in common? Providing role models for girls with (and without) disabilities. In H. Rousso & M. Wehmeyer (Eds.), *Double jeopardy: Addressing gender equity in special education* (pp. 337–360). Albany: State University of New York Press.

Rubin, A., & Peplau, L. (1975). Who believes in a just world? *Journal of Social Issues, 31,* 65–89.

Schriner, K. F., Barnhartt, S. N., & Altman, B. M. (1997). Disabled women and public policy [Special issue]. *Journal of Disability Policy Studies, 8*(1 & 2).

Scotch, R. K. (1988). Disability as the basis for a social movement: Advocacy and the politics of definition. *Journal of Social Issues, 44,* 159–172.

Seligman, M. (1999). Childhood disability and the family. In V. L. Schwean & D. H. Saklofske (Eds.), *Handbook of psychosocial characteristics of exceptional children* (pp. 111–131). New York: Kluwer Academic/Plenum.

Shakespeare, T., Gillespie-Sells, K., & Davies, D. (1996). *The sexual politics of disability: Untold desires.* New York: Cassell.

Smart, J. (2001). *Disability, society, and the individual.* Gaithersburg, MD: Aspen.

Social Security Legislative Bulletin. (1999). *President Clinton signs the Ticket to Work and Work Incentives Improvement Act of 1999.* Retrieved June 10, 2002, from http://www.ssa.gov.legislation/legis_bulletin_121799.html

Stoneman, Z., & Berman, P. W. (Eds.). (1993). *The effects of mental retardation, disability, and illness on sibling relationships: Research issues and challenges.* Baltimore: Paul H. Brookes.

Susman, J. (1994). Disability, stigma and deviance. *Social Science and Medicine, 38,* 15–22.

Trupin, L., Sebesta, D., Yelin, E., & LaPlante, M. (1997). *Trends in labor force participation among persons with disabilities, 1983–1994* (Disability Statistics Report No. 10). Washington, DC: U.S. Department of Education, National Institute on Disability and Rehabilitation Research.

U.S. Bureau of the Census. (1999). *March 1999 current population survey: Disability data* (Tables 1, 2, 3). Retrieved June 10, 2002, from http//www.census.gov/hhes/www/disable/cps/

U.S. Bureau of the Census. (2000). *Official 2000 U.S. Census form.* Retrieved June 10, 2002, from http://www.census.gov/dmd/www/2000quest.html

Vash, C., & McCarthy, H. (Eds.). (1995). Spirituality, disability and rehabilitation [Special issue]. *Rehabilitation Education, 9*(2&3).

Walsh, D. (1999). Coping with a journey toward recovery: From the inside out. In R. Marinelli & A. Dell Orto (Eds.), *The psychological and social impact of disability* (4th ed., pp. 55–61). New York: Springer.

Wates, M. (1997). *Disabled parents: Dispelling the myths*. Cambridge, England: National Childbirth Trust.

Wates, M., & Jade, R. (Eds.). (1999). *Bigger than the sky: Disabled women talk about parenting*. London: Women's Press.

Wright, B. A. (1983). *Physical disability—A psychosocial approach* (2nd ed.). New York: Harper & Row.

Wright, B. (1988). Attitudes and the fundamental negative bias: Conditions and corrections. In H. Yuker (Ed.), *Attitudes toward persons with disabilities* (pp. 3–21). New York: Springer.

Zea, M., Belgrave, F., Townsend, T., Jarama, S., & Banks, S. (1996). The influence of social support and active coping on depression among African Americans and Latinos with disabilities. *Rehabilitation Psychology, 41*, 225–242.

19

TEACHING THE PSYCHOLOGY OF LATER LIFE

ROYDA CROSE

At the turn of the 20th century, the average life expectancy was around 50 years of age. Now, 100 years later, the average life expectancy is 75 years. This increase has resulted primarily from huge decreases in infant mortality, increased hygiene, improved medical technology and pharmacology, and greater economic resources. Although some individuals survived into old age in earlier times, never before have masses of people been living into adulthood and long past middle age and retirement. In fact, the period of life that is labeled *old age* is now much longer than the early part of life that we call *youth*.

However, because human personality is generally believed to stabilize in young to middle adulthood, the development and behaviors of people over the age of 50 have only recently been of interest to psychologists. Human development courses tend to concentrate on the development of children and young adults and essentially ignore midlife and beyond. Yet, our world is rapidly becoming filled with older people whose life experiences have shaped their personalities and whose historical perspectives influence

271

both individual choices and behaviors. As the population becomes older, it is imperative that psychology begin to focus on mental health, personality, and behavior in later life.

IMPORTANT PERSPECTIVES IN THE PSYCHOLOGY OF AGING

Three major perspectives are important in the psychology of aging: (a) several age cohorts exist within the elder population, (b) unique life experiences over time result in a greater variability among older individuals, and (c) a feminization of the older population is occurring due to the greater longevity of women.

Several Age Cohorts Within the Elder Population

With people living so much longer, one cannot view older people as one group. There are, in actuality, several cohorts of aged people (Crose, Leventhal, Haug, & Burns, 1997). Recently retired, active, healthy, 65-year-olds live very different lives from frail, ill, and disabled people in their 90s; they have grown up in different historical climates, and their current opportunities and outlooks are very different. Cross-sectional research has often presented a biased and questionable view of aging, comparing samples of older people over the age of 60 or 65, with an age range of more than 25 years and a wide variety of backgrounds, to younger groups of people who are very close in age, education, and culture. Well-designed longitudinal research is costly and difficult, but it is the best way to determine the effects of age on human existence. Several such longitudinal projects are resulting in valuable knowledge about aging (e.g., Belsky, 1999; Busse & Maddox, 1985; National Institute on Aging, 1989, 1993; Schaie, 1965).

Life Experiences Bring Greater Variability

Psychological development is significantly shaped by life experience that can be acquired only with time. Because older people have more time to acquire unique life experiences, there is greater potential for variability among them than among a sample of younger people. In other words, all 5-year-olds in our culture have much more in common and are more similar in their identity and intellectual development than are a group of 75-year-olds. Thus, even when cohort effects are taken into account, age is less of a marker for behavioral and psychological development in old age than it is in youth.

The Feminization of Older Adults

At present, women have life expectancies that are approximately 7 years longer than men (Crose, 1997), which results in older cohorts that primarily comprise women. Women fill the nursing homes, senior centers, and retirement villages that provide living environments for the aged. Women are the primary recipients of social services and social policies that target the elderly. Because of this greater longevity, women have more health care needs and suffer from more chronic illness and disability. Because they have worked for lesser pay—or, as homemakers, for no pay—they more often live in poverty in their old age than do men. This feminization of aging has important implications for late life psychological theories and mental health treatment policies. Although feminist scholars have challenged traditional theories of human development (e.g., Gilligan, 1982; Miller, 1976), and feminist therapists have questioned many treatment approaches (Worell & Remer, 1992), and although geropsychologists are now publishing treatment strategies for older adults (Duffy, 1999), it remains rare that the views of feminism and gerontology join to address the psychological and mental health issues of older women (Crose, 1999, 2000).

TOPICS IN TEACHING THE PSYCHOLOGY OF AGING

There are 10 key areas to consider when teaching about the psychological aspects of aging; these can be adapted to fit the interests and academic level of students in a particular course.

1. Demographics of an Aging Society

Although most students know about the increase in human longevity, few have stopped to consider its wide-reaching implications. The first unit in any course on the psychology of later life should focus on the demographics of our rapidly aging society (Friedland & Summer, 1999), which are available in gerontological textbooks, census data, and from organizations such as the American Association of Retired Persons (1998). The Internet is also a resource for obtaining the latest demographics, including the Web sites of the National Institute on Aging (http://www.nih.gov.80/nia), the Administration on Aging (http://www.aoa.dhhs.gov), the Gerontological Society of America (http://www.geron.org), Division 20 of the American Psychological Association (http://www.iog.wayne.edu/apadiv20), and Geropsychology (http://www.premier.net/gero/geropsyc). Instructors can assign students a project in which they are to explore the Internet for demographic information on population shifts over last 100 years and predictions for the next 50 years and to discuss the implications for their own lives as well as for society as a whole.

2. Developmental Theories of Aging

Three major developmental theories of aging have emerged over the last 40 years.

Disengagement theory

After World War II, older people were encouraged to retire and make room in the workplace for the younger people who were returning from the war. It was during this time that the *disengagement theory* of aging began to appear in the literature. This theory, influenced by Freud's (1924) psycho-analytic view that people after mid-life had little potential for change or further development, proposed that it was normal in later life to disengage from former roles and activities (Cumming & Henry, 1961). According to disengagement theory, older people were believed to be most healthy and appropriate if they retired to leisure and relative inactivity. Proponents of this theory viewed older people who continued in the work and activities of their youth as resisting normal development and creating a barrier within a youth-dominated society. However, older people who did not want to retreat from life soon forced a countertheory of aging, known as *activity theory*.

Activity theory

Influenced by a behavioral approach to mental health and develop-ment, the activity theory of aging (Lemon, Bengtson, & Peterson, 1972) proposed that healthy and normal aging required one to stay engaged in ac-tive life. According to this theory, later life interests might be different from former activities, but old age should be filled with volunteer work, traveling, projects, and intellectual pursuits. Activity theorists believed that healthy aging meant staying involved and continuing to learn and grow for as long as possible.

Continuity theory

Developmental gerontologists responded to these two theories of aging with the *continuity theory* of aging (Atchley, 1989), which emphasized that behavior does not change drastically as a person ages. Based on perspectives such as Erik Erikson's (1963) life stages, which proposed a progression from infancy to old age, continuity theory held that it was more likely that people would show a continuous pattern of behavior, interests, and activity levels throughout their lifetime. If someone had a tendency to be disengaged when young, then that pattern might be even more evident after retirement, when there were no economic or social reasons to be involved. On the other hand, someone who was actively involved during youth and mid-life was likely to stay active or even increase some forms of an active life after he or she no longer had the responsibilities of family and employment.

Bengtson and Schaie (1999) and Fry (1992) have provided comprehensive overviews of the various theories of aging. To help students understand these theories, the instructor can assign them to observe older people—at family gatherings, at the local mall, or on popular television shows—to determine which theory or theories seem applicable and whether any of the approaches seem to be more associated with positive functioning or life satisfaction.

3. Contributions to Well-Being in Later Life

Whereas genetics are important to health and longevity, well-being in old age also depends on the cumulative effects of what has occurred throughout a person's lifetime. People who have had good relationships, good health care, and adequate economic resources throughout life would be expected to have better well-being in old age than those who have had dysfunctional relationships, poor health care, or inadequate resources. These influences have been shown to be equal to or even greater than genetic predisposition for health and well-being in old age (Berkman & Breslow, 1983). Longitudinal studies of people who have reached old age indicate that social supports and an optimistic outlook appeared to have been as important as physical fitness. Two other areas that have been shown to be significantly related to health, longevity, and well-being are economics and education. Money gives access to resources and health care, while education and knowledge bring greater control over one's life. Resources and control are key elements not only in living longer but also in achieving a higher quality of life in old age (Crose, 1997).

4. Cultural, Ethnic, and Gender Differences in Aging

When the standard for normal aging is set by research on the more privileged individuals in a society (i.e., White men), then individuals who do not fit these standards may be viewed as abnormal or even pathological. This may be further reinforced when the professionals who teach about or oversee care for elders are primarily members of the dominant group. In a youth-oriented, European American- and male-dominated society, women and minorities are placed in double and even triple jeopardy for discrimination in their old age.

In teaching the Psychology of Aging, it is extremely important that cultural, ethnic, and gender differences be acknowledged and discussed. Many textbooks on adult development and aging fail to adequately include these issues, and many textbooks on feminist and multicultural psychology do not adequately address issues for women and minorities in old age. Thus, books and articles that address these issues can provide valuable supplements to the standard texts for Psychology of Aging courses (e.g., Markides, 1989; Miles, 1999; Padgett, 1995; Rosenthal, 1990; Trotman & Brody, 2002).

5. Defining Normal, Optimal, and Pathological Aging

There are many definitions of *normal aging* (Smyer & Qualls, 1999), and little consensus about what changes in health, lifestyle, and mental outlook are the results of aging and which are the results of disease or mental disorder. The one consistent finding that occurs with age is that all aspects of life seem to slow down, including physical responses, cognitive processes, and daily activities (Crose et al., 1997; Knight, 1996). Other things that routinely occur as people get older are the development of chronic, disabling conditions, greater emotional challenges due to losses, and gradual sensory impairments. The majority of older adults over 65 report some level of disability (American Association of Retired Persons, 1998); however, most of these individuals continue to live independently and continue their normal routines of daily life. Even though aging is often equated with disease, dementia, and death, severe disability and major physical diseases or mental disorders are not usual or normal aspects of aging.

A dynamic systems approach can help understand the normal processes of aging, and when and where it may be necessary to intervene (Crose, Nicholas, Gobble, & Frank, 1992; Schroots, 1995). At any age, health and well-being are related to other aspects of life. Physical health may be related to one's psychological state, to the existence of supportive relationships, and to overall outlook on life. These interrelations become stronger in later years, when individuals begin to experience more health problems, life and role changes (such as retirement), and loss of friends and loved ones. When such significant life changes occur very close together, a compression of loss is experienced that takes a toll on all dimensions of life, including physical, mental, occupational, financial, relational, and spiritual health. With age, such compression of loss occurs more frequently and thus provides greater challenges to mental and physical health.

Optimal aging is a relatively new concept that is being discussed under many labels, such as *successful aging* (Rowe & Kahn, 1987), *productive aging*, *vital aging*, *creative aging*, and *conscious aging*. This is a break from traditional concerns with pathology, toward finding ways to age with a high level of well-being. The recently introduced concept of *gerotranscendence* (Tornstam, 1996) points to the potential in the older person for transcending life's travails to realize greater wisdom, spirituality, and life satisfaction than can be known at younger ages. This movement toward considering aging as a normal part of life with much unexplored potential is important to the psychology of aging and to health promotion throughout life. To illustrate these ideas, the instructor can contact retired faculty or a senior center to invite a panel of elders to speak to the class about successful aging. In the class session prior to the panel, it is useful to have students generate a list of their conceptions about growing old, and then in the class session following the panel, to have them consider whether their views have changed.

6. Sensory Changes With Age

Reading, driving, seeing clearly, carrying on a conversation, listening to music, enjoying a good meal, and feeling the textures and detecting the smells of the environment are the things that keep one mentally sharp, motivated, and inspired throughout life. However, sensory losses are common with age, with a wide array of possible effects, including impairment in memory, cognitive processing, orientation, and ability to function independently, as well as a reduction in the level of connection to others.

Some sensory problems are common (see Belsky, 1999, for a concise, comprehensive description of sensory impairment in older adults). For example, a condition known as *presbyopia* reduces the ability to focus on near objects and results in the need for bifocals. Vision problems can often easily be corrected with eyeglasses or minor surgery, such as for retinal detachment or cataracts, and cause no serious impairment in the daily lives of most older adults. More serious visual impairments such as glaucoma (damage to retinal receptors from a buildup of fluid and pressure) and macular degeneration (a loss of central vision) may result in problems such as disorientation, falls, and limited mobility (Marsiske, Klumb, & Baltes, 1997; Rudberg, Furner, Dunn, & Cassel, 1993; Simoneau & Leibowitz, 1996). Hearing problems in old age are more likely to influence emotional and mental health of older adults than vision impairments. Hearing loss affects communication with others and thus interferes with relationships and connections to the outside world in ways that vision impairment does not. The other senses—taste, smell, and touch—are not as crucial to mental well-being as are sight and sound; however, they provide input that improves one's quality of life and are important to overall well-being.

There are several experiential exercises simulating sensory impairment that can be very effective in helping students understand the impact of such disabilities. For vision impairment, they can smear petroleum jelly on an old pair of eyeglasses and try to read a paper. For hearing impairment, they can stuff cotton balls in both ears while the instructor varies the tone and volume of an audiotape. Another possibility is to assign a small-group activity in class, in which one person in each group has their ears blocked with cotton. When the activity is over, students can examine the effects of the induced hearing impairment on the individual's participation and feelings within the group. An organized kit of simulation activities called "Secure Project: Older Adult Sensitivity Program" is available through Lee Memorial Hospital Older Adult Services, 2776 Cleveland Avenue, Fort Myers, FL 33901 (telephone: 941-334-5949; Web site: http://www.leememorial.org).

7. Major Mental Health Issues in Later Life

Although the majority of older people do not suffer from major mental health problems, and a sizable number report that their later life is more sane and satisfying than their earlier years, mental disorders in old age are a concern for many individuals and their families. Cognitive impairment that results from depression, dementia (organic brain disorder), or delirium (acute, reversible confusion and disorientation) is the primary mental health issue in old age.

Careful investigation and psychological assessment are vital to providing appropriate treatment interventions (Smyer & Qualls, 1999). Depression resulting from losses of employment, health, friends, loved ones, sensory acuity, or other abilities may appear very similar to dementia, an irreversible organic condition. Disorientation and confusion may be the results of metabolic imbalances, infections, or medication and not symptoms of dementia. Use of alcohol and nonprescribed drugs is often overlooked in assessment of cognitive impairment in older adults, yet alcohol and drug addiction or dependence is an increasing problem among people over 50 (Substance Abuse and Mental Health Services Administration, 1998).

Actual dementia may result from Alzheimer's disease, cerebral vascular accidents or strokes, Parkinson's disease, AIDS, Huntington's disease, Korsokoff's syndrome, and a variety of other related disorders. These disorders cause permanent and sometimes progressive damage to the brain and cannot be reversed, although there are now some medications that can help slow down their course (Levy & Uncapher, 2000). The care for people with dementia, which can be extremely difficult for family members and other caregivers, benefits from a team approach for intervention with the whole system (Ogland-Hand & Zeiss, 2000). In addition, psychological treatment can be useful; for example, early dementia is often accompanied by depression, which can be treated with behavioral interventions. Behavioral therapy can also help relieve anxiety and prevent dangerous or destructive actions, which in turn can help relieve the stress and burden of the caregivers (Fisher, Harsin, & Hayden, 2000). Instructors can obtain informational materials on dementia from their local Alzheimer's association or from the national Alzheimer's Association at 919 North Michigan Avenue, Chicago, IL 60611 (telephone: 800-272-3900, Web site: http://www.alz.org).

With the improved medical treatment of the past few decades, people with lifelong emotional and mental health problems are now living into old age and needing continued treatment and care. Although schizophrenia, substance abuse, personality disorders, and marriage and family problems occur with less frequency than in younger age groups, they need to be effectively managed and treated when they do occur, and thus they are part of the focus of clinical geropsychology (Nordhus, VandenBos, Berg, & Fromholt, 1998; Smyer & Qualls, 1999).

8. Multigenerational Family Dynamics

With longer life spans, it is not uncommon today to have four-generation families. This creates a different dynamic than in the past, when families were made up of many children and few adults. Modern families may include two children with one or two parents and multiple grandparents. With increases in divorce, adoption, single parenting, and alternative lifestyles, combined with changes in gender roles and work patterns, family structures and caregiving for children and dependent elders have become more complex (Crose, 1997).

Many people now spend more years of their lives caring for parents and grandparents than they do caring for children. On the other hand, more grandparents are the primary caregivers for their grandchildren than ever before in history (Fuller-Thompson, Minkler, & Driver, 1997). Each of these caregiving roles is more likely to be handled by women (Crose et al., 1997), increasing the stress on themselves and their relationships and complicating the functioning of each family. Because of these dramatic changes, more research into family structures and dynamics is needed, as are expanded treatment approaches for family therapy. As an illustration of the increased complexity of caregiving, the instructor can ask students to construct multigenerational genograms (McGoldrick & Gerson, 1985) that trace the caregiving connections within their own families. They might, in particular, examine gender differences in caregiving patterns and include predictions of their own future caregiving relationships.

9. Social Services and Policies

As people are living longer and with more disabilities, there is a need to re-examine social policies and expand social services. Caregiving, quality of life, costs of health care, and the right to die are a few of the issues that will be confronting U.S. society in the coming decades. Many years ago, Maslow and Murphy (1954) described a hierarchy of needs for humans that aptly fits the policies and services required for optimal aging. Basic needs for safety, food, shelter, and socialization must be met first in order for treatments for late-life depression, anxiety, and other mental disorders to be effective. Psychologists must become knowledgeable and proactive in helping older people obtain quality services and care. In this regard, geropsychologists are challenging mainstream psychology to expand research, training, and treatment and to develop team approaches for research and services with professionals from other disciplines that serve the aging population. A

Psychology of Aging instructor can invite a speaker from a local area agency on aging to inform students about governmental policies and social services for older people in their community and to offer suggestions for involvement in advocacy and social action. Students may also wish to know about national organizations concerned with the emerging field of geropsychology, such as Psychologists in Long Term Care; Section II (Geropsychology) of Division 12 (Clinical Psychology) of the American Psychological Association; and the American Psychological Association Office on Aging.

10. Other Issues in Psychology and Aging

Other issues that should be covered in a comprehensive course on the Psychology of Aging include living environments, friendship, productivity, social supports, sexuality, spirituality, financial concerns, and end-of-life decision making. The limits of this chapter do not allow for a discussion of these topics here; however, useful resources are books by Birren, Sloane, and Cohen (1992); Friedman and Wachs (1999); Hazzard, Bierman, Blass, Ettinger, and Halter (1994); Nordhus et al. (1998); and Smyer and Qualls (1999).

Mental health in later life is complex, requiring that psychologists take their research outside the laboratory, and the practice of psychology outside the one-person office, to become engaged in all dimensions of an older person's life experiences. Likewise, the teaching of the Psychology of Aging requires that lessons expand outside the walls of the classroom and into the communities of older people. The best way to overcome the myths, fears, and stereotypes of age is to involve students directly with older adults. This could involve conducting classes at retirement centers or nursing homes. Another possibility is to recruit older people to serve as mentors to the students, with each elder "adopting" one or more students for the semester to help them learn about aging. Mentors and students could meet outside class for various activities throughout the semester. These activities might include (a) interviewing the older person in order to write oral histories, (b) practicing the administration of geriatric assessment instruments, (c) constructing multigenerational family genograms, or (d) experiencing the establishment of a therapeutic relationship between an older client and younger therapist. Then, at the end of the semester, students could host a thank-you party for their mentors. For additional practical methods for teaching about aging in undergraduate psychology courses, see Whitbourne and Cavanaugh (2003).

CONCLUSION

Much of the focus of psychology has centered on development as children move from dependence to independence in the first 20 years of life. In the coming decades, psychology professionals will be attempting to understand and assist with the process of individuals moving from independence back to an interdependent, and perhaps finally a dependent, state at the end of life. Psychologists' role will be to help people live life with a sense of self-worth, dignity, and mental well-being from birth until death. Teaching the Psychology of Aging is not only rewarding and challenging; it also has very important implications for the future of an aging society.

REFERENCES

American Association of Retired Persons. (1998). *A profile of older Americans.* Washington, DC: Author.

Atchley, R. C. (1989). A continuity theory of normal aging. *The Gerontologist, 29,* 183–190.

Belsky, J. (1999). *The psychology of aging: Theory, research, and interventions* (3rd ed.). Pacific Grove, CA: Brooks/Cole.

Bengtson, V. L., & Schaie, K. W. (Eds.). (1999). *Handbook of theories of aging.* New York: Springer.

Berkman, L., & Breslow, L. (1983). *Health and ways of living: The Alameda County study.* New York: Oxford University Press.

Birren, J. E., Sloane, R. B., & Cohen, G. D. (1992). *Handbook of mental health and aging* (2nd ed.). San Diego, CA: Academic Press.

Busse, E. W., & Maddox, G. L. (1985). *The Duke longitudinal studies of normal aging, 1955–1980.* New York: Springer.

Crose, R. (1997). *Why women live longer than men . . . And what men can learn from them.* San Francisco: Jossey-Bass.

Crose, R. (1999). Addressing late life developmental issues for women: Body image, sexuality, and intimacy. In M. Duffy (Ed.), *Handbook of counseling and psychotherapy with older adults* (pp. 57–76). New York: Wiley.

Crose, R. (2000). The impact of culture and gender on mental health. In V. Molinari (Ed.), *Professional psychology in long term care* (pp. 373–400). New York: Hatherleigh Press.

Crose, R., Leventhal, E. A., Haug, M. R., & Burns, E. A. (1997). The challenges of aging. In S. J. Gallant, G. P. Keita, & R. Royak-Schaler (Eds.), *Health care for women: Psychological, social, and behavioral influences* (pp. 221–234). Washington, DC: American Psychological Association.

Crose, R., Nicholas, D., Gobble, D., & Frank, B. (1992). Gender and wellness: A multidimensional model for counseling. *Journal of Counseling and Development, 71,* 149–156.

Cumming, E., & Henry, W. (1961). *Growing old.* New York: Basic Books.

Duffy, M. (Ed.). (1999). *Handbook of counseling and psychotherapy with older adults.* New York: Wiley.

Erikson, E. H. (1963). *Childhood and society*. New York: Norton.

Fisher, J. E., Harsin, C. W., & Hayden, J. E. (2000). Behavioral interventions for patients with dementia. In V. Molinari (Ed.), *Professional psychology in long term care* (pp. 179–200). New York: Hatherleigh Press.

Freud, S. (1924). *On psychotherapy: Collected papers* (Vol. 1). London: Hogarth.

Friedland, R. B., & Summer, L. (1999). *Demography is not destiny*. Washington, DC: Gerontological Society of America.

Friedman, S. L., & Wachs, T. D. (1999). *Measuring environment across the life span: Emerging methods and concepts*. Washington, DC: American Psychological Association.

Fry, P. S. (1992). Major social theories of aging and their implications for counseling concepts and practice: A critical review. *The Counseling Psychologist, 20*, 246–329.

Fuller-Thompson, E., Minkler, M., & Driver, D. (1997). A profile of grandparents raising grandchildren in the United States. *The Gerontologist, 37*, 406–411.

Gilligan, C. (1982). *In a different voice: Psychological theory and women's development*. Cambridge, MA: Harvard University Press.

Hazzard, W. R., Bierman, E. L., Blass, J. P., Ettinger, W. H. Jr., & Halter, J. B. (Eds.). (1994). *Geriatric medicine and gerontology* (3rd ed.). New York: McGraw-Hill.

Knight, B. (1996). *Psychotherapy with older adults*. Thousand Oaks, CA: Sage.

Lemon, B. W., Bengtson, V. L., & Peterson, J. A. (1972). An exploration of the activity theory of aging, activity types and life satisfaction among in-movers to a retirement community. *Journal of Gerontology, 27*, 511–523.

Levy, M. L., & Uncapher, H. (2000). Basic psychopharmacology in the nursing home. In V. Molinari (Ed.), *Professional psychology in long term care* (pp. 279–297). New York: Hatherleigh Press.

Markides, K. S. (Ed.). (1989). *Aging and health: Perspectives on gender, race, ethnicity, and class*. Newbury Park, CA: Sage.

Marsiske, M., Klumb, P., & Baltes, M. M. (1997). Everyday activity patterns and sensory functioning in old age. *Psychology and Aging, 12*, 444–457.

Maslow, A., & Murphy, G. (1954). *Motivation and personality*. New York: Harper.

McGoldrick, M., & Gerson, R. (1985). *Genograms in family assessment*. New York: Norton.

Miles, T. P. (Ed.). (1999). *Full-color aging: Facts, goals, and recommendations for America's diverse elders*. Washington, DC: Gerontological Society of America.

Miller, J. B. (1976). *Toward a new psychology of women*. Boston: Beacon Press.

National Institute on Aging. (1989). *Older and wiser* (NIH Publication No. 89-2797). Bethesda, MD: National Institutes of Health.

National Institute on Aging. (1993). *With the passage of time: The Baltimore Longitudinal Study of Aging* (NIH Publication No. 93-3685). Bethesda, MD: National Institutes of Health.

Nordhus, I. H., VandenBos, G. R., Berg, S., & Fromholt, P. (1998). *Clinical geropsychology*. Washington, DC: American Psychological Association.

Ogland-Hand, S. M., & Zeiss, A. M. (2000). Interprofessional health care teams. In V. Molinari (Ed.), *Professional psychology in long term care* (pp. 257–277). New York: Hatherleigh Press.

Padgett, D. K. (Ed.). (1995). *Handbook on ethnicity, aging, and mental health*. Westport, CT: Greenwood Press.

Rosenthal, E. R. (Ed.). (1990). *Women, aging, and ageism*. New York: Harrington Park Press.

Rowe, J. W., & Kahn, R. L. (July, 1987). Human aging: Usual and successful. *Science, 237*, 143–149.

Rudberg, M. A., Furner, S. E., Dunn, J. E., & Cassel, C. K. (1993). The relationship of visual and hearing impairments to disability: An analysis using the longitudinal study of aging. *Journals of Gerontology, 48A*, M261–M265.

Schaie, K. W. (1965). A general model for the study of developmental problems. *Psychological Bulletin, 64*, 92–107.

Schroots, J. J. F. (1995). Psychological models of aging. *Canadian Journal on Aging, 14*, 44–66.

Simoneau, G. G., & Leibowitz, H. W. (1996). Posture, gaits, and falls. In J. E. Birren & K. W. Schaie (Eds.), *Handbook of the psychology of aging* (4th ed., pp. 204–217). San Diego, CA: Academic Press.

Smyer, M. A., & Qualls, S. H. (1999). *Aging and mental health*. Malden, MA: Blackwell.

Substance Abuse and Mental Health Services Administration. (1998). *Substance abuse among older adults* (Publication No. SMA 98-3179). Rockville, MD: U.S. Department of Health and Human Services.

Tornstam, L. (1996). Gerotranscendence—A theory about maturing into old age. *Journal of Aging and Identity, 1*, 37–49.

Trotman, F. K., & Brody, C. M. (2002). *Psychotherapy and counseling with older women: Cross-cultural, family, and end-of-life issues*. New York: Springer.

Whitbourne, S. K., & Cavanaugh, J. C. (Eds.). (2003). *The aging dimension in undergraduate psychology courses: A practical guide for teaching*. Washington, DC: American Psychological Association.

Worell, J., & Remer, P. (1992). *Feminist perspectives in therapy: An empowerment model for women*. New York: Wiley.

20

LESBIAN, GAY, BISEXUAL, TRANSGENDER, AND INTERSEX ISSUES IN THE PSYCHOLOGY CURRICULUM

JACQUELINE S. WEINSTOCK

Awareness of lesbian, gay, bisexual, transgender, and intersex (LGBTI) issues has substantially increased in the last 10 years; however, it is still uncommon for academic institutions and disciplines to adequately consider LGBTI curriculum content or the needs of LGBTI students (Connolly, 2000; Renn, 1998). Fortunately, psychology is well situated to redress these omissions (Greene & Croom, 2000; Kimmel, 2000). In this chapter, I discuss the challenges that the process may involve, and I present suggestions for ways to incorporate LGBTI issues into the psychology curriculum both in general courses and in individual courses devoted to LGBTI content.

This chapter, and my ideas about lesbian, gay, bisexual, transgender, and intersex teaching issues, have been greatly informed by the undergraduate students I have had the pleasure of working with and learning from over the years. I am also deeply grateful to Lynne Bond, Michelle Clossick, Anthony D'Augelli, Maryalice Elbaum, Rhonda Factor, Diane Felicio, Esther Rothblum, and E. Clark Sheldon for their insights and examples as social justice advocates.

285

INCORPORATING LGBTI ISSUES INTO GENERAL
PSYCHOLOGY COURSES

Teaching and Learning Challenges

> Talk less about gay/lesbian rights. Do less pushing of your life decision. I
> don't want to know about [it].

The above quote, selected from among several similar anonymous end-
of-course student feedback forms, suggests that integrating LGBTI issues into
general psychology courses brings risks for both students and instructors.
Students may view the inclusion of LGBTI materials as irrelevant, inappropriate, or excessive, and they may question the instructor's judgment and
professionalism. Whereas this may be the case for any instructor who brings
these issues into the classroom, additional challenges arise when the instructor self-identifies as (or is presumed to be) other than heterosexual (Browning & Kain, 2000), especially if the institutional climate is less than LGBTI
affirmative (Thoresen, 1998). For all instructors, it can be quite challenging
to teach in a nonheterosexist manner, given the pervasive heterosexism that
defines social structures and norms throughout U.S. society.

Meeting the Challenges: Classroom Strategies

General psychology courses usually offer little opportunity for sus-
tained, interactive engagement with LGBTI issues. The instructor teaching
such a course might best focus on offering accurate information and challenging prevailing myths and stereotypes through lectures, films, or guest
presentations by LGBTI panels or individuals. Drawing more directly on
students' views may elicit negative and hurtful comments that cannot be
adequately processed or refuted—although purposeful generation of myths
and stereotypes may be used constructively, if followed by their critical
examination. Other strategies I have used to engage students in learning
about LGBTI issues include an anonymous survey I designed on LGBTI-related knowledge, beliefs, and attitudes and in-class free-writing assignments
in which students respond privately to selected questions from Rochlin's
(1995) "Heterosexuality Questionnaire" (e.g., "What do you think caused
your heterosexuality?"). I have also constructed a take-home sex, gender, and
sexual orientation self-assessment (adapted from Klein, 1990) that considers
these variables along multiple dimensions and over time. It can be helpful
to note the likely presence of LGBTI people in the class, as long as students
understand this as a general probability statement and not an "outing." In
addition, it is important to focus attention on the negative psychological
impact of homophobia and heterosexism and the benefits—to LGBTIs, heterosexuals, and the field of psychology—in eradicating them (Brown, 1989;

Herek, 1995), which can help demonstrate the relevance of LGBTI issues to the psychology curriculum.

Even when not specifically addressing LGBTI issues, or in courses where such issues may not at first appear to be relevant, psychology instructors can still engage in inclusive, nonheterosexist pedagogy. For example, they can invite LGBTI people to join a parenting panel, or they can use LGBTI examples when discussing psychological concepts besides sexuality. They can—and should—listen for and respond to derogatory comments or stereotypes, thus challenging heterosexism and homophobia (Chestnut, 1998). In addition, as the fifth edition of the *Publication Manual* of the American Psychological Association (2001) indicates, instructors should use preferred language choices that are respectful and inclusive of LGBTI people and avoid the use of comparisons that stigmatize or marginalize particular groups. For example, rather than identify class sessions on families and an additional session on LGBTI families, instructors can include LGBTI families under the generic heading. Even better would be to specifically identify all family types to be studied, including those that reflect the dominant heterosexual form. This avoids placing heterosexual families at the center and challenges the privileging of heterosexuality as the normal way to be.

Suggestions for Course Content

There are many places where it is appropriate and educational to incorporate LGBTI issues into general psychology courses. Courses that examine prejudice and oppression can include homophobia and heterosexism, whereas courses exploring such topics as identity, relationships, family, and sexuality, as well as current research and theory related to sex and gender, can incorporate LGBTI perspectives (e.g., D'Augelli & Patterson, 1995; Dreger, 1999; Greene & Croom, 2000; Kessler, 1998; Koyama & Weasel, 2001; Patterson & D'Augelli, 1998). These courses can also examine popular concerns regarding children raised by same-sex parents. For example, I frequently ask students to generate a list of such concerns (e.g., children's gender identity and sexuality), which can then be compared with the empirical literature (Patterson & Redding, 1996; Stacey & Biblarz, 2001). This sets the stage for a discussion of cultural and psychological assumptions, generating questions such as: "Do mothers and fathers make distinctive contributions to a child's gender identity development?" and "What is healthy gender development?" Such questions also set the stage for examining intersections between heterosexism, sexism, and gender socialization pressures.

To illustrate these issues, I have read students portions of Barlow's Gender Specific Motor Behavior measure (adapted from Burke, 1996), which assesses the way a person stands, walks, and sits in terms of masculinity or femininity (e.g., the distance between one's buttocks and the back of the chair, if more than 4 in. [10.16 cm], is deemed masculine). I also share case stories of children diagnosed with gender identity disorder and relate these to students' own childhood experiences and preferences, to open up discussion of gender rules and gender-related pressures to conform. Finally, if there is time, I discuss the likely causes and typical perpetrators of hate crimes against LGBTI people and demonstrate ways that these crimes may be viewed as extreme but expectable consequences of gender socialization and gender role conformity in a context of heterosexism (Franklin, 1998; Herek, 1993). Burke's (1996) concept of gender independence provides a powerful closing to this examination of gender socialization.

In regard to specific information to include, it is important for instructors to dispel common myths and stereotypes. They need to provide accurate information about LGBTI identities, families, and communities and to articulate LGBTIs' strengths, within-group diversity, and many similarities with—as well as differences from—heterosexuals. Depending on the course focus, I may also cover a variety of LGBTI-preferred terms and key concepts, discuss heterosexism as a form of oppression that negatively affects heterosexuals as well as LGBTIs (Burke, 1996; Hyde & Jaffee, 2000), provide HIV- and AIDS-related information (Grossman, 2001; Herek & Greene, 1995), and offer local contact information and other resources for students. Taken together, this helps make the educational experience safer and more inclusive for LGBTI students. It also prepares heterosexual students to meet their future ethical and professional responsibilities to be knowledgeable about, comfortable with, and respectful of the LGBTI individuals with whom they may interact.

INTRODUCTORY LGBTI-FOCUSED COURSES

Teaching and Learning Challenges

Although students who enroll in LGBTI-focused courses are more likely aware of LGBTI issues, they may still be uncomfortable with course material and class participation. Seemingly simple actions, such as registering for the course, attending the first class, and buying the books, can challenge their own as well as other people's conceptions of their sexual and gender identities. Some students may not want an LGBTI course on their transcript. Despite these challenges, diverse groups have tended to sign up for my LGBTI-focused courses, including openly identified ("out") and not openly identified LGBTI students, students questioning their sexual or gender identity, heterosexual allies, and heterosexuals who do not self-identify as allies. Students have also varied greatly within all these categories in the extent of their LGBTI knowledge and experience and in their comfort in sharing personal thoughts and feelings.

The tendency for LGBTI-focused classes to include visibly LGBTI-identified students presents both great possibilities and unique pedagogical challenges. Unlike in most other courses, LGBTI students may claim the classroom as their own even before the first class begins, possibly making some of the heterosexual and closeted LGBTI students uncomfortable. Whereas this shift in power relations has the potential to provide a great learning opportunity for all students, the challenge of supporting all students to remain in the class must be met before such learning can take place.

Regardless of whether instructors self-identify as LGBTI, there will likely be personal and professional consequences to teaching LGBTI-focused courses. LGBTI and heterosexual students alike may also be concerned about—perhaps even wary of—their instructor's sexual and gender identity, as well as of the perspectives and values guiding the class. Thoresen (1998) noted that some faculty and administrators may view an LGBTI-focused course as "more about politics and/or personal identity than it is about a legitimate subject of academic inquiry" (p. 257), thereby making the course and the teacher suspect.

The course content itself presents personal and intellectual challenges. LGBTI issues and heterosexism are still taboo topics in the United States; as Tatum (1992) noted, this fact interacts with students' desire to believe in the United States as a just society, so that they may initially ignore or deny information to the contrary. When their beliefs are challenged, students may experience—and express—strong emotions. As heterosexual students begin to recognize their own privileges, they may experience embarrassment, shame, and anger about their own complicity in the oppression. LGBTI students may experience strong feelings as they move through various stages of understanding; a full grasp of their oppression may cause powerful reactions, including anger directed at perceived sources of oppression—for example, families, peers, teachers, and administrators (D'Augelli, 1992).

Meeting the Challenges: Classroom Strategies

There are many things an instructor can do to increase students' safety and comfort in LGBTI-focused courses. For example, selecting a relatively nonspecific course name (I call my course "Sexual Identities") that will appear on students' schedules and transcripts, and putting course readings on the Web (so that students don't have to ask for them in the library), may be necessary compromises in the current context of heterosexism (Thoresen, 1998). In addition, I clearly communicate in the course catalogue description that all students are welcome, while at the same time conveying that the course has an LGBTI-affirmative perspective. Perhaps the most important task for the instructor, regardless of personal identity, is to convey an explicitly nonheterosexist perspective, and to place LGBTI voices and perspectives at the course's center, while affirming all students and all identities. It is also critical that the instructor create and maintain a class climate that is attentive to and respectful of all students; that allows for and supports personal expression, struggle, and change; and that encourages critical thinking and the challenging of ideas in a civil manner. It is important to develop shared guidelines with students in the first class session, regarding confidentiality; respect for differences; assumption of best intent; relative safety in sharing personal feelings, reactions, and even (however unintentionally) homophobic or heterosexist assumptions; and challenging each other with care (Olsson & Stuehling, 1999).

To convey the content of the course most effectively, I emphasize my role as the constructor of an interactive learning environment that draws on a diversity of learning styles and activities and that can offer ample opportunity for students to learn about themselves and from one another. In class, these opportunities might include writing exercises, dyadic conversations, small-group activities, and large-group discussions. Because some students may be uncomfortable with class participation, even on a dyadic level, I find it important to clearly convey my expectations about participation early in the semester, along with a willingness to negotiate according to students' differing comfort levels. I also assign weekly reflection papers, which both prepare students for participating in class discussions and provide me with a regular line of communication with every student.

Collaborative in-class and out-of-class activities can encourage the formation of informal support systems, fostering self-acceptance as well as understanding of and respect for others' developmental journeys. Projects that require students to reflect on ways to improve the conditions of LGBTIs' lives can also provide information for allies and support for LGBTIs and allies alike, as together they consider individual and collective actions that might effect positive change. For example, my students have collaborated on the formation of an LGBTI community center, a campus ally support group, and panel presentations on how the Sexual Identities class has affected them. Local LGBTI organizations and agencies can be useful resources for helping students identify and engage in collaborative and action-based projects.

If at some point in the semester everyone has self-identified in the class setting or informed me that I may do so for them, I have found it useful to engage the students in activities that first separate and then bring them together on the basis of their self-described LGBTI identities. This provides small groups with the opportunity to talk among themselves, develop and respond to questions, and explore the similarities and differences in their experiences. Particular activities that have worked using this approach include an examination of LGBTI and heterosexual ally development models, friendship networks and issues for friendships across sexual identities, and a general processing of how the course is going. At the same time, these kinds of activities are best intermixed with ones that divide students randomly—for example, to work together to generate a list of health or political priorities for LGBTIs.

I have also found it useful to incorporate out-of-class LGBTI-related activities—such as cultural events, lectures, and films—into the course. If there are only a few LGBTI students in the class, these activities become a means for introducing a greater diversity of LGBTI voices and perspectives. In addition, attending an LGBTI-related activity can help questioning students explore their identities, and help heterosexual students break through their own barriers around attending LGBTI events, while providing information and reactions for the class to explore. To honor students' differing comfort levels, and the issue of safety itself, a variety of activities should be offered, including some that can be done in relative privacy, such as surfing the Web.

Suggestions for Course Content

Over the last 20 years, there has been increasing interest in supporting LGBTI college students and in teaching about LGBTI issues in college classes (see, e.g., Greene & Croom, 2000; Sanlo, 1998; Wall & Evans, 2000). The content and learning objectives that are important to include in introductory-level LGBTI courses are similar to those important in general psychology courses, although they can be explored in more depth. Overall, I have found it very useful to introduce and discuss early in the semester models of sexual and gender identity development for LGBTIs, and ally development for heterosexual students, and to refer to these models throughout the course; Tatum (1992) used a similar approach in her work with students on race and racism. In this way, students gain important information that may help them anticipate and understand their own and each other's developmental processes. Furthermore, students can compare and contrast their own processes with each other's and with the models in the literature (e.g., Bohan, 1996; Broido, 2000; Savin-Williams, 1998).

In a similar manner, students can explore from personal and research-based perspectives the various forms and functions of heterosexism (e.g., Herek, 1995, 1998); the film *It's Elementary: Talking About Gay Issues in School* (Cohen & Chasnoff, 1997) can increase their understanding of U.S. society's system of privilege and oppression and ways to combat it. The films *Before Stonewall: The Making of a Gay and Lesbian Community* (Rosenberg, Scagliotti, & Schiller, 1994) and *After Stonewall* (Basile, Scagliotti, Baus, & Hunt, 1999) provide both historical information and the opportunity for students to critically examine existing perspectives in the field. One good introductory text that addresses a range of important topics is Bohan's (1996) *Psychology and Sexual Orientation;* additional resources that specifically address LGBTI developmental, family, and health-related concerns include D'Augelli and Patterson (2001), Patterson and D'Augelli (1998), and

Savin-Williams (2001). To introduce students to culturally diverse LGBTI voices and perspectives, reflecting LGBTI experience within different cultural contexts, I bring in guest speakers, assign readings that represent a range of perspectives (e.g., Feinberg, 1998; Howard & Stevens, 2000; Ochs, 2001; Savin-Williams, 1998), and show the film *Speaking for Ourselves: Portraits of Gay and Lesbian Youth* (Coppel & Mifsud, 1994).

The experiences and challenges of being transgendered in LGBTI communities and in the larger U.S. society also warrant careful attention in LGBTI courses. Some of the personal, developmental, and relationship issues can be effectively illuminated with Feinberg's (1993) novel *Stone Butch Blues*, in combination with the film *Ma Vie en Rose* (Scotta & Berliner, 1999), or the films *Different for Girls* (Chapman & Spence, 1998) and *You Don't Know Dick: Courageous Hearts of Transsexual Men* (Schermerhorn & Cram, 1997), or by guest speakers who are transgendered. Other useful introductory readings and activities can be found in Bornstein (1994, 1998).

For introducing and exploring bisexuality, I have found it helpful to engage the class in a critical examination of prevailing myths and stereotypes about bisexual people, as well as the ways that antibisexual oppression operates among both heterosexuals and gay men and lesbians. A panel of bisexual-identified people representing diverse experiences and perspectives is another way of breaking down myths and developing a better understanding of bisexualities. Selected resources to draw on include Firestein (1996), Ochs (2001), and Rust (1995).

ADVANCED LGBTI-FOCUSED COURSES: CHALLENGES, ACTIVITIES, AND SUGGESTIONS FOR CONTENT

Advanced LGBTI-focused courses offer opportunities to delve more deeply into specific topics. An advanced course should still include students' personal experiences and perspectives, but it ought to emphasize complex theoretical and empirical issues to a greater extent than does an introductory course. The instructor can provide background readings (e.g., Bohan, 1996) in conjunction with more advanced-level texts (e.g., D'Augelli & Patterson, 1995; Savin-Williams & Cohen, 1996), which may be especially helpful to students with little LGBTI knowledge.

Upper level seminars can expand on topics addressed above, focusing on particular identities, developmental experiences, or relationships forms, or they examine key historical, sociopolitical, or theoretical issues relevant to LGBTI communities. As examples, "Challenging Sex and Gender" and "Born or Made: LGBTI Identity Issues," could be taught as special seminars drawing on such resources as Chase (1998), Colapinto (2000), Dreger (1999), Feinberg (1998), Queen and Schimel (1997), Wilchins (1997), and the films *Adventures in the Gender Trade* (Marenco & Mason, 1993),

Transsexual Menace (Praunheim, 1996), and *Hermaphrodites Speak!* (Intersex Society of North America, 1996). Another seminar title might be "Multiple and Intersecting Identities Among LGBTIs" that could use such resources as Clare (1999), Conerly (1996), Greene (1997), Lee (1996), and the film *Tongues Untied* (Riggs, 1996). Other possible seminars might include "Theorizing Heterosexuality" (Hyde & Jaffee, 2000; Kitzinger, Wilkinson, & Perkins, 1992) and "Preventing Heterosexism and Developing LGBTI Allies" (Broido, 2000; Rothblum & Bond, 1996; Sears & Williams, 1997).

In addition to the opportunities that advanced LGBTI-focused courses offer for more in-depth analysis of LGBTI-related issues, they provide an opportunity to reflect critically on the ways that psychological theory, research, and clinical practice have been influenced by heterosexual assumptions and privileges. Furthermore, they allow for an examination of the ways that various identities interact to shape LGBTIs' experiences, which informs students not only about LGBTIs and heterosexism but also about the influences of various contexts and interactions among multiple forms of oppression.

CONCLUSION

Academic silence about LGBTI issues has contributed to the perpetuation of heterosexism (Chestnut, 1998). As D'Augelli (1992) noted, LGBTI young people "find themselves deleted from most relevant courses" (p. 214), and this omission devalues their existence and contributions. LGBTI-focused courses (and "out" LGBTI instructors; Allen, 1995) may be especially important in that they offer LGBTI students material that, as one student put it on an end-of-course anonymous evaluation form, "really pertained to my life." A learning environment that affirms all sexual and gender identities will enhance self-esteem, self-understanding, and respect for diverse others, for all students. To date, psychological knowledge has typically reflected and reinforced heterosexual assumptions and heterosexual privileges. By making these invisible assumptions visible (Brown, 1989), instructors can help students develop a better understanding of the various ways that psychology is embedded in a context of heterosexism, and thus—because students are the professionals of tomorrow—move the field of psychology forward in developing multicultural theories, research, therapeutic approaches, and pedagogical practice.

REFERENCES

Allen, K. R. (1995). Opening the classroom closet: Sexual orientation and self-disclosure. *Family Relations, 44,* 136–141.

American Psychological Association. (2001). *Publication manual of the American Psychological Association* (5th ed.). Washington, DC: Author.

Basile, V. (Producer), Scagliotti, J. (Producer and Director), Baus, J., & Hunt D., (Directors). (1999). *After Stonewall* [Videotape]. New York: First Run Features.

Bohan, J. S. (1996). *Psychology and sexual orientation.* New York: Routledge.

Bornstein, K. (1994). *Gender outlaw: On men, women and the rest of us.* New York: Routledge.

Bornstein, K. (1998). *My gender workbook: How to become a real man, a real woman, the real you, or something else entirely.* New York: Routledge.

Broido, E. (2000). Ways of being an ally to lesbian, gay, and bisexual students. In V. A. Wall & N. J. Evans (Eds.), *Toward acceptance: Sexual orientation issues on campus* (pp. 345–369). Lanham, MD: University Press of America.

Brown, L. S. (1989). New voices, new visions: Toward a lesbian/gay paradigm for psychology. *Psychology of Women Quarterly, 13,* 272–277.

Browning, C., & Kain, C. (2000). Teaching lesbian, gay, and bisexual psychology: Contemporary strategies. In B. Greene & G. L. Croom (Eds.), *Education, research, and practice in lesbian, gay, bisexual, and transgendered psychology: A resource manual* (pp. 46–58). Thousand Oaks, CA: Sage.

Burke, P. (1996). *Gender shock: Exploding the myths of male and female.* New York: Anchor Books/Doubleday.

Chapman, J. (Executive Producer), & Spence, R. (Director). (1998). *Different for girls* [Videotape]. New York: Fox & Lorber.

Chase, C. (1998). Hermaphrodites with attitude: Mapping the emergence of intersex political activism. *GLQ: A Journal of Lesbian and Gay Studies, 4,* 189–211.

Chestnut, S. (1998). Queering the curriculum or what's Walt Whitman got to do with it? In R. L. Sanlo (Ed.), *Working with lesbian, gay, bisexual, and transgender college students: A handbook for faculty and administrators* (pp. 221–230). Westport, CT: Greenwood Press.

Clare, E. (1999). *Exile and pride: Disability, queerness and liberation.* Cambridge, MA: South End Press.

Cohen, H. S. (Producer), & Chasnoff, D. (Producer and Director). (1997). *It's elementary: Talking about gay issues in school* [Videotape]. Hohokus, NJ: New Day Films.

Colapinto, J. (2000). *As nature made him: The boy who was raised as a girl.* New York: HarperCollins.

Conerly, G. (1996). The politics of Black lesbian, gay, and bisexual identity. In B. Beemyn & M. Eliason (Eds.), *Queer Studies: A lesbian, gay, bisexual, and transgender anthology* (pp. 133–144). New York: New York University Press.

Connolly, M. (2000). Issues for lesbian, gay, and bisexual students in traditional college classrooms. In V. A. Wall & N. J. Evans (Eds.), *Toward acceptance: Sexual orientation issues on campus* (pp. 109–130). Lanham, MD: University Press of America.

Coppel, A., & Mifsud, J. (Producers and Directors). (1994). *Speaking for ourselves: Portraits of gay and lesbian youth* [Videotape]. Seattle, WA: Diversity Productions. (Distributed by Intermedia, Inc., 8490 Sunset Blvd., Suite 700, West Hollywood, CA 90069.)

D'Augelli, A. R. (1992). Teaching lesbian/gay development: From oppression to exceptionality. In K. M. Harbeck (Ed.), *Coming out of the classroom closet: Gay and lesbian students, teachers, and curricula* (pp. 213–227). New York: Harrington Park Press.

D'Augelli, A. R., & Patterson, C. J. (Eds.). (1995). *Lesbian, gay, and bisexual identities over the lifespan: Psychological perspectives.* New York: Oxford University Press.

D'Augelli, A. R., & Patterson, C. J. (Eds.). (2001). *Lesbian, gay, and bisexual identities and youth: Psychological perspectives.* New York: Oxford University Press.

Dreger, A. D. (Ed.). (1999). *Intersex in the age of ethics.* Hagerstown, MD: University Publishing Group.

Feinberg, L. (1993). *Stone butch blues.* Ithaca, NY: Firebrand Books.

Feinberg, L. (1998). *Trans liberation: Beyond pink or blue.* Boston: Beacon Press.

Firestein, B. A. (Ed.). (1996). *Bisexuality: The psychology and politics of an invisible minority.* Thousand Oaks, CA: Sage.

Franklin, K. (1998). Unassuming motivations: Contextualizing the narratives of antigay assaults. In G. M. Herek (Ed.), *Stigma and sexual orientation: Understanding prejudice against lesbians, gay men, and bisexuals* (pp. 1–23). Thousand Oaks, CA: Sage.

Greene, B. (Ed.). (1997). *Ethnic and cultural diversity among lesbians and gay men.* Thousand Oaks, CA: Sage.

Greene, B., & Croom, G. L. (Eds.). (2000). *Education, research, and practice in lesbian, gay, bisexual, and transgendered psychology: A resource manual.* Thousand Oaks, CA: Sage.

Grossman, A. H. (2001). Avoiding HIV/AIDS and the challenge of growing up gay, lesbian, and bisexual. In A. R. D'Augelli & C. J. Patterson (Eds.), *Lesbian, gay, and bisexual identities and youth* (pp. 155–180). New York: Oxford University Press.

Herek, G. M. (1993). The context of antigay violence: Notes on cultural and psychological heterosexism. In L. D. Garnets & D. C. Kimmel (Eds.), *Psychological perspectives on lesbian and gay male experiences* (pp. 89–107). New York: Columbia University Press.

Herek, G. M. (1995). Psychological heterosexism in the United States. In A. R. D'Augelli & C. J. Patterson (Eds.), *Lesbian, gay, and bisexual identities over the lifespan* (pp. 321–346). New York: Oxford University Press.

Herek, G. M. (Ed.). (1998). *Stigma and sexual orientation: Understanding prejudice against lesbians, gay men, and bisexuals.* Thousand Oaks, CA: Sage.

Herek, G. M., & Greene, B. (Eds.). (1995). *AIDS, identity, and community: The HIV epidemic and lesbians and gay men.* Thousand Oaks, CA: Sage.

Howard, K., & Stevens, A. (2000). *Out and about campus: Personal accounts by lesbian, gay, bisexual, and transgendered college students.* Los Angeles: Alyson Books.

Hyde, J. S., & Jaffee, S. R. (2000). Becoming a heterosexual adult: The experiences of young women. *Journal of Social Issues, 56,* 283–296.

Intersex Society of North America (Producer). (1996). *Hermaphrodites speak!* [Videotape]. (Available from the Intersex Society of North America, P.O. Box 3070, Ann Arbor, MI 48106-3070.)

Kessler, S. (1998). *Lessons from the intersexed.* New Brunswick, NJ: Rutgers University Press.

Kimmel, D. C. (2000). Including sexual orientation in life span developmental psychology. In B. Green & G. L. Croom (Eds.), *Education, research, and practice in lesbian, gay, bisexual, and transgendered psychology: A resource manual* (pp. 59–73). Thousand Oaks, CA: Sage.

Kitzinger, C., Wilkinson, S., & Perkins, R. (Eds.). (1992). Heterosexuality [Special issue]. *Feminism & Psychology, 2*(3).

Klein, F. (1990). The need to view sexual orientation as a multivariable dynamic process: A theoretical perspective. In D. P. McWhirter, S. A. Saunders, & J. M. Reinisch (Eds.), *Homosexuality/heterosexuality* (pp. 277–282). New York: Oxford University Press.

Koyama, E., & Weasel, L. (2001, June). *Teaching intersex issues: Teaching kit for Women's, Gender & Queer Studies.* Petaluma, CA: Intersex Society of North America (Available from http://www.isna.org/store/store-teaching.html)

Lee, J. Y. (1996). Why Suzie Wong is not a lesbian: Asian and Asian American lesbian and bisexual women and femme/butch/gender identities. In B. Beemyn & M. Eliason (Eds.), *Queer Studies: A lesbian, gay, bisexual, and transgender anthology* (pp. 115–132). New York: New York University Press.

Marenco, S. (Producer and Director), & Mason, J. (Director). (1993). *Adventures in the gender trade* [Videotape]. New York: Filmakers Library.

Ochs, R. (Ed.). (2001). *Bisexual resource guide* (4th ed.). Boston: Bisexual Resource Center.

Olsson, J., & Stuehling, J. (1999). *Dismantling oppression and forging justice: Training of trainers training manual.* (Available from cultural bridges, HC81 Box 7015, Questa, NM 87556.)

Patterson, C. J., & D'Augelli, A. R. (Eds.). (1998). *Lesbian, gay, and bisexual identities in families: Psychological perspectives.* New York: Oxford University Press.

Patterson, C. J., & Redding, R. E. (1996). Lesbian and gay families with children: Implications of social science research for policy. *Journal of Social Issues, 52*(3), 29–50.

Praunheim, R., von (Producer and Director). (1996). *Transsexual menace* [Videotape]. (Available from Video Data Bank, 112 S. Michigan Ave., Chicago, IL 60603.)

Queen, C., & Schimel, L. (Eds.). (1997). *Pomosexuals: Challenging assumptions about gender and sexuality.* San Francisco: Cleis Press.

Renn, K. A. (1998). Lesbian, gay, bisexual, and transgender students in the college classroom. In R. L. Sanlo (Ed.), *Working with lesbian, gay, bisexual, and trans-*

gender college students: A handbook for faculty and administrators (pp. 231–237). Westport, CT: Greenwood Press.

Riggs, M. T. (Producer and Director). (1996). *Tongues untied* [Videotape]. New York: Frameline.

Rochlin, M. (1995). The Heterosexual Questionnaire. In M. S. Kimmel & M. A. Messner (Eds.), *Men's lives* (3rd ed., p. 405). Boston: Allyn & Bacon.

Rosenberg, R. (Producer and Director), Scagliotti, J. (Producer), & Schiller, G. (Producer and Director). (1994). *Before Stonewall: The making of a gay and lesbian community* [Videotape]. New York: Cinema Guild.

Rothblum, E. D., & Bond, L. A. (Eds.). (1996). *Preventing heterosexism and homophobia*. Thousand Oaks, CA: Sage.

Rust, P. C. (1995). *The challenge of bisexuality to lesbian politics: Sex, loyalty, and revolution*. New York: New York University Press.

Sanlo, R. L. (Ed.). (1998). *Working with lesbian, gay, bisexual, and transgender college students: A handbook for faculty and administrators*. Westport, CT: Greenwood Press.

Savin-Williams, R. C. (1998). *". . . And then I became gay": Young men's stories*. New York: Routledge.

Savin-Williams, R. C. (2001). *Mom, Dad. I'm gay. How families negotiate coming out*. Washington, DC: American Psychological Association.

Savin-Williams, R. C., & Cohen, K. M. (Eds.). (1996). *The lives of lesbians, gays, and bisexuals: Children to adults*. Fort Worth, TX: Harcourt Brace.

Schermerhorn, C., & Cram, B. (Producers and Directors). (1997). *You don't know Dick: Courageous hearts of transsexual men* [Videotape]. Berkeley: University of California Extension Center for Media and Independent Learning.

Scotta, C. (Executive Producer), & Berliner, A. (Director). (1999). *Ma vie en rose* [Motion picture]. Culver City, CA: Sony Pictures.

Sears, J. T., & Williams, W. L. (Eds.). (1997). *Overcoming heterosexism and homophobia: Strategies that work*. New York: Columbia University Press.

Stacey, J., & Biblarz, T. J. (2001). (How) does the sexual orientation of parents matter? *American Sociological Review, 66*, 159–183.

Tatum, B. D. (1992). Talking about race, learning about racism: The application of racial identity development theory in the classroom. *Harvard Educational Review, 62*, 1–24.

Thoresen, J. H. (1998). "Do we have to call it that?" Planning, implementing, and teaching an LGBTI course. In R. L. Sanlo (Ed.), *Working with lesbian, gay, bisexual, and transgender college students: A handbook for faculty and administrators* (pp. 255–263). Westport, CT: Greenwood Press.

Wall, V. A., & Evans, N. J. (Eds.). (2000). *Toward acceptance: Sexual orientation issues on campus*. Lanham, MD: University Press of America.

Wilchins, R. A. (1997). *Read my lips: Sexual subversion and the end of gender*. Ithaca, NY: Firebrand Books.

21

A COURSE ON MEN
AND MASCULINITY

ALBERT J. LOTT

For the past 10 years, I have been teaching an upper division under-graduate course titled "Men and Masculinity" at the University of Rhode Island. In this chapter, I describe my approach to this course as well as the various topics covered and resources used. It is of interest to note at the outset that every time the course has been offered (one time each academic year), female students have far outnumbered men; once, when it was offered as a special topics course in the university's honors program, only women were enrolled. In class discussions over the years, students have told me that women are more interested in gender roles than are men and that women are more interested in understanding men than men are in understanding themselves!

My personal pedagogical orientation to the course is from a gender-aware perspective articulated early on by Pleck (1981) and from a men's studies critique of gender by Brod (1987). In addition, I incorporate a book by Kimmel and Messner (1995), to provide a social constructionist, life course perspective on men from various cultural groups in the United States. I begin with a feminist and social psychological analysis of gender role learning (Geis, 1993; B. Lott & Maluso, 1993) and raise a variety of questions about the psychology of men within that context. Throughout the course, I ask students to examine male experiences within the U.S. cultural context, with a recognition of diversity mediated by social class, ethnicity, and sexual orientation. As part of this sociocultural approach (Clatterbaugh, 1990), I also look at the political discourse and influence of contemporary male-oriented social movements, such as the Promise Keepers (Silverstein, Auerbach, Grieco, & Dunkel, 1999), Gay Male Liberation, the Men's Rights Movement, and Profeminist Men (Messner, 1997).

FRAMEWORKS FOR UNDERSTANDING MEN

Before I conduct detailed analyses of particular issues in men's lives, I spend the first part of the course developing a framework and social analysis of masculinity into which specific topical areas are later incorporated. I have used two different textbooks over the years: *The Male Experience* (Doyle, 1994) and *The Masculine Self* (Kilmartin, 1999); each presents a useful organization of topics around which to construct a course. For example, Doyle examined Western historical ideals of masculinity (epic male, spiritual male, chivalric male, renaissance male, bourgeois male, male as partner) to make the point that male gender is a changing social phenomenon. (See also Rotondo, 1993, for a historian's view of American manhood over the last 200 years, and Kimmel, 1996, for a cultural history of American masculinity.) Kilmartin, on the other hand, looked at broad theories of human development for understanding masculinity, introduced the concept of gender roles, and reviewed three psychological models that focus on masculinity: (a) gender identity (Pleck, 1987), (b) androgyny (Bem, 1974, 1981), and (c) gender role strain (O'Neil, Good, & Holmes, 1995; Pleck, 1995a).

Within this broader framework, I include examinations of masculinity from the perspective of four different academic disciplines, which I describe next.

Biological Perspective

Issues of masculinity and gender raised by sociobiology are a good example of biologically based notions of sex differences that rely heavily on studies of animal behavior. The sociobiological view (Caporael & Brewer, 1991) of men as destined by biology to be promiscuous, aggressive, selfish, and so on, can be contrasted dramatically with a social constructionist analysis that demonstrates how social factors influence these same behaviors (Beall, 1993). Fausto-Sterling (1992) presented an excellent critique of the biological perspective, demonstrating that simplistic theories of biological or hormonal determinants of gendered behaviors lack scientific support.

Starting from the position that a frequently occurring behavior among men does not necessarily mean that the behavior is genetically based, she helps students understand how biological and social influences interact to produce gendered behavior.

Sociological Perspective

Doyle (1994) presented a good discussion of sociological approaches to masculinity, focusing on the social categories of male and female as analyzed by role theory. Within the role theory context, he discussed socializing agents and societal gender role prescriptions that "shape a boy's gender development: his parents, the media, the educational system, and his peers" (p. 105). Another application of this approach can be found in Carrigan, Connell, and Lee's (1987) chapter, in which they used basic sociological role analysis to develop a new understanding of gender relations, gay liberation, and masculinity. They criticized abstract views of gender role issues that neglect or evade the importance of power differences between men and women in a patriarchal context. In addition, they credited gay activists with providing a clear understanding of the reality of power hierarchies among men and, like Pleck (1995b), discussed *hegemonic masculinity*, the subordination of ethnic men, young men, and gay men, in addition to women.

Anthropological Perspective

An anthropological approach looks at cultural variations of male behavior to show the wide range of male activities across cultures. This approach helps to emphasize a social constructionist perspective on masculinity, enabling students to see that definitions of masculinity are a product of culture and history. Gilmore (1990) provided an insightful cross-cultural analysis of the standards, ideologies, and anxieties associated with culturally imposed ideals of masculinity. After reviewing manhood dynamics in a wide variety of world cultures, he presented a provocative description of a quasi-global masculinity:

> To be a man in most societies . . . one must impregnate women, protect dependents from danger and provide for kith and kin. So although there may be no "Universal Male," we may perhaps speak of a "Ubiquitous Male" based on these criteria of performance. (p. 223)

A consideration of Gilmore's proposed global model can stimulate class discussions of its validity, as well as its relevance to men in the United States from different socioeconomic and ethnic backgrounds and with different sexual orientations. Another interesting perspective is Mackey's (2001) cross-cultural case for a nontrivial, independent, man-to-child affiliative bond that is separate from a woman-to-child bond.

Psychological Perspectives

Some traditional psychological theories of human development can be adapted to focus on males. For example, Kilmartin (1999) conducted a masculinity analysis within several theoretical systems: psychoanalysis, social learning, and phenomenology. These and other traditional theories provide a context for considering male development and behavior; however, in their basic formulations they neglect to include information on cultural diversity. Instructors teaching a course on the Psychology of Men will need to add multicultural information at this time or else re-examine the theories in relation to multicultural material introduced later in the course. I have found that it works well to present a section on men from culturally diverse backgrounds immediately after the examination of theoretical systems.

DIVERSITY AMONG AMERICAN MEN

The representations of diversity that I include are African American men and gay men, with some attention to Latino and Asian men as well. This choice in part reflects the amount of male-oriented literature currently available about each group. In addition to the resources on African American and gay men that I present below, instructors might find useful a general overview of ethnocultural variations in the male role (and male role strain) in four cultures of color in the United States (Lazur & Majors, 1995); a study of men's feelings of ethnic belonging and traditional masculinity in African American, European American, and Latino men (Abreu, Goodyear, Campos, & Newcomb, 2000); and individual readings on Mexican American men (Baca Zinn, 1992; Fragoso & Kashubeck, 2000), American Indians (Trimble, 1988), and Asian Americans (Sue & Sue, 1993).

African American Men

The lives of African American men must be examined within the context of a largely racist culture that leads to stresses that are reflected in outcomes such as higher rates of unemployment, poverty, crime victimization, premature death by violence, and prison incarceration. Gibbs (1992) provided a useful backdrop of the historical, sociocultural, economic, and political factors that have contributed to the "deteriorating status of young Black males" (p. 60). However, there is currently an effort to balance this "endangered species" focus (Parham & McDavis, 1987) with more positive analyses of Black masculinity (Marable, 1995) and proposals to move beyond the stereotypes Whites impose on Black men. For example, McAdoo and McAdoo (1995) found that economically secure African American fathers were warm, loving, and nurturant toward their children, while viewing themselves as being strict. They expected their children to obey them, but they also provided explanations for the behaviors they wanted their children to exhibit. In a similar vein, Cazenave (1979) found that with increasing economic security, African American men became more involved in child rearing and participated more in the care of their children than their own fathers had. In this context, Cazenave and Leon (1987) highlighted the importance of economic security (i.e., a stable job) for African American fathers. These findings illustrate how the larger cultural context affects men's behaviors in the more intimate family culture.

Majors and Billson (1992) proposed that Black men, especially those living in adverse social and economic conditions, may tend to adopt a "cool pose," a demeanor that projects a feeling of self-worth and dignity in the face of pervasive disrespect and injustices in everyday life. They reasoned that because African American males cannot freely, spontaneously, or safely be themselves in White-dominated society, they may adopt a behavioral style that connotes pride, strength, and invulnerability (e.g., African American athletes dancing in the end zone or engaging in high-five handshakes). However, the authors introduced a cautionary note into their cool-pose analysis: They suggested that African American men who become overdependent on "coolness" may also find it difficult to engage in meaningful self-disclosure with other people in their lives. The same reasoning would apply to any men, regardless of ethnicity, who overindulge in stereotypic masculine aloofness or toughness. A psychological challenge for African American men, then, may be to develop an adaptive identity and interpersonal style without falling prey to a narrow masculinity that will end up undermining effective interactions with others. Watts, Abdul-Adil, and Pratt (2002) designed a multifaceted psychoeducational program to develop critical thinking skills in young African American men, to help them understand and deal with the sociopolitical forces that oppress them. For other information on African American men, see Gary (1981, 1987), Majors (1994), and Majors and Gordon (1993).

Gay Men

An extensive literature is available on gay men overall, as well as on ethnic and cultural diversity among gay men (Greene, 1997; Greene & Herek, 1994). Within this section of the course it is important to consider heterosexuals' perceptions of and attitudes toward gay men (Herek, 1994; Kite, 1994) and to explain how societal homophobia and heterosexism are used to validate heterosexual masculinity and to oppress gay and bisexual men (Herek, 1987; Pleck, 1995b). Herek (1998) edited a volume analyzing antigay stigma and prejudice that includes discussions of cultural heterosexism, homophobia (societal and internalized), and developmental issues for gay youth. Harrison (1995) discussed the relevance of a role strain paradigm for understanding the experiences of gay and bisexual men, with reference to factors such as religion, language, and social norms that have historically been sources of antigay oppression. Other issues to include are the dynamics of gay male identity development (D'Augelli, 1994; D'Augelli & Patterson, 1995) and coming out (Gonsiorek, 1995; Gonsiorek & Rudolph, 1991), and gay male relationships (Kurdek, 1994; Peplau, 1991).

SOME SALIENT ISSUES IN MEN'S LIVES

Once students have a solid foundation in new approaches to the psychology of men and the role of diversity in men's lives, I turn to an analysis of particular issues that are important to men, such as the three I describe next.

Self-Disclosure and Emotionality

A common issue explored in practically all discussions of masculinity is the relative (compared to women) inability of most men to express or perhaps even identify their emotions and to disclose to others intimate parts of their inner lives. Such emotional restrictiveness reflects an antifeminist and antigay norm that is part of traditional masculinity (Brannon, 1976; O'Neil, 1981). It may also help men avoid feelings of vulnerability, based on their perceptions of what is appropriate hegemonic masculinity. By adopting these strict gender role norms, boys and men learn to suppress their more vulnerable feelings (e.g., sadness, fear, embarrassment, need for love), which predisposes them to later difficulties with interpersonal relationships. Derlega (1984) documented many ways in which self-disclosure is an essential ingredient in forming and maintaining intimate relationships; Levant (1995) developed an intervention program to help men overcome what he called *emotional numbness*.

Aggression and Violence

The topic of aggression and violence ranges widely, from discussions of biology to the role of aggression as part of male gender role learning and standards (Brannon, 1976; Kaufman, 1995). It includes a consideration of rape (Browne, 1993; Koss, 1993), pornography (Brod, 1995; Kimmel, 1990), and other predominantly male negative behaviors (e.g., sexual harassment) that Brooks and Silverstein (1995) called the "dark side of masculinity." The major goal of this section is to ask why violence is such an ingrained aspect of traditional masculinity and to understand the social and psychological forces acting on men that make aggression such an easily available way of controlling others. In addition, I examine the interpersonal and emotional issues that may underlie male violence (Graham & Wells, 2001; Jennings & Murphy, 2002), and I consider ways of reducing it within this social psychological context (Brooks & Silverstein, 1995; Levant, 1995).

Work and Family Life

Men tend to evaluate their personal worth on the basis of work roles or paycheck, and this meshes with family life, including fatherhood. Brooks and Gilbert (1995) presented a useful historical overview of men in families, pointing to new, contemporary roles for men in the home, and Bronstein and Cowan (1988), Coltrane (1996), and Lamb (1997) have addressed a range of issues related to fathering and fathers' roles. Silverstein and Auerbach (1999) offered an analysis of responsible fathering across different family structures (e.g., gay fathers, teenage fathers, divorced fathers, middle-class fathers) and concluded that paternal involvement will be enhanced by "reconstructing traditional masculinity ideology, restructuring societal institutions, and providing a comprehensive program of governmental subsidies to all families with children" (p. 405). Critical responses to their article can be found in a later issue of the journal ("Commentary," 2000). Barnett and Rivers (1996) examined the increasing participation in family work of fathers in dual-career families; Bowman and Forman (1998) looked at expressive and instrumental family roles of African American fathers; Pleck (1993) examined men's work and family roles as influenced by employment policies; and Snarey (1993) presented longitudinal findings suggesting that involved fathering builds interpersonal skills that transfer to other areas of men's lives. Several authors have offered insightful analyses of how diversity and poverty influence men's work and family lives (Coltrane, 1995; McAdoo & McAdoo, 1995; Miller, 1995; Nonn, 1995).

CLASSROOM ACTIVITIES AND ASSIGNMENTS

Of the many outside-of-class projects I have developed over the years, one stands out as most successful in terms of student interest and learning. I have required each student to interview 20 men on a topic covered in the course that is of particular interest to her or him. The interviews are conducted with two different groups of men, defined by variables such as age, ethnicity, education, or sexual orientation. For example, a student might interview 10 White men and 10 Black men on the same topic and summarize and interpret the similarities and differences in their responses. I then set aside class times to discuss the results of the interview projects. The depth, variety, and insights of the respondents' answers provide a very effective basis for evaluating course materials compared with what men outside of the classroom are thinking.

In the all-women honors version of the course, mentioned earlier, I had each of the 15 students bring a man to class every 3 weeks to join the discussion, which turned out to be a marvelous learning experience for all of us. This technique could be adapted to bring to class individuals (e.g., a gay father, a single mother raising sons, a divorced father) whose lives reflect some of the situations being studied in class. It not only puts a human face on the issue but also presents a model for open discussion of social situations that may be difficult to raise.

Videos about men's lives have also been a useful (and popular) course activity. A good introduction to gender issues early in the course is *Gender: The Enduring Paradox* (Bradley, 1996). Other excellent and engaging films are *Tough Guise: Violence, Media, and the Crisis in Masculinity* (Jhally, 1999), which is about the influence of the public media on men's and boys' lives; *The Male Couple* (Weissman & Frisch, 1985), which is about the development of long-term gay relationships; and *How Far Home: Veterans After Vietnam* (Robert & Cram, 1983), which is about men's postwar experiences. Free study guides to *Tough Guise* can be downloaded from the Media Education Foundation Web site (http://www.mediaed.org).

In recent years, a number of popular books on men have been published (e.g., Bly, 1990; Gray, 1992; Keen, 1991) and have received media attention. I now spend part of the course discussing these books and comparing some of their conclusions to what is known from the academic literature. Students enjoy this exercise and are amazingly perceptive in finding useful ideas as well as gender stereotypes, overgeneralizations, and hidden sexist assumptions in these works. Kimmel (1995) edited a book offering a systematic critique of Bly (1990) and Keen (1991) from a male profeminist perspective. Faludi (1999) raised all kinds of subtle and provocative issues about masculinity today, using an approach that students should find accessible, informative, and controversial.

CONCLUSION

In the United States today, frequent discussions of masculinity issues appear in the public media—often with a focus on the fathering role and, more recently, on male youth violence. This attention speaks to an urgent need to understand the constraints and misdirections of traditional masculine norms and values and to explore possibilities for societywide change. Furthermore, as Cazenave (1984) pointed out, to understand the dynamics of masculinity, one must consider the relative position a man occupies in the prestige and power structures of his society; thus, it is essential to include sociocultural factors in one's analyses. The new subfield within psychology that focuses on the study of men and masculinity (as opposed to the traditional approach within psychology of focusing almost exclusively on White males) offers the promise of new paradigms and new possibilities for social transformation. Teaching the Psychology of Men from this new perspective provides students with the opportunity to understand men's development and behaviors within social and historical contexts, gives them tools for interpreting real world events, and invites them to become change agents in the new century—both within psychology and in the world at large.

REFERENCES

Abreu, J. M., Goodyear, R. K., Campos, A., & Newcomb, M. D. (2000). Ethnic belonging and traditional masculinity ideology among African Americans, European Americans, and Latinos. *Psychology of Men and Masculinity, 1,* 75–86.

Baca Zinn, M. (1992). Chicano men and masculinity. In M. S. Kimmel & M. A. Messner (Eds.), *Men's lives* (pp. 67–76). New York: Macmillan.

Barnett, R. C., & Rivers, C. (1996). *She works/he works.* San Francisco: Harper.

Beall, A. E. (1993). A social constructionist view of gender. In A. E. Beall & R. J. Sternberg (Eds.), *The psychology of gender* (pp. 127–147). New York: Free Press.

Bem, S. (1974). The measurement of psychological androgyny. *Journal of Counseling and Clinical Psychology, 42,* 165–174.

Bem, S. (1981). Gender schema theory: A cognitive account of sex-typing. *Psychological Review, 88,* 353–361.

Bly, R. (1990). *Iron John.* Reading, MA: Addison-Wesley.

Bowman, P. J., & Forman, T. A. (1998). Instrumental and expressive family roles among African American fathers. In R. Taylor, J. Jackson, & L. M. Chatters (Eds.), *Family life in Black America* (pp. 216–261). Newbury Park, CA: Sage.

Bradley, S. W. (Producer and Director). (1996). *Gender: The enduring paradox* [Videotape]. New York: Unapix Consumer Products.

Brannon, R. (1976). The male sex role: Our culture's blueprint of manhood, and what it's done for us lately. In D. David & R. Brannon (Eds.), *The forty-nine percent majority* (pp. 1–45). Reading, MA: Addison-Wesley.

Brod, H. (1987). The case for men's studies. In H. Brod (Ed.), *The making of masculinities: The new men's studies* (pp. 39–62). Boston: Allen & Unwin.

Brod, H. (1995). Pornography and the alienation of male sexuality. In M. S. Kimmel & M. A. Messner (Eds.), *Men's lives* (3rd ed., pp. 393–404). Boston: Allyn & Bacon.

Bronstein, P., & Cowan, C. P. (1988). *Fatherhood today: Men's changing role in the family.* New York: Wiley.

Brooks, G. R., & Gilbert, L. A. (1995). Men in families: Old constraints, new possibilities. In R. F. Levant & W. S. Pollack (Eds.), *A new psychology of men* (pp. 252–279). Boston: Unwin.

Brooks, G. R., & Silverstein, L. B. (1995). Understanding the dark side of masculinity: An interactive systems model. In R. F. Levant & W. S. Pollack (Eds.), *A new psychology of men* (pp. 280–333). Boston: Unwin.

Browne, A. (1993). Violence against women by male partners: Prevalence, outcomes, and policy implications. *American Psychologist, 48*, 1077–1087.

Caporael, L. R., & Brewer, M. B. (Eds.). (1991). Issues in evolutionary psychology [Special issue]. *Journal of Social Issues, 47*(3).

Carrigan, T., Connell, B., & Lee, J. (1987). Toward a new sociology of masculinity. In H. Brod (Ed.), *The making of masculinities: The new men's studies* (pp. 63–100). Boston: Allen & Unwin.

Cazenave, N. A. (1979). Middle-income Black fathers: An analysis of the provider role. *Family Coordinator, 28*, 583–593.

Cazenave, N. A. (1984). Race, socioeconomic status, and age: The social context of American masculinity. *Sex Roles, 11*, 139–156.

Cazenave, N. A., & Leon, G. H. (1987). Men's work and family roles and characteristics: Race, gender, and class perceptions of college students. In M. S. Kimmel (Ed.), *Changing men: New directions in research on men and masculinity* (pp. 244–262). Newbury Park, CA: Sage.

Clatterbaugh, K. (1990). *Contemporary perspectives on masculinity: Men, women, and politics in modern society.* San Francisco: Westview.

Coltrane, S. (1995). Stability and change in Chicano men's lives. In M. S. Kimmel & M. A. Messner (Eds.), *Men's lives* (3rd ed., pp. 461–468). Boston: Allyn & Bacon.

Coltrane, S. (1996). *Family man.* New York: Oxford University Press.

Commentary. (2000). *American Psychologist, 55*, 678–684.

D'Augelli, A. R. (1994). Lesbian and gay male development: Steps toward an analysis of lesbian's and gay men's lives. In B. Greene & G. M. Herek (Eds.), *Lesbian and gay psychology: Theory, research, and clinical applications* (pp. 118–132). Thousand Oaks, CA: Sage.

D'Augelli, A. R., & Patterson, C. J. (Eds.). (1995). *Lesbian, gay, and bisexual identities over the lifespan: Psychological perspectives.* New York: Oxford University Press.

Derlega, V. J. (Ed.). (1984). *Communication, intimacy, and close relationships.* New York: Academic Press.

Doyle, J. A. (1994). *The male experience* (3rd ed.) New York: McGraw-Hill.

Faludi, S. (1999). *Stiffed: The betrayal of the American male.* New York: Morrow.

Fausto-Sterling, A. (1992). *The myths of gender: Biological theories about women and men* (2nd ed.). New York: Basic Books.

Fragoso, J. M., & Kashubeck, S. (2000). Machismo, gender role conflict, and mental health in Mexican American men. *Psychology of Men & Masculinity, 1*, 87–97.

Gary, L. E. (Ed.). (1981). *Black men.* Beverly Hills, CA: Sage.

Gary, L. E. (1987). Predicting interpersonal conflict between men and women: The case of Black men. In M. S. Kimmel (Ed.), *Changing men: New directions in research on men and masculinity* (pp. 232–243). Beverly Hills, CA: Sage.

Geis, F. L. (1993). Self-fulfilling prophecies: A social psychological view of gender. In A. E. Beall & R. J. Sternberg (Eds.), *The psychology of gender* (pp. 9–54). New York: Guilford Press.

Gibbs, J. T. (1992). Young Black males in America: Endangered, embittered, and embattled. In M. S. Kimmel & M. A. Messner (Eds.), *Men's lives* (2nd ed., pp. 50–66). New York: Macmillan.

Gilmore, D. D. (1990). *Manhood in the making: Cultural concepts of masculinity.* New Haven, CT: Yale University Press.

Gonsiorek, J. C. (1995). Gay male identities: Concepts and issues. In A. D'Augelli & C. J. Patterson (Eds.), *Lesbian, gay, and bisexual identities over the lifespan: Psychological perspectives* (pp. 24–47). New York: Oxford University Press.

Gonsiorek, J. C., & Rudolph, J. R. (1991). Homosexual identity: Coming out and other developmental events. In J. C. Gonsiorek & J. D. Weinrich (Eds.), *Homosexuality: Research implications for public policy* (pp. 101–176). Newbury Park, CA: Sage.

Graham, K., & Wells, S. (2001). The two worlds of aggression for men and women. *Sex Roles, 45,* 595–622.

Gray, J. (1992). *Men are from Mars, women are from Venus.* New York: HarperCollins.

Greene, B. (Ed.). (1997). *Ethnic and cultural diversity among lesbians, gay men.* Thousand Oaks, CA: Sage.

Greene, B., & Herek, G. M. (Eds.). (1994). *Lesbian and gay psychology: Theory, research, and clinical implications.* Thousand Oaks, CA: Sage.

Harrison, J. (1995). Roles, identities, and sexual orientation: Homosexuality, heterosexuality, and bisexuality. In R. F. Levant & W. S. Pollack (Eds.), *A new psychology of men* (pp. 257–382). New York: Basic Books.

Herek, G. M. (1987). On heterosexual masculinity: Some psychical consequences of the social construction of gender and sexuality. In M. S. Kimmel (Ed.), *Changing men: New directions in research on men and masculinity* (pp. 68–82). Beverly Hills, CA: Sage.

Herek, G. M. (1994). Assessing heterosexuals' attitudes toward lesbians and gay men: A review of empirical research with the ATLG Scale. In B. Greene & G. M. Herek (Eds.), *Lesbian and gay psychology: Theory, research, and clinical applications* (pp. 206–382). Thousand Oaks, CA: Sage.

Herek, G. M. (Ed.). (1998). *Stigma and sexual orientation: Understanding prejudice against lesbians, gay men, and bisexuals.* Thousand Oaks, CA: Sage.

Jennings, J. L., & Murphy, C. M. (2000). Male–male dimensions of male–female battering: A new look at domestic violence. *Psychology of Men and Masculinity, 1,* 21–29.

Jhally, S. (Producer and Director). (1999). *Tough guise: Violence, media, and the crisis in masculinity* [Videotape]. Northampton, MA: Media Education Foundation.

Kaufman, M. (1995). The construction of masculinity and the triad of men's violence. In M. S. Kimmel & M. A. Messner (Eds.), *Men's lives* (3rd ed., pp. 13–25). Boston: Allyn & Bacon.

Keen, S. (1991). *Fire in the belly: On being a man.* New York: Bantam.

Kilmartin, C. T. (1999). *The masculine self* (2nd ed.). New York: McGraw-Hill.

Kimmel, M. S. (Ed.). (1990). *Men confront pornography.* New York: Meridian.

Kimmel, M. S. (Ed.). (1995). *The politics of manhood.* Philadelphia: Temple University Press.

Kimmel, M. S. (Ed.). (1996). *Manhood in America: A cultural history.* New York: Free Press.

Kimmel, M. S., & Messner, M. A. (Eds.). (1995). *Men's lives* (3rd ed.). Boston: Allyn & Bacon.

Kite, M. (1994). When perceptions meet reality: Individual differences in reactions to lesbians and gay men. In B. Greene & G. M. Herek (Eds.), *Lesbian and gay psychology: Theory, research, and clinical applications* (pp. 25–53). Thousand Oaks, CA: Sage.

Koss, M. P. (1993). Rape: Scope, impact, interventions, and public policy responses. *American Psychologist, 48,* 1062–1069.

Kurdek, L. A. (1994). The nature and correlates of relationship quality in gay, lesbian, and heterosexual cohabiting couples: A test of the individual difference, interdependence, and discrepancy models. In B. Greene & G. M. Herek (Eds.), *Gay and lesbian psychology: Theory, research, and clinical applications* (pp. 133–154). Thousand Oaks, CA: Sage.

Lamb, M. E. (Ed.). (1997). *The role of the father in child development* (3rd ed.). New York: Wiley.

Lazur, R. F., & Majors, R. (1995). Men of color: Ethnocultural variations of male gender role strain. In R. F. Levant & W. S. Pollack (Eds.), *A new psychology of men* (pp. 337–358). New York: Basic Books.

Levant, R. F. (1995). *Masculinity reconsidered: Changing rules of manhood at work, in relationships and in family life.* New York: Dutton.

Lott, B., & Maluso, D. (1993). The social learning of gender. In A. E. Beall & R. J. Sternberg (Eds.), *The psychology of gender* (pp. 99–123). New York: Guilford Press.

Mackey, W. C. (2001). Support for the existence of an independent man-to-child affiliative bond: Fatherhood as a biocultural invention. *Psychology of Men and Masculinity, 2,* 51–66.

Majors, R. (1994). *The American Black male: His present status and future.* Chicago: Nelson Hall.

Majors, R., & Billson, J. M. (1992). *Cool pose: The dilemma of Black manhood in America.* New York: Lexington.

Majors, R., & Gordon, J. (Eds.). (1993). *The American Black male.* Chicago: Nelson Hall.

Marable, M. (1995). The Black male: Searching beyond the stereotypes. In M. S. Kimmel & M. A. Messner (Eds.), *Men's lives* (3rd ed., pp. 26–33). Boston: Allyn & Bacon.

McAdoo, J. L., & McAdoo, J. B. (1995). The African-American father's role within the family. In M. S. Kimmel & M. A. Messner (Eds.), *Men's lives* (3rd ed., pp. 485–494). Boston: Allyn & Bacon.

Messner, M. A. (1997). *Politics of masculinities: Men in movements.* Thousand Oaks, CA: Sage.

Miller, B. (1995). Lifestyles of gay husbands and fathers. In M. S. Kimmel & M. A. Messner (Eds.), *Men's lives* (3rd ed., pp. 461–468). Boston: Allyn & Bacon.

Nonn, T. (1995). Hitting bottom: Homelessness, poverty, and masculinity. In M. S. Kimmel & M. A. Messner (Eds.), *Men's lives* (3rd ed., pp. 225–234). Boston: Allyn & Bacon.

O'Neil, J. M. (1981). Patterns of gender role conflict and strain: Sexism and fear of femininity in men's lives. *Personnel and Guidance Journal, 60,* 203–210.

O'Neil, J. M., Good, G. E., & Holmes, S. (1995). Fifteen years of theory and research on men's gender role conflict: New paradigms for empirical research. In R. F. Levant & W. S. Pollack (Eds.), *A new psychology of men* (pp. 164–206). New York: Basic Books.

Parham, T. A., & McDavis, R. J. (1987). Black men, an endangered species: Who's really pulling the trigger? *Journal of Counseling and Development, 62,* 24–27.

Peplau, L. A. (1991). Lesbian and gay relationships. In J. C. Gonsiorek & J. D. Weinrich (Eds.), *Homosexuality: Research implications for public policy* (pp. 177–196). Newbury Park, CA: Sage.

Pleck, J. H. (1981). *The myth of masculinity.* Cambridge, MA: MIT Press.

Pleck, J. H. (1987). The theory of male sex-role identity: Its rise and fall, 1936 to the present. In H. Brod (Ed.), *The making of masculinities: The new men's studies* (pp. 21–38). Boston: Unwin.

Pleck, J. H. (1993). Are "family supportive" employer policies relevant to men? In J. C. Hood (Ed.), *Men, work, and family* (pp. 217–237). Newbury Park, CA: Sage.

Pleck, J. H. (1995a). The gender role strain paradigm: An update. In R. F. Levant & W. S. Pollack (Eds.), *A new psychology of men* (pp. 11–32). New York: Basic Books.

Pleck, J. H. (1995b). Men's power with women, other men, and society: A men's movement analysis. In M. S. Kimmel & M. A. Messner (Eds.), *Men's lives* (3rd ed., pp. 5–12). Boston: Allyn & Bacon.

Robert, S. (Producer), & Cram, B. (Director). (1983). *How far home: Veterans after Vietnam* [Videotape]. Boston: Northern Light Productions.

Rotondo, E. A. (1993). *American manhood: Transformations in masculinity from the Revolution to the modern era.* New York: Basic Books.

Silverstein, L. B., & Auerbach, C. F. (1999). Deconstructing the essential father. *American Psychologist, 54,* 397–407.

Silverstein, L. B., Auerbach, C. F., Grieco, L., & Dunkel, F. (1999). Do Promise Keepers dream of feminist sheep? *Sex Roles, 40,* 665–688.

Snarey, J. (1993). *How fathers care for the next generation: A four decade study.* Cambridge, MA: Harvard University Press.

Sue, D., & Sue, D. W. (1993). Ethnic identity: Cultural factors in the psychological development of Asians in America. In D. W. Atkinson, G. Morten, & D. W. Sue (Eds.), *Counseling American minorities: A cross-cultural perspective* (4th ed., pp. 199–210). Dubuque, IA: William C. Brown.

Trimble, J. E. (1988). Stereotypic images, American Indians, and prejudice. In P. A. Katz & D. A. Taylor (Eds.), *Eliminating racism: Profiles in controversy* (pp. 181–202). New York: Plenum.

Watts, R. J., Abdul-Adil, J. K., & Pratt, T. (2002). Enhancing critical consciousness in young African American men: A psychoeducational approach. *Psychology of Men and Masculinity, 3,* 41–50.

Weissman, F. W. (Producer), & Frisch, P. (Director). (1985). *The male couple* [Videotape]. Los Angeles: Humanus Home Video.

III

PROGRAMMATIC AND
PEDAGOGICAL ISSUES

22

BUILDING A MULTICULTURAL COMMUNITY: ONE DEPARTMENT'S TRANSFORMATION

VONDA DIONNE JONES-HUDSON

An increasing awareness of the importance and value of diversity has led many colleges and universities to seek strategies for change. This has in particular meant efforts to increase multicultural representation among faculty and students and to incorporate multiculturalism into the curriculum. Along with this has come a responsibility to ensure a safe and comfortable climate for all people, irrespective of roles and individual differences related to age, gender, race, ethnicity, national origin, religion, sexual orientation, age, disability, language, and socioeconomic status (Alcalde & Walsh-Bowers, 1996; McEwen & Roper, 1994).

However, progress has been slow on all three fronts. Many well-intentioned faculty and administrators are unaware of the ways in which the dominant culture has shaped their notions of scholarship and pedagogy and the ways in which their cultural biases affect their perceptions of and behaviors toward members of cultural groups different from their own. Often the concerns of faculty or students of color regarding their treatment in academic departments have gone unheeded or have been viewed as rationalizations to excuse substandard performance—and this nonreceptivity has been a major barrier to creating environments that are truly committed to multiculturalism.

Yet there are institutions, departments, and programs that have been willing to meet the problems head on, have gone through the sometimes-painful process of self-examination as a first step toward change, and are attempting to take further steps on that journey. The Department of Psychology at the University of Rhode Island (URI) in Kingston provides such a model.

A CASE STUDY

In the spring of 1995, a group of female students of color in the URI psychology graduate program came together to discuss an all-too-familiar assumption they had encountered in their department—that the terms *people of color* and *intellectual* are mutually exclusive (Harrington-Austin & DiBona, 1993). What follows is the story of their efforts to obtain fair treatment and justice in the academic environment in which they lived and learned, and the ongoing outcomes of those efforts. These students exemplified courage and foresight at a time when most people viewed them as overreactive, rabble rousing, and collectively crazy for speaking out against what they saw as injustices embedded in the academic system.

Students in previous years had experienced the same feelings but had not been able to achieve change. For the first few months, these graduate students also kept silent, not even sharing their experiences with each other. To some extent, they felt that perhaps they were not measuring up, and private thoughts that prejudice was operating tended to be viewed as individual battles. However, several elements helped them coalesce and become a successful force. One was that the number of minority students reached a critical mass, so that a group could form and patterns in their experiences could be seen more clearly. Another was that students were told about a comment allegedly made by a faculty member criticizing minority students' ability, which provided the impetus for the initial discussions. Once together, their discussions rapidly progressed to deeper sharing and the awareness of a need for action.

Initial Events

After a series of meetings in which they discussed their common experiences, this small group of students drafted a statement of their concerns and recommendations for change. They then presented their statement to the psychology department's Affirmative Action Committee. It read:

We, the graduate students of color in the psychology department, would like to address the members of this department concerning matters regarding the performance of graduate students of color. It has come to our attention that there have been statements made by certain faculty suggesting that our performance is "suboptimal." We would like to address these issues and would like to begin with clarification as to what, if anything, about our performance has been "suboptimal." In addition, we deem it necessary that we, the students, faculty and staff of this department, cultivate a relationship that is respectful and sensitive to multiculturalism. We feel that we can begin to meet this challenge by:

- addressing our concerns to the entire psychology department at a departmental meeting;
- having a liaison between faculty and students of color;
- having sensitivity workshops throughout the course of the year using professors and other qualified individuals from diverse ethnic backgrounds and institutions;
- developing a clear protocol to deal with discrimination in the department;
- looking closely at the issues surrounding grading multicultural students on a monoculturally based grading system.

The concerns that have been addressed at this time are a small representation of the many issues faced by graduate students of color in the psychology department and within the university. We feel confident that these issues will be addressed in a timely manner which exhibits support, sensitivity, and commitment to the tasks that are before us.

The statement then listed specific areas of concern:

- routine interactions with professors often tinged with racial overtones;
- unsubstantiated allegations of academic dishonesty;
- faculty being ambiguous when critiquing the writing style of minority students, without providing clear and salient notations, remarks, and suggestions, thereby giving students a reasonable opportunity for redress and improvement;
- inconsistencies and inequity with regard to grading policy;
- general failure to provide concrete and or explicit feedback, forcing students to make assumptions or guesses as to instructor expectations;
- professors, whether consciously or unconsciously, creating a classroom environment that is insensitive to and often hostile for students of color;
- treating individual or personal concerns raised by one minority student as an issue for all students of color, thereby nullifying our individuality;

- no safe or unbiased venue available for investigating complaints of racial discrimination;
- little or no encouragement for exploring multicultural and diversity issues as they might pertain to a chosen field of study;
- a *Bell Curve*-like attitude (cf. Herrnstein & Murray, 1994) among the faculty with regard to the intellectual ability of students of color. This limited thinking denigrates, demoralizes, and demeans each of us and suggests that this institution is less than forthright in its recruitment practices.

The chair of the psychology department invited the students to bring their concern to the department. With the support of the Affirmative Action Committee and representatives of both the university's multicultural center and the graduate school, the students presented the statement to the entire department faculty at its next meeting. Although most faculty were silent, a few responded with a willingness to address the issues by joining a task force and agreeing to work over the summer months.[1]

From that moment in time, the students of color and other supporters began to lead the way on a journey through uncharted waters. They spent countless hours in meetings with faculty, including the chair, recounting their experiences and discussing options. At first, other faculty in the department seemed unconcerned, and in fact several negative comments circulated back to the students of color (e.g., they were upset because they got low grades, they were rabble rousers). However, when a rumor circulated that the American Psychological Association, the accrediting body for two of the three graduate programs in the department, had been contacted, most of the unconcerned faculty decided that perhaps this was in fact a noteworthy cause.

Because of the general atmosphere of mistrust, and because no expertise was readily available in the university, the department faculty, in consultation with the students, decided that their efforts to address these issues would benefit from outside consultation. Recommendations for a consultant were obtained from the American Psychological Association Office of Ethnic Minority Affairs, and together the students and department representatives selected two experienced diversity sensitivity trainers.[2] Limited funding was provided by reallocating the departmental budget to make this a priority, with additional funds provided by the dean.

---

[1]The document, of which I am the author, can be found in Jones-Hudson (2001). Thanks are extended to the following individuals who participated in the initial stages of the process: Janet Kulberg, psychology department chair; Harold Bibb, associate dean of the graduate school; Melvin Wade, director of the multicultural center; members of the Graduate Students of Color Association (now the MultiEthnic Graduate Association, or MEGA); my fellow students Danielle Cutter, Susan Kang, Michelle Kemp, Trisha Suggs, and Maria Vasquez; and the late Sandra Gainer Wood; as well as other faculty members from the psychology department and friends from the university community.

[2]Don Pope-Davis and Will Liu performed this service admirably and with highly positive feedback from the department.

Consultation Process

The consultants were asked to assess the department and to initiate a process by which the psychology department could actively pursue its agenda to transform its curriculum and environment (Pope-Davis & Liu, 1995). The goal was for faculty, students, and staff to become more knowledgeable about and sensitive to multicultural issues. During the initial assessment, the consultants visited the department for 2 days early in the fall of 1995, speaking with individuals and groups representing all constituents (students of color, majority-group students, faculty, administrators, and staff). In a detailed report to the department, the consultants identified six areas of concern: (a) conflict resolution; (b) cross-cultural communication; (c) professional development; (d) trust and confidentiality; (e) student feedback; and (f) multicultural education courses, training and evaluation. Soon after the report was distributed, the department held a full-day retreat. A group of graduate students and faculty members served as facilitators, with the consultants present to advise and assist. Most of the department's 24 faculty, and many graduate students, attended and engaged in thoughtful, sometimes difficult discussions. At the end of the day, each was asked to make a commitment to a multicultural effort, and most did so.

The next step was to create a mechanism to implement the changes recommended in the report. A task force on multiculturalism and diversity, which would focus on the six areas identified by the consultants, was envisioned as a way to meet the challenge. One staff member, one faculty member, and one graduate student, representing each of the department's three graduate programs, were selected in departmentwide elections. By the spring of 1996, the task force was in full action. "Friends of the Department" (university colleagues from outside the department) were invited to participate. Open meetings were held frequently and were well attended. Within the task force, members adopted a consensus model, agreeing that students would hold the same power as faculty. They also set up procedures, such as checklists, to monitor task assignments and to allow ongoing feedback on their progress, and they addressed individual concerns when they arose.

Students and faculty who were not on the task force participated in subcommittees chaired by members of the task force. Their specific missions, based on the original areas of concern as outlined by the consultants, were as follows:

1. *Grievance procedure/conflict resolution:* to develop a sequence of steps for the management of conflicts among members of the department community and specific procedures for situations when conflict resolution proves impossible.
2. *Cross-cultural communication:* to generate a definition of multiculturalism; enhance interpersonal relations within the de-

partment community; and increase awareness, knowledge, and understanding of and sensitivity to diverse cultures.

3. *Curriculum:* to address tasks such as developing a course on multicultural issues in psychology, enhancing multicultural perspectives in existing courses, and identifying practicum settings serving diverse populations.

4. *Evaluation:* to design and implement measures for monitoring performance on multicultural issues, including feedback on courses, student training, and departmental atmosphere.

As the task force crafted recommendations, they were forwarded directly to the department faculty for a vote. Most of the recommendations were passed unanimously.

The Beginning of a Metamorphosis

Thus the URI psychology department became a laboratory grappling with real world problems pertaining to the acknowledgment of diverse backgrounds, perspectives, and talents. In those early weeks, months, and years, the department began to undergo a metamorphosis. The diversity consultants had outlined a 3-year plan. Some of the suggestions were carried out immediately, whereas others have yet to be actualized. At present, the task force has completed its sixth year. The interim conflict resolution guidelines that the department adopted in the first year are currently being revisited by a new URI Center for Nonviolence and Peace Studies, which is closely affiliated with the department. "Community chats" have brought together students and faculty within and across the three graduate psychology programs for topical discussions and food. Each semester, in-service trainings or retreats have been offered to faculty and graduate students, usually facilitated by an expert from outside the department, to address difficult dialogues such as "Does multiculturalism ignore racism?" Department members are core participants in the planning and presentation of a universitywide Diversity Week, which features programs on multicultural issues and challenging prejudice. The task force made a presentation of the department's model for change to deans and department chairs across the university.

Having fun together has been an important aspect of the process. At the annual Holiday Heritage parties, students and faculty vie for prizes for the best ethnic foods. This year, a department multicultural fair, featuring informational displays from diversity groups around the campus; an international bingo game, which encouraged mixing and meeting others; and friendly "hellos" in seven languages, welcomed new graduate students.

The department voted that the next faculty person hired would be one specializing in the area of multicultural psychology, and the university administration responded positively and funded the position. This new faculty member has substantially contributed to the change process, through workshop presentations, new courses on diversity issues, mentoring, and individual discussions with colleagues and students. Each graduate program has made active efforts to increase diversity among its constituents, resulting in two more minority hires and substantial increases in minority group representation in each of the graduate programs. Several new practicum sites offer students a greater range of experience with urban and minority clients. A graduate assistant was assigned part time to affirmative recruitment and retention activities, such as updating Web site information and mailing information about the programs to minority college seniors.

Curriculum change has been slower. In the first year, a graduate course in multicultural psychology was developed and introduced into the core curriculum. Last year, 8 hr of department meetings each semester were devoted to discussing ways of integrating multicultural content into other courses. Although the concept of a multicultural competency requirement for PhD candidates was favorably received, the specifics of such a requirement were more difficult to agree on. However, in 2000, a set of competency requirements that should enhance graduate students' multicultural knowledge and practice in teaching, research, and clinical work was unanimously approved by the faculty. These requirements include didactic (at least one multicultural course or equivalent) and applied (multicultural teaching, research, practica, or some combination of these) components. In addition, in thesis and dissertation proposals, the department now requires students to specify the population under study and to justify their choices of research methods and participants in regard to diversity and external validity.

The task force is also beginning to address the needs, curricula, and environments of undergraduate students; it has added an undergraduate representative and identified areas of potential concern and is discussing ways to encourage students' participation in the multicultural initiative. Multiculturalism clearly is not a product but an ongoing process with much work yet to be done.

THE PROGRAM AS A MODEL

Today, some view the URI psychology department's multicultural initiative as a model—not in the ideal sense, but as a preliminary pattern.[3] Models are useful in any field where much remains to be discovered, because they provide a framework in which investigators can formulate new hypotheses to be tested, plan their research, and evaluate their findings (Zimbardo,

---

[3]More information about the model is available from the Multicultural Task Force, University of Rhode Island, Department of Psychology, Kingston, RI 02881, or on the psychology department's Web site: http://www.uri.edu/artsci/psy/

1985). Multicultural models for organizational development make visible the invisible structures within institutions (see, e.g., the cultural environment transitions model developed by Manning, 1994). By understanding "how things work," departments can see the changes necessary for becoming multicultural environments. It is then up to the members of the department—with support from those in power and energy from everyone—to make the changes to transform themselves.

By recruiting and admitting students of diverse backgrounds into institutions of higher education, campuses have accepted a moral responsibility to create and maintain an environment that maximizes opportunities for learning (Corrigan, 1995). Yet, as institutions of higher education increasingly seek to build multicultural communities on campus and foster a celebration of differences, they also experience a resurgence of oppressive "isms" or a confirmation of their enduring presence. Consequently, the goal of multiculturalism is challenging and revolutionary and requires careful, comprehensive planning. As John Dewey proclaimed, "We never educate directly, but indirectly by means of the environment, and whether we permit chance environment to do the work, or whether we design environments for the purpose makes a great difference" (1933, quoted in King, 1992, p. 6).

REFERENCES

Alcalde, J., & Walsh-Bowers, R. (1996). Community psychology values and the culture of graduate training: A self-study. *American Journal of Community Psychology, 24*, 389–411.

Corrigan, R. (1995). Diversity, public and institutional. *Liberal Education*, 21–31.

Harrington-Austin, E., & DiBona, J. (1993). Bringing multiculturalism to the historically Black university in the United States. *Educational Horizons, 71*, 150–156.

Herrnstein, R. J., & Murray, C. (1994). *The bell curve: Intelligence and class structure in American life*. New York: Free Press.

Jones-Hudson, V. D. (2001). *Movin' on up to the 21st century: Multiculturalism . . . Making the abstract applied*. Unpublished doctoral dissertation, University of Rhode Island, Kingston.

King, P. M. (1992). How do we know? Why do we believe? Learning to make reflective judgment. *Liberal Education, 78*, 2–9.

Manning, K. (1994). Multicultural theories for muticultural practice. *NASPA Journal, 31*, 176–185.

McEwen, M. K., & Roper, L. D. (1994). Incorporating multiculturalism into student affairs preparation programs: Suggestions from the literature. *Journal of College Student Development, 35*, 46–53.

Pope-Davis, D., & Liu, W. (1995). *Multicultural issues and concerns in the department of psychology at the University of Rhode Island.* Unpublished report. University of Maryland at College Park.

Zimbardo, P. G. (1985). *Psychology and life.* Glenview, IL: Scott, Foresman.

23

CONTINUING EDUCATION

MARY ZAHM AND KATHRYN QUINA

More than 40% of the college students in the United States are over the age of 25, and the proportion of students who are enrolled part time has increased dramatically at both the undergraduate and graduate levels (Dortch, 1995). Women, who now make up the majority of college students, are particularly likely to attend part time (Bae, Choy, Geddes, Sable, & Snyder, 2000). Variously called *re-entry, resumed ed, continuing education,* or *perpetual learning* students, adults are no longer an oddity, but a fact of life in most college classrooms (Dolence & Norris, 1995).

We tend to regard students as if they are in school to develop their identities and prepare to enter society. Among older students, the motivations for attending college in a nontraditional way are as varied as the students (Paluda, 1994). They may be retraining for a new career, perhaps to

---

In this chapter, *URI* refers to the students, employees, and programs of the Alan Shawn Feinstein College of Continuing Education of the University of Rhode Island. We have not named individuals because there are so many; however, special appreciation is extended to Dr. Walter Crocker, recently retired Dean of Continuing Education, whose enthusiasm and support fueled many of the programs described here and energized those of us who had the good fortune to have worked with him.

Information on the URI programs described in this chapter can be obtained from the URI Web site: http://www.uri.edu/prov/

accommodate an adult-onset disability (Matthews, 1995) or in preparation for self-sufficiency necessitated by divorce or the death of a spouse. They may be moving from welfare to work (Kates, 1999), pursuing a lifelong dream of a college degree, or simply seeking the stimulation of new ideas and new learning (Johnson, 1995). Regardless of their specific reasons for returning to school, the experience has been described as transformative for adult students (Knowles, 1994), who often view their new knowledge and skills as routes to intellectual and personal emancipation (Fingeret & Drennon, 1997).

In this chapter we discuss some of the approaches we and our colleagues have developed for adult and nontraditional students at the Alan Shawn Feinstein College of Continuing Education of the University of Rhode Island (URI), located in the heart of "downcity" Providence. As is typical for continuing education (CE) programs, our average student age is 40, most students attend part time, and they are more likely to be women or minorities (or both) than are students on the main campus. Flexibility in course hours, locations, and budgets, along with a willingness to risk new ventures, have allowed us to offer educational opportunities to diverse populations.

JOYS AND CHALLENGES OF TEACHING ADULTS

The literature on adult learning has focused on various dimensions, including developmental processes, learning styles, intellectual skills, relevance of life experiences, and the meaning of the educational experience to the individual (e.g., Donaldson & Graham, 1999; Kasworm, 1990). Although age or "stage" is not necessarily a determining factor (Rossiter, 1999), an older student's approach to learning may be different from that of a younger student.

Cognitive Style

Smith and Pourchot's (1998) edited volume presents theories and research approaches from educational psychology as they apply to adult learners. The authors have offered strategies for learning and teaching, ranging from mnemonic devices for enhancing memory to incorporating personal forgiveness into the overall learning experience. Additional resources can be found in *Adult Education Quarterly, American Journal of Distance Education, Journal of Continuing Higher Education*, and the Web site of the National University Continuing Education Association (http://www.nucea.edu/).

Belenky, Clinchy, Goldberger, and Tarule (1986/1997) posited that adults often take a more relativistic, deeper approach (not rote memorization) to material. Buerk (1985) suggested that some of the anxiety expressed by older students about mathematics arises from the effort to "make meaning" out of abstract material—an indication of high, not low, cognitive ability. Statistics and methodology instructors can address this anxiety by taking time to answer student questions in ways that explain the reasons behind the answer. Kolb and Kolb (2001) offered a free on-line bibliography of resources on experiential learning and learning styles. Understanding the different ways in which students tend to learn can help instructors diversify their classrooms and evaluation strategies, in order to make learning more active and accessible to all students.

Mentkowski (2000) described an exciting program for adult female students built on active learning experiences that target communication, analysis, problem solving, values, and personal responsibility. Other CE programs provide innovative interdisciplinary opportunities that enable adults to integrate their life and work experiences with academic material they are learning in their classes. Interdisciplinary courses also can help students grasp connections between theoretical factors and applications in daily life and help prepare them for collaborative, interdisciplinary teamwork in the workplace (Dinmore, 1997).

A number of authors have recognized the significance of the educational experience for individual growth and meaning-making in life (Kroth & Boverne, 2000; LeBlanc, Brabnt, & Forsyth, 1996). Friere (1998), Mezirow (1996), and Rassool (1999) have each provided nontraditional models of literacy education that inform other areas of teaching adult students, incorporating multicultural awareness into non-Western teaching formats. These approaches offer ways to help students become aware of oppression and to increase their voice in relationships, public participation, and ultimately in creating social change (Fingeret & Drennon, 1997).

Academic Preparation

Among our students, some hold advanced degrees, whereas others earned equivalency diplomas after dropping out of high school years ago. Performance-based admissions procedures allow students who may not meet formal criteria for admission to take 12 credits on a probationary basis, to demonstrate their ability to successfully complete college-level work; thus, CE programs can provide a fresh start for everyone. However, instructors must be conscious of the fact that study skills, particularly "test-wisdom," decline with time elapsed since formal education, so that CE students often have academic deficiencies (Culross, 1996; Smith & Pourchot, 1998) or do not fully understand what higher education involves (Dinmore, 1997). Witherspoon and Nickell (1991) offered a thorough, well-written guide for adult students about what to expect and how to maximize the higher education experience, including developing study skills.

Although well-developed verbal skills, general knowledge, and writing ability often balance out academic deficiencies, specific tasks may be problematic. Re-entry courses such as the proseminar offered at URI can help students identify their scholastic strengths and interests and provide training and assistance to rebuild both academic skills and confidence. We have found that it is essential to describe to our students the conceptual skills we expect them to develop and to help them practice these skills through exercises and discussion. Timed exams and multiple-choice questions may not be good measures of learning for these students; they generally perform better on assignments and exams that are clearly based on the learning objectives, have varied formats that they have had practice in using, and do not rely on memorization. When appropriate, we give take-home essay exams that require integration of ideas from several sources of information. Teaching handbooks such as those by Bloom (1984) and McKeachie and Gibbs (1999) offer instructors helpful techniques for defining learning objectives and ways to promote and evaluate learning.

Time

A survey by the American Association of University Women (1999) found that 69% of adult female students, and a smaller but significant number of men, are concerned about flexibility of scheduling. In addition to attending school, most hold part- or full-time jobs and have families. Thus, arranging class and study schedules can be a serious problem, particularly when caring for children or elderly relatives is involved (Hagedorn, 1999; Home, 1998). Yet, in spite of these demands, most adult students manage time for their studies quite effectively (Kaplan & Saltiel, 1997). It is not surprising, though, that women over the age of 25 experience more interruptions and slowing in academic progress than do men (Robertson, 1991).

CE programs can respond to this challenge with evening and weekend courses, classes that meet fewer times each week, and increased use of electronic communications. A well-thought-out syllabus, with assignment and exam dates, is essential. Students schedule their precious study hours well in advance, and any changes should be negotiated with the class. Reserve readings should be available early, where they can be easily copied, because many students cannot spend long hours in the library. If outside activities such as attending a talk during nonclass hours are assigned, options must be provided for those whose work or family schedules conflict.

In our experience, supplementary readings and homework assignments are pursued enthusiastically when they increase understanding of the material. However, "busywork," work not tied to the course goals, ambiguous instructions, and assignments that are not evaluated are viewed dimly, as is the instructor who assigns them. A number of strategies for motivating adult students' learning can be found in Wlodkowski's (1998) book.

Undetected Learning Disabilities

Some returning students with persisting academic difficulties may have difficulty processing and retaining information that is presented and assessed in traditional modes (Matthews, 1995). Such students may fear the stigma of having a label, so identifying a learning problem requires instructor sensitivity. Furthermore, because testing for disabilities can be very expensive, institutional support is needed. However, testing can be worthwhile; several of our students went from near failure to Dean's List in a relatively short time after receiving a boost from an integrated approach. At URI, entry-level instructors and advisors identify potential referrals and discuss options with those students, including the benefits of acquiring greater self-understanding and obtaining assistance in order to enhance future learning. Testing is free at an on-campus academic skills center, thanks to a generous benefactor who appreciated this need, and the center staff work with each student to develop the most appropriate and comfortable learning plan. As instructors, we have met the challenges of a wide array of student learning and writing styles by offering all students multiple format options, such as audiotaped or computer-based presentations, especially in writing-intensive classes. In lieu of traditional term papers, students can create a class presentation using the guided outline structure of a software program such as Microsoft PowerPoint, allowing them to demonstrate their knowledge by identifying the key points and presenting them to others in a logical, visually effective manner, and answering questions from other students. By offering these options to the whole class, individuals who may have a learning disability are not stigmatized by "different" treatment, and other students enjoy the opportunity to express themselves in their most comfortable mode. More information on maximizing learning effectiveness for adults with learning disabilities may be found in Westby's (2000) article.

Family and Social Support

Bauer and Mott (1990) found that resolving conflicts with family, friends, and self was an important goal among re-entry students. Indeed, most studies have found that lack of family support is one of the most serious deterrents to satisfaction with the adult educational experience (Paluda, 1994), especially for mothers of young children and first-generation college attendees (Home, 1998). At the same time, research has shown that achieving in a multidimensional world, and managing different domains successfully, can be healthier than having fewer challenges (Baruch & Barnett, 1986).

Edwards (1993) discussed the various ways in which family and educational spheres impinge on each other for adult female students. She particularly identified the issue of guilt—over wanting time for oneself, being angry when family matters arise during crucial study periods, or having fun when one should be studying. Husbands, children, and friends can be important sources of social and instrumental support, regardless of their educational level (Novacki & Thacker, 1991; Suitor & Keeton, 1997). However, friends and partners of comparable educational levels are particularly important in providing school-related support, such as encouragement to succeed academically. Academic encouragement is especially important for students whose family's educational attainment has been limited in the past (Kaplan & Saltiel, 1997). The movie *Educating Rita* (Oakes & Gilbert, 1983), which depicts interpersonal and existential crises faced by a free-spirited cockney hairdresser pursuing a college degree, reflects some of the experiences of adult female students.

Student activities and peer support systems can increase a sense of belonging in the institution. Our active peer counseling program provides drop-in advising about careers, financial aid, and other academic matters; referrals for more complex personal issues; and often just a friendly ear from a welcoming advocate. The benefactor for whom the college is named, Alan Shawn Feinstein, funds scholarships for low-income parents and quality care for their young children on site, and parents, staff, and other students are encouraged to stop by and read to the children. Thanks to the creative energy of an artist in residence, in recent years monthlong campuswide events around such relevant themes as domestic violence, the legacy of Vietnam, and "family matters," have drawn in students, family members, and friends through art exhibits, plays, and weekend events. Each of these opportunities strengthens the connection students feel to the academic sphere, while widening that same sphere to include their outside support systems.

Acknowledging and Incorporating Life Experience

Enrolled in our program have been engineers, scientists, teachers, and legislators, and students from many countries. Some students have done extensive volunteer work, including coaching national championship teams, running a drug and alcohol treatment program, and founding a homeless shelter. Others have achieved quieter greatness, through parenting, caring for others, surviving illness or injury, resisting oppression, or overcoming childhood traumas (LeBlanc et al., 1996). Instructors can stimulate discussions without the grueling efforts often needed to get younger students to talk (Poppenga & Prisbell, 1996), and classroom interaction can incorporate learning from each others' experiences. When presenting formal definitions of a concept, instructors can solicit examples from students' own lives, or from magazines and newspapers—and students can be encouraged to apply concepts to their everyday or work lives in essays and class discussions. Furthermore, discussions need to be balanced in such a way that all views and all students are included and respected, and students of different age cohorts can learn from one another. Younger students, whose life experiences have generally been more limited, may need to engage in their own active discovery process—although some young adults have already led remarkable lives.

Older students' interests may differ from those of younger students. For example, in developmental psychology, we have found that younger students are often fascinated by infant development, whereas most parents are more concerned about their maddening teens and their aging parents. Instructors should incorporate later life topics and examples into the course material (see chapter 19, this volume), and provide opportunities for students to enhance the personal meaning of the material through journals or projects. One assignment we use in many of our courses is to ask students to review a contemporary popular book in the context of both the scholarly literature and personal experiences, including validity (or lack thereof) for their own lives. Particularly well-liked examples are Crose (1997); Pipher (1994); Prochaska, Norcross, and DiClemente (1995); Sheehy (1995); and Tannen (1991).

Motivating and Retaining Students

The presence of highly motivated students in the classroom is a joy as well as a challenge. Eagerness to learn means attentive, active listening, but the eager learner also demands that the instructor provide new information and be prepared. The teaching role we have found most effective is not that of a traditional authority figure, but rather of an expert in our particular field of study—a consultant to the learning process, facilitating knowledge and understanding (Dinmore, 1997; Fleming, 1997), empowerment, and lifelong learning (Ferrari & Mahalingam, 1998). Each of us serves as a mentor and a role model of a professional in our field (see suggestions in Backes, 1997; Collins, Chrisler, & Quina, 1998). In fact, we find that by midsemester, our students virtually take over some courses, such as the Psychology of Women, because they are so engaged in the material.

A high grade point average is a strong predictor of persistence and satisfaction in school (Hagedorn, 1999; Novacki & Thacker, 1991), but for many adult students grades also demonstrate—to themselves and to others—that they are capable thinkers. As well, external recognitions of achievement, such as awards and honors, are important to adult students. Yet at URI (as at other schools), most awards were not available to our part-time students, until a group of students, faculty, staff and administrators worked together to install an adult student honorary organization, Alpha Sigma Lambda, and to change university policies. For example, Dean's List eligibility is now evaluated for each block of 12 successive credits for part-time students.

Helping CE students identify effective strategies for managing stress has also proven to be useful (Kaplan & Saltiel, 1997; Witherspoon & Nickell, 1991). These might include effective time management and test-taking strategies as well as cognitive–behavioral self-help techniques such as engaging in positive self-talk and maintaining an optimistic attitude. In addition, although older students are more self-directed, they are more likely to indicate a need for help with anxiety management than are younger students, for example, by asking more questions about assignments and wanting very specific guidelines. Instructors can help by providing detailed written instructions for assignments, taking the time to explain assignments as fully as needed, setting aside time to review students' preliminary plans for projects and papers, allowing home phone calls or e-mail messages to clarify questions about assignments, reviewing drafts of papers, and encouraging revisions. Another approach that can enhance motivation is to offer courses on personally relevant topics, which may also attract students who might otherwise not have thought of higher education. For example, among our successful graduates are several persons with alcohol-troubled histories, who were initially attracted to our campus by a certificate program in working with substance abuse problems. Courses on gender, ethnicity, and culture regularly draw a diversity of students. "Toward Self-Understanding," an entry-level personal adjustment course designed by Zahm (1996), draws adults at all levels who wish to develop skills for life planning, goal setting, problem solving, and self-management.

Overcoming Oppression

For us, perhaps the most exciting transformation occurs when students find ways to overcome past oppressions, particularly when they discover their power to make a difference beyond their own lives. We have seen students move from welfare to university staff, from being abused to managing shelters for others who are abused. Indeed, empowerment is the goal many see for education (Friere, 1998). However, instructors need to be aware of oppressive elements that may exist within the academic setting itself. Black women interviewed by Johnson-Bailey and Cervero (1996) reported that they regularly experienced racism, sexism, and other forms of class and color discrimination at their universities. They often chose to be silent rather than address these oppressions, for fear of losing their opportunity for an education. The very place that empowerment should have happened was instead yet another source of stress and harm.

There are several ways to try to reduce the likelihood that discrimination will occur. URI has hired peer counselors, advisors, faculty, and other staff members who will reach out and establish personal relationships with minority students. Every effort is made to recruit and retain a diverse student body, something that is made more possible by performance-based admissions, courses in English as a second language, and other entry-level skill-building courses. A semester-long precollege learning assessment program offers men and women who have had no previous higher education experience an opportunity to brush up on skills and to determine which educational institution is the best starting point for them, while helping them feel that they belong in college. Diversity is celebrated, as in our annual student-led multicultural food-and-fun day for students and their families. However, most important is the availability of financial aid—not just the funding itself, but also staff to help students negotiate what can be a complicated system of forms and requirements. These actions cannot ensure a nondiscriminating environment, but they can help identify problem areas, give students who experience difficulty a place to be heard, and assure that appropriate action will be taken when incidents arise. We believe that the increasing minority enrollment and retention in our program reflect these kinds of actions; in fact, in some minority communities, our best recruitment has been word of mouth from other students.

ALTERNATIVE FORMATS FOR CONTINUING EDUCATION: DISTANCE LEARNING

A growing number of students are enrolling in psychology courses and degree programs at both the undergraduate and graduate levels using distance technologies; in response, the American Psychological Association has created a Task Force on Distance Education and has issued guidelines for good practice and assessment (retrieved September 30, 2002 from http://www.apa.org/ed/exec_summary.html). Several Web sites list currently available programs (e.g., *Peterson's Guide*, retrieved January 4, 2003 from http://www.petersons.com/distancelearning/). Such programs provide another way to reach out to individuals who might not be able to come to traditional classes. We have successfully taught several Web based psychology courses: the previously mentioned entry-level "Toward Self-Understanding," an upper level Psychology of Women course, and a collaborative undergraduate–graduate course in History and Systems. Mary Zahm designed a domestic violence Web site, "STOP the Violence, Break the Cycle—Locally and Globally with Education," which provides her community college students with historical, sociological, psychological, and legal information on issues associated with domestic violence and the wider community with practical strategies for stopping relationship violence and sources of help for victims and batterers (http://dl.mass.edu/stoptheviolence/).

The challenge is to be able to use the gifts of technology without being dominated by it (Peinovich, 1997). We use a variety of approaches: weekly discussions on assigned topics; weekly open-book quizzes (with the express objective of having students learn the material in a timely fashion); individual or group essays; and, in all classes, an independent paper or project. We also find it helpful to be explicit about the kinds of demands the course makes, including how often and for how long the student can expect to be on-line (usually four 60-min sessions on-line per week, not including major assignments). When possible, we hold two or three optional face-to-face meetings, and many students enjoy the opportunity to see the instructors and other students with whom they have become good e-friends.

We have found that on-line class discussions are often even more congenial, lively, and thoughtful than those in actual classrooms. Individual instructor–student interactions can be more casual, personal, and frequent than in traditional classroom settings. Several of our students, including some with learning disabilities, have told us that they are able to participate in class discussions as intellectual equals for the first time in their lives, because they are able to take extra time to polish their contributions.

Unlike people who fear that distance learning courses and programs will "take over" higher education, we believe that they have the potential to strengthen our connections to students and our abilities as teachers. Many of our students are highly motivated adult women with limited time to attend campus-based classes; along with two to three courses in "real time," an additional one to two "virtual" courses per semester means an earlier completion of their degree that would not have been possible otherwise because of scheduling conflicts. However, we caution that teaching on-line is more work, not less, for the students and the instructor; class size limits are important, because of the increased individual contact.

Another concern for us is the potential for widening the gap between individuals with computer access and those without. Although more women and minorities have joined the ranks of regular computer users (Hoffman & Novak, 1998), we have found that distance-based courses are considerably less manageable for students—often women and minorities—who do not have a computer in their home (Blumenstyk, 1997). One solution is to identify conveniently located and user-friendly sites for students to use computers, such as community agencies or offices during off-peak hours. At times, our student government has been able to make a computer available in a room where children can read or play nearby without bothering others.

CONCLUSION

Working with older students has taught us to take no aspect of what we do for granted, and we are constantly challenged to be systematic, thoughtful, and flexible. The changes we have had to make, however, have been richly rewarded by the growth and learning we and our students have experienced. Furthermore, the awareness and skills we have gained from working with adult students have made us better teachers and learners with students of all ages and learning styles. We have been fortunate to work in institutions that have taken seriously their mission to educate diverse students. We hope that more colleges and universities will extend their commitments to include greater access—physically, financially, and psychologically. It is essential to make higher education available to those groups for whom it has often seemed out of reach, thereby reducing the educational and income gaps between minorities and nonminorities and between poorer and more privileged sectors of society.

REFERENCES

American Association of University Women. (1999). *Gaining a foothold: Women's transitions through work and college*. Washington, DC: Author.

American Psychological Association 2001 Task Force on Distance Education. (2002). *Executive summary*. Retrieved Septemeber 30, 2002 from http:///www.apa.org/ed/exec_summary.html

Backes, C. E. (1997). The do's and don'ts of working with adult learners. *Adult Learning, 8*(3), 29–31.

Bae, Y., Choy, S., Geddes, C., Sable, J., & Snyder, T. (2000). *Trends in educational equity of girls and women*. Washington, DC: U.S. Department of Education, National Center for Education Statistics.

Baruch, G. K., & Barnett, R. (1986). Role quality, multiple role involvement, and psychological well-being in midlife women. *Journal of Personality and Social Psychology, 51*, 578–585.

Bauer, D., & Mott, D. (1990). Life themes and motivations of re-entry students. *Journal of Counseling and Development, 68*, 555–560.

Belenky, M. F., Clinchy, B. M., Goldberger, N. R., & Tarule, J. M. (1997). *Women's ways of knowing: The development of self, voice, and mind*. New York: Basic Books. (Original work published 1986)

Bloom, B. S. (Ed.). (1984). *Taxonomy of educational objectives: Cognitive domain*. New York: Longman.

Blumenstyk, G. (1997). Colloquy: A feminist scholar questions how women fare in distance education. *Chronicle of Higher Education, 44*, A36.

Buerk, D. (1985). The voices of women making meaning in mathematics. *Journal of Education, 167*(3), 59–70.

Collins, L. H., Chrisler, J. C., & Quina, K. (Eds.). (1998). *Career strategies for women in academe: Arming Athena*. Thousand Oaks, CA: Sage.

Crose, R. (1997). *Why women live longer than men, and what men can learn from them*. San Francisco: Jossey-Bass.

Culross, R. (1996). Remediation: Real students, real standards. *Change, 28*(6), 50–52.

Dinmore, I. (1997). Interdisciplinary and integrative education: An imperative for adult education. *Education, 117*, 452–468.

Dolence, M. E., & Norris, D. M. (1995). *Transforming higher education, a vision for learning in the 21st century*. Ann Arbor, MI: Society for College and University Planning.

Donaldson, J. F., & Graham, S. (1999). A model of college outcomes for adults. *Adult Education Quarterly, 50,* 24–40.

Dortch, S. (1995). Colleges come back. *American Demographics, 17*(5), 4–6.

Edwards, R. (1993). *Mature women students: Separating or connecting family and education.* London: Taylor & Francis.

Ferrari, M., & Mahalingam, R. (1998). Personal cognitive development and its implications for teaching and learning. *Educational Psychologist, 33,* 35–44.

Fingeret, H. A., & Drennon, C. (1997). *Literacy for life: Adult learners, new practices.* New York: Teachers College Press.

Fleming, J. (1997). Successful life skills. *Adult Learning, 8*(5–6), 10, 31.

Friere, P. (1998). The adult literacy process as cultural action for freedom. *Harvard Educational Review, 68,* 480–498.

Hagedorn, L. S. (1999). Factors related to the retention of female graduate students over 30. *Journal of College Student Retention, 1,* 99–114.

Hoffman, D. L., & Novak, T. P. (April, 1998). Information access: Bridging the racial divide on the Internet. *Science, 280,* 390–391.

Home, A. M. (1998). Predicting role conflict, overload and contagion in adult women university students with families and jobs. *Adult Education Quarterly, 48,* 85–97.

Johnson, M. L. (1995). Lessons from the Open University: Third age learning. *Educational Gerontology, 21,* 415–427.

Johnson-Bailey, J., & Cervero, R. M. (1996). An analysis of the educational narratives of reentry Black women. *Adult Education Quarterly, 46,* 142–157.

Kaplan, P. L., & Saltiel, I. M. (1997). Adults who do it all: Balancing work, family, and schooling. *Adult Learning, 8*(5–6), 17–18, 31.

Kasworm, C. E. (1990). Adult undergraduates in higher education: A review of past research perspectives. *Review of Educational Research, 60,* 345–372.

Kates, E. (1999). Defining a supportive educational environment for low-income women. In S. N. Davis, M. Crawford, & J. Sebrechts (Eds.), *Coming into her own: Educational success in girls and women* (pp. 328–359). San Francisco: Jossey Bass.

Knowles, M. S. (1994). *The history of the adult education movement in the United States.* Malabar, FL: Krieger.

Kolb, A., & Kolb, D. A. (2001). *Experiential learning theory bibliography 1971–2001.* Boston: McBer. Retrieved September 30, 2002, from http://trgmcber.haygroup.com/Products/learning/bibliography.htm.

Kroth, M., & Boverne, P. (2000). Life mission and adult learning. *Adult Education Quarterly, 50,* 134–149.

LeBlanc, J. B., Brabnt, S., & Forsyth, C. J. (1996). The meaning of college for survivors of sexual abuse: Higher education and the older female college student. *American Journal of Orthopsychiatry, 66,* 468–473.

Matthews, M. A. (1995). The ever-changing face of the adult learner. *Adult Learning, 7*(2), 19, 30.

McKeachie, W. J., & Gibbs, G. (1999). *Teaching tips: Strategies, research, and theory for college and university teachers* (10th ed.). Boston: Houghton Mifflin.

Mentkowski, M. (2000). *Learning that lasts: Integrating learning, development, and performance in college and beyond.* San Francisco: Jossey Bass.

Mezirow, J. (1996). Contemporary paradigms of learning. *Adult Education Quarterly, 46*, 158–173.

Novacki, M., & Thacker, C. (1991). Satisfaction and role strain among middle-age women who return to school: Replication and extension of findings in a Canadian context. *Educational Gerontology, 17*, 323–342.

Oakes, H. L. (Executive Producer), & Gilbert, L. (Director). (1983). *Educating Rita* [Motion picture]. Burbank, CA: Columbia/Tristar Studios.

Paluda, M. A. (1994). Reentry women: A literature review with recommendations for counseling and research. *Journal of Counseling and Development, 73*, 10–16.

Peinovich, P. E. (1997). Changing the rules: Access and accessibility in an information age. *Journal of Continuing Higher Education, 45*, 34–37.

Peterson's (2003). Petersons.com distance learning page. Retrieved January 4, 2003 from http://www.petersons.com/distancelearning

Pipher, M. (1994). *Reviving Ophelia: Saving the selves of adolescent girls.* New York: Ballentine Books.

Poppenga, J., & Prisbell, M. (1996). Differences in apprehension about communicating in the classroom between traditional and nontraditional students. *Psychological Reports, 78*(3, Part 1), 802.

Prochaska, J. O., Norcross, J. C., & DiClemente, C. (1995). *Changing for good.* New York: Avon.

Rassool, N. (1999). *Literacy for sustainable development in the age of information.* Philadelphia: Multilingual Matters.

Robertson, D. (1991). Gender differences in the academic progress of adult undergraduates: Patterns and policy implications. *Journal of College Student Development, 32*, 490–496.

Rossiter, M. (1999). A narrative approach to development: Implications for adult education. *Adult Education Quarterly, 50*, 56–71.

Sheehy, G. (1995). *New passages: Mapping your life across time.* New York: Random House.

Smith, M. C., & Pourchot, T. (Eds.). (1998). *Adult learning and development: Perspectives from educational psychology.* Mahwah, NJ: Erlbaum.

Suitor, J. J., & Keeton, S. (1997). Once a friend, always a friend? Effects of homophily on women's support networks across a decade. *Social Networks, 19*, 51–62.

Tannen, D. (1991). *You just don't understand! Women and men in conversation.* New York: Ballentine Books.

Westby, C. (2000). Who are adults with learning disabilities and what do we do about them? *Topics in Language Disorders, 21*, 1–14.

Witherspoon, D., & Nickell, E. (1991). *Back to school at my age? A guide for both the returning student and the college administrator*. Lanham, MD: University Press of America.

Wlodkowski, R. (1998). *Enhancing adult motivation to learn*. San Francisco: Jossey-Bass.

Zahm, M. (1996). *Create your ideal life: Applied psychology of personal adjustment and growth*. Dubuque, IA: McGraw-Hill.

24

INTEGRATING MULTICULTURAL ISSUES INTO GRADUATE CLINICAL PSYCHOLOGY TRAINING

ELIZABETH DAVIS-RUSSELL

Clinical and counseling programs seeking to incorporate ethnic minority issues into the curriculum have wrestled with how best to do so. A number of training models have recently been suggested that include a multicultural focus (e.g., Adams, 2002; Taylor et al., 2002). Earlier, Copeland (1982), operating from the premise that theories and practices traditionally taught in graduate programs were relevant mainly to White, middle-class clients, proposed four different approaches by which materials relevant to ethnic minority populations could be integrated into those programs. Although she specifically targeted counselor education, the models she presented can be applied to graduate programs in clinical psychology as well. In this chapter, I discuss each of the models and then present a case study describing the application of one of them within a clinical doctoral program. Additional ideas about core curriculum transformation can be found in Davis-Russell, Bascuas, Duran, and Forbes (1991) and Stricker et al. (1990).

FOUR MODELS FOR ADDRESSING ETHNIC MINORITY ISSUES

Separate-Course Model

This model involves an addition to the existing curriculum of one multicultural course, which may vary widely in its goals, design, and content. Copeland (1982) described some of the variations:

> Some courses provide a historical perspective (i.e., ethnic studies approach), others focus on the study of appropriate theoretical models, others are more active oriented in nature and assume the form of encounter or sensitivity groups, and still others are comprehensive in nature, addressing each of the aforementioned topics. (p. 189)

Within some programs, the course focus has been on a single ethnic or cultural group because it is the largest minority in that locale, whereas in others, when a number of ethnic minority groups have been well represented in the surrounding population, the course has focused on each of those groups. The separate-course model is less effective if the course is taught in a single semester, because this time frame does not permit intensive study of even one group. However, it can be meaningful if it has clearly defined objectives and is regarded as a central requirement of the program. Furthermore, the faculty member teaching the course must have expertise in the area. She or he may be an adjunct or visiting instructor if the institution does not already have someone sufficiently qualified among its regular faculty; however, a disadvantage of using adjunct or visiting faculty is that it absolves the regular faculty of responsibility, involvement, and commitment, thereby perpetuating the mindset that ethnic minority issues are the province and responsibility of a select few. The separate-course model may appear attractive to many institutions, because it ensures coverage of ethnic minority content without requiring a total program evaluation or overhaul in this area.

Area-of-Concentration Model

This model is designed for training students whose goal is to work with specific minority populations. The curriculum includes basic clinical psychology training, with the added option of an interrelated core of courses in ethnic minority issues. Compared with the separate-course model, this option provides students who choose it with exposure to more diversity and more in-depth study of ethnic minority populations, with the opportunity to study the similarities and differences in approaches to working with each group. It also provides prepractica skill building, and practica and internships in settings with ethnic minority populations along with supervision from professionals with appropriate expertise, so that students get to have direct experience working with ethnic minority clients. In addition, their dissertations may focus on this aspect of their training, which can then contribute to the discourse and research literature on ethnic minority mental health.

However, the area-of-concentration model has some drawbacks. First, although it reaches students who specifically want to develop proficiencies in this area, it does not reach many others who will in fact end up working with ethnic minority populations. Also, because the model requires a core of courses in addition to the basic clinical psychology curriculum, it may extend the length of training. Finally, given that the 1996 American Psychological Association's Committee on Accreditation Guidelines and Principles (retrieved December 25, 2000 from http://2222.apa.org/ed/g&p.html) stresses that specialization at the predoctoral level be very limited, the implementation of this model could presumably evoke criticism when the program is evaluated for reaccreditation.

Interdisciplinary Model

Within this model, students take courses outside the clinical psychology curriculum, in disciplines such as anthropology, sociology, economics, political science, and ethnic studies. This eliminates the concern that clinical psychology programs do not have the expertise and resources to provide a sufficient variety of courses with multicultural content. In universities, the model relies heavily on interdepartmental cooperation, but it can avoid redundancy in course offerings while more fully utilizing the institution's resources. In free-standing professional schools, the model requires contracting with outside faculty to teach the needed courses. However, no matter what the setting, if these courses are not required, only a select few students will choose to take them.

Integration Model

The major weakness of the area-of-concentration and interdisciplinary models is their dependence on students electing to take the courses. The integration model addresses this weakness and offers other benefits as well; however, it is also the most difficult to implement. For an existing clinical program, the adoption of the integration model means the redesigning of courses and field experiences, thereby involving the commitment and time of administration, faculty, students, and field coordinators and supervisors.

A specific positive outcome is that the model elicits cooperation and input from all individuals involved, with faculty, students, practicing professionals, and potential client populations taking an active role in program evaluation. For this to happen, these groups need to have the opportunity to interact on a continuing basis at the sites that serve diverse groups. In addition, faculty, student, and administrative review of course offerings, along with comments from supervisors in the field, provides useful information to assess what modifications are needed.

Basic Requirements for All Models

Whichever model an institution selects to implement, success entails careful planning and evaluation. Both the necessary resources and the unwavering support and commitment of the administration are critical. In addition, trainees must have contact with individuals from a variety of cultural groups at all levels, including fellow students with whom to study and interact on a daily basis, faculty and administrators, field supervisors, and clients. Methods of evaluating changes in students' beliefs and attitudes as well as their knowledge and skills must be built into the chosen model. Such evaluation not only provides vital data for the continuing development and refining of the program but also generates important information about what does and does not work that can be disseminated to clinical and counseling training professionals.

CASE STUDY: AN INTEGRATED MODEL

The California School of Professional Psychology, Fresno (CSPP–Fresno), is one of four branches of the California School of Professional Psychology (CSPP). A free-standing institution that offers a PsyD in clinical psychology, it is striving to create a program with diversity as a central goal. *Diversity* has been defined inclusively to incorporate ethnicity, race, culture, national origin, language, gender, sexual orientation, religious orientation, physical condition, socioeconomic class, and age. Specifically, CSPP–Fresno's ultimate aim is to reflect with its student body and faculty the diverse reality of the state of California.

Institutional Commitment to Diversity

Essential to the achievement of this goal was the establishment of an institutional commitment, the foundation upon which all the other steps in the process were built. Such a commitment requires that individuals in positions of leadership work to alter long-established institutional procedures, involving such things as hiring and evaluation of personnel and the allocation of institutional resources. An important initial demonstration of this commitment was CSPP–Fresno's search for a new chancellor. The campus, through the search committee, made a commitment to diversity a major criterion in the qualifications. Each candidate interviewed was asked to provide further evidence of his or her record of promoting diversity and to articulate an agenda for the future. In addition, the MERIT (Multicultural Education,

Research, Intervention, and Training) Council, part of a CSPP system-wide MERIT Institute, reviewed and revised all institutional policies and procedures to make them consistent with this commitment. Some of the changes that were made included the policy and practice to advertise position vacancies in journals and newsletters of underrepresented groups and to include questions pertaining to one's past work in diversity in hiring interviews. In admission requirements, applicants were asked to include their perspectives on diversity in their written statements.

Faculty Issues

Recruitment of a diverse faculty

Faculty diversity plays an important role in the development of a multicultural institution. It provides a broad range of cultural perspectives, knowledge, and experience to enrich both the educational and interpersonal domains. In addition, a diverse faculty is more likely to attract a diverse student body, which further enhances the learning experience for all, as well as providing increased opportunity for training ethnic minority professionals. Accordingly, at CSPP–Fresno, the MERIT Council was charged with reviewing procedures for faculty recruitment and designing new approaches. For example, they developed a list of diversity-related journals to be used when advertising any new positions and specific interview questions to access candidates' competence and commitment regarding diversity.

Training

Faculty education and training are essential factors in creating and delivering a curriculum that reflects an institution's commitment to diversity. At CSPP–Fresno, the first step in this direction was a monthly meeting of the faculty as a whole throughout the academic year, to examine obstacles to the inclusion of diversity issues in courses. The faculty identified pedagogical, content, and social and emotional obstacles. For pedagogical and content obstacles, teaching and reference materials were developed, and regular in-service meetings were held. For the social emotional obstacles, consciousness-raising meetings were held.

Next, a permanent diversity committee was formed as a subcommittee of the faculty senate, which received funds from the institution to provide continuing faculty education. This educational process consists in part of retreats and in-service training to develop cultural awareness and sensitivity. However, awareness and sensitivity alone do not produce a multicultural curriculum. Therefore, the major emphasis is on multicultural competence in teaching about assessment, intervention, and research, which has been achieved through in-service education focusing on diversity topics for all core faculty. For example, in assessment, the use of moderator variables when working with culturally diverse populations is stressed, as is developing competence in the use of culturally specific instruments.

As a final part of the process, the institution is moving toward including multicultural competence as a criterion in the evaluation of faculty performance. A list of competencies developed for all four CSPP campuses can be found on the Web site for this volume (see introduction).

TRANSFORMING THE CURRICULUM

It is vital that the core curriculum in clinical and counseling psychology provide a thorough understanding of the paradigms that traditionally have guided the production of psychological knowledge, as well as a new paradigm for work in this area. The range of events to which people attend can be limited by the paradigms they accept, and the adoption of a new paradigm can open them up to what they have not seen before. In regard to traditional paradigms, CSPP–Fresno offers a concentration in psychodynamic approaches. This consists of a series of courses in Jungian psychology and ego psychology that students can add on to their programs.

The new paradigm, on the other hand, emphasizes the importance of culture, race, and ethnicity in defining the constructs of psychology. Built into it is the recognition that clients receiving counseling or therapy are knowing individuals who shape their destinies through conceptual frameworks that they develop about the world and their lives—and that the social system and individual interactions affect how they function and organize their lives.

This new paradigm is being incorporated into the core curriculum. The first step in the process was the development of specialized coursework for students whose career paths will lead to work with minority groups. Some of these courses include Cross-Cultural Families, Cross-Cultural Mental Health, and Intercultural Psychotherapy Lab. The second step was the development of multicultural competencies in research, assessment, and intervention for various year levels. The third step—integration of these multicultural competencies into the core curriculum—is still being implemented. A detailed description of these competencies and a plan for their integration into the curriculum can be found on the Web site for this volume.

In addition to the core requirements, CSPP–Fresno faculty developed a required experiential diversity sequence with different goals for each level of the academic program. The institution funds faculty for their involvement in these activities, which they do in addition to their usual teaching. Year 1 includes self-assessment in small groups with a faculty facilitator monitoring student responses. Year 2 is an immersion experience, in which students, working with a faculty mentor, become involved in a culture other than their own. They are encouraged to participate in activities of the cultural group and then are able to process the experience with the faculty and a small group of peers in a small-group format. Year 3 is a series of clinical case conferences focusing on diversity issues in assessment and psychotherapy.

CREATING SUPPORT SYSTEMS FOR STUDENTS

Two underlying premises of CSPP–Fresno are that support systems are natural phenomena and that instructors provide support for all students. In keeping with their diversity goals, the faculty have developed several student support groups, sponsored by faculty and run by students, including a cross-cultural student association, a gay/lesbian/bisexual student organization, and a Christian student group. These organizations provide a forum for the discussion of issues of identity as faced by graduate students in psychology. They also provide opportunities for social interaction with faculty members who represent a specific diversity interest. Thus, these organizations can be identity enhancing for the students in a context separate from the daily academic environment.

The development of a group identity can influence the campus in a number of positive ways. Sometimes it has resulted in specific academic recommendations to the campus at large, such as the need for clinical case conferences focused on gay/lesbian/bisexual issues. Activities organized by these groups can provide an immersion experience for the rest of the campus. An example is the International Fair that happens on campus each year. The Multicultural Student Association holds a daylong fair with food, dress, exhibits, music, dance, and speakers from different cultural groups. Speakers address healing traditions in their culture, and the whole campus has the opportunity to attend these lectures and to participate in the social–cultural events. In addition, students have found constructive avenues for focusing their group's concerns or frustrations over a lack of progress. For example, international students generated a list of needs that they presented to the chancellor; included among these were their concerns that they were seen by some faculty and peers as less competent because of the differences in culture and their accents. The Christian student group identified a need for the discussion and ethical integration of belief systems into clinical work.

EVALUATION OF THE EFFORTS

Thus far CSPP–Fresno faculty have used a number of strategies to evaluate the effectiveness of the efforts. To assess the level of integration of diversity content in the curriculum, courses were evaluated over a 5-year period with an instrument developed by a faculty member and her research students (Kuba & Bluestone, 2002). The results of their study showed that not all courses were integrated and that gay/lesbian and ethnic/racial issues were more often included than were issues pertaining to aging, disability, and religion. An evaluation of the first-year diversity experience, a pre–post assessment utilizing an Intercultural Sensitivity Inventory (Davis-Russell, 2002) that I designed, showed some modest changes at the end of the experience. To evaluate campus climate, a faculty member and his class conducted an ethnographic study of the campus. Their findings revealed that although there had been some changes toward building an inclusive community, many students of color still felt alienated.

The results are promising. CSPP–Fresno faculty have learned that commitment must come from all segments of the institution, and the president/chancellor must be highly visible in demonstrating the institution's commitment. Resources must be provided to enhance faculty competence, because sensitivity alone is insufficient to deliver a quality curriculum.

REFERENCES

Adams, D. (2002). A metastructure for multicultural professional psychology education and training: Standards and philosophy. In E. Davis-Russell (Ed.), *Multicultural education, research, intervention, and training* (pp. 20–36). San Francisco: Jossey-Bass.

Copeland, E. J. (1982). Minority populations and traditional counseling programs: Some alternatives. *Counselor Education and Supervision, 21*, 187–193.

Davis-Russell, E. (2002). Preparation for training: Assessing attitudes toward difference using the ISI. In E. Davis Russell (Ed.), *Multicultural education, research, intervention, and training* (pp. 287–295). San Francisco: Jossey-Bass.

Davis-Russell, E., Bascuas, J., Duran, E., & Forbes, W. (1991). Ethnic diversity and the core curriculum. In R. L. Peterson, J. D. McHolland, R. J. Bent, E. Davis-Russell, G. E. Edwall, K. Polite, et al. (Eds.), *The core curriculum in professional psychology* (pp. 126–137). Washington, DC: American Psychological Association.

Kuba, S., & Bluestone, H. (2002). Integrating diversity content across the curriculum: Evaluation in a clinical graduate program. In E. Davis-Russell (Ed.), *Multicultural education, research, intervention, and training* (pp. 67–87). San Francisco: Jossey-Bass.

Stricker, G., Davis-Russell, E., Bourg, E., Duran, E., Hammond, W., McHolland, J., et al. (1990). *Toward ethnic diversification in psychology education and training.* Washington, DC: American Psychological Association.

Taylor, S., Parks, C., Shorter-Gooden, K., Johnson, P., Burke, E., Ashing, K., et al. (2002). In and out of the classroom: A model for multicultural training in clinical psychology. In E. Davis-Russell (Ed.), *Multicultural education, research, intervention, and training* (pp. 54–66). San Francisco: Jossey-Bass.

25

DEALING WITH DIFFICULT
CLASSROOM DIALOGUE

GALE YOUNG

Imagine this scenario: Your class is discussing the day's reading assignments on how families have viewed children differently over the centuries. A European American student, drawing from her own experience working in a social service agency with people of color, says "It seemed like those people didn't really care about their children." Several African American students in the class take offense and demand "What do you mean by 'those people'?" The student who made the comment is puzzled and feels put on the spot. The students who are offended by her comment are not going to be put off; they want to deal directly with her for what they perceive as her racism. Everyone else in the room is waiting to see what happens. Welcome to a difficult dialogue!

This chapter is a revised version of a module, "Facilitating Difficult Dialogues in the Classroom," that was part of the CD ROM *Diversity, Distance, Dialogue* © 1998 by California State University, Hayward; licensed and distributed by Public Broadcasting Service. I am grateful to Benjamin Bowser, Terry Jones, and Derald Sue for their support and their review of the original module.

The possibility that a difficult dialogue will occur is heightened whenever course materials reflect a multicultural perspective; when students are racially or culturally diverse; and/or when the instructor's ethnicity, gender, and/or sexual orientation is different from the students. In this chapter, I consider ways to transform these kinds of emotionally charged classroom encounters into opportunities for meaningful dialogues. I explore the dynamics that can make such discussions difficult, and I present a model of effective strategies for engaging students in cognitive and emotional inquiry and open-minded discussion about multicultural issues.

THE DYNAMICS OF DIFFICULT DIALOGUE

Difficult classroom dialogues occur when differences in perspectives are challenged or judged to be offensive—often with intense emotions aroused among participants and observers. Such dialogues immediately spotlight the race, gender, culture, and sexual orientation of the participants. The normal classroom conversation stops, and verbal exchanges are no longer student to student or faculty to student, but White to Black, male to female, gay to heterosexual, and so on. The interaction calls attention to these identities, and students and faculty alike can find themselves experiencing a strong personal reaction. Confronted with a different cultural perspective, students may experience a variety of responses, from anger to disbelief or dismissal. Instructors may feel threatened by the awareness that some of their students know more about certain subjects than they do and that their ignorance or biased perspective may become all too apparent to the class.

Difficult dialogues can take different forms. The normal classroom conversation can explode into an intense exchange, characterized by friendly intellectual debate, or it can veer toward strongly worded disagreement, angry confrontation, or personal attack. From mild to mean, these exchanges have the potential for serious polarization, in which the educational process comes to a standstill. In the worst-case scenario, all attempts at dialogue fail, and verbal (or even physical) violence occurs; some students storm out of the room and go so far as to withdraw from the course or file a complaint. When the class meets again, tension fills the air like fumes that any spark could ignite.

Difficult dialogues can also brew in silence. Ironically, one signal that a difficult dialogue is simmering is the absence of visible emotion. Students are dutiful and respectful but apparently uninterested in discussion. Feelings are heating up, but there is a lid of polite and deadening silence over them. In this situation, little or nothing is communicated among the students. They leave the class muttering, "Man, am I glad this class is over," "I hate these PC classes," or "I'm not about to say anything and have everyone jump all over me." Day after day, the instructor finds the same silent resistance. It's a long semester, and the teaching evaluations are a disaster.

However, difficult dialogues can also become exciting educational opportunities. In the best-case scenario, a difficult dialogue occurs and the students and instructor move beyond the discomfort, the fear of confrontation, and the tendency to be judgmental. The students become energized and curious, taking conversational risks and inquiring about what others know and feel. The tension in the situation is not only recognized but used as a lightning rod for cognitive inquiry and insight.

An example of this happened in a class of mine, in which the students were discussing stereotypes as learned behavior. A Latino student said,

> I don't like this about myself, but when I see a White man driving a Lexus, I say to myself, "There goes a CEO, a lawyer, a successful person." But when I see a Black man in a Lexus, I say, "There goes a drug dealer." I learned all this from the media.

An African American young woman replied, "I say 'Go Man,' and I say to you [the Latino student] 'You're wrong and you should know better.'" She then burst into tears and ran out of the room. An older African American woman followed her, signaling to me that she would comfort her. The bell rang, and class was over.

Before class convened 2 days later, I prepared a structure for continuing the discussion, to be followed by a period for reflective writing. In class, each student was invited to share one question or feeling they experienced during or after the encounter. The tension, curiosity, or pain that they felt were thus brought out into the open, and the lesson that stereotypes are learned, alive in each of us, and a cause of suffering was more real than any lecture could ever have made it.

Why Are Dialogues About Gender, Race, and Culture So Difficult?

When in a diverse group, people often avoid discussions of race, class, gender, and sexual identity for fear of creating discomfort, embarrassment, or hostility. The avoidance, in the guise of politeness, can take such forms as making light of the topic, shifting topics, or simply ignoring anything said that happens to relate to the topic. This "code of silence" is a reflection of a societal denial that cultural factors matter and that such things as sexism, racism, and White privilege exist. To avoid feeling awkward or making others uncomfortable, faculty often perpetuate the code of silence.

Race relations in the United States are both an intensely intellectual and an extremely emotional issue, triggering deep feelings about identity and self-worth. The racial divide is wide, with sharp and jagged edges. Many European Americans feel guilty for the legacy of oppression or defensive over their position of historical privilege—and even when they acknowledge their White privilege, they do not know what to do about it. In addition, because in mainstream U.S. culture the principle of equality is regarded as sacred, to be called a racist packs the same punch as being called a child molester. On the other hand, most people of color must navigate a daily tide of racist projections. In subtle and obvious ways, members of other cultural groups question their worth and judge them to be less qualified, tokens, or a commodity. Thus it is understandable that it seems safer to avoid race-related topics.

Moreover, because of the inextricable emotional dimension of race relations, most faculty view difficult dialogues as violating academic protocol. The Western academic tradition has typically held emotions to be irrational and not appropriate to the intellectual pursuits of academia. Faculty are trained to emphasize cognitive processes in the classroom and to treat emotions as private and personal.

Finally, for both students and faculty, difficult dialogues heighten an awareness of personal vulnerability. From a psychological perspective, people craft their identities from the stories they have been told (by family, peers, religious leaders, and society) about what it means to be of a certain race, culture, gender, or sexual identity. Usually, they don't question these identities until others challenge them, which can happen when one is feeling attacked or spotlighted. However, when instructors deny or ignore the importance of these identities, they communicate a message to students that feelings in these areas don't belong in the classroom and that perhaps their experiences and knowledge about their ethnicity are not worthy of academic attention. This can lead students to question their overall worth and acceptability to the academic world.

During difficult dialogues, instructors may feel vulnerable because they don't know when to be the expert and when to let go, when to refer to their own identity and when to refer to the cognitive content. The faculty with whom I work speak of their lack of intercultural competence. They are embarrassed by how little they really know about the different cultures in the United States. They are often horrified when they realize how few, if any, friends they have from a different race or culture, and how few, if any books, movies, or plays they have read or seen by and about members of a different culture. When they have friendly intercultural relationships with colleagues, the topic of race or culture rarely arises. Faculty are trained to be the experts, in charge of a subject matter—but most are not experts in race and culture issues. When confronted with a lack of knowledge and very different experience, they may begin to question their identity and place. No wonder instructors want to defend against this vulnerability by attempting to avoid or contain difficult dialogues. Yet paradoxically, instructors' awareness and acceptance of their own vulnerability can increase their empathy for their students' vulnerability.

How Can Difficult Dialogues Have Successful Outcomes?

One indication that a difficult dialogue is successful is when students come to integrate cognitive knowledge with emotional responses. Despite the feelings that may be aroused, they become curious about what they don't know or understand, and curious about the feelings as well. As they strive to get to know, communicate with, and understand one another, they gain respect for themselves and for their classmates.

Another indication of success is when students begin talking to each other about issues they would normally find threatening. They demonstrate the courage and willingness to ask questions, listen carefully to the responses, and speak honestly about their own perspective. I regularly do a "fishbowl" exercise after students read Peggy McIntosh's (1988) classic essay on White privilege, first with White students discussing the essay and students of color observing, and then with the process reversed. When the White students discuss the essay, there are two dominant themes: (a) they are truly surprised that not everyone shares the same privileges (e.g., not being followed in a store, and being able to assume you can rent an apartment anywhere you can afford) and (b) they get defensive and try to pick apart the essay. When the students of color discuss the essay, there are three dominant themes: (a) genuine disbelief and mistrust that Whites don't know they have White privilege, (b) anger about White privilege, and (c) appreciation for McIntosh laying it out so clearly. At the end, I put the students together and ask them to re-enact the fishbowl conversations by role playing each other. After the role play, the difficult dialogue begins; it is most successful when students begin asking questions that reveal their own vulnerability and true curiosity. Examples might include: "What do you see when you look in the mirror, a woman or a White woman?" "How do you instruct your children on how to handle racial name-calling?" "Help me understand what it feels like to be White;" "How is your life at school different from your life at home?" "How do you handle always wondering if someone is being friendly to you in a store so they can help you or guard you?" Taking a risk might also take the form of self-disclosure, such as a story about how the person was oblivious to White privilege or wrongly assumed they were being stereotyped.

A further indication of successful dialogue is when students and instructors begin seeing their vulnerability as a strength. They become aware of the desire to be understood and to understand other human beings across race, culture, and gender lines—and this urge to speak genuinely and to understand others becomes stronger than the urge to protect their own perspectives. Paradoxically, successful difficult dialogues often occur when individuals become aware of their defensiveness and have the courage to acknowledge it (e.g., "Wow, I'm feeling so defensive right now. I wonder why."). Instructors can encourage this practice by giving examples from their own experiences that disclose their own defensiveness and stereotyping.

DEALING WITH DIFFICULT DIALOGUE: A MODEL FOR MULTICULTURAL INQUIRY

The following model for facilitating difficult dialogues is grounded in my 20 years of teaching race-related courses at a racially diverse campus, incorporating ideas from ongoing discussions with many colleagues. It contains four elements: (a) creating a climate for inquiry, (b) focusing on cognitive inquiry, (c) focusing on emotional inquiry, and (d) developing skills for mindful listening.

Creating a Climate for Inquiry

To prepare students for a difficult dialogue, it is important to create a climate for inquiry within the classroom. This means encouraging students to develop an enthusiasm for seeking, exploring, and loving the questions more than the answers. The following questions can help introduce them to this idea of inquiry:

- What is the goal of inquiry—to find answers, or questions, or both?
- How are self-reflection and speculation involved?
- What kind of questions do you ask when you are truly interested in inquiry?
- What is involved in an attitude of inquiry?

I offer a perspective from Chodron (1991), who regards the willingness to inquire as "not caring whether the object of our inquisitiveness is bitter or sweet" (p. 3). Genuine inquiry involves the courage to question what one thinks one already knows to be true—or, to put it another way, inquiry is finding the questions to one's answers. I ask students to consider what it might mean to not have a vested interest in whether they liked or did not like the answer. Would that be possible? What might be the benefits and drawbacks of this attitude?

One way to demonstrate how to transform answer-driven statements into inquiry-driven questions is for the instructor to put a topic on the board, such as "therapy and the single mother," and then ask the students to generate statements that reflect what they think they know to be true. Students will generally say things like, "Most single mothers are African Americans" and "Most are on welfare." After several statements are on the board, the instructor then can ask the students for their sources. Students rarely quote a source; rather, they just assume it is true from the media or from hearsay. Even when a more accurate answer is given (e.g., "Most single mothers are White"), the instructor does not give away the "right" answer. At this point she continues to encourage the students to inquire more specifically into what they truly know and do not know about the topic. They can also be asked to consider what they know about different perspectives on the topic—for example, how men and women, various cultural groups, gays and heterosexuals, and different socioeconomic classes may understand this issue. Finally, the instructor can ask students: If they didn't have to worry about being right or smart, what additional questions might they have?

Focusing on Cognitive Inquiry

Cognitive inquiry in this model means going beyond learning about the theories and research findings that make up a discipline, to investigate the underlying contexts and assumptions that shape its knowledge base. It is useful to invite students to consider such things as the origin of the concept of Whiteness and color that continues to be maintained as a social construct within the United States, and the development and significance of ethnic identity within a color-conscious society (Alba, 1990; Allen, 1994; Bowser & Hunt, 1996; Roediger, 1994; Wildman, 1996). Instructors can guide students toward an understanding of differences in values, attitudes, beliefs, and communication norms among ethnic, national, racial, and gender groups and the effects of economic scarcity or abundance on human development and behavior.

Although most instructors are not experts in the cultural, historical, socioeconomic, and social identity dimensions for each controversial issue, they can model and stimulate inquiry by telling students what they themselves do not know and the questions they want to explore. The goal is to cultivate students' curiosity for discovering knowledge. It would be useful, for example, if during a difficult dialogue on "therapy and single mothers" students would want to explore such questions as: What is the ethnic breakdown of single mothers? Where do single mothers live? Compared with married mothers, what is their average level of education? What support (e.g., financial, housing, child care) do grandparents and other extended family members play in the life of single parents? What community support is available to single mothers and their children? How does a mother's race, culture, and socioeconomic background influence the responses to the above questions. How do society's values on marriage affect its policies on single mothers? How does the stress of being a single mother affect her mental health? Asking such questions involves courage: the courage to reveal what one does not know. It takes courage and self-awareness to resist getting caught up in an opinion war or a code of silence. This means noticing feelings—of inadequacy, fear, anger, or guilt—that may come up and knowing how to consider them in ways that enhance rather than undermine cognitive inquiry.

Focusing on Emotional Inquiry

Although many people believe that knowledge automatically translates into appropriate attitudes and behavior, racist and culturally based prejudices—which are, essentially, emotional reactions—can exist along with substantive knowledge to the contrary. Goleman (1995) made a persuasive case that emotional intelligence is in fact interdependent with and as important as cognitive intelligence; if instructors do not take the emotional dimension into account in the classroom, they may not achieve their cognitive goals. In addition, if emotional inquiry is going to be part of the class, the instructor should discuss it at the outset. The following are basic points I have found to be helpful in teaching about emotional inquiry, along with methods for facilitating students' inquiry into their own and other's emotional responses. In developing this approach, I have relied heavily on Gendlin (1978) and the writings of Welwood (e.g., *Toward a Psychology of Awakening*, 2000).

Feelings are temporal

People can talk about feelings in the past or imagine them in the future, but they occur only in the present moment, and in that present moment they may feel many emotions simultaneously or in rapid succession—emotions that may be conflicting, intense, and confusing, or gentle and easily understood. If a feeling is particularly strong, it may feel like a permanent state, leading to the conviction that something must be done to attend to or alleviate it.

Feelings are not inferences

It is important to help students learn to distinguish between a feeling, such as discomfort, and inferences about the feeling, such as, "You are making me uncomfortable." White students who feel remorse or anger about racism may begin spinning inferences—for example, that this is a terrible country, that racism is not their fault, that people of color must hate them. What happens is that the feeling becomes translated into a particular inference, which allows them to bypass the actual experience of remorse and anger. If unexamined, this kind of inference can solidify and numb other emotions in the process. Students often need assistance discerning the feeling from the inference.

Feelings are often reactive

Feelings are often responses to past experiences as well as to current stimuli. An emotional reaction to an outspoken classmate may be shaped more by one's cultural background, earlier family dynamics, or previous life experiences than by the actual content of the classmate's utterance. Students need to learn that because feelings are so affected by one's own personal histories, they may not be the most trusted guides for taking rational action in the present.

Emotions and reactions in response to multicultural material

Sue and Sue (1990) and Sue, Arredondo, and McDavis (1992) have identified the six most common reactions students experience when working with multicultural curricula. They include

1. *Anger*, which is often expressed as "Why blame me?", "How dare you?", and "It's your fault."
2. *Sadness* and *remorse*, which often translate into "I am bad" and "I feel so guilty."
3. *Despair*, which is often communicated as "I can't do anything to change this", "I feel ashamed of being White", and "I feel like racism will never end."
4. *Fear*, which is often expressed as "You can't expect me to give up what I've earned", "They control everything", and "They will just assume I'm like other Whites and try to hurt me."
5. *Intellectualization*, which may take the form of denying the relevance of feelings or claiming the primacy of the content issues.
6. *Withdrawal*, which may be expressed by lowered eyes, silence, or leaving the room.

Noticing and acknowledging feelings

It is important for faculty to give students an opportunity to practice acknowledging their feelings in the moment, learning to listen to their feelings before they engage in inquiry. To notice one's own or another's feelings is to take that moment and check in: "What is going on with me right now?" "What am I sensing is going on with this person right now?" Usually what happens here is a jumble of unidentified physical sensations or confused observations, but when given a few moments, the stimuli will settle into a discernible pattern that can be acknowledged—such as "I feel nervous, scattered, and tired." It is important to tell students that the feelings will change.

Once students have noticed and labeled their feelings, they can then begin to notice the difference between the feelings themselves and the inferences identified with them. For example, a student reported on this process by saying:

> At first, I noticed feelings of hunger and weariness, and then resentment and guilt set in. I first began to think about what I wanted to eat and when I might be able to get a rest. Then the resentment came in that you were making me think about race when I was working so hard and

didn't even have time to eat. Then I felt guilty for being so self-centered and for all the racial injustices in the world and that I really had it easy.

When the student reported on this experience in class, I was able to assist the class in discerning the differences between her feelings, (hunger, weariness, anger, and guilt) and her inferences (I will eat, rest, blame the instructor for making me think about these things, blame myself for thinking my hunger is more important than racial injustice).

As the feelings and inferences are identified, the instructor can ask students to explore the emotional content further. Some questions might be: "What else is going on underneath this feeling (e.g., anger)?" "What am I angry about, really?" "Why do I want to blame the instructor?" "What am I afraid of?" "Why do I get angry when this issue comes up?" Unlike cognitive inquiry, where questions get asked and strategies generated for finding out answers, emotional inquiry encourages the asking and holding of the questions. It involves waiting and listening to the responses.

It is helpful to remind students that they do not need to judge, change, deny, or indulge their feelings; rather, they can continue to acknowledge and inquire, and just notice what emerges. It is essential to provide enough time for students to process the feelings they have acknowledged as well as to invite students to inquire into the relationship between the cognitive content and their emotions.

Developing Mindful Listening

Listening, once defined by a radio disc jockey as waiting for your turn to interrupt, is better practiced as the full and mindful attention to understanding one's own or another's message. Listening, when done mindfully, is the key to establishing an open and inquisitive environment, and it is a prerequisite for all the other teaching and learning methods discussed here. Mindfulness, in the Western tradition (Gudykunst & Kim, 1997; Langer, 1989), is the ability to see and transcend the stereotypes, scripts, and automatic reactions that prevent people from responding appropriately, thus allowing them to become more open to information and to others whom they might have perceived as different or threatening (Trungpa, 1988). Mindful listening to another involves placing the attention on the other and his or her message. The following are the basic instructions for this method.

1. *Focusing on the other person.* By holding attention on what the other person is saying and feeling, the listener tries to understand the other's message from the other's perspective.
2. *Trying to be nonjudgmental.* The listener attempts to communicate the desire to understand, which is markedly different than expressing agreement or disagreement.
3. *Paraphrasing.* The listener tries to clarify his or her level of

understanding, by repeating back in his or her own words what the other person has said.

4. *Engaging in gentle inquiry.* The listener asks questions that will allow her or him to put her- or himself in the other person's shoes. Gentle inquiry is not interrogation.

5. *Noticing.* The listener seeks conscious awareness of her or his own internal dialogue and external behavior, which brings her or him back to focusing on the other person. In this sense it is a self-correcting step.

Because even the most skilled listeners forget these principles, it is useful to remind students of the guidelines and allow them practice time during each difficult dialogue. Once learned, it can become a useful habit.

Putting the Model Into Practice

When a difficult dialogue arises—or when the instructor anticipates that it might—the following systematic approach of combining mindful listening to self with mindful listening to others can be very useful.

1. *Sit comfortably.* Ask students to sit respectfully (whatever that means to them) but comfortably, and to put down pens, pencils, drinks, and such. They can close their eyes or look diffusely at the floor.

2. *Noticing.* Ask students to notice their feelings—both physical and emotional—and their thoughts. Invite them to be gentle with themselves as they notice the feelings and thoughts they are experiencing.

3. *Breathing.* Ask students to notice their breathing, which may help them to become more aware of their thoughts and feelings, rather than simply being immersed in them. (Allow 2–5 min for this.)

4. *Focusing.* Ask students to focus their attention on a potentially difficult question (posed by the instructor) that is derived from a reading, lecture, or class discussion. A helpful metaphor is to have the students ask themselves the question and then, as if their mind were a movie screen, to watch what shows up without getting caught up in it.

5. *Waiting.* Remind students to wait and hold the question and to try not to analyze or search their minds. Rather, the purpose of waiting is to clear a space so that many thoughts and feelings can make themselves known to the individual. The instructor can remind students that if they notice they are making inferences by judging or arguing with themselves or another, or if

they have drifted off into a daydream, they can just acknowledge what they were thinking and return to their breathing and to the question. Similarly, if they feel sleepy and distracted, or if intense feelings come up, they can acknowledge it and return to their breath and the question. Remind them that there is no right answer and no need to fix or change anything. Their only assignment right now is to notice and acknowledge that they are responding to this particular topic. (Allow 2–5 min for this.)

6. *Emotional inquiry.* At this point, encourage students to engage in gentle inquiry in the same way they would if they were listening to another person. The questions might be: What is going on here? Why am I so angry? Why did I wander off and not want to think about the material? Why did I feel so nervous (or tired)?

7. *Cognitive inquiry.* Here again, encourage students to focus their inquiry toward the cognitive knowledge. The questions might be: What do I know? What troubles me about this concept? What more do I need to know in order to understand this idea?

8. *Writing.* Ask students to write down what they noticed and to describe their experience with this mode of inquiry.

9. *Discussion.* At this point, instructors can use any number of teaching and learning strategies. For example, they can pose a question and divide students into pairs or groups to discuss it, or ask for a word, a sentence, or a question from each person that relates to the student's experience with the question. In this situation, it is helpful to remind students about practicing mindful listening to others.

Taking the Plunge: An Example

Imagine this scenario: It is early in the course, and you have just barely begun to address the concept of mindful listening. After a brief presentation that touches on a multicultural topic, you ask for questions and comments on the lecture and readings. An African American man who is older than most of the other students consistently responds to your questions; he doesn't really answer them, but instead, uses them to espouse his beliefs and views. His statements invariably begin or end with "the White Man." He says the "White Man" did this, "the White Man" did that, and "the White Man" is responsible for whatever. None of the other students, regardless of ethnicity, want to respond to him or draw his attention for fear of being accused of being "the White Man" or "the White Man's lackey."

What do you do? How might you evoke the spirit of inquiry into this situation? Addressing possible cognitive issues and questions, you might begin by:

- discussing that "The White Man" is a shorthand way of saying institutional racism;
- establishing a definition of institutional racism;
- asking all the students what "the White Man" means to them;
- asking the students what questions they have about the phrase "the White Man";
- asking students to identify the kind of information they need to know in order to more fully understand what "the White Man" means;
- inviting emotional inquiry; this might involve asking the students to take a moment to notice and acknowledge what goes on inside of them when they hear "the White Man" and then inviting them to inquire into their feelings, in the manner discussed earlier.

After students have had to chance to notice and inquire into their emotions, the instructor can then make fruitful use of one of the writing, discussing, or sharing options described above.

CONCLUSION

I close this chapter on a personal note. Awhile ago, in the academic senate at my institution, a contentious colleague spoke out about the uselessness of establishing a standing committee for equity and diversity. Identifying with my judgments, I immediately stopped listening and began my plan of attack. I spoke not in response to him but in response to all the other people I knew who had similar opinions. In an "academically civil" way, I matched his arrogance with my own and lost touch with my own feelings. What would have happened if I had just listened with an open heart, noticed his feelings and thoughts, and my own? How might I have responded? I don't know, but it would have been different and less arrogant. In those rare moments when I allow myself to feel and be present in the jagged racial divide, I feel so intensely the differences that separate and simultaneously the commonalties that bind.

Increasingly I find that in those moments when I befriend my own prejudice, ignorance, and emotional tides, I am awed, humbled, and often sad or full of wrath, but I am also more honest and compassionate with my students and colleagues, no matter what their attitude or message. Situations hurt, anger, and disturb more. Sometimes the feelings scare me, but they no longer scare me off, or not for long. My students' feelings are no longer un-wanted, ignored, or intellectualized away but are a welcome addition to the classroom. As W.E.B. Du Bois (1973) argued, education, to be relevant, must grow out of the life experiences of those being educated. So the more we can practice listening to our own experiences and each other's, we will see, hear, feel, and understand how different and how similar we are. By bringing the confusions and emotions of race relations into the center of the class, we ac-knowledge and feel the truth of the racial divide and, paradoxically, by doing so, we begin to feel more connected to ourselves and to each other.

REFERENCES

Alba, R. D. (1990). *Ethnic identity: The transformation of White America*. New Haven, CT: Yale University Press.

Allen, T. (1994). *The invention of the White race: Racial oppression and social control*. London: Verso.

Bowser, B., & Hunt, R. (Eds.). (1996). *Impacts of racism on White Americans*. New-bury Park, CA: Sage.

Chodron, P. (1991). *The wisdom of no escape and the path of loving–kindness*. Boston: Shambhala.

Du Bois, W. E. B. (1973). *The education of Black people: Ten critiques, 1906–1960* (H. Aptheker, Ed.). New York: Monthly Review Press.

Gendlin, E. T. (1978). *Focusing*. New York: Bantam Books.

Goleman, D. (1995). *Emotional intelligence: Why it can matter more than IQ*. New York: Bantam.

Gudykunst, W. B., & Kim, Y. Y. (Eds.). (1997). *Communicating with strangers: An approach to intercultural communication*. New York: McGraw-Hill.

Langer, E. J. (1989). *Mindfulness*. Reading, MA: Addison-Wesley.

McIntosh, P. (1988). *White privilege and male privilege: A personal account of coming to see correspondences through work in women' studies*. Working Paper 189, Welles-ley College Center for Research on Women.

Roediger, D. R. (1994). *Towards the abolition of Whiteness: Essays on race, politics, and working class history*. New York: Verso.

Sue, D. W., Arredondo, P., & McDavis, R. J. (1992). Multicultural organizational development: Implications for the counseling profession. *Journal of Counseling and Development, 70*, 477–486.

Sue, D. W., & Sue, D. (1990). *Counseling the culturally different: Theory and practice*. New York: Wiley.

Trungpa, C. (1988). *Shambhala: The sacred path of the warrior*. Boston: Shambhala.

Welwood, J. (2000). *Toward a psychology of awakening*. Boston: Shambhala.

Wildman, S. (1996). *Privilege revealed: How invisible preference undermines America*. New York: New York University Press.

INDEX

health effects of stress, 130–131
introductory course, 16–17
personality psychology topics, 75–76
racial issues in, 106
research methodology, 106–107
Bipolar disorder, 105
Biracial identity. *See* Multiracial identity
Bisexuality, 292, See also Sexual
    Orientation
Bitter Wind (video), 229
Blaming of victim, 258
Bless Me, Ultima (book), 215
Boring, E. G., 115
Born on the Fourth of July (film), 41
Brazil, 22
Broken Cord, The (book/video), 228–229

Cambodia, 182, 188
Candid Camera (television series), 81
Cardiovascular problems, 130–131
Caregiver–child relationship
    Asian American culture, 183
    attachment, 18
    cultural context, 48
    Jewish psychology, 244–245
    See also Child-rearing practices
Carry Me Like Water (book), 215
Case Management Society of America,
    265
Castillo, R. J., 38
Cattell, R. B., 76
*Changing Our Minds: The Story of Evelyn
    Hooker* (video), 24
Chicks in White Satin (film), 247
Child-rearing practices
    African American, 302–303
    Asian American, 183
    bed-sharing, 18
    gender role socialization, 76–77
    introductory psychology course topics,
        18
    limitations of current conceptualizations
        in psychology, 46
    nonheterosexual parenting, 287
    See also Caregiver-child relationship
Child sexual abuse, 75
Children of Wind River (video), 228
Chinese immigrant experience, 180
Cigarette smoking, 128–129, 130
Class Divided, A (video), 23
Classroom techniques, 8

abnormal psychology studies, 35–42
African American psychology course,
    199–200
American Indian psychology, 230–231
with Asian American students, 189–190
cognitive inquiry, 353
community interviews, 53–54, 80
creating climate of inquiry, 352–353
disability issues, 263–265
discussion of racism and prejudice,
    23–24
emotional inquiry, 354–356
establishing a safe climate for
    discussion, 38–39, 67
examination of social privilege, 51
examination of student bias, 51–52
exploring student ethnocultural
    identity, 157–159
exploring student sameness and
    difference, 40, 50
graduate level courses, 114
individual research on specific culture,
    52
introducing diversity topics in
    developmental psychology, 49–55
Jewish psychology, 247–248
managing classroom dynamics, 24,
    67–68
managing difficult dialogue, 9, 347–359
mindful listening, 356–357
social psychology course, 64–66
student journals, 53
student role in choice of, 64
teaching men's issues, 305–306
teaching nonheterosexual orientation
    topics, 288–291
Clinical training, multicultural studies in
    as area of concentration, 340–341
    basic requirements, 342, 344
    curriculum design, 344–345
    departmental transformation for,
        342–344
    integration model, 341–342
    interdisciplinary approach, 341
    models for, 339
    program evaluation, 345–346
    as separate course, 340
    student support system, 345
*Closing: Future Steps and Celebrating
    Ethnocultural Diversity* (textbook),
    164
Clothesline (film), 143

Geropsychology, 273. See also Aging,
    psychology of
Gerotranscendence, 276–277
Goddard, H. H., 119–120
Grandmothers, Mothers, and Daughters
    (video), 147
Greece, 23

Half the Kingdom (video), 247
Hand gestures, 22–23
Handbook of Cross-Cultural Psychology
    (textbook), 174
Handbook of Culture and Psychology
    (textbook), 174
Handicap, 254–255
Hassidic Jews, 20
Health psychology, 8
    alcohol abuse studies, 126–127
    conceptualization of health behavior,
        131–132
    effects of discrimination, 130–131
    exercise behavior, 127–128
    sociocultural context of health and
        sickness, 125–126, 132–133
    tobacco use, 128–129, 130
    violence against women, 129–130
Hearing loss, 277
Help-seeking behaviors, 189
    Latino psychology, 212–213
Hermaphrodites Speak! (film), 293
*Hispanic Psychology: Critical Issues in
    Theory and Research* (textbook),
    63
History of Experimental Psychology, A
    (textbook), 115
History of psychology
    conceptualizations of race, 120–121
    contextual analysis, 115–116
    contributions of women, 113, 116–117
    cultural context, 121–122
    goals of new history, 113, 122
    impact of psychotherapy, 118–119
    limitations of traditional course, 113,
        122
    psychological testing, 119–120
    psychology as social force, 117–120
    social psychology, 65
    textbooks, 114–115
    U.S. influence in, 122
    Zeitgeist concept, 115
History of Psychology (journal), 116

Homosexuality
    pathologization of, 24, 65, 104, 105
    See also Sexual orientation
Honigmann, J., 226–227
Hormonal system, 105–106
House Made of Dawn (book/video), 229
How Far Home: Veterans After Vietnam
    (film), 306
Human Genome Project, 104–105
Huntington's disease, 278
Hypertension, 104, 130, 131

Immigrant experience
    Asian Americans, 180–182, 188–189
    Latino population, 208–209
    mental health effects, 208
Immigration Act, 181
Immigration and Naturalization Act, 181
Immune function, 130–131
Impairment, biological, 254–255
*In Our Own Words: Writings from Women's
    Lives* (textbook), 63
*In the Shadow of the Past: Psychology
    Portrays the Sexes* (textbook), 117
*Indigenous Psychologies: Research Experience
    in Cultural Context* (textbook),
    225
Industrial psychology, 262–263
Infant mortality, 47
Infibulation, 25–26
Institutional Review Boards, 92
Insurance, 37
Intelligence testing, 36, 119–120, 197–198
    introductory course topics, 20–21
    sociocultural factors, 21
    stereotype threat effects, 20–21, 198
    test design bias, 20
Interdisciplinary study, 341
International Academy of Intercultural
    Research, 174
International Association for Cross-
    Cultural Psychology, 174
International Council of Psychologists,
    175
*International Journal of Intercultural
    Relations* (journal), 174
International Society of Psychologists, 175
Interpersonal relations
    Asian American, 184–185
    communication psychology, 22–23
    Latino psychology, 211–212

people with disability, 258–259, 262
promoting sense of student
   commonality, 40, 50
See also Social psychology
Interviews, research, 53–54, 80
   disability studies, 264
   studying men's issues, 305
Intracultural variability, 5, 48–49, 61
   American Indians, 222, 223
   among Asian Americans, 179
Introductory course, 8
   abnormal psychology topics, 24–25
   biology content, 16–17
   developmental psychology, 18–20
   goals, 15–16
   intelligence testing topics, 20–21
   personality theory, 21–22
   recitation section, 16
   significance of, 15
   social psychology topics, 22–24
   student discomfort with multicultural
      topics, 24, 25–26
Ireland, 23
Italy, 23
*It's Elementary: Talking About Gay Issues in
   School* (film), 291

Japanese immigrant experience, 180–181
Jewish population
   Ashkenazi, 237, 238, 247
   demographics, 237–238
   developmental psychology, 241–242
   family structure and functioning,
      244–245
   Hassidim, 20
   identity, 238
   intermarriage, 241–242
   need for expanded psychology
      curriculum, 237, 239, 248
   prejudice and persecution, 237,
      238–239, 242, 248
   psychological researchers and theorists,
      240–241
   psychology course
      classroom activities, 247–248
      limitations of current curriculum, 237
      obstacles to inclusion, 239–240
      resources, 240
      strategies for inclusion, 240
      topics, 240–246
   Sephardim, 237–238

sexual identity issues, 242
social psychology, 243
socioeconomic status, 238
therapeutic issues, 245–246
women's issues, 243–245
Journal of Bisexuality (journal), 6
Journal of Cross-Cultural Psychology
   (journal), 174
Journal of Lesbian Studies (journal), 6
Journal of Social Issues (journal), 6
Joy Luck Club (book/video), 80, 190
Jungle Fever (film), 200

Kampuchea, 182
Kaufman Assessment Battery for Children,
   20
Kitano, M. K., 60, 62
Klein, Melanie, 118–119
Korean immigrant experience, 181
Korsakoff's syndrome, 278

Language
   of clinical diagnosis, 24, 37–38
   cross-cultural psychology research, 173
   gender differences, 94
   labels of sexual identity, 17
   nonheterosexist, 287
   translation, 173
   See also Communication
Laos, 182
Latino population, 25
   acculturation, 211, 213, 215–216
   assessment issues, 215–216
   demographics, 208
   educational attainment, 209
   ethnic and racial identity, 214
   family structure and functioning,
      210–211, 212
   health effects of discrimination, 130
   immigrant experience, 208–209
   interpersonal relations, 211–212
   mestizos, 207, 208
   psychology course content, 207,
      210–214, 215–216
   psychology course resources, 214–215
   psychology student population, 3
   religion and spirituality, 212–213
   socioeconomic status, 209–210
Learning disability, sexism in assessment
   of, 24
Lecturing, 64

Lesbian population. *See* Sexual orientation
Low-birthweight babies, 100

Ma Vie en Rose (film), 292
Majority culture
    classroom discussion of racism and
        prejudice, 23–24, 347–359
    examination of social privilege, 51
    unconscious assumption of racial
        superiority, 19
Male Couple, The (film), 306
Male Experience, The (textbook), 300
Manifest Anxiety Scale, 77
Margaret Cho–I'm The One That I Want
    (film), 146
Masculine Self, The (textbook), 300
Mass media depictions of psychological
    science, 40–42, 93
Masturbatory insanity, 65
McCarran-Walters Act, 181
Measure of Acculturation for Chicano
    Adolescents, 213
*Measuring Minds: Henry Herbert Goddard
    and the Origins of American
    Intelligence Testing*, 119
Media Education Foundation, 306
Medicine at the Crossroads: Disordered States
    (video), 40
Men and masculinity
    African American psychology, 302–303
    aggressive behavior and, 304–305
    anthropological perspective, 301
    biological perspective, 300–301
    classroom activities, 305–306
    course design, 299–300
    emotional functioning, 304
    ethnocultural diversity, 302
    family issues, 305
    gay issues, 303–304
    goals of psychology course, 306–307
    Latino psychology, 210–211
    psychological development, 302
    sociological perspective, 301
    teaching resources, 306
    work roles, 305
    See also Gender
Menstruation, 90
Mestizos, 207, 208
Methodological technique, 49
Mexican people, 208–209
Mi Familia (film), 215

Mindful listening, 356–357
Minority groups, 6
    classification, 4–5
    classroom discussion of racism and
        prejudice, 23–24, 347–359
    ethnic identity development, 19–20
    inadequacies in current developmental
        psychology research, 46
    people with disabilities as, 255
    psychology student population, 3
    research bias, 91–92
    risk of alcohol abuse, 127
    risk of tobacco use, 128–129
    social context of mental distress in, 39
    socioeconomic status, 46
    student discomfort with multicultural
        topics, 25–26
    U.S. demographic profile, 19
    See also specific minority group
Mismeasure of Man, The (textbook), 91
Mismeasure of Woman, The (textbook), 91
Mood disorders, 35
Multiculturalism, generally, 89
    case study of departmental
        implementation, 316–322
    definition and scope, 4–5, 60–61
    goals of introductory psychology course,
        16
    levels of course content, 61–62
    resistance to, in psychology
        departments, 315–316
    trends in psychology, 5–6
    See also Cultural diversity topics in
        teaching of psychology
Multiracial identity, 19–20
    American Indian self-identification,
        222–223
    Jewish population, 241–242
Murphy, Gardner, 120
Murphy, Lois Barclay, 120
My Knees Were Jumping (film), 247

Naming the Mind (textbook), 121
Nappy (film), 200
National Association to Advance Fat
    Acceptance, 146
National Institute on Aging, 273
National Rehabilitation Information
    Center, 265
National University Continuing
    Education Association, 326

Neighborhood context
  exercise behavior and, 127–128
  racial segregation in U.S., 131
  risk of alcohol abuse, 126–127
Nepal, 17
Neurasthenia, 65
Nonverbal communication, 22–23, 185
Now That the Buffalo's Gone (video), 229
Number Our Days (film), 247

Obesity, 144–146, 254
Oedipal theory, 75
On-line learning, 333–334
One Week (film), 200
Organizational psychology, 262–263
Overcoming Fear of Fat (book), 145

Park, R. E., 224
Parkinson's disease, 278
Personal Attributes Questionnaire, 77
Personal narrative, 49
  African American, 77
  as research material, 78–79
Personality psychology
  African American, 198
  American Indian, 226–227
  course content, 21–22, 73–81
  disability topics, 261–262
  feminist theory, 21–22
  gender topics, 75, 76, 80–81
  limitations of traditional approach,
    73–74, 81
  measures of personality, 77–79
  nature–nurture debate, 75–77
  psychoanalytic theory, 75
  race and ethnicity topics, 76
  race-specific personality types, 226–227
  sociocultural factors in development,
    79
Physical activity, 127–128
Picture Bride (film), 80
Planning fallacy, 132
Polyandry, 17
Pomo Shaman (film), 227
Population genetics, 104–105
Postmodernism, 89
Posttraumatic stress disorder, 188
Prejudice and discrimination
  against African Americans, 130, 198
  against American Indians, 229–230

against Asian Americans, 180, 181,
    186, 187–188
  against fat women, 144–146
  against Jews, 237, 238–239, 242, 248
  against people with disability, 255–256,
    258, 261–262
  bias in research methods, 65–66, 88–91,
    105–106
  biological reductionism and, 16
  effects on health, 130–131
  effects on presentation and course of
    mental problems, 199
  ethnic identity as protective factor
    against, 19
  historical development of racism/
    sexism, 100–101
  inadequacies in current developmental
    psychology research, 46
  in intelligence testing, 20–21
  introductory course topics, 23–24
  in military, 78
  obstacles to continuing education,
    332–333, 334–335
  in psychiatric diagnostic practice,
    24–25, 37–38
  racial attitudes of therapist, 199
  sexual orientation-based, 287, 288
  student anger in classroom, 24
  student self-examination, 51–52
  women's psychology studies, 140–141
  See also Racism; Stereotyped thinking
Presbyopia, 277
Primate research, 92, 102
Professional identity, 94
Proteomics, 102, 103
Psychoanalytic theory, 75
Psychological Testing and American Society
    (textbook), 119
Psychology and Sexual Orientation
    (textbook), 291–292
Psychology of Men and Masculinity
    (journal), 6
Psychology of Women course, 8
  class-based studies, 141–144
  disability topics in, 262
  gender difference studies, 138–139
  incorporating diversity topics in,
    139–148
  issues for Jews, 243–245
  limitations of current courses, 137
  need for diversity topics in, 137–139
  sizism research, 144–146

Psychology of Women Quarterly (journal), 116–117
Puerto Rican people, 208

Qualitative research, 65–66, 78–79, 88
Question of Color, A (film), 200

Race and ethnicity
    in abnormal psychology, 34
    associated personality types, 226–227
    bias in research methods, 91–92
    biopsychology research, 106
    communication style and, 22
    conceptual evolution in psychological research, 120–121
    difficult dialogue in class, 25–26, 347–359
    diversity in women's psychology research, 137–139
    ethnic identity development, 19–20, 214
    in gender role socialization, 18–19
    health effects of discrimination, 130–131
    Latino identity, 214
    personality psychology topics, 76, 79–80
    psychology of aging topics, 275–276
    psychology of men, 302–303
    segregation in U.S., 131
    socioeconomic status and, 46
    student discomfort with classroom discussions, 25–26
    therapist's, 199, 215–216
    tobacco use patterns, 128–129
    See also Cultural diversity in teaching of psychology; Culture, Ethnicity, and Mental Health Project; Minority groups; Racism; Researchers of color; *specific racial or ethnic group*
Race relations
    American Indian, 224
    model of, 224
Racism
    historical development, 100–101
    in psychology research, 66, 120–121
    See also Prejudice and discrimination
Recovered memory, 93–94
Rehabilitation Act, 263
Rehabilitation psychology, 265

Relativism, 171–172
Religion and spirituality
    American Indian, 227
    among Asian Americans, 179–180
    in gender role socialization, 19
    Jewish identity, 238, 245–246
    Latino psychology, 212–213
    seasonal dissonance, 245–246
    women's psychology studies, 141
Research methodologies
    American Indian psychology, 225–226
    animal models, 92, 101–102, 107
    bias in, 65–66, 88–91
    in biopsychology, 106–107
    community interviews, 53–54, 80
    cross-cultural psychology, 172–173, 225, 226
    cultural equivalence issues, 225–226
    cultural identity of research subjects, 169
    developmental psychology pilot projects, 54–55
    ethical practice, 92–93
    external validity, 91–92
    fundamental attribution error, 131–132
    gender of research subjects, 105–106
    historical development, 121, 169
    mass media presentations of research findings, 93–94
    measures of personality, 77–79
    Process Model, 89
    qualitative approaches, 65–66, 78–79, 88
    selection and definition of variables, 89–90
    social power relations in, 49
    study design, 88
    See also Experimental psychology course
Researchers, women, 77, 94
    in history of psychology textbooks, 114–115
Researchers of color, 34, 36, 94, 117, 160, 161–162, 199
    in history of psychology textbooks, 114–115
Return to Oulad Moumen (film), 247
Romance of American Psychology, The (textbook), 118

Sankofa (film), 200
Schizophrenia, 105

Scotland, 23
Self concept
    American Indian psychology, 222, 226
    collectivism and individualism, 21
    ethnic identity development, 19, 214
    exploring student ethnocultural
        identity, 157–159
    Jewish identity, 241–242, 246
    Jewish women, 243–244
    multiracial identity, 19–20, 222–223,
        241–242
    people with disability, 257
    physical impairment experienced as
        handicap, 254–255
    professional identity, 94
    social psychology course exercise, 66
    women's, 146
Self-esteem, ethnic identity and, 19
Sensory impairments
    aging effects, 277–278
    intelligence testing and, 20
Separation anxiety, 18
Sexism, 101
Sexual orientation
    clinical conceptualization, 24
    course name and description, 289
    determinants of, 16–17
    diversity in women's psychology
        research, 137–138
    family issues, 287
    gay men's issues, 303–304
    genetic basis, 104
    goals of psychology course, 16, 17, 293
    inadequacies of current psychology
        training in, 285, 293
    Jewish identity and, 242
    language of, 4, 17
    Latino psychology, 211
    nonheterosexist teaching, 286, 287
    nonheterosexual student, 286, 289,
        290–291
    nonheterosexual teacher, 286, 289
    obstacles to incorporation in psychology
        course, 285
    pathologization of, 24, 65, 104, 105
    prejudice and stereotypes, 287, 288
    teaching resources, 291–292
    topics and techniques for teaching
        about, 286–293
    See also Sexuality/sexual behavior
Sexuality/sexual behavior
    animal research models, 92, 102

Asian American stereotypes, 187–188
cultural diversity, 17
gender conceptualizations, 4, 17
gender role socialization, 18–19
Latino psychology, 210
personality development, 80–81
student self-assessment, 286
traditional evolutionary theory, 76
See also Gender; Sexual orientation
Shadow on a Tightrope (book), 145
She's Gotta Have It (film), 200
Simulation exercises
    disability experience, 264
    sensory impairment, 277–278
Sizism, 144–146
Slaying the Dragon (film), 188
Social constructionism, 5, 89, 171
Social context
    American Indian psychology, 224
    collectivism and individualism, 21
    community interviews, 53–54, 80
    concepts of masculinity, 300, 301
    in developmental psychology, 47–48
    exercise behavior and, 127–128
    gender identity development, 18–19,
        47, 301
    health psychology conceptualizations
        of health and sickness, 125–126,
        132–133
    impact of psychological testing,
        119–120
    intelligence testing and, 20–21
    introductory course instruction on
        influence of, 15–16
    media portrayals of abnormal
        psychology, 40–42
    psychological assessment and diagnosis,
        36, 39
    psychology as social force, 117–120
    risk of alcohol abuse, 126–127
    See also Social constructionism
Social learning theory, 259
Social Perspectives in Lesbian and Gay
        Studies: A Reader (textbook), 63
Social psychology
    classroom dynamics, 67–68
    course goals, 62
    course materials, 62–64
    disability topics, 257–259
    evaluation of course by students, 68–69
    evaluation of student performance,
        66–67

historical development, 65
instructional activities, 64–66
introductory course topics, 22–24
Jewish culture, 243
with multicultural foundation, 59–60
Social Psychology: Exploring Universals Across Cultures (textbook), 63
Social Psychology (textbook), 63
Society for the Psychological Study of Social Issues, 7
Sociobiology, 102
Sociocultural Perspectives in Social Psychology: Current Reading (textbook), 63
Socioeconomic status
  African American psychology, 198
  developmental outcomes and, 47
  diversity in women's psychology research, 137–138, 141–144
  gender role socialization and, 19
  health and, 125–126
  inadequacies in current developmental psychology research, 46
  intelligence testing and, 21
  Jewish population, 238
  Latino population, 209–210
  minority status and, 46
  people with disabilities, 255–256
  prenatal care and, 100
  racial segregation and, 131
  risk of alcohol abuse, 127
Sourcebook on the Teaching of Black Psychology (book), 196
Speaking for Ourselves: Portraits of Gay and Lesbian Youth (film), 291
Specialized study
  African American psychology, 195–196
  in clinical work with specific minority, 340–341, 344
  gender and cultural diversity as, 16
Stereotype threat, 20–21, 198
Stereotyped thinking, 6
  about American Indians, 226–227, 229–230
  about Asian Americans, 186–188
  about Jews, 239
  about marginalized women, 146
  about people with disability, 257
  examination of student bias, 51–52
  in psychiatric diagnostic practice, 24–25, 37–38
  racial superiority, 19

student conceptions of abnormal psychology, 39–40
Sterilization, forced, 76
Stigma, 258
Stone Butch (book), 292
Strange Situation Test, 18
Strom, L., 143
Student behavior and attitudes
  advocating for multicultural curriculum, 316–318
  Asian Americans, 189–190
  conceptions of abnormal psychology, 39–40
  continuing education students, 325–328
  discomfort with multicultural topics, 24, 25–26
  establishing a safe climate for classroom discussion, 38–39
  evaluation of course by students, 68–69
  evaluation of performance in course, 66–67
  examination of social privilege, 51
  examination of student's ethnocultural identity, 157–159
  exploring student sameness and difference, 40, 50
  Latino population, 212
  learning styles, 64, 74
  managing classroom dynamics, 67–68
  managing difficult dialogue, 9, 347–359
  reactions elicited by multicultural material, 355–356
  role in course design, 64
  sexual orientation topics, 286, 288, 289–291
  stress of examining diversity topics, 157, 159
  student support programs, 345
Substance use
  American Indian psychology, 228–229
  See also Alcohol abuse
Sudden Infant Death Syndrome, 18
Sullivan, Harry S., 118–119

Teacher characteristics
  implementing a multicultural curriculum, 343–344
  nonheterosexual, 286, 289
  obstacles to incorporating diversity studies, 170–171
  See also Training of educators

Teacher self-appraisal, 68
Teaching About Culture, Ethnicity, and Diversity (book), 174
Teaching assistants, preparation for multicultural studies, 16
Teen pregnancy, 49
Television shows, 74, 80–81
Testosterone, 106
Textbooks
  cross-cultural psychology, 174
  cultural diversity topics in, 171
  Culture, Ethnicity, and Mental Health Project, 164
  history of psychology, 114–115
  psychology of women, 140, 142, 144–145, 147
Thematic Apperception Test, 77
Therapy
  acculturation effects, 215–216
  African American psychology, 198–199
  American Indian psychology, 227–228
  disability issues, 261, 262
  Jewish psychology, 245–246
  media portrayals, 42
  sensitivity to diverse populations, 34, 37
  social impact, 118–119
  therapist race/ethnicity, 199, 215–216
Thinking Critically About Research on Sex and Gender (textbook), 90
Thompson, Veronique, 157
Tobacco use, 128–129, 130
Tongues Untied (film), 293
Tough Guise: Violence, Media, and the Crisis in Masculinity (film), 306
Towards Intimacy (video), 146
Training of educators
  for multicultural curriculum, 343–344
  teaching assistants, 16
Transgender issues, 292, See also Sexual Orientation
Translation, 173, 225–226
Transsexual Menace (film), 293
True Colors (video), 23
28-Up (video), 79

Underserved populations, 37
Urban populations, 19
  American Indian, 223

Vietnamese people, 182
Vision impairment, 20
  aging effects, 277

Way Home, The (video), 146
Wechsler Intelligence Scale for Children, 20
Wedding Banquet, The (video), 80
What About Bob? (film), 41
When Shirley Met Florence (film), 247
White Shamans, Plastic Medicine Men (film), 227
Whose Honor? American Indian Mascots in Sports (video), 229
Without Reservations: Notes on Racism in Montana (video), 229–230
Woman Warrior: Memoirs of a Childhood Among Ghosts (book), 190
Women
  aging issues, 273
  AIDS risk, 130
  Asian American stereotypes, 187–188
  with disability, 146
  fat, 144–146
  health effects of discrimination, 130
  Latino psychology, 210
  psychology student population, 3
  violence against, 129–130, 245
  See also Gender; Psychology of Women course
Work Incentive Improvement Act, 263
World of Differences: Understanding Cross-Cultural Communication (film), 63
Writings by Women on Fat Oppression (book), 145

You Don't Know Dick: Courageous Hearts of Transsexual Men (film), 292

ABOUT THE EDITORS

Phyllis Bronstein is a professor of clinical psychology at the University of Vermont. She received her PhD in social psychology from Harvard University in 1979. Her research and writing have been in two main areas. The first is family relationships—in particular, parenting and its long-term effects on child and adolescent development. In line with this interest, she is currently conducting a 27-year follow-up on a study of Mexican families, in which the children she initially studied now have children of their own. The second area relates to gender and multicultural issues in academia, including diversifying the curriculum and examining and promoting the career advancement of women and faculty of color. In line with this, she is the faculty ombudsperson for her institution and has created and directs an extensive mentoring program there for junior faculty, focusing in particular on the retention and advancement of female and minority faculty. She is the author of numerous articles and chapters in these areas, and the coeditor of *Fatherhood Today: Men's Changing Role in the Family* and *Teaching a Psychology of People: Resources for Gender and Sociocultural Awareness.* She is also the mother of three adult children.

Kathryn Quina, PhD, is a professor of psychology and women's studies at the University of Rhode Island. She coordinates the psychology degree program at the Alan Shawn Feinstein College of Continuing Education. Her teaching and research address sexual victimization, gender and multicultural issues, HIV risk and women's health, and incarcerated women. She coauthored *Rape, Incest and Harassment: A Guide to Helping Survivors* and *Child-*

hood *Trauma and HIV: Women at Risk*. Quina coedited *Teaching a Psychology of People: Towards Gender and Sociocultural Awareness* and *Career Strategies for Women in Academe: Arming Athena*. She has also published chapters and journal articles and has presented over 150 papers at professional conferences.